# accounting

5. Use the following information to present the stockholders' equity section in good form:

| | |
|---|---|
| Common Stock, $1.00 par, 2,000,000 shares authorized, 1,205,000 issued | 1,205,000 |
| Donated Capital | 267,500 |
| Paid-in Capital in Excess of Par - Common | 5,620,000 |
| Preferred Stock, $10 par, 100,000 shares authorized, 50,000 issued | 500,000 |
| Retained Earnings | 10,418,000 |
| Treasury Stock-Common (30,000 shares) | 465,000 |
| Treasury Stock-Preferred (5,000 shares) | 90,000 |

*[Handwritten worksheet:]*

| PIC | | | |
|---|---|---|---|
| Preferred Stock | | | 500,000 |
| Common Stock | | 1,205,000 | |
| PIC Common | | 5,620,000 | 6,825,000 |
| | | | 7,325,000 |
| Donated Capital | | | 267,500 |
| | | | 7,592,500 |
| R/E | | | 10,418,000 |
| | | | 18,010,500 |
| Less | | | |
| T/S Preferred | | | 90,000 |
| T/S Common | | | 465,000 |
| | | | 17,455,500 |

6. Using the information in Exercise #5 above, calculate book value assuming the preferred stock has a redemption value of $14 a share.

## VI. Beyond the Numbers

Review the facts in Exercise 3 with the following changes:

4/4   Declared a 3 for 2 stock split. The market price was $60 per share.
4/26  Issued the shares.

Present the journal entries for the above stock split.

4/4   Declared a 50% stock dividend. The market price was $60 per share.

4/26  Issued the stock dividend.

| Date | Account and Explanation | PR | Debit | Credit |
|------|-------------------------|----|-------|--------|
|      |                         |    |       |        |
|      |                         |    |       |        |
|      |                         |    |       |        |
|      |                         |    |       |        |
|      |                         |    |       |        |
|      |                         |    |       |        |

4. Prepare journal entries for the following transactions:

2/10   Purchased 800 shares of $5 par treasury stock for $24 per share.
7/1    Sold 500 shares of treasury stock for $28 per share.
12/12  Sold 300 shares of treasury stock for $16 per share.

| Date | Account and Explanation | PR | Debit | Credit |
|------|-------------------------|----|-------|--------|
| 2/10 | T/S Common              |    | 19200 |        |
|      | Cash                    |    |       | 19200  |
| 7/1  | Cash                    |    | 14000 |        |
|      | T/S                     |    |       | 12000  |
|      | PIC                     |    |       | 2000   |
| 12/12| Cash                    |    | 4800  |        |
|      | PIC                     |    | 2000  |        |
|      | R/E                     |    | 400   |        |
|      | T/S                     |    |       | 7200   |
|      |                         |    |       |        |
|      |                         |    |       |        |
|      |                         |    |       |        |

# study guide

**Stephen C. Sheafer**
Contra Costa College

# accounting

**CHAPTERS 12 – 26**
*fourth edition*

**Charles T. Horngren** | **Walter T. Harrison** | **Linda Smith Bamber**

Prentice Hall, Upper Saddle River, NJ 07458

Acquisitions editor: **Deborah Emry**
Associate editor: **Natacha St. Hill Moore**
Senior editorial assistant: **Jane Avery**
Project editor: **Richard Bretan**
Manufacturer: **Banta Book Group**

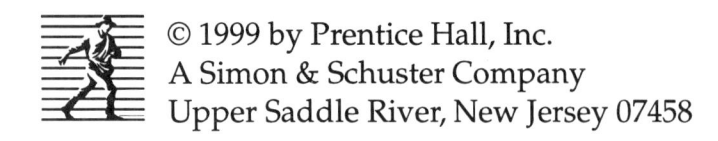

© 1999 by Prentice Hall, Inc.
A Simon & Schuster Company
Upper Saddle River, New Jersey 07458

All rights reserved. No part of this book may be
reproduced, in any form or by any means,
without permission in writing from the publisher.

Printed in the United States of America

10  9  8  7  6  5  4  3  2

ISBN 0-13-080788-5

Prentice-Hall International (UK) Limited, *London*
Prentice-Hall of Australia Pty. Limited, *Sydney*
Prentice-Hall Canada Inc., *Toronto*
Prentice-Hall Hispanoamericana, S.A., *Mexico*
Prentice-Hall of India Private Limited, *New Delhi*
Prentice-Hall of Japan, Inc., *Tokyo*
Simon & Schuster Asia Pte. Ltd., *Singapore*
Editora Prentice-Hall do Brasil, Ltda., *Rio de Janeiro*

# Contents

*Preface*
*Acknowledgments*

| Chapter 12 | Accounting for Partnerships | 306 |
| --- | --- | --- |
| Chapter 13 | Corporate Organization, Paid-In Capital, and the Balance Sheet | 337 |
| Chapter 14 | Retained Earnings, Treasury Stock, and the Income Statement | 361 |
| Chapter 15 | Long-Term Liabilities | 389 |
| | *Chapter 15 Appendix* | 394 |
| Chapter 16 | Accounting for Investments and International Operations | 418 |
| Chapter 17 | Preparing and Using the Statement of Cash Flows | 444 |
| Chapter 18 | Financial Statement Analysis | 466 |
| Chapter 19 | Introduction to Management Accounting | 491 |
| Chapter 20 | Job Costing | 516 |
| Chapter 21 | Process Costing | 538 |
| Chapter 22 | Cost-Volume-Profit Analysis and the Contribution Margin Approach to Decision Making | 567 |
| Chapter 23 | The Master Budget and Responsibility Accounting | 594 |
| Chapter 24 | Flexible Budgets and Standard Costs | 617 |
| Chapter 25 | Activity-based Costing and Other Tools for Cost Management | 642 |
| Chapter 26 | Special Business Decisions and Capital Budgeting | 666 |

# Preface

This Study Guide will assist you in mastering ACCOUNTING, Fourth Edition, by Horngren, Harrison, and Bamber. The 15 chapters in the second volume of this Study Guide correspond to Chapters 12 to 26 in the textbook. Each chapter of this Study Guide contains three sections: Chapter Review, Test Yourself, and Demonstration Problems.

**Chapter Review.** The Chapter Review parallels the chapter in you textbook. It is organized by learning objective and provides a concise summary of the major elements in each objective. Emphasis is given to new terms and concepts because it is essential for the student to be conversant with accounting terminology. A Chapter Overview links each chapter to previous or subsequent topics.

**Test Yourself.** The test yourself section is divided into six parts: matching, multiple choice, completion, daily exercises, exercises, and beyond the numbers. Answers are provided for each section along with explanations, when appropriate. The six sections provide a comprehensive review of the material in each chapter and should be used after you have read each chapter thoroughly to determine which topics you understand and those requiring further study.

**Demonstration Problems.** Two demonstration problems are provided for each chapter. These problems attempt to incorporate as many of the topics in the chapter as possible. For some chapters, the first demonstration problem must be completed before the second one is attempted. For those chapters, complete the first one, check your answers, make any necessary corrections, then go on to the second problem. The solutions to the demonstration problems provide explanations as well.

THIS STUDY GUIDE IS NOT A SUBSTITUTE FOR YOUR TEXTBOOK. It is designed as an additional support tool to assist you in succeeding in your accounting course.

Comments about the Study Guide are encouraged and should be sent to me in care of the publisher.

Stephen C. Schaefer
*Contra Costa College*

# Acknowledgments

Thanks to Loc Huynh, a former student and graduate of the Walter A. Haas School of Business at the University of California-Berkeley, for his invaluable assistance in the preparation of this Study Guide. Loc did all the word processing and his comments and suggestions were always thought provoking and worthwhile. Thanks also to Joseph Marshman, a current student at the Walter A. Haas School of Business, for his help with proofreading and error checking. Thanks to current and former students who are a constant source of inspiration and challenge.

# Chapter 12 - Accounting for Partnerships

## CHAPTER OVERVIEW

In Chapter 1 you were introduced to the three legal forms of business organization: sole proprietorships, partnerships, and corporation. Since then, the focus has been on either sole proprietorships or corporations. We now turn our attention to the third type, partnerships. This topic can be covered in one chapter because the differences are not all that great and most of the topics covered so far apply to all three forms. The learning objectives for this chapter are to

1. Identify the characteristics of a partnership.
2. Account for partner's initial investments in a partnership.
3. Allocate profits and losses to the partners by different methods.
4. Account for the admission of a new partner to the business.
5. Account for the withdrawal of a partner from the business.
6. Account for the liquidation of a partnership.
7. Prepare partnership financial statements.

## CHAPTER REVIEW

### Objective 1 - Identify the characteristics of a partnership.

A **partnership** is an association of two or more persons who are co-owners of a business for profit. Partners frequently draw up a **partnership agreement**, also called **articles of partnership**. This agreement is a contract between the partners which sets forth the duties and rights of each partner.

The **characteristics of a partnership** are:

1. **Limited life**. The addition or withdrawal of a partner dissolves the partnership.
2. **Mutual agency**. Every partner has the authority to obligate the business to contracts within the scope of regular business operations.
3. **Unlimited liability**. If the partnership cannot pay its debts, the partners are personally responsible for payment.
4. **Co-ownership**. Assets of the business become the joint property of the partnership.
5. **No partnership income taxes**. The net income of a partnership is divided among the partners, who individually pay income taxes on their portions of the partnership's income.
6. **Partners' owner's equity accounts**. Separate owner's equity accounts will be set up for each partner, both a Capital account and Withdrawal account.

Exhibit 12-2 in your text summarizes the advantages and disadvantages of partnerships.

## Objective 2 - Account for partner's initial investments in a partnership.

Partners may invest assets and liabilities in a business. The simplest investment to account for is cash:

| Cash | XX | |
| Partner's Name, Capital | | XX |

Assets other than cash are recorded at their current market value. Suppose Craine invests land in a partnership. The land cost $60,000 several years ago and has a current market value of $95,000. The correct entry on the partnership's books is:

| Land | 95,000 | |
| Craine, Capital | | 95,000 |

## Objective 3 - Allocate profits and losses to the partners by different methods.

If there is no partnership agreement, or the agreement does not specify how profits and losses are to be divided, then the partners share profits and losses equally. If the agreement specifies a method for sharing profits, but not losses, then losses are shared in the same manner as profits.

Several methods exist to allocate profits and losses. Partners may share profits and losses according to a stated fraction or percentage. If the partnership agreement allocates 2/3 of the profits and losses to Chang, and 1/3 to Estrada, then the entry to record the allocation of $60,000 of income is:

| Income Summary | 60,000 | |
| Chang, Capital | | 40,000 |
| Estrada, Capital | | 20,000 |

The partnership agreement may provide that profits and losses be allocated in proportion to the partner's capital contributions to the business. To find the income allocated to a particular partner, use this formula:

$$\text{Income allocated to a partner} = \frac{\text{Partner's capital}}{\text{Total capital}} \times \text{Net income}$$

Suppose Chang and Estrada have the capital balances listed below:

| Chang, Capital | 240,000 |
| Estrada, Capital | 160,000 |
| Total Capital balances | 400,000 |

Partnership income of $60,000 will be allocated as follows:

| Chang: | (240,000 / 400,000) 60,000 = | 36,000 |
| Estrada: | (160,000 / 400,000) 60,000 = | 24,000 |
| Total income allocated to partners | | 60,000 |

The entry to record the allocation of profits is:

| | | |
|---|---|---|
| Income Summary | 60,000 | |
|     Chang, Capital | | 36,000 |
|     Estrada, Capital | | 24,000 |

Sharing of profits and losses may also be allocated based on a combination of capital contributions, service to the business, and/or interest on capital contributions. The important point to remember is to follow the exact order of allocation specified by the partnership agreement.

When a loss occurs the process does not change. Simply follow the terms of the agreement (or divide the loss equally in the absence of an agreement) in the order specified.

Partners generally make periodic withdrawals of cash from a partnership. If Estrada withdraws $5,000 from the partnership, the entry is:

| | | |
|---|---|---|
| Estrada, Drawing | 5,000 | |
|     Cash | | 5,000 |

The drawing accounts must be closed to the capital accounts at the end of the period. If Estrada's $5,000 withdrawal is the only withdrawal during the period, the closing entry is:

| | | |
|---|---|---|
| Estrada, Capital | 5,000 | |
|     Estrada, Drawing | | 5,000 |

## Objective 4 - Account for the admission of a new partner to the business.

Remember that a partnership is dissolved when a new partner is added or an existing partner withdraws. Often a new partnership is immediately formed to replace the old partnership. CPA firms and law firms often admit new partners and have existing partners retire during the course of a year.

A new partner may be admitted into an existing partnership either by purchasing a present partner's interest or by investing in the partnership. The new partner must be approved by all the current partners in order to participate in the business.

When **purchasing a partnership interest**, the new partner pays the old partner directly, according to the terms of the purchase agreement. The purchase transaction has no effect on the partnership's books. The only entry the partnership will make is to close the old partner's capital account and open the new partner's capital account:

| | | |
|---|---|---|
| Old Partner, Capital | XX | |
|     New Partner, Capital | | XX |

A person may also be admitted to a partnership by directly **investing in the partnership**. This investment can be a simple investment, and is recorded as:

    Cash and Other assets              XX
        New Partner, Capital                XX

The new partner's interest in the business will equal:

$$\text{New partner's interest} = \frac{\text{New partner's capital}}{\text{Total capital}}$$

Note that sharing of profits and losses is determined by the new partnership agreement, and not by the proportion of total capital allotted to the new partner.

Successful partnerships frequently require incoming partners to pay a **bonus** to existing partners. In this situation, the incoming partner will pay more for a portion of the partnership interest than the amount of capital he receives. The difference, which is a bonus to the existing partners, is computed by a three-step calculation:

1)      Total capital before new partner's investment
      + New partner's investment
      = Total capital after new partner's investment

2)      New partner's capital = Total capital after new partner's investment new partner's interest in the partnership

3)      Bonus to existing partners = New partner's investment - New partner's capital

The entry on the partnership books to record the transaction is:

    Cash                               XX
        New Partner, Capital                XX
        Old Partners, Capital               XX

Note that the bonus paid by the new partner is credited to the old partners' Capital account. The allocation of the bonus to existing partners is based on the partnership agreement of the existing partners.

In some cases, a potential new partner may bring substantial future benefits to a partnership, such as a well-known reputation. In this situation, the existing partners may offer the newcomer a partnership share that includes a bonus. The calculation is similar to the calculation for a bonus to the existing partners:

1)      Total capital before new partner's investment
      + New partner's investment
      = Total capital after new partner's investment

2)      New partner's capital = Total capital after new partner's investment
New partner's interest in the partnership

3)      Bonus to new partner = New partner's investment - New partner's investment

The entry on the partnership books to record the transaction is:

| | | |
|---|---|---|
| Cash and Other Assets | XX | |
| Old Partners, Capital | XX | |
|     New Partner, Capital | | XX |

Note that the bonus paid to the new partner is debited to the old partners' Capital accounts. The allocation of the bonus to the new partner is based on the partnership agreement of the existing partners.

## Objective 5 - Account for the withdrawal of a partner from the business.

Partners may **withdraw from a partnership** due to retirement, partnership disputes, or other reasons. The withdrawing partner may sell his or her interest or may receive the appropriate portion of the business directly from the partnership in the form of cash, other partnership assets, or notes.

The first step is to determine whether the partnership assets are to be valued at book value or market value. If assets are to be valued at market value, they must be revalued, often by an independent appraiser. Increases in asset values are debited to asset accounts and credited to the partners capital accounts (according to the profit-and-loss sharing ratio). Decreases in asset values are debited to the partners' capital accounts and credited to asset accounts. The revalued assets then become the new book value of the assets.

A partner may withdraw from a partnership at book value, at less than book value, or at more than book value. (Remember that book value may or may not be equal to current market value, depending upon whether the assets have been revalued or not.) A partner willing to withdraw at less than book value may be eager to leave the partnership. A partner withdrawing at more than book value may be collecting a bonus from the remaining partners, who may be eager to have the partner withdraw.

Withdrawal at book value is recorded as:

| | | |
|---|---|---|
| Withdrawing Partner, Capital | XX | |
|     Cash, Other Assets, or Note Payable | | XX |

Withdrawal at less than book value is recorded by:

| | | |
|---|---|---|
| Withdrawing Partner, Capital | XX | |
|     Cash, Other Assets, or Note Payable | | XX |
|     Remaining Partners, Capital | | XX |

When a partner withdraws at less than book value, the difference between the withdrawing partner's capital and the payment to the withdrawing partner is allocated to the remaining partners based on the new profit-and-loss ratio.

Withdrawal at more than book value is recorded by:

| | | |
|---|---|---|
| Withdrawing Partner, Capital | XX | |
| Remaining Partners, Capital | XX | |
|     Cash, Other Assets, or Note Payable | | XX |

When a partner withdraws at more than book value, the difference between the payment to the withdrawing partner and the withdrawing partner's capital is allocated to the remaining partners based on the new profit-and-loss ratio.

The death of a partner also dissolves the partnership. The books are closed to determine the deceased partner's capital balance on the date of death. Settlement with the partner's estate is made according to the partnership agreement. The entry is:

| | | |
|---|---|---|
| Deceased Partner, Capital | XX | |
|     Liability Payable to Estate | | XX |

## Objective 6 - Account for the liquidation of a partnership.

**Liquidation** is the process of going out of business and involves three basic steps:

1. Selling the partnership assets and allocating gains or losses to the partners' capital accounts based on the profit-and-loss ratio.
2. Paying the partnership liabilities.
3. Distributing the remaining cash to the partners based on their capital balances.

When selling assets, gains result in credits (increases) to partners' capital accounts. Losses result in debits (decreases) to partners' capital accounts.

The general worksheet for liquidation of a partnership is:

| | Cash | + | Noncash Assets | = | Liabilities | + | Capital | |
|---|---|---|---|---|---|---|---|---|
| Balances before sale of assets | XX | | XX | | XX | | XX | |
| Sale of assets and sharing of | | | | | | | XX | if gain |
|     gains and (losses) | XX | | (XX) | | | | (XX) | if loss |
| Balances after sale of assets | XX | | -0- | | | | XX | |
| Payment of liabilities | (XX) | | | | (XX) | | | |
| Balances after payment of | | | | | | | | |
|     liabilities | XX | | -0- | | -0- | | XX | |
| Disbursement of cash to | | | | | | | | |
|     partners | (XX) | | | | | | (XX) | |
| Ending balances | -0- | | -0- | | -0- | | -0- | |

Accounting for Partnerships 311

Occasionally, allocation of losses on the sale of assets results in a capital deficiency for one or more partners. The deficient partner should contribute personal assets to eliminate the deficiency. If not, the deficiency must be allocated to the remaining partners.

## Objective 7 - Prepare partnership financial statements.

Partnership financial statements are similar to the financial statements of a proprietorship. The exceptions are that a partnership income statement includes a section showing the division of net income to the partners, and the owners' equity section of the balance sheet includes accounts for each partner.

# TEST YOURSELF

All the self-testing materials in this chapter focus on information and procedures that your instructor is likely to test in quizzes and examinations.

**I. Matching**  *Match each numbered term with its lettered definition.*

\_\_\_\_\_ 1. partnership agreement or articles of partnership
\_\_\_\_\_ 2. capital deficiency
\_\_\_\_\_ 3. unlimited personal liability
\_\_\_\_\_ 4. dissolution
\_\_\_\_\_ 5. liquidation
\_\_\_\_\_ 6. mutual agency
\_\_\_\_\_ 7. bonus
\_\_\_\_\_ 8. limited partner
\_\_\_\_\_ 9. general partner

A. a contract among partners specifying such things as the name, location, and nature of the business; the name, capital investment, and the duties of each partner; and the method of sharing profits and losses by the partners
B. a debit balance in a partner's capital account
C. ending of a partnership
D. the ability of every partner to bind the business to a contract within the scope of the partnership's regular business operations
E. the process of going out of business
F. when partnership (or a proprietorship) cannot pay its debts with business assets, the partners (or the proprietor) must use personal assets to meet the debt
G. a partner in a limited partnership whose liability is unlimited
H. a partner in a limited partnership whose liability is limited
I. results when assets contributed (or withdrawn) do not equal the amount credited (or debited) to a partner's capital account

**II. Multiple Choice**  *Circle the best answer.*

1. Which of the following provisions will *not* be found in the partnership agreement?

   A. liquidation procedures
   B. profit-and-loss ratio
   C. withdrawals allowed to partners
   D. dividends payable to partners

2. Which of the following does *not* result in dissolution of a partnership?

   A. addition of a new partner
   B. withdrawal of a partner
   C. marriage of a partner
   D. death of a partner

3. Assets and liabilities contributed by a partner to a partnership are recorded at:

   A. expected future value
   B. fair market value
   C. original cost
   D. book value

Accounting for Partnerships

4. Profits and losses are usually shared by partners according to

   A. verbal agreements
   B. the balance in partners' equity accounts
   C. partners' personal wealth
   D. the partnership agreement

5. When a partner takes money out of the partnership, the partner's:

   A. drawing is credited
   B. drawing is debited
   C. capital is debited
   D. capital is credited

6. A new partner may be admitted to a partnership:

   A. only by investing in the partnership
   B. only by purchasing a partner's interest
   C. by purchasing common stock of the partnership
   D. either by investing in the partnership or by purchasing a partner's interest

7. In a partnership liquidation, a gain from the sale of assets is allocated to the:

   A. payment of partnership liabilities
   B. partners based on their capital balances
   C. partner with the lowest capital balance
   D. partners based on their profit-and-loss ratio

8. If a partner has a debit balance in his capital account and is personally insolvent, then the other partners:

   A. absorb the deficiency based on their personal wealth
   B. absorb the deficiency based on their capital balances
   C. absorb the deficiency based on their profit-and-loss ratio
   D. sue the insolvent partner's spouse

9. ABC partnership shares profits and losses in a 5:4:3 ratio respectively. This means:

   A. partner A receives 5/12 of the profits
   B. partner A receives 5/9 of the profits
   C. partner B receives 1/4 of the profits
   D. partner C receives 1/3 of the profits

10. In a limited partnership, which of the following is false?

    A. there must be more than one partner
    B. there must be at least one general partner
    C. all partners have unlimited liability
    D. some partners have limited liability

### III. Completion   *Complete each of the following statements.*

1. If the partnership agreement does not specify a profit-and-loss ratio, profits and losses are allocated _____.

2. The five characteristics of a partnership are: 1) _____, 2) _____, 3) _____, 4) _____, and 5) _____.

3. The difference between a partnership and sole proprietorship is that a partnership has _____ _____ owners, while a sole proprietorship has _____ owner.

4. _____ refers to the ability of any partner to contract on behalf of the partnership.
5. A _____ occurs when a new partner is admitted or an existing partner leaves a partnership.
6. A partnership undergoes _____ when it ceases operations and settles all its affairs.
7. A debit balance in a partner's capital account is called _____.
8. The steps in liquidating a partnership are:
   1) _____
   2) _____
   3) _____
   4) _____
9. A partner with limited liability is called a _____.
10. When liquidating, cash is distributed to the partners according to the _____.

## IV. Daily Exercises

1. Two sole proprietors, Wells Co. and Bank Co., decide to form a partnership called Wells Bank. Wells will contribute the following to the proprietorship:

   | | |
   |---|---|
   | Cash | 8,000 |
   | Inventory | 7,200 |
   | Equipment | 11,700 |
   | Liabilities | 6,100 |

   The current market value of the equipment is $9,000 and the current market value of the inventory is $7,600. Record the journal entry to reflect Wells' investment.

   | Accounts and Explanation | Debit | Credit |
   |---|---|---|
   | | | |
   | | | |
   | | | |
   | | | |
   | | | |
   | | | |

2. The ACE partnership reported $45,000 net income its first year of operations If the partners neglected to agree on the distribution of profits, how much should partners A, C, and E receive?

3. Refer to the information in Daily Exercise #2 above, but assume the partners agreed to a $12,000 per partner salary allowance, with any balance divided 3:2:1 among A, C, and E. Calculate the amount owed to each partner.

Accounting for Partnerships

4. Review the information in Daily Exercises #3 above, but assume the first year resulted in net income of $6,000. Calculate the amount A, C, and E should receive.

5. Record the journal entry for Daily Exercise #4 above.

| Accounts and Explanation | Debit | Credit |
|---|---|---|
|  |  |  |
|  |  |  |
|  |  |  |
|  |  |  |
|  |  |  |

6. A partnership has decided to liquidate. After selling the assets and paying the debts, $9,000 in liabilities remain outstanding. To whom should the creditors look for payment?

7. Assume the same information in Daily Exercise #5, except the partnership is a limited partnership. How would your answer change?

## V. Exercises

1. Lewis and Clark formed a partnership. Lewis contributed cash of $9,000 and land with a fair market value of $65,000 that had cost $14,000. The partnership also assumed Lewis's note payable of $24,000. Clark contributed $20,000 in cash, equipment with a fair market value of $14,000 that had cost $22,000, and the partnership assumed his accounts receivable of $3,200.

Make journal entries to show each partner's contribution to the business.

| Date | Accounts and Explanation | PR | Debit | Credit |
|---|---|---|---|---|
|  |  |  | 9000 |  |
|  |  |  | 65000 |  |
|  |  |  |  |  |
|  |  |  |  |  |
|  |  |  |  |  |
|  |  |  |  |  |
|  |  |  |  |  |
|  |  |  |  |  |

316 Chapter 12

2. Price and Cost formed a partnership. Price invested $75,000 and Cost invested $50,000. Price devotes most of his time on the road developing the business, while Cost devotes some of his time to managing the home office and the rest of his time watching television. They have agreed to share profits as follows:

   - The first $50,000 of profits is allocated based on the partner's capital contribution.
   - The next $50,000 of profits is allocated 3/4 to Price and 1/4 to Cost based on their service to the partnership.
   - Any remaining amount is allocated equally.

   A. If the partnership profits are $110,000, how much will be allocated to Price, and how much will be allocated to Cost?
   B. If the partnership has a loss of $70,000, how much will be allocated to Price, and how much will be allocated to Cost?
   C. If the partnership profits are $62,000, how much will be allocated to Price, and how much will be allocated to Cost?

A.

|  | Price | Cost | Total |
|---|---|---|---|
|  |  |  |  |
|  |  |  |  |
|  |  |  |  |
|  |  |  |  |
|  |  |  |  |
|  |  |  |  |
|  |  |  |  |
|  |  |  |  |
|  |  |  |  |
|  |  |  |  |
|  |  |  |  |
|  |  |  |  |
|  |  |  |  |
|  |  |  |  |
|  |  |  |  |
|  |  |  |  |

B.

|  | Price | Cost | Total |
|---|---|---|---|
|  |  |  |  |
|  |  |  |  |
|  |  |  |  |
|  |  |  |  |
|  |  |  |  |
|  |  |  |  |
|  |  |  |  |
|  |  |  |  |
|  |  |  |  |
|  |  |  |  |
|  |  |  |  |
|  |  |  |  |

C.

|  | Price | Cost | Total |
|---|---|---|---|
|  |  |  |  |
|  |  |  |  |
|  |  |  |  |
|  |  |  |  |
|  |  |  |  |
|  |  |  |  |
|  |  |  |  |
|  |  |  |  |
|  |  |  |  |
|  |  |  |  |
|  |  |  |  |
|  |  |  |  |
|  |  |  |  |

3. Keith and Vince are partners in a landscaping business. Their capital balances are $24,000 and $16,000 respectively. They share profits and losses equally. They admit Amy to a one-fourth interest with a cash investment of $8,000. Make the journal entry to show the admission of Amy to the partnership.

| Date | Accounts and Explanation | PR | Debit | Credit |
|---|---|---|---|---|
|  |  |  |  |  |
|  |  |  |  |  |
|  |  |  |  |  |
|  |  |  |  |  |

4. Anne, Barbara, and Cathy are partners with capital balances of $15,000, $45,000, and $30,000 respectively. They share profits and losses equally. Barbara decides to retire.

   A. Make the journal entry to show Barbara's retirement if she is allowed to withdraw $25,000 in cash.

   | Date | Accounts and Explanation | PR | Debit | Credit |
   |------|--------------------------|----|-------|--------|
   |      |                          |    |       |        |
   |      |                          |    |       |        |
   |      |                          |    |       |        |
   |      |                          |    |       |        |
   |      |                          |    |       |        |

   B. Make the journal entry to show Barbara's retirement if she is allowed to withdraw $45,000 in cash.

   | Date | Accounts and Explanation | PR | Debit | Credit |
   |------|--------------------------|----|-------|--------|
   |      |                          |    |       |        |
   |      |                          |    |       |        |
   |      |                          |    |       |        |
   |      |                          |    |       |        |
   |      |                          |    |       |        |

   C. Make the journal entry to show Barbara's retirement if she is allowed to withdraw $55,000 in cash.

   | Date | Accounts and Explanation | PR | Debit | Credit |
   |------|--------------------------|----|-------|--------|
   |      |                          |    |       |        |
   |      |                          |    |       |        |
   |      |                          |    |       |        |
   |      |                          |    |       |        |
   |      |                          |    |       |        |

5. The following balance sheet information is given for Three Ts Company:

   | | | | |
   |---|---|---|---|
   | Cash | 16,000 | Liabilities | 28,000 |
   | Noncash assets | 56,000 | Tom, Capital | 6,000 |
   |  |  | Tran, Capital | 24,000 |
   |  |  | Tony, Capital | 14,000 |
   | Total assets | 72,000 | Total liabilities and capital | 72,000 |

   Tom, Tran, and Tony use a profit and loss ratio of 3:4:1, respectively. Assume that any partner with a deficit in his or her capital account is insolvent.

Prepare the journal entries for liquidation assuming the noncash assets are sold for $20,000.

| Date | Accounts and Explanation | PR | Debit | Credit |
|------|--------------------------|----|-------|--------|
|      |                          |    |       |        |

## VI. Beyond the Numbers

Review the information in Exercises 5. Assume all information is the same except Tom is a limited partner. Prepare journal entries to record the liquidation.

| Date | Accounts and Explanation | PR | Debit | Credit |
|------|--------------------------|----|-------|--------|
|      |                          |    |       |        |

## VII. Demonstration Problems

### Demonstration Problem #1

The partnership of Russell and Stoner is considering admitting Wayne as a partner on April 1, 1999. The partnership general ledger includes the following balances on that date:

| | | | |
|---|---|---|---|
| Cash | 40,000 | Total liabilities | 50,000 |
| Other assets | 85,000 | Russell, Capital | 25,000 |
| | | Stoner, Capital | 50,000 |
| Total assets | 125,000 | Total liabilities and capital | 125,000 |

Russell's share of profit and losses is 1/3 and Stoner's share is 2/3.

### Required:

1. Assume that Wayne pays Stoner $75,000 to acquire Stoner's interest of the business, and that Russell has approved Wayne as a new partner.

   a. Prepare the journal entries for the transfer of partner's equity on the partnership books.
   b. Prepare the partnership balance sheet immediately after Wayne is admitted as a partner.

2. Suppose Wayne becomes a partner by investing $75,000 cash to acquire a one-fourth interest in the business.

   a. Prepare a schedule to compute Wayne's capital balance. Record Wayne's investment in the business.
   b. Prepare the partnership balance sheet immediately after Wayne is admitted as a partner.

### Requirement 1

a. (Journal entry)

| Date | Accounts and Explanation | PR | Debit | Credit |
|------|--------------------------|----|----|----|
| | | | | |
| | | | | |
| | | | | |

b.

Russell, Stoner, and Wayne<br>Balance Sheet<br>April 1, 1999

| | | | |
|---|---|---|---|
| | | | |
| | | | |
| | | | |
| | | | |

Accounting for Partnerships

## Requirement 2

a. Computation of Wayne's capital balance:

(Journal entry)

| Date | Accounts and Explanation | PR | Debit | Credit |
|------|--------------------------|----|-------|--------|
|      |                          |    |       |        |
|      |                          |    |       |        |
|      |                          |    |       |        |
|      |                          |    |       |        |
|      |                          |    |       |        |

b. (Balance Sheet)

Russell, Stoner, and Wayne<br>Balance Sheet<br>April, 1999

|   |   |   |   |
|---|---|---|---|
|   |   |   |   |
|   |   |   |   |
|   |   |   |   |
|   |   |   |   |

## Demonstration Problem #2

The partnership of B, T, and U is liquidating. The partnership agreement allocated profits to the partners in the ratio of 3:2:1. In liquidation, the noncash assets were sold in a single transaction for $120,000 on August 31, 1999. The partnership paid the liabilities the same day. The partnership accounts are presented at the top of the liquidation schedule which follows.

1. Complete the schedule summarizing the liquidation transactions. See the format on the next page. You may wish to refer to the partnership liquidation exhibits in the text. Assume that U invests cash of $4,000 in the partnership in partial settlement of any capital account deficiency. This cash is distributed to the other partners. The other partners must absorb the remainder of the capital deficiency.
2. Journalize the liquidation transactions.
3. Post the liquidation entries.

**Requirement 1 (Summary of liquidation transactions)**

|   | Cash | + | Noncash Assets | = | Liabilities | + | B (1/2) | + | Capital T (1/3) | + | U (1/6) |
|---|---|---|---|---|---|---|---|---|---|---|---|
| Balance before sale of assets | 30,000 | | 240,000 | | 120,000 | | 90,000 | | 50,000 | | 10,000 |
| a) Sale of assets and sharing of loss | | | | | | | | | | | |
| Balances | | | | | | | | | | | |
| b) Payment of liabilities | | | | | | | | | | | |
| Balances | | | | | | | | | | | |
| c) U's investment of cash to share part of his deficiency | | | | | | | | | | | |
| Balances | | | | | | | | | | | |
| d) Sharing of deficiency by remaining partners in ratio of 3/5 to 2/5 | | | | | | | | | | | |
| Balances | | | | | | | | | | | |
| e) Distribution of cash to partners | | | | | | | | | | | |
| Balances | | | | | | | | | | | |

**Requirement 2 (Journal entries to record the liquidation transactions)**

a.

| Date | Accounts and Explanation | PR | Debit | Credit |
|------|--------------------------|----|-------|--------|
|      |                          |    |       |        |
|      |                          |    |       |        |
|      |                          |    |       |        |
|      |                          |    |       |        |
|      |                          |    |       |        |
|      |                          |    |       |        |

b.

| Date | Accounts and Explanation | PR | Debit | Credit |
|------|--------------------------|----|-------|--------|
|      |                          |    |       |        |
|      |                          |    |       |        |
|      |                          |    |       |        |

c.

| Date | Accounts and Explanation | PR | Debit | Credit |
|------|--------------------------|----|-------|--------|
|      |                          |    |       |        |
|      |                          |    |       |        |
|      |                          |    |       |        |

d.

| Date | Accounts and Explanation | PR | Debit | Credit |
|------|--------------------------|----|-------|--------|
|      |                          |    |       |        |
|      |                          |    |       |        |
|      |                          |    |       |        |
|      |                          |    |       |        |

e.

| Date | Accounts and Explanation | PR | Debit | Credit |
|------|--------------------------|----|-------|--------|
|      |                          |    |       |        |
|      |                          |    |       |        |
|      |                          |    |       |        |
|      |                          |    |       |        |

## Requirement 3 (Post the liquidation transactions)

| Cash | Noncash Assets | Liabilities |
|---|---|---|
| 30,000 | 240,000 | 120,000 |

| B, Capital | T, Capital | U, Capital |
|---|---|---|
| 90,000 | 50,000 | 10,000 |

# SOLUTIONS

## I. Matching

1. A
2. B
3. F
4. C
5. E
6. D
7. I
8. H
9. G

## II. Multiple Choice

1. D  Dividends are distributions of earnings paid by corporations to their shareholders. It is a term that is strictly applicable to corporate accounting and as such cannot apply to partnership accounting.

2. C  The marriage of a partner is an event of the partner's personal life and has no direct bearing on the partnership entity. All of the other items listed cause a dissolution of the partnership.

3. B  Using fair market value is appropriate to accurately measure exactly what each partner is bringing into the partnership.

4. D  The partnership agreement can specify the distribution of profits and losses in any manner to which the partners have agreed.

5. B  Withdrawing money from the partnership requires a credit to cash which is balanced with a debit to the partner's Drawing account. The balance of the partner's Drawing account will be closed to his Capital account at the end of the period.

6. D  Of the items listed, answer C "purchasing common stock of the partnership" is inappropriate since partnerships do not have stock; answers A and B are incorrect because of the use of the word "only" in the answers.

7. D  Gains and losses incurred in liquidation are distributed as are any other gains and losses, in accordance with the partnership agreement.

8. C  The deficiency in a partner's capital account balance is distributed as if it were a loss, in accordance with the partnership agreement.

9. A  To determine a partner's fractional share, create a denominator by summing the integers (5 + 4 + 3 = 12) and use the partner's ratio as the numerator. Thus, A receives 5/12, B receives 4/12 or 1/3, and C receives 3/12 or 1/4.

10. C  The key distinction is the limitation of liability by at least one of the partners, who is identified as a limited partner.

## III. Completion

1. equally
2. limited life, mutual agency, unlimited liability, co-ownership of property, no partnership income taxes
3. two or more, one
4. mutual agency
5. dissolution
6. liquidation
7. deficit
8. close the books, sell the assets, pay the debts, distribute the cash (order is important)
9. limited partner
10. the balance in the capital accounts (*not* the profit/loss ratio)

## IV. Daily Exercises

1.

| | | |
|---|---|---|
| Cash | 8,000 | |
| Inventory | 7,600 | |
| Equipment | 9,000 | |
| Liabilities | | 6,100 |
| Wells, Capital | | 18,500 |

Assets contributed are recorded at their current market value. Wells's net investment is $18,500, the difference between the value of the assets ($8,000 + $7,600 + $9,000) less the liabilities.

2. Each partner receives an equal share. When the partners fail to specify, the distribution of profits (and losses) is always equal.

3.

| | Partners | | | Amount |
|---|---|---|---|---|
| | A | C | E | 45,000 |
| Salary Allowance | 12,000 | 12,000 | 12,000 | (36,000) |
| Balance | | | | 9,000 |
| 3:2:1 | 4,500 | 3,000 | 1,500 | (9,000) |
| | 16,500 | 15,000 | 13,500 | 0 |

Proof: $16,500 + $15,000 + $13,500 = $45,000

**Study Tip:** After the calculating, always verify the individual amounts sum back to the original amount.

4.

|  | Partners | | | Amount |
|---|---|---|---|---|
|  | A | C | E | 6,000 |
| Salary Allowance | 12,000 | 12,000 | 12,000 | (36,000) |
| Balance | | | | (30,000) |
| 3:2:1 | (15,000) | (10,000) | (5,000) | (30,000) |
|  | (3,000) | 2,000 | 7,000 | 6,000 |

Proof:  $-3,000 + $2,000 + $7,000 = $6,000

5.
```
A, Capital                3,000
Income Summary            6,000
     C, Capital                    2,000
     E, Capital                    7,000
```

6. The partnership's creditors can look to any of the partners for payment. In a general partnership, each partner has unlimited personal liability for partnership's debts. Creditors would be wise to enforce their claims against the partner with the largest net worth.

7. In a limited partnerships, two classes of partners exist—general and limited. The liability of a limited partner extends only to the amount invested. The fact that liabilities remain after all the assets have been sold and the cash proceeds distributed to creditors indicates the limited partners' obligations have been met. Therefore, the creditors can look only to the general partner(s) for payment.

## V. Exercises

1.

GENERAL JOURNAL

| Date | Accounts and Explanation | PR | Debit | Credit |
|---|---|---|---|---|
|  | Land |  | 65,000 |  |
|  | Cash |  | 9,000 |  |
|  |    Notes Payable |  |  | 24,000 |
|  |    Lewis, Capital |  |  | 50,000 |
|  |  |  |  |  |
|  | Cash |  | 20,000 |  |
|  | Equipment |  | 14,000 |  |
|  | Account Receivable |  | 3,200 |  |
|  |    Clark, Capital |  |  | 37,200 |

2.

A.

|  | Price | Cost | Total |
|---|---|---|---|
| Total net income |  |  | 110,000 |
| Sharing of first $50,000 of net income, based on capital contribution: |  |  |  |
|     Price (75,000/125,000 50,000) | 30,000 |  |  |
|     Cost (50,000/125,000 50,000) |  | 20,000 |  |
|     Total |  |  | 50,000 |
| Net income remaining for allocation |  |  | 60,000 |
| Sharing of the next $50,000 based on service: |  |  |  |
|     Price (3/4 50,000) | 37,500 |  |  |
|     Cost (1/4 50,000) |  | 12,500 |  |
|     Total |  |  | 50,000 |
| Net income remaining for allocation |  |  | 10,000 |
| Remainder shared equally: |  |  |  |
|     Price (1/2 10,000) | 5,000 |  |  |
|     Cost (1/2 10,000) |  | 5,000 |  |
|     Total |  |  | 10,000 |
| Net income remaining for allocation |  |  | -0- |
| Net income allocated to the partners | 72,500 | 37,500 | 110,000 |

B.

|  | Price | Cost | Total |
|---|---|---|---|
| Total net income (loss) |  |  | (70,000) |
| Sharing of first $50,000 of net income (loss), based on capital contribution: |  |  |  |
|     Price (50,000/125,000 50,000) | (30,000) |  |  |
|     Cost (50,000/125,000 50,000) |  | (20,000) |  |
|     Total |  |  | (50,000) |
| Net income (loss) remaining for allocation |  |  | (20,000) |
| Sharing of the remainder based on service: |  |  |  |
|     Price (3/4 20,000) | (15,000) |  |  |
|     Cost (1/4 20,000) |  | (5,000) |  |
|     Total |  |  | (20,000) |
| Net income (loss) remaining for allocation |  |  | -0- |
| Net income (loss) allocated to the partners | (45,000) | (25,000) | (70,000) |

C.

|  | Price | Cost | Total |
|---|---|---|---|
| Total net income |  |  | 62,000 |
| Sharing of first $50,000 of net income, based on capital contribution: |  |  |  |
|    Price (50,000/125,000 50,000) | 30,000 |  |  |
|    Cost (50,000/125,000 50,000) |  | 20,000 |  |
|    Total |  |  | 50,000 |
| Net income remaining for allocation |  |  | 12,000 |
| Sharing of the remainder based on service: |  |  |  |
|    Price (3/4 12,000) | 9,000 |  |  |
|    Cost (1/4 12,000) |  | 3,000 |  |
|    Total |  |  | 12,000 |
| Net income remaining for allocation |  |  | -0- |
| Net income allocated to the partners | 39,000 | 23,000 | 62,000 |

3. Total new partnerships equity is $48,000 ($24,000 + $16,000 + $8,000). One fourth of $48,000 is $12,000.

| Date | Accounts and Explanation | PR | Debit | Credit |
|---|---|---|---|---|
|  | Cash |  | 8,000 |  |
|  | Keith, Capital [1/2 (12,000 - 8,000)] |  | 2,000 |  |
|  | Vince, Capital |  | 2,000 |  |
|  | Amy, Capital [1/4 (24,000 + 16,000 + 8,000)] |  |  | 12,000 |

4.
A.

| Date | Accounts and Explanation | PR | Debit | Credit |
|---|---|---|---|---|
|  | Barbara, Capital |  | 45,000 |  |
|  | Cash |  |  | 25,000 |
|  | Anne, Capital |  |  | 10,000 |
|  | Cathy, Capital |  |  | 10,000 |

B.

| Date | Accounts and Explanation | PR | Debit | Credit |
|---|---|---|---|---|
|  | Barbara, Capital |  | 45,000 |  |
|  | Cash |  |  | 45,000 |

C.

| Date | Accounts and Explanation | PR | Debit | Credit |
|---|---|---|---|---|
|  | Barbara, Capital |  | 45,000 |  |
|  | Anne, Capital |  | 5,000 |  |
|  | Cathy, Capital |  | 5,000 |  |
|  | Cash |  |  | 55,000 |

5.

| Date | Accounts and Explanation | PR | Debit | Credit |
|------|--------------------------|----|-------|--------|
|      | Cash                     |    | 20,000 |       |
|      | Tom, Capital             |    | 13,500 |       |
|      | Tran, Capital            |    | 18,000 |       |
|      | Tony, Capital            |    | 4,500  |       |
|      | Noncash assets           |    |        | 56,000 |

Loss on sale = 36,000 (56,000 - 20,000). Therefore,
- Tom  = 36,000 × 3/8 = 13,500
- Tran = 36,000 × 4/8 = 18,000
- Tony = 36,000 × 1/8 =  4,500

| Date | Accounts and Explanation | PR | Debit | Credit |
|------|--------------------------|----|-------|--------|
|      | Liabilities              |    | 28,000 |       |
|      | Cash                     |    |        | 28,000 |
|      |                          |    |        |        |
|      | Tran, Capital            |    | 6,000  |       |
|      | Tony, Capital            |    | 1,500  |       |
|      | Tom, Capital             |    |        | 7,500  |

Tom's deficit = 7,500 (6,000 - 13,500)
Tran = 4/5 × 7,500 = 6,000
Tony = 1/5 × 7,500 = 1,500

| Date | Accounts and Explanation | PR | Debit | Credit |
|------|--------------------------|----|-------|--------|
|      | Tony, Capital            |    | 8,000  |       |
|      | Cash                     |    |        | 8,000  |
|      | Tran's balance = 0 (24,000 - 18,000 - 6,000 = 0) | | | |

## VI. Beyond the Numbers

| Date | Accounts and Explanation | PR | Debit | Credit |
|------|--------------------------|----|-------|--------|
|      | Cash                     |    | 20,000 |       |
|      | Tom, Capital             |    | 6,000  | *     |
|      | Tran, Capital            |    | 24,000 | **    |
|      | Tony, Capital            |    | 6,000  |       |
|      | Noncash Assets           |    |        | 56,000 |

\* Because Tom is a limited partner, the amount of loss he must absorb is limited to the balance in his capital account.

\*\* After debiting Tom's account for $6,000, the remaining loss is distributed between Tran and Tony, as follows:
- Tran  = 30,000 × 4/5 = 24,000
- Tony  = 30,000 × 1/5 =  6,000

| Date | Accounts and Explanation | PR | Debit | Credit |
|------|--------------------------|----|-------|--------|
|      | Liabilities              |    | 28,000 |       |
|      | Cash                     |    |        | 28,000 |
|      |                          |    |        |        |
|      | Tony, Capital            |    | 8,000  |       |
|      | Cash                     |    |        | 8,000  |

## VII. Demonstration Problems

## Demonstration Problem #1 Solved and Explained

### Requirement 1

a.  July 1   Stoner, Capital                 50,000           Debit closes Stoner's account
             Wayne, Capital                               50,000   Credit opens Wayne's account
    To transfer Stoner's equity in the partnership to Wayne.

Note that the book value of Stoner's capital account ($50,000) is transferred, not the price Wayne paid ($75,000) to buy into the business. Since the partnership received no cash from the transaction, the entry would be the same no matter what Wayne paid Stoner for the interest.

b.

Russell and Wayne<br>Balance Sheet<br>April 1, 1999

| | | | | |
|---|---|---|---|---|
| Cash | 40,000 | Total liabilities | | 50,000 |
| Other assets | 85,000 | Russell, Capital | | 25,000 |
| | | Wayne, Capital | | 50,000 |
| Total assets | $125,000 | Total liabilities and capital | | $125,000 |

### Requirement 2

a.  Computation of Wayne's capital balance:
    Partnership capital before Wayne is admitted
        (25,000 + 50,000)                              $ 75,000
    Wayne's investment in the partnership                75,000
    Partnership capital after Wayne is admitted        $150,000
    Wayne's capital in the partnership
        (100,000 1/4)                                  $ 37,500

| Date | Accounts and Explanation | PR | Debit | Credit |
|---|---|---|---|---|
| April 1 | Cash | | 75,000 | |
| | Wayne, Capital | | | 37,500 |
| | Russell, Capital (1/3 of $37,500) | | | 12,500 |
| | Stoner, Capital (2/3 of $37,500) | | | 25,000 |
| | To admit Wayne as a partner with a one-fourth interest in the business. | | | |

Note that Russell's capital account increased by $12,500 and Stoner's capital account increased by $25,000. These amounts represent Russell and Stoner's proportionate share of the $37,500 amount by which Wayne's $75,000 payment exceeded his $37,500 capital account credit. When a partner is admitted by investment in the partnership, often the investment exceeds the new partner's capital account credit, and the original partners share proportionately in the difference.

b.

Russell, Stoner, and Wayne
Balance Sheet
April, 1999

| | | | |
|---|---|---|---|
| Cash (40,000 + 75,000) | $115,000 | Total liabilities | $ 50,000 |
| Other assets | 85,000 | Russell, Capital | 37,500 |
| | | Stoner, Capital | 75,000 |
| | | Wayne, Capital | 37,500 |
| Total assets | $200,000 | Total liabilities and capital | $200,000 |

Points to Remember

1. Partners may specify any profit or loss sharing method they desire. Common arrangements include:

    a. Sharing equally - unless the partners agree otherwise, profits and losses are required by law to be divided equally
    b. Sharing based on a stated fraction
    c. Sharing based on capital contributions
    d. Sharing based on salaries and interest
    e. Sharing based on a combination of the above and/or other factors

**Study Tip:** Be alert to problems requiring an allocation of profits and losses when the capital account balances are given for each partner, but nothing is specified about the sharing method. When the sharing method is not specified, each partner receives an equal share.

2. New partners are often admitted to established partnerships. Technically, a new partnership is formed to carry on the former partnership's business, and the old partnership ceases to exist (it is dissolved). Although the old partnership dissolves, the business is not normally terminated, nor are the assets liquidated.

**Study Tip:** Be sure you can distinguish between the admission of a partner by purchase of a partner's interest (Requirement 1) and admission by making a direct investment in the proprietorship (Requirement 2).

# Demonstration Problem #2 Solved and Explained

## Requirement 1 (Summary of liquidation transactions)

|  |  | Cash | + | Noncash Assets | = | Liabilities | + | B (1/2) | + | Capital T (1/3) | + | U (1/6) |
|---|---|---|---|---|---|---|---|---|---|---|---|---|
|  | Balance before sale of assets | 30,000 |  | 240,000 |  | 120,000 |  | 90,000 |  | 50,000 |  | 10,000 |
| a) | Sale of assets and sharing of loss | 120,000 |  | (240,000) |  |  |  | (60,000) |  | (40,000) |  | (20,000) |
|  | Balances | 150,000 |  | -0- |  | 120,000 |  | 30,000 |  | 10,000 |  | (10,000) |
| b) | Payment of liabilities | (120,000) |  |  |  | (120,000) |  |  |  |  |  |  |
|  | Balances | 30,000 |  | -0- |  | -0- |  | 30,000 |  | 10,000 |  | (10,000) |
| c) | U's investment of cash to share part of his deficiency | 4,000 |  |  |  |  |  |  |  |  |  | 4,000 |
|  | Balances | 34,000 |  | -0- |  | -0- |  | 30,000 |  | 10,000 |  | (6,000) |
| d) | Sharing of deficiency by remaining partners in ratio of 3/5 to 2/5 |  |  |  |  |  |  | (3,600) |  | (2,400) |  | 6,000 |
|  | Balances | 34,000 |  | -0- |  | -0- |  | 26,400 |  | 7,600 |  | -0- |
| e) | Distribution of cash to partners | (34,000) |  |  |  |  |  | (26,400) |  | (7,600) |  |  |
|  | Balances | -0- |  | -0- |  | -0- |  | -0- |  | -0- |  | -0- |

## Requirement 2 (Journal entries to record the liquidation transactions)

a.

| Date | Accounts and Explanation | PR | Debit | Credit |
|------|--------------------------|----|----|----|
|  | Cash |  | 120,000 |  |
|  | B, Capital [(240,000 - 120,000) 3/6] |  | 60,000 |  |
|  | T, Capital [(240,000 - 80,000) 2/6] |  | 40,000 |  |
|  | U, Capital [(200,000 - 80,000) 1/6] |  | 20,000 |  |
|  | Noncash Assets |  |  | 240,000 |
|  | To record the sale of noncash assets in liquidation, and to distribute loss to partners. |  |  |  |

b.

| Date | Accounts and Explanation | PR | Debit | Credit |
|------|--------------------------|----|----|----|
|  | Liabilities |  | 120,000 |  |
|  | Cash |  |  | 120,000 |
|  | To pay liabilities in liquidation. |  |  |  |

c.

| Date | Accounts and Explanation | PR | Debit | Credit |
|------|--------------------------|----|----|----|
|  | Cash |  | 4,000 |  |
|  | U, Capital |  |  | 4,000 |
|  | T's contribution to pay part of the capital deficiency in liquidation. |  |  |  |

After posting the entries above, U's capital account reveals a $6,000 deficiency, indicated by its debit balance:

```
                     U, Capital
     Loss on sale   20,000  | Bal.         10,000
                            | Investment    4,000
     Bal.    6,000          |
```

d.

| Date | Accounts and Explanation | PR | Debit | Credit |
|------|--------------------------|----|----|----|
|  | B, Capital ($6,000 3/5) |  | 3,600 |  |
|  | T, Capital ($4,000 2/5) |  | 2,400 |  |
|  | U, Capital |  |  | 6,000 |
|  | To allocate U's capital deficiency to the other partners in their profit and loss ratios. |  |  |  |

Prior to U's withdrawal from the partnership, the partners shared profits and losses as follows:

Ratio:   B   3 = 1/2
         T   2 = 1/3
         U   1 = 1/6

Accounting for Partnerships

The remaining partners are required to absorb the deficiency left by a partner who is unable to contribute sufficient capital to cover the deficiency. After a $4,000 contribution, U's deficiency was reduced to $6,000. Note that between B and T, profits and losses are shared in the ratio of 3 to 2 (or 60% and 40%). As a result, U's uncovered deficiency is allocated to B and T by reducing their capital accounts by $3,600 ($6,000÷60%) and $2,400 ($6,000÷40%), respectively.

e.

| Date | Accounts and Explanation | PR | Debit | Credit |
|---|---|---|---|---|
| | B, Capital | | 26,400 | |
| | T, Capital | | 7,600 | |
| | Cash | | | 34,000 |
| | To distribute cash to partners on liquidation of partnership. | | | |

**Requirement 3 (Post the liquidation transactions)**

Cash
| | | | |
|---|---|---|---|
| Bal. | 30,000 | Payment of liabilities | 120,000 (b) |
| (a) Sale of assets | 120,000 | | |
| (c) U's contribution | 4,000 | | |
| Bal. | 34,000 | Final distribution | 34,000 (e) |
| Bal. | 0 | | |

Noncash Assets
| | |
|---|---|
| Bal. 240,000 | 240,000 (a) |

Liabilities
| | |
|---|---|
| (b) 120,000 | Bal. 120,000 |

B, Capital
| | | | |
|---|---|---|---|
| (a) Loss of sale | 60,000 | Bal. | 90,000 |
| (c) Loss on U | 3,600 | | |
| Final distribution | 26,400 | Bal. | 26,400 |
| | | Bal. | 0 |

T, Capital
| | | | |
|---|---|---|---|
| (a) Loss on sale | 40,000 | Bal. | 50,000 |
| (d) Loss on U | 2,400 | | |
| (e) Final distribution | 7,600 | Bal. | 7,600 |
| | | Bal. | 0 |

U, Capital
| | | | |
|---|---|---|---|
| (a) Loss on sale | 20,000 | Bal. | 10,000 |
| | | Investment | 4,000 (c) |
| Bal. | 6,000 | Bal. | 6,000 (d) |
| | | Bal. | 0 |

# Chapter 13 - Corporate Organization, Paid-In Capital, and the Balance Sheet

## CHAPTER OVERVIEW

In Chapter 12 you learned about the partnership form of organization. In this chapter, we begin an in-depth discussion of the corporate form of organization. Because the corporate form is more complex than either sole proprietorships or partnerships, our discussion of corporations continues in Chapter 14, 15, and 16. Therefore, an understanding of the topics in this chapter is important before continuing to the next chapter. The learning objectives for this chapter are to

1. Identify the characteristics of a corporation.
2. Record the issuance of stock.
3. Prepare the stockholders' equity section of a corporation balance sheet.
4. Account for cash dividends.
5. Use different stock values in decision making.
6. Evaluate a company's return on assets and return on stockholders' equity.
7. Account for a corporation's income tax.

## CHAPTER REVIEW

### Objective 1 - Identify the characteristics of a corporation.

1. A corporation is a **separate legal entity** chartered and regulated under state law. The owners' equity of a corporation is held by stockholders as shares of stock.
2. A corporation has **continuous life**. A change in ownership of the stock does not affect the life of the corporation.
3. **Mutual agency of owners is not present** in corporations. A stockholder cannot commit a corporation to a binding contract (unless that stockholder is also an officer of the corporation).
4. Stockholders have **limited liability**. That is, they have no personal obligation for the debts of the corporation.
5. **Ownership and management are separated**. Corporations are controlled by boards of directors who appoint officers to manage the business. Boards of directors are elected by stockholders. Thus, stockholders are not obligated to manage the business; ownership is separate from management.
6. **Corporations pay taxes**: state franchise taxes and federal and state income taxes. Corporations pay dividends to stockholders who then pay personal income taxes on their dividends. This is considered double taxation of corporate earnings.

Exhibit 13-1 in your text summarizes the advantages and disadvantages of a corporation.

Corporations come into existence when a **charter** is obtained from a relevant state official. **Bylaws** are then adopted. The stockholders elect a **board of directors**, who appoint the officers of the corporation. (Review Exhibit 13-2 in your text.)

Owners receive **stock certificates** for their investment. The basic unit of investment is a **share**. A corporation's outstanding stock is the shares of its stock that are held by stockholders. Stockholders' equity is reported differently than owners' equity of a proprietorship or a partnership because corporations must report the sources of their capital. These sources are **paid-in or contributed capital** from sale of stock, and **retained earnings**. Generally, paid-in capital is not subject to withdrawal. Retained Earnings is the account that at any time is the sum of earnings accumulated since incorporation, minus any losses, and minus all dividends distributed to stockholders. Revenues and expenses are closed into Income Summary and then Income Summary is closed to Retained Earnings. To close net income, debit Income Summary and credit Retained Earnings. To close net loss, debit Retained Earnings and credit Income Summary.

**Stockholders** have four basic **rights**:

1. to participate in management by voting their shares,
2. to receive a proportionate share of any dividend,
3. to a proportionate share of the remaining assets after payment of liabilities in the event of liquidation, and
4. to maintain a proportionate ownership in the corporation (**preemptive right**).

**Stock** may be **common** or **preferred** and have a **par value** or **no-par value**. **Par value** is an arbitrary value that a corporation assigns to a share of stock. Different classes of common or preferred stock may also be issued. Each class of common or preferred stock is recorded in a separate general ledger account. Preferred stockholders receive their dividends before common stockholders and take priority over common stockholders in the receipt of assets if the corporation liquidates.

The corporate charter specifies the number of shares a corporation is authorized to issue. The corporation is not required to issue all the stock it is authorized to issue.

Exhibit 13-6 in your text compares common stock, preferred stock, and long-term debt.

## Objective 2 - Record the issuance of stock.

If a corporation sells common stock for a cash receipt equal to the par value, the entry to record the transaction is:

| | | |
|---|---|---|
| Cash | XX | |
|     Common Stock | | XX |

Par value is usually set low enough so that stock will not be sold below par. A corporation usually sells its common stock for a price above par value, that is, at a premium. The **premium** is also paid-in capital, but is recorded in a separate account called **Paid-In Capital in Excess of Par Value**. A premium is not a gain, income, or profit to the corporation. A corporation cannot earn a profit or incur a loss by buying or selling its own stock. The entry to record stock issued at a price in excess of par value is:

| | | |
|---|---|---|
| Cash | XX | |
|     Common Stock | | XX |
|     Paid-in Capital in Excess | | |
|         of Par - Common Stock | | XX |

If no-par common stock has no stated value, the entry is the same as for a cash selling price equal to par value (above). Accounting for no-par common stock with a **stated value** is identical to accounting for par-value stock. When a corporation receives non-cash assets as an investment, the assets are recorded by the corporation at their current market value.

Accounting for preferred stock follows the same pattern as accounting for common stock. The difference is that instead of the word "Common," the word "Preferred" will appear in the titles of the general ledger accounts.

Occasionally a corporation will receive a donation such as land or some other asset. The donated asset is recorded at its current market value. If the donation is received from a governmental agency, the account Donated Capital is credited. Donated Capital is a separate category of Paid-in Capital and is listed on the balance sheet. If the donation is received from someone other than a governmental agency, the account credited is Revenue from Donations and reported as Other Revenue on the income statement.

## Objective 3 - Prepare the stockholders' equity section of a balance sheet.

Preferred stock always appears before common stock in the stockholders' equity section of the balance sheet.

The format of the stockholders' equity section of the balance sheet is:

                    Stockholders' Equity
Paid-in capital:
  Preferred stock, $ par, number of shares authorized,
    number of shares issued                                XX
  Paid-in capital in excess of par - preferred stock       XX
  Common stock, $ par, number of shares authorized,
    number of shares issued                                XX
  Paid-in capital in excess of par - common stock          XX
  Donated capital                                          XX
      Total paid-in capital                                XX
  Retained earnings                                        XX
      Total stockholders' equity                           XX

**Study Tip:** Review the Decision Guidelines *Reporting Stockholders' Equity on the Balance Sheet* in your text.

A **dividend** is a distribution of cash to the stockholders of a corporation. A corporation must have Retained Earnings and sufficient cash in order to declare a dividend. A dividend must be declared by the board of directors before the corporation can pay it. Once a dividend has been declared, it is a legal liability of the corporation.

On the **date of declaration** the board also announces the **date of record** and the **payment date**. Those owning the shares on the date of record will receive the dividend. The payment date is the date the dividends are actually mailed.

## Objective 4 - Account for cash dividends.

When a dividend is declared, this entry is recorded:

| | | |
|---|---|---|
| Retained Earnings | XX | |
|     Dividends Payable | | XX |

Dividends Payable is a current liability.

The date of record falls between the declaration date and the payment date and requires no journal entry. The dividend is usually paid several weeks after it is declared. When it is paid, this entry is recorded:

| | | |
|---|---|---|
| Dividends Payable | XX | |
|     Cash | | XX |

Preferred stockholders have priority over common stockholders for receipt of dividends. In other words, common stockholders do not receive dividends unless the total declared dividend is sufficient to pay the preferred stockholders first.

Preferred stock usually carries a stated percentage rate or a dollar amount per share. Thus, if par value is $50 per share, "5% preferred" stockholders receive a $2.50 ($50 × 5%) annual dividend. Stockholders holding "$3 preferred" stock would receive a $3 annual cash dividend regardless of the par value of the stock. The dividend to common stockholders will equal:

**Common dividend = Total dividend - Preferred dividend**

A dividend is passed when a corporation fails to pay an annual dividend to preferred stockholders. Passed dividends are said to be in arrears. **Cumulative preferred stock** continues to accumulate annual dividends until the dividends are paid. Therefore, a corporation must pay all dividends in arrears to cumulative preferred stockholders before it can pay dividends to other stockholders.

Dividends in arrears are not liabilities, but are disclosed in notes to the financial statements. Preferred stock is considered cumulative unless it is specifically labeled as noncumulative. Noncumulative preferred stock does not accumulate dividends in arrears.

**Convertible preferred stock** can be exchanged by the holder for another class of stock. Suppose you have 200 shares of preferred stock and each share can be converted to four shares of common stock. If the market value of 800 shares of common stock exceeds the market value of 200 shares of convertible preferred stock, conversion would be to your advantage.

The entry to record conversion, assuming that the par value of the preferred stock is greater than the par value of the common stock, is:

| | | |
|---|---|---|
| Preferred stock | XX | |
|     Common stock | | XX |
|     Paid-in capital in excess of par - | | |
|         common stock | | XX |

## Objective 5 - Use different stock values in decision making.

**Market value (market price)** is the price at which a person could buy or sell a share of the stock. Daily newspapers report the market price of many publicly traded stocks.

Sometimes preferred stock can be redeemed by the corporation for a stated amount per share. This amount, which is set when the stock is issued, is called **redemption value**.

Preferred stock may also be issued with a **liquidation value**. This is the amount the corporation agrees to pay preferred stockholders if the company liquidates. Dividends in arrears are added to liquidation value to determine the amount to be paid if liquidation occurs.

Book value is the amount of stockholders' equity per share of stock. If only common stock is outstanding:

$$\text{Book value} = \frac{\text{Total stockholders' equity}}{\text{Number of shares outstanding}}$$

If both preferred and common stock are outstanding, preferred stockholders equity must be calculated first. If preferred stock has no redemption value, then total preferred equity in the equation below is equal to the balance in Preferred Stock plus Paid-in Capital in Excess of Par-Preferred. If preferred stock has a redemption value, then total preferred equity in the equation below equals the total redemption value (redemption value per share × number of preferred shares).

$$\text{Preferred book value} = \frac{\text{Total preferred equity} + \text{Dividends in arrears}}{\text{Number of preferred shares outstanding}}$$

$$\text{Common book value} = \frac{\text{Total equity} - (\text{Total preferred equity} + \text{Dividends in arrears})}{\text{Number of common shares outstanding}}$$

## Objective 6 - Evaluate a company's return on assets and return on stockholders' equity.

1. **Rate of return on total assets** = $\dfrac{\text{Net income} + \text{Interest expense}}{\text{Average total assets}}$

The return on total assets (or return on assets) measures how successfully the company was in using its (average) assets to earn a profit.

2. **Rate of return on common stockholders' equity** = $\dfrac{\text{Net income} - \text{Preferred dividends}}{\text{Average common stockholders' equity}}$

The denominator, average common stockholders' equity, is equal to total stockholders' equity minus preferred equity.

The rate of return on common stockholders' equity also measures profitability of the company. The return on equity should always be higher than the return on assets.

## Objective 7 - Account for a corporation's income tax.

Because corporations have a distinct legal identity (they have the right to contract, to sue, and be sued--just as individuals have these rights), their income is taxed just like individuals. However, unlike individuals, the amount of tax actually paid will differ from the expense incurred for the period (for individuals, these amounts are generally the same). The difference results from the following:

**Income tax expense** is calculated by multiplying the applicable tax rate times the amount of pre-tax accounting income as reported on the income statement, while **income tax payable** is calculated by multiplying the applicable tax rate times the amount of taxable income as reported on the corporate tax return. Because these results will differ, a third account, **Deferred Income Tax**, is used to reconcile the entry, as follows:

| | | |
|---|---|---|
| Income Tax Expense | XX | |
|    Income Tax Payable | | XX |
|    Deferred Income Tax | XX | |

(When the expense is greater than the liability.)

| | | |
|---|---|---|
| Income Tax Expense | XX | |
| Deferred Income Tax | XX | |
|    Income Tax Payable | | XX |

(When the expense is less than the liability.)

# TEST YOURSELF

All the self-testing materials in this chapter focus on information and procedures that your instructor is likely to test in quizzes and examinations.

**Matching**  *Match each numbered term with its lettered definition.*

_____ 1. authorized stock
_____ 2. book value
_____ 3. chairperson of the board
_____ 4. convertible stock
_____ 5. cumulative stock
_____ 6. legal capital
_____ 7. revenue from donations
_____ 8. liquidation value
_____ 9. market value
_____ 10. outstanding stock
_____ 11. stated value
_____ 12. preferred stock
_____ 13. stockholders' equity
_____ 14. retained earnings
_____ 15. deferred income tax

_____ 16. board of directors
_____ 17. bylaws
_____ 18. charter
_____ 19. common stock
_____ 20. deficit
_____ 21. dividends
_____ 22. limited liability
_____ 23. paid-in capital
_____ 24. par value
_____ 25. preemptive right
_____ 26. premium on stock
_____ 27. contributed capital
_____ 28. income tax expense
_____ 29. income tax payable

A. an account which reconciles the difference between income tax expense and income tax payable
B. a corporation's capital that is earned through profitable operation of the business
C. a corporation's capital from investments by the stockholders
D. a debit balance in the retained earnings account
E. a group elected by the stockholders to set policy for a corporation and to appoint its officers
F. another term for paid-in capital
G. the account created when a corporation receives a gift from a donor who receives no ownership interest in the company
H. a stockholder's right to maintain a proportionate ownership in a corporation
I. an arbitrary amount assigned to a share of stock
J. an elected person on a corporation's board of directors who is usually the most powerful person in the corporation
K. the portion of stockholders' equity that cannot be used for dividend
L. distributions by a corporation to its stockholders
M. means that the most that a stockholder can lose on his investment in a corporation's stock is the cost of the investment
N. owners' equity of a corporation
O. similar to par value
P. preferred stock that may be exchanged by the stockholders, if they choose, for another class of stock in the corporation
Q. preferred stock whose owners must receive all dividends in arrears before the corporation pays dividends to the common stockholders
R. pre-tax accounting income times the tax rate
S. shares of stock in the hands of stockholders
T. stock that gives its owners certain advantages such as the priority to receive dividends and the priority to receive assets if the corporation liquidates

U. the amount that a corporation agrees to pay a preferred stockholder per share if the company liquidates
V. the amount of owners' equity on the company's books for each share of its stock
W. taxable income times the tax rate
X. the constitution for governing a corporation
Y. the document that gives the state's permission to form a corporation
Z. the excess of the issue price of stock over its par value
AA. the most basic form of capital stock
BB. the price for which a person could buy or sell a share of stock
CC. the maximum number of shares of stock a corporation may issue

## II. Multiple Choice   *Circle the best answer.*

1. The corporate board of directors is:

   A. appointed by the state
   B. elected by management
   C. elected by the stockholders
   D. appointed by corporate officers

2. A stockholder has no personal obligation for corporation liabilities. This is called:

   A. mutual agency
   B. limited agency
   C. transferability of ownership
   D. limited liability

3. Stated value has the same meaning as:

   A. market value
   B. par value
   C. book value
   D. redemption value

4. A stock certificate shows all of the following except:

   A. additional paid-in capital
   B. stockholder name
   C. par value
   D. company name

5. The ownership of stock entitles common stockholders to all of the following rights except:

   A. right to receive guaranteed dividends
   B. voting right
   C. preemptive right
   D. right to receive a proportionate share of assets in a liquidation

6. When a corporation declares a cash dividend:

   A. liabilities decrease, assets decrease
   B. assets decrease, retained earnings decreases
   C. assets decrease, retained earnings increases
   D. liabilities increase, retained earnings decrease

7. When a corporation pays a cash dividend:

   A. liabilities decrease, assets increase
   B. assets decrease, retained earnings decreases
   C. liabilities decrease, assets decrease
   D. retained earnings decrease, liabilities increase

8. When a company issues stock in exchange for assets other than cash, the assets are recorded at:

   A. market value
   B. original cost
   C. book value
   D. replacement cost

9. Dividends Payable is a(n):

   A. expense
   B. current liability
   C. paid-in capital account
   D. stockholders' equity account

10. Dividends in arrears on preferred stock are reported:

    A. on the balance sheet
    B. as a reduction of retained earnings
    C. on the income statement
    D. as a footnote to the financial statements

## III. Completion  *Complete each of the following.*

1. Every corporation issues _____ stock.
2. The corporation's constitution is called the _____.
3. Preferred stockholders have preference over common stockholders in _____ and _____.
4. Dividends are declared by _____.
5. Taxable income times the applicable tax rate equals _____.
6. Stockholders' equity minus preferred equity equals _____.
7. The date of _____ determines who receives the dividend.
8. The date of _____ establishes the liability to pay a dividend.
9. The price at which a share of stock is bought or sold is called the _____ value.
10. Corporations come into existence when a _____ is approved by the _____ government.

## IV. Daily Exercises

1. Arrange the following stockholders' equity items in the correct sequence.

    Donated capital  5
    Common stock  3
    Paid-in capital in excess of par - preferred  2
    Retained earnings  6
    Preferred stock  1
    Paid-in capital in excess of par - common  4

2. Assets donated to a corporation are recorded at their current market value. However, the account credited is determined by the source of the donation. Which two accounts could be credited and what circumstances dictate which to use? How are both reported on the financial statements?

3. A company issues 40,000 shares of common stock for $30 per share. Record this transaction (omit explanation) assuming

    a. the stock had a par value of $1 per share
    b. the stock had no par value, but a stated value of $1 per share
    c. the stock had no par or stated value

|  |  |  |
|---|---|---|
|  |  |  |
|  |  |  |
|  |  |  |
|  |  |  |
|  |  |  |
|  |  |  |
|  |  |  |
|  |  |  |
|  |  |  |
|  |  |  |

4. On September 10, the board of directors declares an annual dividend of $30,000 payable on October 30 to stockholders of record on September 30. Make the journal entries to record the declaration date, record date, and payment date.

|   |   |   |   |
|---|---|---|---|
|   |   |   |   |
|   |   |   |   |
|   |   |   |   |
|   |   |   |   |
|   |   |   |   |
|   |   |   |   |
|   |   |   |   |

5. Refer to the information in Daily Exercise #4 and assume the company has 4,000 shares of $50 par, 4% preferred stock issued and 10,000 shares of $1 par common stock. The preferred stock is non-cumulative and this is the first dividend the corporation has declared since the stock was issued four years ago. Calculate the amount due to each class of shareholder.

6. Refer to the information in Daily Exercise #5, but assume the preferred stock is cumulative. Calculate the amount due each class of shareholder.

## V. Exercises

1. The charter of Berger Corporation authorizes the issuance of 25,000 shares of preferred stock and 300,000 shares of common stock. During the first year of operation, Berger Corporation completed the following stock-issuance transactions:

   March 1   Issued 40,000 shares of $1 par common stock for cash of $15 per share.
   March 10  Issued 5,000 shares of 6%, no-par preferred stock with stated value of $50 per share. The issue price was cash of $60 per share.
   March 28  Received inventory valued at $25,000 and equipment with a market value of $60,000 in exchange for 2,000 shares of $1 par common stock.

   Prepare the journal entries for March 1, 10, and 28.

|   |   |   |
|---|---|---|
|   |   |   |
|   |   |   |
|   |   |   |
|   |   |   |
|   |   |   |
|   |   |   |
|   |   |   |
|   |   |   |
|   |   |   |
|   |   |   |
|   |   |   |

2. Review the information in Exercise #1 and assume retained earnings has a balance of $95,000. Prepare the stockholders' equity section of the Berger Corporation balance sheet at the end of the first year.

|   |   |
|---|---|
|   |   |
|   |   |
|   |   |
|   |   |
|   |   |
|   |   |
|   |   |
|   |   |
|   |   |

3. Coles Corporation has 2,000 shares of $50 par, cumulative, 8% preferred stock outstanding. There were no dividends in arrears at the end of 1996, and no dividends were paid in 1997 or 1998. Coles also has 10,000 shares of $5 par common stock outstanding.

   A. If Coles pays a total of $60,000 in dividends in 1999, how much will each class of stockholders receive?

   B. If Coles pays a total of $20,000 in dividends in 1999, how much will each class of stockholders receive?

4. The balance sheet of Winter House Corporation reports total stockholders' equity of $719,500, consisting of the following:

   a. Redeemable preferred stock; redemption value $22,000; 400 shares issued and outstanding
   b. Common stockholders' equity, 15,500 shares issued and outstanding.
   c. Winter House has paid preferred dividends for the current year and there are no dividends in arrears.

   Compute the book value per share of the preferred stock and the common stock.

5. Natural Fibers Corporation reported pre-tax income of $242,000 on their income statement and $186,000 taxable income on their tax return. Assuming a corporate tax rate of 35%, present the journal entry to record Natural Fibers taxes for the year.

| Date | Accounts and Explanation | PR | Debit | Credit |
|------|--------------------------|----|-------|--------|
|      |                          |    |       |        |
|      |                          |    |       |        |
|      |                          |    |       |        |
|      |                          |    |       |        |
|      |                          |    |       |        |

## VI. Beyond the Numbers

Using the information in Daily Exercise #5 and #6, state the effect (increase, decrease, no effect), as of 12/31 on the return on assets, return on stockholders' equity, and book value in each situation. Assume preferred's redemption value is its par value.

Corporate Organization, Paid-in Capital, and the Balance Sheet

## VII. Demonstration Problems

### Demonstration Problem #1

On January 1, 1999, California authorized Video Productions, Inc. to issue 100,000 shares of 6%, $25 par preferred stock and 1,000,000 shares of common stock with a $1 par value. During January, the company completed the following selected transactions related to its stockholders' equity:

1/10  Sold 50,000 shares of common stock at $15 per share.
1/11  Issued 6,000 shares of preferred stock for cash at $25 per share.
1/17  Issued 20,000 shares of common stock in exchange for land valued at $420,000.
1/24  An old building and small parcel of land was donated to the corporation by a town for a future office site that would employ 60 people. The site value was $125,000; the building was worthless.
1/27  Sold 2,000 shares of preferred stock at $31 a share.
1/31  Earned a small profit for January and closed the $3,800 credit balance of Income Summary into the Retained Earnings account.

### Required

1. Record the transactions in the general journal.
2. Post the journal entries into the equity accounts provided.
3. Prepare the stockholders' equity section of Video Productions, Inc. balance sheet at Jan 31, 1999.
4. Compute the book value per share of the preferred stock and the common stock. The preferred stock has a liquidation value of $30 per share. No dividends are in arrears.

### Requirement 1 (journal entries)

| Date | Accounts and Explanation | PR | Debit | Credit |
|------|--------------------------|----|----|----|
|      |                          |    |    |    |

|   |   |   |   |   |
|---|---|---|---|---|
|   |   |   |   |   |
|   |   |   |   |   |
|   |   |   |   |   |
|   |   |   |   |   |
|   |   |   |   |   |
|   |   |   |   |   |

**Requirement 2 (postings)**

**Requirements 3 (Stockholders' equity section)**

Video Productions, Inc.
Balance Sheet - Stockholders' Equity Section
January 31, 1999

|   |   |
|---|---|
|   |   |
|   |   |
|   |   |
|   |   |
|   |   |
|   |   |
|   |   |
|   |   |
|   |   |
|   |   |
|   |   |

**Requirement 4 (book value per share)**

**Demonstration Problem #2**

Wilcox Corporation has the following capital structure: 5,000 shares of $25 par, 4% preferred stock authorized and outstanding, and 100,000 authorized shares of $2 par common stock, 20,000 shares issued. During years X1 through X4, the corporation declared the following dividends:

| | |
|---|---|
| X1 | $0 |
| X2 | 2,000 |
| X3 | 40,000 |
| X4 | 120,000 |

A. Assume the preferred stock is noncumulative, calculate the amount of dividends per share for each share of stock for each year.

| Year | Dividend Amount | Preferred | Common |
|---|---|---|---|
| | | | |
| | | | |
| | | | |
| | | | |
| | | | |
| | | | |
| | | | |
| | | | |
| | | | |

B. Assume the preferred stock is cumulative, calculate the amount of dividends per share each year for each share of stock.

| Year | Dividend Amount | Preferred | Common |
|---|---|---|---|
| | | | |
| | | | |
| | | | |
| | | | |
| | | | |
| | | | |
| | | | |
| | | | |
| | | | |

# SOLUTIONS

## I. Matching

| | | | | | | | |
|---|---|---|---|---|---|---|---|
| 1. CC | 5. Q | 9. BB | 13. N | 17. X | 21. L | 25. H | 29. W |
| 2. V | 6. K | 10. S | 14. B | 18. Y | 22. M | 26. Z | |
| 3. J | 7. G | 11. O | 15. A | 19. AA | 23. C | 27. F | |
| 4. P | 8. U | 12. T | 16. E | 20. D | 24. I | 28. R | |

## II. Multiple Choice

1. C   Each share of common stock usually gives the stockholder one vote in the election of the board of directors.
2. D   Recall that mutual agency is a characteristic of partnerships not present in corporations. Transferability of ownership is a characteristic that the corporate form of organization simplifies as compared with partnerships. Limited agency has no meaning.
3. B   Stated value, like par value, is an arbitrary value assigned to a share of stock.
4. A   Additional paid-in capital is the excess of the price paid to the corporation over the par value of the stock.
5. A   Dividends represent the distribution of the earnings of the corporation and are not guaranteed.
6. D   The declaration of a dividend reduces Retained Earnings and increases the liability account, Dividends Payable.
7. C   The payment of a cash dividend results in cash being paid to stockholders to settle the liability created by the declaration of the dividend.
8. A   When capital stock is issued in exchange for non-cash assets, the transaction should be recorded at fair market value.
9. B   The declaration of a dividend by the board of directors creates a current liability.
10. D   Dividends in arrears is not a liability since a dividend must be declared to create a liability. However, dividends in arrears do impair the amount of capital available to common stockholders. Dividends in arrears are usually disclosed by a footnote.

## III. Completion

1. common (Corporations may also issue preferred stock, but that is optional.)
2. bylaws
3. receiving dividends and in event of a liquidation
4. the board of directors
5. Income Tax Payable
6. common stockholders' equity
7. record
8. declaration
9. market
10. charter; state

## IV. Daily Exercises

1.
   Preferred stock
   Paid-in capital in excess of par - preferred
   Common stock
   Paid-in capital in excess of par - common
   Donated capital
   Retained earnings

> **Study Tip:** Paid-in (contributed) capital is always listed first, followed by Retained Earnings.

2. Either Revenue from Donations or Donated Capital will be credited when assets are donated to the company. Donated Capital is credited when the source of the donations is a governmental agency; otherwise, Revenue from Donations is credited. Donated Capital is a stockholders' equity account on the balance sheet while Revenues from Donations appears as Other Revenue on the Income Statement.

3.
   | | | | | |
   |---|---|---|---|---|
   | a. | Cash | | 1,200,000 | |
   | |     Common Stock | | | 40,000 |
   | |     Paid-in Capital in Excess of Par - Common | | | 1,160,000 |
   | b. | Cash | | 1,200,000 | |
   | |     Common Stock | | | 40,000 |
   | |     Paid-in Capital in Excess of Stated Value - Common | | | 1,160,000 |
   | c. | Cash | | 1,200,000 | |
   | |     Common Stock | | | 1,200,000 |

4.
   | | | | |
   |---|---|---|---|
   | 9/10 | Retained Earnings | 30,000 | |
   | |     Dividends Payable | | 30,000 |
   | 9/20 | No entry | | |
   | 10/30 | Dividends Payable | 30,000 | |
   | |     Cash | | 30,000 |

> **Study Tip:** Remember no entry is required on the record date. This simply determines who will receive the dividends when mailed.

5.
   Preferred: $50 × 4% = $2 per share × 4,000 shares = $8,000.
   Common: $30,000 - $8,000 = $22,000, or $2.20 per share.

   Since the preferred stock is noncumulative, the preferred shareholders are only entitled to the current year's dividend ($8,000). The balance is distributed to the common stock.

6.
 Preferred: $8,000 per year (see above) × 4 years = $32,000.

 Since the board of directors only declared $30,000 for dividends, preferred shareholders receive the entire amount ($7.50 per share) and still have a $2,000 arrearage. The common stock receives nothing!

## V. Exercises

1.

| 3/1 | Cash | 600,000 | |
|---|---|---|---|
| | Common Stock | | 40,000 |
| | Paid-in Capital in Excess of Par - Common | | 560,000 |
| | | | |
| 3/10 | Cash | 300,000 | |
| | Preferred Stock | | 250,000 |
| | Paid-in Capital in Excess of Par - Preferred | | 50,000 |
| | | | |
| 3/28 | Inventory | 25,000 | |
| | Equipment | 60,000 | |
| | Common Stock | | 2,000 |
| | Paid-in Capital in Excess of Par - Common | | 83,000 |

2.

       Stockholders' Equity

| | |
|---|---|
| Paid-in capital: | |
|  Preferred stock, 6%, no-par, $50 stated value, 25,000 shares authorized, 5,000 shares issued | 250,000 |
|  Paid-in capital in excess of par – preferred stock | 50,000 |
|  Common stock, $1 par, 300,000 shares authorized, 42,000 shares issued | 42,000 |
|  Paid-in capital in excess of par – common stock | 643,000 |
|   Total paid-in capital | 985,000 |
| Retained earnings | 95,000 |
|   Total stockholders' equity | 1,080,000 |

3.
 A. Preferred: 3 years × 2,000 shares × $50 par × 8% = $24,000
   Common: $60,000 - $24,000 = $36,000

 B. Preferred: 3 years × 2,000 shares × $50 par × 8% = $24,000
   Since $20,000 is less than the $24,000 preferred stockholders must receive before common stockholders receive anything, all $20,000 goes to the preferred stockholders.

4.

| Preferred book value | = | $\dfrac{\text{Total preferred equity + Dividends in arrears}}{\text{Number of preferred shares outstanding}}$ |

Preferred book value = $\dfrac{\$22,000 + \$0}{400}$ = $55

Common book value = $\dfrac{\text{Total equity - (Total preferred equity + Dividends arrears)}}{\text{Number of common shares outstanding}}$

Common book value = $\dfrac{\$719,500 - (\$22,000 + \$0)}{15,500}$ = $45.00

5.
| | | |
|---|---|---|
| Income Tax Expense | 84,700 | |
| Income Tax Payable | | 65,100 |
| Deferred Income Tax | | 19,600 |

Income Tax Expense = $242,000 × 35% = $84,700
Income Tax Payable = $186,000 × 35% = $65,100
Deferred Income Tax = $84,700 - $65,100 = $19,600

## VI. Beyond the Numbers

Here's the solution—see below for the explanation. This is more difficult than you might have thought.

| Situation | Return on Assets | Return on Stockholders' Equity | Common Book Value |
|---|---|---|---|
| a. preferred stock is non-cumulative | increase | decrease | decrease |
| b. preferred stock is cumulative | increase | decrease | decrease |

The formulas are:

Rate of return on total assets = $\dfrac{\text{Net income + Interest expense}}{\text{Average total assets}}$

Rate of return on common stockholders' equity = $\dfrac{\text{Net income - Preferred dividends}}{\text{Average common stockholders' equity}}$

Common book value = $\dfrac{\text{Total equity - (Total preferred equity + Dividends arrears)}}{\text{Number of common shares outstanding}}$

For the return on assets, neither net income nor interest expense change because dividends of $20,000 were paid (regardless of who got how much.) However, average total assets will decrease because of the $30,000 reduction in cash. Therefore, return on assets will increase in both situations.

For return on stockholders' equity, the numerator (net income less preferred dividends) is smaller because of the dividend payment. The denominator (average stockholders' equity) is also decreasing because the total dividends are debited to Retained Earnings. In Exercise #5, the numerator is decreasing by $8,000 while the denominator is decreasing by $30,000. In Exercise #6, the numerator is decreasing by $30,000 while the denominator is decreasing by $32,000 (the $30,000 dividends recorded plus the $2,000 still in arrears to the preferred shareholders).

For common book value, the numerator in both exercises is decreasing while the denominator remains constant.

## VII. Demonstration Problems

### Demonstration Problem #1 Solved and Explained

**Requirement 1**

| 1/10 | Cash | 750,000 | |
| --- | --- | --- | --- |
| | Common Stock (50,000 × $1) | | 50,000 |
| | Paid-in Capital in Excess of Par - | | |
| | Common Stock (50,000 × $14) | | 700,000 |
| | Sold common stock at $14 per share. | | |

The payment of cash is recorded by debiting Cash and crediting Common Stock for the number of shares times the par value of the stock (50,000 × $1). The balance is recorded in the premium account, Paid-in Capital in Excess of Par - Common Stock.

| 1/11 | Cash (6,000 × $25) | 150,000 | |
| --- | --- | --- | --- |
| | Preferred Stock (6,000 × $25) | | 150,000 |
| | Issued preferred stock at par. | | |

Preferred Stock is credited for the shares times par (6,000 × $25).

| 1/17 | Land | 420,000 | |
| --- | --- | --- | --- |
| | Common Stock (20,000 × $1) | | 20,000 |
| | Paid-in Capital in Excess of Par - | | |
| | Common Stock ($420,000 - $20,000) | | 400,000 |
| | To issue common stock at a premium price. | | |

When a corporation issues stock in exchange for an asset other than cash, it debits the asset received (in this case, land) for its fair market value and credits the capital accounts as it would do if cash were the asset received.

| 1/24 | Land | 125,000 | |
| --- | --- | --- | --- |
| | Donated Capital | | 125,000 |
| | To record land received as a donation from the town. | | |

The donation of land by a town is a gift. Since the donor is a governmental entity, the donation is recorded by debiting the asset received at its current market value and by crediting Donated Capital. Since the building is worthless, the debit should be made to the Land account.

| 1/27 | Cash | 62,000 | |
| --- | --- | --- | --- |
| | Preferred Stock (2,000 × $25) | | 50,000 |
| | Paid-in Capital in excess of par - Preferred ($62,000 - $50,000) | | 12,000 |

The amount received above the stock's par value is recorded in a premium account, Paid-in Capital in excess of par - Preferred Stock.

| 1/31 | Income Summary | 3,800 | |
| --- | --- | --- | --- |
| | Retained Earnings | | 3,800 |

To close Income Summary by transferring net income into Retained Earnings.

At the end of each month or year, the balance of the Income Summary account is transferred to Retained Earnings. Video Productions, Inc. earned a small profit in January. The closing entry will debit Income Summary (to reduce it to zero) and credit Retained Earnings (increasing stockholders' equity to reflect profitable operations).

## Requirement 2

| Preferred Stock | |
| --- | --- |
| | 1/11  150,000 |
| | 1/27   50,000 |
| | Bal. 200,000 |

| Common Stock | |
| --- | --- |
| | 1/11  50,000 |
| | 1/17  20,000 |
| | Bal. 70,000 |

| Paid-in Capital in Excess of Par - Preferred Stock | |
| --- | --- |
| | 1/27  12,000 |
| | Bal. 12,000 |

| Paid-in Capital in Excess of Par – Common Stock | |
| --- | --- |
| | 1/11   700,000 |
| | 1/17   400,000 |
| | Bal. 1,100,000 |

| Retained Earnings | |
| --- | --- |
| | 1/31  3,800 |
| | Bal. 3,800 |

| Donated Capital | |
| --- | --- |
| | 1/24   125,000 |
| | Bal.   125,000 |

**Requirements 3**

Video Productions, Inc.
Balance Sheet - Stockholders' Equity Section
January 31, 1999

| | |
|---|---:|
| Stockholders' equity: | |
|    Preferred stock, 6%, $25 par, 100,000 shares authorized | $ 200,000 |
|    Paid-in capital in excess of par - Preferred stock | 12,000 |
|    Common stock, $1 par, 1,000,000 shares authorized | 70,000 |
|    Paid-in capital in excess of par - Common stock | 1,100,000 |
|    Donated capital | 125,000 |
|    Total paid-in capital | 1,507,000 |
|    Retained earnings | 3,800 |
|    Total stockholders' equity | $1,510,800 |

**Requirement 4**

| | |
|---|---:|
| Preferred: | |
|    Liquidation value (8,000 shares × $30) | $ 240,000 |
|    Dividends in arrears | 0 |
|    Stockholders' equity allocated to preferred | 240,000 |
|    Book value per share ($240,000 ÷ 8,000 shares) | $ 30.00 |
| | |
| Common: | |
|    Total stockholders' equity | $1,510,800 |
|    Less: Stockholders' equity allocated to preferred | 240,000 |
|    Stockholders' equity allocated to common | 1,270,800 |
|    Book value per share ($1,270,800 ÷ 70,000 shares) | $18.15 (rounded) |

Calculated as follows:

| Date | No. of Shares | Transactions |
|---|---:|---|
| 1/10 | 50,000 | Issued |
| 1/17 | 20,000 | Issued |
| | 70,000 | Shares |

## Demonstration Problem #2 Solved and Explained

A. Preferred stock is noncumulative.

| Year | Dividend Amount | Preferred | Common |
|------|-----------------|-----------|--------|
| X1 | $0 | $0 | $0 |
| X2 | $2,000 | $0.40 per share ($2,000 ÷ 5,000 shares) | $0 |
| X3 | $40,000 | $1.00 per share 5,000 shares × $25 par × 4% | $1.75 per share $35,000 ÷ 20,000 |
| X4 | $120,000 | $1.00 per share 5,000 shares × $25 par × 4% | $5.75 $115,000 ÷ 20,000 |

The preferred stock is noncumulative so the shareholders are only entitled to the current year's dividend, which is $1/share for a total of $5,000. Any (and all) excess goes to the common shareholders.

B. The preferred stock is cumulative.

| Year | Dividend Amount | Preferred | Common |
|------|-----------------|-----------|--------|
| X1 | $0 | $0 | $0 |

There are now $5,000 of preferred dividends in arrears.

| | | | |
|---|---|---|---|
| X2 | $2,000 | $0.40 per share ($2,000 ÷ 5,000 shares) | $0 |

There are now $8,000 of preferred dividends in arrears.

| | | | |
|---|---|---|---|
| X3 | $40,000 | $2.60 per share | $1.35 per share |

First, the preferred shares get their arrearage which is $1 each from X1 and $.60 from X2 for a total of $1.60. Then they get their $1 for X3, so a total of $2.60. The balance $27,000 ($40,000 - $13,000) goes to common.

| | | | |
|---|---|---|---|
| X4 | $120,000 | $1.00 per share | $5.75 |

Preferred has no arrearage so they receive $1.00 per share with the remainder going to common.

**Study Tip:** Most preferred stock is cumulative. The term has no meaning when applied to common stock.

# Chapter 14 - Retained Earnings, Treasury Stock, and the Income Statement

## CHAPTER OVERVIEW

In Chapter 13 you learned about capital stock, cash dividends, stock values, corporate income taxes, and other topics related to corporations. We expand those topics in this chapter and learn about stock dividends, treasury stock and a corporation income statement, among other topics. The learning objectives for this chapter are to

1. Account for stock dividends.
2. Distinguish stock splits from stock dividends.
3. Account for treasury stock.
4. Report restrictions on retained earnings.
5. Identify the elements of a corporation income statement.
6. Prepare a statement of stockholders' equity.

## CHAPTER REVIEW

**Retained Earnings** is the account that holds all the corporation's net incomes less net losses and less dividends declared, accumulated over the life of the business. A deficit or debit balance means net losses have exceeded net incomes. Income Summary is closed to Retained Earnings at the end of each period. Retained Earnings is not a fund of cash.

### Objective 1 - Account for stock dividends.

Corporation declare **stock dividends** instead of cash dividends when they want to conserve cash or reduce the market price per share of stock. Unlike cash dividends, stock dividends are not distributions of corporate assets. A stock dividend is a proportional distribution of the corporation's stock to its stockholders. Thus, a stock dividend affects only a corporation's stockholders' equity accounts; the result of a stock dividend is a reduction in Retained Earnings, an increase in contributed capital, and total stockholders' equity stays the same.

The effect of declaring a stock dividend is to capitalize or transfer a portion of Retained Earnings to Common Stock. In the event of a small stock dividend, a portion of Retained Earnings is also transferred to Paid-in Capital in Excess of Par - Common in order to reflect the excess of market value over par.

A **small stock dividend** is one that comprises less than 20-25% of shares issued. A **large stock dividend** comprises 25% or more of shares issued. Small stock dividends are accounted for at market value on the declaration date. The entry is:

| | | |
|---|---|---|
| Retained Earnings | XX | |
|     Common Stock Dividend Distributable | | XX |
|     Paid-in Capital in Excess of Par - Common | | XX |

The amount of the debit to Retained Earnings is equal to:

Number of Shares Outstanding × Dividend % × Market Price Per Share

The credit to Common Stock Dividend Distributable is equal to:

Number of Shares Outstanding × Dividend % × Par Value Per Share

The credit to Paid-in Capital in Excess of Par - Common is equal to:

Number of Shares Outstanding × Dividend % × (Market Price - Par)

On the date of distribution of a small stock dividend, the par value of the issued stock is transferred from the dividend distributable account to the stock account:

| | | |
|---|---|---|
| Common Stock Dividend Distributable | XX | |
| Common Stock | | XX |

Large stock dividends (25% or more of the outstanding shares) are usually accounted for at par value. On the declaration date, this entry is recorded:

| | | |
|---|---|---|
| Retained Earnings | XX | |
| Common Stock Dividend Distributable | | XX |

When the dividend is issued, this entry is recorded:

| | | |
|---|---|---|
| Common Stock Dividend Distributable | XX | |
| Common Stock | | XX |

Note that these entries are all based on par rather than market value.

A **stock split** increases the number of outstanding shares and proportionately reduces the par value of the stock. A stock split affects only the par value of the shares and the number of shares outstanding. No account balances are affected.

## Objective 2 - Distinguish stock splits from stock dividends.

Both stock splits and stock dividends increase the number of shares outstanding and may decrease the market price per share. The difference between stock splits and stock dividends is that a stock split changes the par value of the stock, while a stock dividend leaves the par value of the stock unchanged; also a stock dividend requires a transfer from Retained Earnings while a stock split requires no journal entry.

Carefully review Exhibit 14-3 in your text for a summary of the stockholders' equity effects of cash dividends, stock dividends and stock splits.

## Objective 3 - Account for treasury stock.

Stock which a corporation issues and later reacquires is called **treasury stock**. Treasury stock does not receive dividends and has no voting rights. Corporations may want treasury stock for distribution within the company, to support or raise the market price, to try to increase net assets by buying low and selling high, or to avoid a takeover. The entry to record the purchase of treasury stock is:

| | | |
|---|---|---|
| Treasury Stock, Common | XX | |
|     Cash | | XX |
| (Shares × market price per share) | | |

The debit balance in the Treasury Stock account reduces total stockholders' equity. Note that treasury stock is *not* an asset, and that a corporation *never* incurs a gain or loss by dealing in its own stock.

The purchase of treasury stock does not alter the number of shares authorized or issued. To determine the number of shares outstanding, take the issued number and deduct the number of shares of treasury stock. The result is the number of shares outstanding.

When treasury stock is sold, the entry to record the transaction depends on the relationship between the selling price and the cost of the Treasury Stock. The entry to record the sale of treasury stock at cost is:

| | | |
|---|---|---|
| Cash | XX | |
|     Treasury Stock, Common | | XX |

The entry to record the sale of Treasury Stock above cost is:

| | | |
|---|---|---|
| Cash (Shares × Current price) | XX | |
|     Treasury Stock, Common (Shares × Orig. price) | | XX |
|     Paid-in Capital from Treasury Stock | | XX |

The entry to record the sale of Treasury Stock below cost is:

| | | |
|---|---|---|
| Cash | XX | |
| Paid-in Capital from Treasury Stock | XX | |
|     Treasury Stock, Common | | XX |

Note that when treasury stock is sold, the Treasury Stock account is credited for the original cost of the treasury stock. Any difference between cost and selling price is recorded in the Paid-in Capital from Treasury Stock account. However, this Paid-In Capital Account cannot have a debit balance. If necessary, the Retained Earnings account may be debited if there is no balance in the Paid-In Capital account and the treasury stock's reissue price is less than its original cost.

A corporation that is replacing issues of stock or is liquidating may repurchase its own stock and retire it. Like treasury stock, retired stock produces neither a gain nor a loss.

## Objective 4 - Report restrictions on retained earnings.

Many corporations obtain financing through long-term loans. Creditors wish to ensure that funds will be available to repay these loans. Thus, loan agreements frequently **restrict** the amount of retained earnings that can be used to pay dividends and purchase treasury stock. These restrictions are usually reported in notes to the financial statements.

A corporation may also **appropriate** a portion of retained earnings for a specific purpose by debiting Retained Earnings and crediting Retained Earnings Appropriated.

Review Exhibit 14-5 in your text so you understand how a detailed stockholders' equity presentation can be condensed.

## Objective 5 - Identify the elements of a corporation income statement.

Investors may want to examine the trend of a company's earnings and the makeup of its net income. Therefore, the corporation income statement starts with income from continuing operations, follows with income or loss from special items, and concludes with earnings per share of common stock. See Exhibit 14-6 in your text.

**Continuing operations** are expected to continue in the future. Income from continuing operations helps investors make predictions about future earnings. Income from continuing operations is shown both before and after income tax has been deducted.

When a corporation sells one of its segments, the sale is reported in a section of the income statement called **discontinued operations**. Such sales are viewed as one-time transactions, and are therefore not a future source of income. Discontinued operations are separated into an operating component and a disposal component. Each is shown net of its related tax effect.

**Extraordinary gains and losses** are both unusual and infrequent, and are reported net of tax. Extraordinary items are those which are unusual and not likely to occur in the future. Examples are natural disasters and expropriations by foreign governments of business assets.

On occasion companies change an accounting method. When this occurs, it is difficult for financial statement users to compare consecutive years' activity unless they are informed of changes. For this reason, the cumulative (total) effect of any **changes in accounting principles** is reported separately. This cumulative effect is also reported net of its related tax effect.

**Earnings per share** of common stock is computed for each source of income or loss. To compute EPS divide net income by the weighted average number of shares of common stock outstanding.

**Weighted Average = Shares outstanding × Fraction of year that shares were held**

Review the example in your text to be certain that you understand how to compute the weighted average number of shares.

When preferred dividends exist, they must be subtracted from income subtotals (income from continuing operations, income before extraordinary items and cumulative effect of accounting change, and net income)

364    Chapter 14

in the computation of EPS. Preferred dividends are not subtracted from income or loss from discontinued operations, and they are not subtracted from extraordinary gains and losses.

**Dilution** must be considered if preferred stock can be converted into common stock because there is the potential for more common shares to be divided into net income. Corporations therefore provide **basic EPS** and **diluted EPS** information.

**Comprehensive income** refers to the change in total stockholders' equity from all sources other than from the owners of the business (the shareholders). In addition to net income, comprehensive income includes unrealized gains/losses on certain investments and foreign currency translation adjustments (both of these are discussed in greater detail in Chapter 16). FASB Statement 130, which dictates the reporting of comprehensive income, does not require EPS calculations for these additional components.

**Prior period adjustments** usually occur as the result of correcting an error in a previous accounting period. Prior period adjustments that decrease income from a prior period are debited to Retained Earnings:

| | | |
|---|---|---|
| Retained Earnings | XX | |
|     Asset or Liability account | | XX |

Prior period adjustments that increase prior period income are credited to Retained Earnings:

| | | |
|---|---|---|
| Asset or Liability account | XX | |
|     Retained Earnings | | XX |

Note that, because of the matching principle, prior period adjustments *never* affect revenue or expense accounts in the current period.

## Objective 6 - Prepare a statement of stockholders' equity.

A **statement of stockholders' equity** reports the changes in all elements of equity. Therefore, it contains the details of any changes in stock (both preferred and common), retained earnings, and treasury stock. Review Exhibit 14-9 in your text as an example.

Many of the changes listed on the statement of stockholders' equity will also be listed on the statement of cash flow (the cash flows statement is discussed in detail in Chapter 17.) Stockholders' equity are transactions classified as financing activities on the cash flows statement because owners (stockholders) are a major source of funds used to finance the company. Examples of cash inflows from stockholders' equity transactions are the sale of common, preferred, and treasury stock. The purchase of treasury stock is a cash outflow as is the payment of cash dividends.

# TEST YOURSELF

All the self-testing materials in this chapter focus on information and procedures that your instructor is likely to test in quizzes and examinations.

**I. Matching**   *Match each numbered term with its lettered definition.*

_____ 1. stock dividend
_____ 2. earnings per share (EPS)
_____ 3. extraordinary item
_____ 4. prior period adjustments
_____ 5. small stock dividend
_____ 6. appropriation of retained earnings
_____ 7. date of record
_____ 8. declaration date
_____ 9. large stock dividend
_____ 10. segment of a business
_____ 11. stock split
_____ 12. treasury stock
_____ 13. deficit
_____ 14. dilution
_____ 15. comprehensive income

A. a correction to Retained Earnings for an error of an earlier period
B. gain or loss that is both unusual for the company and nonrecurring
C. a significant part of a business
D. a stock dividend of 25% or more of the corporation's issued stock
E. a stock dividend of less than 20-25% of the corporation's issued stock
F. a proportional distribution by a corporation of its own stock that affects only the owners' equity section of the balance sheet
G. amount of a company's net income per share of its outstanding common stock
H. an increase in the number of outstanding shares of stock coupled with a proportionate reduction in the par value of the stock
I. date on which the board of directors announces the intention to pay a dividend
J. date on which the owners of stock to receive a dividend are identified
K. restriction of retained earnings that is recorded by a formal journal entry
L. the stock that a corporation issues and later reacquires
M. the change in total stockholders' equity from all sources other than from the owners of the business
N. when a corporation has outstanding equity which may be converted to common stock
O. a debit balance is Retained Earnings

**II. Multiple Choice**   *Circle the best answer.*

1. The correct order for pertinent dividend dates is:

   A. declaration date, record date, payment date
   B. record date, declaration date, payment date
   C. declaration date, payment date, record date
   D. record date, payment date, declaration date

2. Large stock dividends are recorded at:

   A. par value
   B. market value
   C. book value
   D. carrying value

3. The market price of a share of Moule Corporation's common stock is $60. If Moule declares and issues a 50% stock dividend, the market price will adjust to approximately:

   A. $30
   B. $12
   C. $90
   D. $40

4. The Common Stock Dividend Distributable account is reported in which section of the balance sheet?

   A. current liabilities
   B. long-term liabilities
   C. current assets
   D. stockholders' equity

5. The purchase of treasury stock will:

   A. decrease assets
   B. increase liabilities
   C. increase stockholders' equity
   D. have no effect on stockholders' equity

6. The purchase of treasury stock decreases the number of:

   A. authorized shares
   B. outstanding shares
   C. issued shares
   D. both B and C

7. When a company retires common stock:

   A. the number of shares outstanding decreases
   B. the number of shares issued is unchanged
   C. the number of shares authorized increases
   D. total assets increase

8. An appropriation of retained earnings will:

   A. decrease total retained earnings
   B. increase total retained earnings
   C. not affect total retained earnings
   D. increase total assets

9. All of the following would usually be reported as extraordinary items on the income statement *except:*

   A. a flood loss
   B. the loss on assets taken by a foreign government
   C. the loss from a strike by workers
   D. a tornado loss

10. Prior period adjustments are found on the:

    A. balance sheet
    B. income statement
    C. statement of cash flows
    D. statement of retained earnings

## III. Completion  *Complete each of the following statements.*

1. Earnings per share is calculated by dividing _____ by _____.
2. _____ stock does not receive cash dividends.

Retained Earnings, Treasury Stock, and the Income Statement    367

3. Extraordinary gains and losses on the income statement are both _____ and _____.

4. A corporation may buy treasury stock in order to:
   _____
   _____
   _____

5. The change in total stockholders' equity from all sources other than from the owners of the business is called _____.

6. The P/E is the acronym for the _____.

7. The denominator for the P/E ratio is _____.

8. A(n) _____ occurs when a stockholder returns shares to the corporation and receives more shares in the exchange.

9. An error affecting net income in a previous accounting period is called a _____.

10. A(n) _____ occurs when a stockholder returns shares to the corporation and receives fewer shares in the exchange.

## IV. Daily Exercises

1. Number the following income statement categories to show the order in which they should appear. Use * to indicate those categories that should be shown net of tax.

   _____ A. Discontinued Operations

   _____ B. Continuing Operations

   _____ C. Extraordinary Items

   _____ D. Cumulative Effect of Change in Accounting Principle

2. A stockholder owns 4,000 shares of Utronics, Inc. If the company declares and issues a 25% stock dividend, how many shares will the stockholder own?

3. Examine the information in Daily Exercise #2 above, but assume a 5 for 4 stock split. How many shares will be owned after the split?

4. A corporation's equity includes the following:

   Preferred Stock                              300,000
   Paid-in Capital in Excess of Par - Preferred 100,000

   The company decides to purchase and retire its outstanding preferred stock and is able to do so for a total of $360,000. Record the journal entry to purchase the preferred stock.

   | | | |
   |---|---|---|
   | Pfd St. | 300,000 | |
   | PIC | 100,000 | |
   |     Cash | | 360,000 |
   |     R/E | | 40,000 |
   | | | |

5. Review the information in #4 above, but assume the cost to purchase and retire the preferred stock is $440,000. Record the journal entry to purchase the preferred stock.

   | | | |
   |---|---|---|
   | P/S | 300,000 | |
   | PIC | 100,000 | |
   | R/E | 40,000 | |
   |     Cash | | 440,000 |
   | | | |

6. Pure-Flo had 450,000 shares of common stock outstanding on January 1. On April 1, an additional 150,000 shares were issued and on September 15, 75,000 more shares were issued. Assuming Pure-Flo's net income for the year was $981,750, calculate earnings per share.

## V. Exercises

1. Indicate the effect of each of the following transactions on Assets, Liabilities, Paid-in Capital, and Retained Earnings. Use + for increase, - for decrease, and 0 for no effect.

|  | Assets | Liabilities | Paid-in Capital | Retained Earnings |
|---|---|---|---|---|
| A. Declaration of a cash dividend | _____ | _____ | _____ | _____ |
| B. Payment of a cash dividend | _____ | _____ | _____ | _____ |
| C. Declaration of a stock dividend | _____ | _____ | _____ | _____ |
| D. Issuance of a stock dividend | _____ | _____ | _____ | _____ |
| E. A stock split | _____ | _____ | _____ | _____ |
| F. Cash purchase of treasury stock | _____ | _____ | _____ | _____ |
| G. Sale of treasury stock below cost | _____ | _____ | _____ | _____ |

2. Wholesome Corporation had 400,000 shares of $5 par common stock outstanding on October 1. Prepare journal entries for the following transactions:

   10/15  Declared a 15% stock dividend. The market price was $20 per share.

   10/30  Issued the stock dividend.

| Date | Account and Explanation | PR | Debit | Credit |
|---|---|---|---|---|
|  |  |  |  |  |
|  |  |  |  |  |
|  |  |  |  |  |
|  |  |  |  |  |
|  |  |  |  |  |
|  |  |  |  |  |
|  |  |  |  |  |

# VII. Demonstration Problems

**Demonstration Problem #1**

Digital Data Systems, Inc., reported the following stockholders' equity:

| | |
|---|---:|
| Stockholders' Equity: | |
| Preferred stock, 8%, $25 par value | |
|     Authorized - 1,000,000 shares | |
|     Issued 150,000 shares | $3,750,000 |
| Common stock $1 par value | |
|     Authorized - 5,000,000 shares | |
|     Issued - 800,000 shares | 800,000 |
| Paid-in capital in excess of par - common | 6,000,000 |
| Retained earnings | 6,855,180 |
| Less: Treasury stock, at cost (2,000 common shares) | 14,000 |
| Total stockholders' equity | $17,419,180 |

**Required:** (Work space to complete each of these questions is provided on the following pages.)

1. What was the average issue price per share of the common stock?
2. What was the average issue price per share of the preferred stock?
3. Assume that net income for the year was $825,000 and that issued shares of both common and preferred stock remained constant during the year. Journalize the entry to close net income to Retained Earnings. What was the amount of earnings per share?
4. Journalize the issuance of 10,000 additional shares of common stock at $22.50 per share. Use the same account titles as shown in the problem.
5. How many shares of common stock are outstanding after the 10,000 additional shares have been sold?
6. How many shares of common stock would be outstanding after the corporation split its common stock 2 for 1? What is the new par value?
7. Journalize the declaration of a stock dividend when the market price of the common stock is $22.50 per share. Consider each of the following stock dividends independently:
   a. Digital Data Systems, Inc., declares a 10% common stock dividend on shares outstanding after the 2-for-1 split.
   b. Digital Data Systems, Inc., declares a 40% common stock dividend on shares outstanding after the 2-for-1 split.
8. Journalize the following treasury stock transactions in the order given:
   a. Digital Data Systems, Inc., purchases 2,500 shares of treasury stock at $25 per share.
   b. One month later, the corporation sells 1,000 shares of the same treasury stock for $27 per share (credit Paid-in Capital from Treasury Stock Transactions).
   c. An additional 1,000 shares of treasury stock acquired in 8a are sold for $22 per share.
9. The board of directors has voted to appropriate $800,000 of retained earnings for future expansion of foreign operations. Prepare the journal entry to record this event.
10. Set up the balances in the following T-accounts using the information provided in the Stockholders' Equity section for Digital Data Systems, Inc.
11. Post the journal entries from instructions 3, 4, 7a, 8a, 8b, 8c, and 9 to the T-accounts above.
12. Prepare a current Stockholders' Equity section for Digital Data Systems, Inc.

**Requirement 1**

**Requirement 2**

**Requirement 3**

| Date | Account and Explanation | PR | Debit | Credit |
|---|---|---|---|---|
|  |  |  |  |  |
|  |  |  |  |  |
|  |  |  |  |  |

**Requirement 4**

| Date | Account and Explanation | PR | Debit | Credit |
|---|---|---|---|---|
|  |  |  |  |  |
|  |  |  |  |  |
|  |  |  |  |  |
|  |  |  |  |  |
|  |  |  |  |  |
|  |  |  |  |  |
|  |  |  |  |  |

**Requirement 5**

Requirement 6

Requirement 7

a.

| Date | Account and Explanation | PR | Debit | Credit |
|---|---|---|---|---|
|  |  |  |  |  |
|  |  |  |  |  |
|  |  |  |  |  |
|  |  |  |  |  |
|  |  |  |  |  |

b.

| Date | Account and Explanation | PR | Debit | Credit |
|---|---|---|---|---|
|  |  |  |  |  |
|  |  |  |  |  |
|  |  |  |  |  |
|  |  |  |  |  |
|  |  |  |  |  |

Requirement 8

a.

| Date | Account and Explanation | PR | Debit | Credit |
|---|---|---|---|---|
|  |  |  |  |  |
|  |  |  |  |  |
|  |  |  |  |  |
|  |  |  |  |  |
|  |  |  |  |  |

b.

| Date | Account and Explanation | PR | Debit | Credit |
|---|---|---|---|---|
|  |  |  |  |  |
|  |  |  |  |  |
|  |  |  |  |  |
|  |  |  |  |  |
|  |  |  |  |  |

c.

| Date | Account and Explanation | PR | Debit | Credit |
|---|---|---|---|---|
|  |  |  |  |  |
|  |  |  |  |  |
|  |  |  |  |  |
|  |  |  |  |  |
|  |  |  |  |  |

Requirement 9

| Date | Account and Explanation | PR | Debit | Credit |
|------|-------------------------|----|-------|--------|
|      |                         |    |       |        |
|      |                         |    |       |        |
|      |                         |    |       |        |
|      |                         |    |       |        |
|      |                         |    |       |        |

Requirements 10 and 11

Preferred Stock

Common Stock

Paid-in Capital in Excess of Par - Common Stock

Retained Earnings

Treasury Stock

Requirement 12

|   |   |   |
|---|---|---|
|   |   |   |
|   |   |   |
|   |   |   |
|   |   |   |
|   |   |   |
|   |   |   |
|   |   |   |
|   |   |   |
|   |   |   |
|   |   |   |
|   |   |   |
|   |   |   |
|   |   |   |
|   |   |   |
|   |   |   |
|   |   |   |
|   |   |   |
|   |   |   |
|   |   |   |
|   |   |   |

**Demonstration Problem #2**

The following items, listed alphabetically, were taken from the records of Atlas Manufacturing, Inc., for the year ended December 31, 1999.

| | |
|---|---:|
| Administrative Expenses | 185,000 |
| Cost of Goods Sold | 2,648,000 |
| Cumulative Effect of Change in Accounting Principle | 82,000 |
| Extraordinary Loss | (296,000) |
| Gain on Sale of Equipment | 48,000 |
| Gain on Sale of Discontinued Operations | 137,400 |
| Operating Loss - Discontinued Operations | (91,680) |
| Sales (net) | 5,014,200 |
| Selling Expenses | 305,000 |

Atlas Manufacturing is subjected to a combined 45% tax rate.

**Required**

1. Present the income statement in good form for Atlas Manufacturing
2. Assume Atlas began the year with 225,000 shares of common stock outstanding. On March 1, the corporation issued 75,000 additional shares of common stock. On October 1, Atlas re-purchased 50,000 shares. Present earnings per share information.

**Requirement 1 (income statement)**

|  |  |  |
|---|---|---|
|  |  |  |
|  |  |  |
|  |  |  |
|  |  |  |
|  |  |  |
|  |  |  |
|  |  |  |
|  |  |  |
|  |  |  |
|  |  |  |
|  |  |  |
|  |  |  |
|  |  |  |
|  |  |  |
|  |  |  |
|  |  |  |
|  |  |  |
|  |  |  |
|  |  |  |
|  |  |  |
|  |  |  |
|  |  |  |
|  |  |  |
|  |  |  |

**Requirement 2 (earnings per share)**

|  |  |
|---|---|
|  |  |
|  |  |
|  |  |
|  |  |
|  |  |
|  |  |
|  |  |
|  |  |

# SOLUTIONS

## I. Matching

1. F
2. G
3. B
4. A
5. E
6. K
7. J
8. I
9. D
10. C
11. H
12. L
13. O
14. N
15. M

## II. Multiple Choice

1. A  The board of directors declares a dividend on the declaration date, to stockholders of record on the record date that is paid on the payment date.

2. A  A large stock dividend (more than 25%) is accounted for at par value on the date of declaration.

3. D  If the market price for one share of pre-dividend stock is $60, then approximately the same market value will apply to the 1.5 shares of post dividend stock since the stockholder's percentage ownership in the corporation has not changed. $60 / 1.5 shares = $40 per share.

4. D  Common Stock Dividend Distributable represents the new shares of stock that will be issued as a result of the declaration of the stock dividend.

5. A  Treasury Stock, a contra stockholders' equity account, is acquired by purchasing it; cash is decreased and stockholders' equity is decreased.

6. B  Treasury stock has been, and still is, authorized and issued, but it is no longer outstanding.

7. A  When a company retires stock, it purchases its own outstanding stock and cancels the stock certificates. The number of shares issued and outstanding both decrease.

8. C  Appropriating retained earnings has no effect on total retained earnings. It merely indicates that some retained earnings are not available for dividends.

9. C  To be treated as an extraordinary item on the income statement an event must be unusual and infrequent. In today's business environment worker strikes are neither, whereas the other listed items can be considered both.

10. D  By its definition, prior period adjustments are corrections to retained earnings for errors of an earlier period.

## III. Completion

1. net income less preferred dividends; weighted average number of common shares outstanding
2. Treasury (For practical purposes, treasury stock is like unissued stock, neither is in the hands of stockholders, nor do they receive dividends.)
3. unusual in nature; infrequent in occurrence (Note that extraordinary items must be unusual and infrequent.)
4. avoid a takeover; support the market price of the stock; distribute to employees; buy low and sell high

5. comprehensive income
6. price-to-earnings ratio
7. earnings per share
8. stock split
9. prior period adjustment
10. reverse split

## IV. Daily exercise

1. A. 2*
   B. 1 (Note, however, that income from continuing operations is shown both before and after income taxes.)
   C. 3*
   D. 4*

2. Current holdings          4,000 shares
   Dividend (.25 × 4,000)     1,000 shares
      Total                    5,000 shares

3. The answer is 5,000 shares—the same answer. A 5 for 4 split means the stockholder receives 1 additional share for cash for 4 held. In other words, in terms of number of shares, there's no difference between a 25% stock dividend and a 5 for 4 split. However, the split results in shares of a proportionally lower par value while the dividend results in shares of the same par value.

4. Preferred Stock                         300,000
   Paid-in Capital in Excess of Par-Preferred   100,000
      Cash                                           360,000
      Retained Earnings                       40,000

5. Preferred Stock                         300,000
   Paid-in Capital in Excess of Par-Preferred   100,000
   Retained Earnings                        40,000
      Cash                                           440,000

6. 450,000 × 3/12   =   112,500
   600,000 × 5.5/12 =   275,000
   675,000 × 3.5/12 =   196,875
                                  584,375

   EPS = $981,754 ÷ 584,375 = $1.68

## V. Exercises

1.

|   | Assets | Liabilities | Paid-in Capital | Retained Earnings |
|---|---|---|---|---|
| A. Declaration of a cash dividend | 0 | + | 0 | - |
| B. Payment of a cash dividend | - | - | 0 | 0 |
| C. Declaration of a stock dividend | 0 | 0 | + | - |
| D. Issuance of a stock dividend | 0 | 0 | 0 | 0 |
| E. A stock split | 0 | 0 | 0 | 0 |
| F. Cash purchase of treasury stock | - | 0 | 0* | 0* |
| G. Sale of treasury stock below cost | + | 0 | -* | -** |

\* While a cash purchase of treasury stock does not affect Paid-in Capital or Retained Earnings, it does reduce stockholders' equity.

\*\* The sale may reduce one or the other, or both. In addition, the sale also increases total stockholders' equity, by the amount of the credit to Treasury Stock.

2.

| Date | Account and Explanation | PR | Debit | Credit |
|---|---|---|---|---|
| 10/10 | Retained Earnings | | 1,200,000 | |
| | (400,000 ×.15 × $20) | | | |
| | Common Stock Dividend Distributable | | | 300,000 |
| | (400,000 ×.15 × $5) | | | |
| | Paid-in Capital in Excess of Par - Common | | | 900,000 |
| | [400,000 ×.15 × ($20 - $5)] | | | |
| | | | | |
| 10/30 | Common Stock Dividend Distributable | | 300,000 | |
| | Common Stock | | | 300,000 |

3.

| Date | Account and Explanation | PR | Debit | Credit |
|---|---|---|---|---|
| 4/4 | Retained Earnings | | 5,000 | |
| | Common Stock Dividend Distributable | | | 5,000 |
| | (10,000 × .50 × $1) | | | |
| | | | | |
| 4/26 | Common Stock Dividend Distributable | | 5,000 | |
| | Common Stock | | | 5,000 |

4.

| Date | Account and Explanation | PR | Debit | Credit |
|---|---|---|---|---|
| 2/10 | Treasury Stock (800 × $24) | | 19,200 | |
| | Cash | | | 19,200 |
| | | | | |
| 7/1 | Cash | | 14,000 | |
| | Treasury Stock (500 × $24) | | | 12,000 |
| | Paid-in Capital from Treasury Stock Transactions | | | 2,000 |
| | [($28 - 24) × 500] | | | |
| | | | | |
| 12/12 | Cash (300 × $16) | | 4,800 | |
| | Paid-in Capital from Treasury Stock Transactions | | 2,000 | |
| | Retained Earnings | | 400 | |
| | Treasury Stock (300 × $24) | | | 7,200 |
| The July 1 transaction resulted in a $2,000 balance in the Paid-in Capital account. This credit balance is not large enough to absorb the entire $2,400 difference between the Treasury Stock cost and its selling price (300 shares × $8). Therefore, the Paid-in Capital account is debited up to its credit balance ($2,000) and the excess is charged against Retained Earnings. The Paid-in Capital account cannot carry a debit balance. ||||

## 5.

| | | |
|---|---:|---:|
| Paid-in Capital | | |
| Preferred Stock, $10 par, 100,000 shares authorized, 50,000 issued | | 500,000 |
| Common Stock, $1.00 par, 2,000,000 shares authorized, 1,205,000 issued | 1,205,000 | |
| Paid-in Capital in Excess of Par - Common | 5,620,000 | 6,825,000 |
| Donated Capital | | 267,500 |
| Total Paid-In Capital | | 7,592,500 |
| Retained Earning | | 10,418,000 |
| Subtotal | | 18,010,500 |
| Less: | | |
| Treasury Stock (5,000 shares preferred) | 90,000 | |
| Treasury Stock (30,000 shares common) | 465,000 | 555,000 |
| Total Stockholders' Equity | | $17,455,500 |

## 6.

Book Value = $\dfrac{\text{Total Stockholders' Equity - Preferred Equity}}{\text{\# of common shares outstanding}}$

Preferred Equity = # of shares outstanding × Redemption Value

= 45,000 shares × $14/share = $630,000

Book Value = ($17,455,500 - $630,000) ÷ (1,205,000 - 30,000)

= $16,825,500 ÷ 1,175,000 = $14.32 (rounded)

> **Study Tip:** Remember book value (for both classes of stock) is based on outstanding shares, not issued shares. When a company has treasury stock, outstanding shares will equal issued less treasury.

## VI. Beyond the Numbers

No journal entries are required when a company declares a stock split. The outstanding shares are returned to the company and replaced with new shares. Each new share will have a par value of 66 2/3 cent ($1 par ÷ 3/2). The total paid-in capital remains unchanged, however. The market price will drop proportionately (to $40 per share). Stock splits have the same effect on market price as large stock dividends.

### Demonstration Problem #1 Solved and Explained

1. Average issue price of the common stock was $8.50 per share:

| | |
|---|---:|
| Common stock at par ($1 × 800,000 shares) | $800,000 |
| Paid-in capital in excess of par - common | 6,000,000 |
| Total paid in for common stock | 6,800,000 |
| ÷ number of issued shares | ÷ 800,000 |
| Average issue price | $8.50 |

2. Average issue price of the preferred stock was $25 per share:

| | |
|---|---|
| Preferred stock at par ($25 × 150,000 shares) | $3,750,000 |
| Paid-in capital in excess of par - preferred | 0 |
| Total paid in for preferred stock | 3,750,000 |
| ÷ number of issued shares | ÷150,000 |
| Average issue price | $25.00 |

3. Income Summary                825,000
     Retained Earnings                         825,000

Earnings per share is $0.66:

| | |
|---|---|
| Net income | $825,000 |
| Less: Preferred dividends (150,000 × $2) | 300,000 |
| Net income available to common stock | 525,000 |
| ÷ average outstanding shares (800,000 issued - 2,000 treasury stock) | ÷ 798,000 |
| Earnings per share (rounded) | $0.66 |

4. Cash (10,000 shares × $22.50 selling price)     225,000
    Common Stock (10,000 × $1)                      10,000
    Paid-in Capital in Excess of Par - Common         215,000
To issue common stock at a premium.

5. Shares outstanding = 808,000
810,000 shares issued* less 2,000 shares treasury stock = 808,000
* 800,000 shares issued, plus 10,000 shares from answer 4 above.

6. Shares outstanding after 2-for-1 split = 1,616,000:
808,000 shares outstanding immediately before split × 2/1 = 1,616,000 shares outstanding
The new par value of the common stock is $0.50 ($1.00 × 1/2)

7.
   a. Retained Earnings (1,616,000 outstanding shares ×
       10% × $22.50)                                      3,636,000
       Common Stock Dividend Distributable                    80,800
       (161,600 × $.50)
       Paid-in Capital in Excess of Par - Common              3,555,200
       (161,600 shares × $22.00 premium)
      To declare a 10% stock dividend.

When a *small stock dividend* occurs (GAAP defines a small dividend as one for less than 25%), Retained Earnings should be capitalized for the *fair market* value of the shares to be distributed (in this case, 3,636,000). Note that 1,616,000 shares were outstanding after answer 6 above, and that the 2-for-1 stock split reduces par value to $0.50 per share. The 10% distribution was for 161,600 shares (1,616,000 × 10% = 161,600).

b.  Retained Earnings (1,616,000 outstanding shares ×
    40% × $0.50)                                              323,200
        Common Stock Dividend Distributable                           323,200
    To declare a 40% common stock dividend.

When a *large stock dividend* occurs (GAAP defines a large dividend as one for 25% or more), Retained Earnings should be capitalized for the *par value* of the shares issued. 40% × 1,616,000 = 646,400 shares to be distributed × $0.50 par = 323,200.

8.  a.  Treasury Stock (2,500 × $25)                           62,500
            Cash                                                       62,500
        To purchase 2,500 shares of treasury stock at $27 per share.

    b.  Cash (1,000 × $27)                                      27,000
            Treasury Stock (1,000 × $25)                               25,000
            Paid-in Capital from Treasury Stock Transactions            2,000
        To sell 1,000 shares of treasury stock at $27 per share.

    c.  Cash (1,000 × $22)                                      22,000
        Paid-in Capital from Treasury Stock Transactions         2,000
        Retained Earnings                                        1,000
            Treasury Stock (1,000 × $25)                               25,000
        To sell 1,000 shares of treasury stock at $22 per share.

A company does not earn income on the purchase and sale of its own stock. The sale of treasury stock results in an increase to paid-in capital, not income. Paid-in Capital from Treasury Stock Transactions (a paid-in capital account is *credited* for sales in excess of cost (as in answer 8b) and *debited* for a sale below cost. If the account balance is not large enough to cover a sale below cost, it may be necessary to debit Retained Earnings (as in answer 8c).

9.      Retained Earnings                                      800,000
            Retained Earnings Appropriated
                for Future Expansion                                  800,000
        To appropriate retained earnings for future expansion of foreign operations.

10 & 11.

| Preferred Stock | |
|---|---|
| | Bal. 3,750,000 |

| Common Stock | |
|---|---|
| | Bal. 800,000 |
| | (5) 10,000 |
| | Bal. 810,000 |

| Paid-in Capital in Excess of Par - Common Stock | |
|---|---|
| | Bal. 6,000,000 |
| | (4) 215,000 |
| | (7a) 3,555,200 |
| | Bal. 9,770,200 |

| Retained Earnings | |
|---|---|
| (7a) 3,636,000 | Bal. 6,855,180 |
| (8c) 1,000 | (3) 825,000 |
| (9) 800,000 | |
| | Bal. 3,243,180 |

| Treasury Stock | |
|---|---|
| Bal. 14,000 | (8b) 25,000 |
| (8a) 62,500 | (8c) 25,000 |
| Bal. 26,500 | |

| Common Stock Dividend Distrib. | |
|---|---|
| | (7a) 80,800 |

| Retained Earnings Appropriated | |
|---|---|
| | (9) 800,000 |

| Paid-in Cap. from Treasury Stock | |
|---|---|
| (8c) 2,000 | (8b) 2,000 |

12.

| Stockholders' Equity: | | |
|---|---|---|
| Preferred Stock, 8%, $25 par value | | |
| Authorized - 1,000,000 shares | | |
| Issued 150,000 shares | $3,750,000 | |
| Common Stock $0.50 par value | | |
| Authorized - 5,000,000 shares | | |
| Issued - 1,620,000 shares | 810,000 | |
| Common Stock Dividend Distributable | 80,800 | |
| Paid-in Capital in Excess of Par - Common | 9,770,200 | |
| Total Paid-in Capital | | 14,411,000 |
| Retained earnings | | |
| Appropriated | 800,000 | |
| Unappropriated | 3,243,180 | |
| Total Retained Earnings | | 4,043,180 |
| Total Paid-in Capital and Retained Earnings | | $18,454,180 |
| Less: Treasury stock, at cost (4,500 common shares) | | 26,500 |
| Total Stockholders' Equity | | $18,427,680 |

Explanation:

All the amounts were taken directly from the ending T-account balances. These ending balances are the result of requirements a and b. Remember, the common shares split 2 for 1, thereby reducing the par value of each from $1.00 to $.50. Therefore, the ending balance in the common stock account of $810,000 must represent 1,620,000 shares ($810,000 ÷ $.50 par = 1,620,000 shares). When the common stock dividend of 161,600 shares is distributed, the total number of issued shares will increase to 1,781,600 (1,620,000 + 161,600). The Treasury Stock balance represents the original balance of $14,000 plus the 500 shares remaining from the transactions in entry 8. The total shares are now 4,500 because the original 2,000 shares were affected by the 2 for 1 split in #6 (2,000 × 2 = 4,000 + 500 = 4,500).

**Demonstration Problem #2 Solved and Explained**

**Requirement 1 (income statement)**

Atlas Manufacturing<br>Income Statement<br>1999

| | | |
|---|---|---|
| Sales | | $5,014,200 |
| Cost of Goods Sold | | 2,648,000 |
| Gross Margin | | 2,366,200 |
| Less: Operating Expenses | | |
| Selling | 305,000 | |
| Administrative | 185,000 | 490,000 |
| Operating Income | | 1,876,200 |
| Other gains (losses) | | |
| Gain on Sales of Equipment | | 48,000 |
| Income from continuing operations before income tax | | 1,924,200 |

| | | |
|---|---|---|
| Income tax expense | | 865,890 |
| Income from continuing operations | | 1,058,310 |
| | | |
| Discontinued Operations: | | |
|    Operating Loss $91,680, less income tax savings of $41,256 | (50,424) | |
|    Gain on Sale, $137,400, less income tax of $61,830 | 75,570 | 25,146 |
| Income before extraordinary items and cumulative effect of change in accounting principle | | 1,083,456 |
| Extraordinary Loss, $296,000, less income tax saving of $133,200 | | (162,800) |
| Cumulative Effect of Change in Accounting Principle, $82,00, less income tax of $36,900 | | 45,100 |
| | | |
| Net Income | | $ 965,756 |

**Requirement 2 (earning per share)**

Weighted average # of shares outstanding =
   225,000 × 2/12 =   37,500
   300,000 × 7/12 =  175,000
   250,000 × 3/12 =   62,500
                      275,000

| | |
|---|---|
| Income from continuing operations | $3.85 (rounded) |
| Income from discontinued operations | 0.09 |
| Income before extraordinary loss and cumulative effect of change in accounting principle | $3.94 |
| Extraordinary loss | (0.59) |
| Cumulative effect of change in accounting | 0.16 |
| Net income | $3.51 (rounded) |

**Study Tip:** Proof = $965,756 ÷ 275,000 = $3.51

# Chapter 15 - Long-Term Liabilities

## CHAPTER OVERVIEW

In Chapters 13 and 14 you learned about topics related to stockholders' equity. Paid-in capital is a major source of funds for corporations. However, companies obtain funds from other sources as well. Hopefully, profitable operations will supply a significant amount of these funds. Corporations can also obtain additional funds by borrowing. In this chapter we examine long-term liabilities, particularly bonds and leases. The learning objectives for the chapter are to

1. Account for basic bonds payable transactions by the straight-line amortization method.
2. Amortize bond discount and premium by the effective-interest method.
3. Account for the retirement of bonds payable.
4. Account for conversion of bonds payable.
5. Show the advantages and disadvantages of borrowing.
6. Report lease and pension liabilities.

The chapter 15 appendix covers these additional objectives:

A1. Compute the future value of an investment made in a single amount.
A2. Compute the future value of annuity-type investment.
A3. Compute the present value of a single future amount.
A4. Compute the present value of an annuity.
A5. Determine the cost of an asset acquired through a capital lease.

## CHAPTER REVIEW

### Objective 1 - Account for basic bonds payable transactions by the straight-line amortization method.

Corporations issue **bonds** (typically in $1,000 units) to raise large amounts of money from multiple lenders. Bonds are long-term liabilities. The **bond certificate** states the 1) principal amount, 2) interest rate, 3) maturity date, and 4) dates that interest payments are due. Exhibit 15-1 in your text presents a typical bond certificate.

**Term bonds** mature at the same time. **Serial bonds** mature in installments over a period of time. Unsecured bonds are called **debentures**. **Secured bonds** may be referred to as mortgage bonds (i.e., used to purchase a building). The owners of a secured bond have the right to take specified assets of the issuer in the event of default.

Bonds are often traded on bonds markets. Bond prices are quoted at a percentage of their maturity value. For example, a $10,000 bond selling for 97 would sell for $9,700.

Four factors set the **price of bonds**: 1) the length of time until the bond matures, 2) the company's ability to meet interest and principal payments, 3) the maturity value, and 4) the rates of other available investment plans.

A basic understanding of the concept of **present value** is necessary to understand bond prices. When companies borrow money they have to pay interest on the debt. To the lender this represents the time value of money. Therefore a lender would not be interested in giving up $500 today only to receive $500 five years from now. If the lender wants to receive $500 years from now, the question is, how much would the lender be willing to give up today to do so? The answer to the question represents the present value of that future amount ($500). Present value is discussed in detail in the chapter 15 Appendix.

The price at which bonds are sold is determined by the **contract interest (stated)** rate and the **market (effective) interest rate**. The contract rate is the amount (expressed as a percent) listed on the bond certificate. The market rate is the amount that potential investors are currently demanding for their money. When the contract rate is less than the market rate the bonds have to be sold are less than their face value (called a **discount**) to attract investors. Conversely, when the contract price is greater than the market rate, the bonds will sell at a **premium**. Exhibit 15-3 in your text illustrates this relationship.

The simplest transaction occurs when bonds are issued on an interest date and no difference exists between the stated rate and the market rate. Debit Cash and credit Bonds Payable. When interest is paid, debit Interest Expense and credit Cash. When the bonds mature and are paid off, debit Bonds Payable and credit Cash.

When **bonds are issued between interest dates**, (or sold "plus accrued interest") the corporation collects the accrued interest from the purchaser, in addition to the selling price of the bonds. Debit Cash, credit Bonds Payable, and credit Interest Payable.

The first interest payment is recorded with a debit to Interest Expense, a debit to Interest Payable, and a credit to Cash (for the full 6 months' interest payment).

Interest payments are not prorated based on the issue date. The interest payment to the purchaser is composed of the accrued interest collected from the purchaser plus the interest expense from the sale date to the next interest date; in other words, the full 6 months' interest.

Issuing Bonds at a Discount

If the market interest rate is higher than the stated rate of a bond issue, then the issuer must **sell the bonds at a discount**, that is at less than face value, in order to attract buyers. The entry debits Cash, debits Discount on Bonds Payable, and credits Bonds Payable.

**Discount on Bonds Payable** is a contra account to Bonds Payable. On the balance sheet, the discount balance is subtracted from Bonds Payable to equal the book value or carrying amount of the bond issue. The issuer will have to repay the face value of the bonds when they mature. Therefore, a discount is additional interest expense to the issuer.

The discount is allocated to Interest Expense over the life of the bonds, in accordance with the matching principle. **Straight-line amortization** of the discount is computed by dividing the discount by the number of accounting periods during the life of the bonds. On each interest date the entry to record interest expense debits Interest Expense, credits Cash, and credits Discount on Bonds Payable. Therefore, the total cost to the corporation of borrowing the money is the sum of the interest payments plus the discount.

Issuing Bonds at a Premium

If the market rate is lower than the stated rate of a bond issue, then the issuer can **sell the bonds at a premium**, that is, for more than face value. The entry debits Cash, credits Bonds Payable and credits Premium on Bonds Payable. **Premium on Bonds Payable** is added to Bonds Payable on the balance sheet to show the book value or carrying amount. The issuer will have to repay only the face value of the bonds when they mature. Therefore, a premium is treated as a reduction of the issuer's interest expense. The premium is allocated to reduce interest expense over the life of the bonds, in accordance with the matching principle.

Straight-line amortization of the premium is computed by dividing the premium by the number of accounting periods during the life of the bonds. On each interest date the entry to record interest expense debits Interest Expense, debits Premium on Bonds Payable and credits Cash.

**Adjusting entries** are prepared to accrue interest and amortize the discount or premium for the period from the last interest date to the end of the accounting period. Debit Interest Expense, credit Interest Payable, and either debit Premium on Bonds Payable or credit Discount on Bonds Payable.

## Objective 2 - Amortize bond discount and premium by the effective-interest method.

GAAP requires that discounts and premiums be amortized using the **effective interest method**. However, when the difference between the straight-line and effective interest methods is not material, either method may be used.

The objective of the effective interest method is to match interest expense as a constant percentage of the changing carrying value of the bonds rather than as a constant amount each period. The effective interest rate is the market rate in effect when the bonds are sold. Three steps are followed when using the effective interest method:

1. Interest expense is calculated by multiplying the effective interest rate by the carrying value of the bonds. (This amount changes each period.)

**Study Tip:** Carrying value equals principal plus premium or minus discount.

2. The cash paid to bondholders is calculated by multiplying the stated interest rate by the principal amount of the bonds. (This amount is the same each period.)

3. The difference between the interest expense and the cash paid is the amount of discount or premium amortized.

Remember that amortization of bond discount or premium will change the carrying value of the bonds before the next calculations are made. If a premium is amortized, the carrying value of the bonds will decrease; if a discount is amortized, the carrying value will increase.

Carefully study Exhibits 15-5 and 15-6 in your text in order to understand the effective interest method.

As with straight-line amortization, adjusting entries must be prepared for a partial period from the last interest date to the end of the accounting period in order to accrue interest and amortize bond discount or premium. Debit Interest Expense, credit Interest Payable, and either debit Premium on Bonds Payable or credit Discount on Bonds Payable.

## Objective 3 - Account for the retirement of bonds payable.

Sometimes corporations retire bonds prior to the maturity date. **Callable bonds** may be retired at the option of the issuer. **Noncallable bonds** may be bought back on the open market and retired. If interest rates have dropped, the issuer may compare the book value of the bonds to the market price to decide whether to retire the bonds. When bonds are retired and the bonds were initially sold at either a premium or discount, the entry to retire the bonds must also remove the unamortized premium or discount from the books. A **gain (or loss) on retirement** results when the carrying value of the bonds is greater (or lesser for a loss) than the cash paid for the bonds. Any gain or loss on the retirement of bonds payable is an extraordinary item according to GAAP.

> **Study Tip:** Remember from Chapter 14 that extraordinary items are reported separately on the income statement, net of tax.

## Objective 4 - Account for conversion of bonds payable.

Bonds which can be converted into common stock are called **convertible bonds**. Investors will convert the bonds when the stock price of the issuing company increases to the point that the stock has a higher market value than the bonds. The entry transfers the bond carrying amount into stockholders' equity:

| | | |
|---|---|---|
| Bonds Payable | XX | |
| Premium on Bonds Payable (if applicable) | XX | |
|     Discount on Bonds Payable (if applicable) | | XX |
|     Common stock | | XX |
|     Paid-in Capital in Excess of Par - Common | | XX |

> **Study Tip:** Note both Premium and Discount cannot appear in the same entry.

There will never be a gain or loss recorded on the conversion of bonds. The credit to Paid-in Capital is the difference between the carrying value of the bonds (Bonds Payable + Premium or Bonds Payable - Discount) and the par value of the shares issued.

## Objective 5 - Show the advantages and disadvantages of borrowing.

**Advantages of borrowing**:

1. Borrowing does not affect ownership; bondholders are creditors, not stockholders.
2. Interest on debt is deductible for tax purposes.
3. **Trading on the equity** usually increases EPS. This means that the corporation earns a return on the borrowed funds that is greater than the cost of the borrowed funds.

**Disadvantages of borrowing:**

1. High interest rates
2. Interest on debt must be paid; dividends on stock are optional.

## Objective 6 - Report lease and pension liabilities.

A **lease** is a rental agreement in which the tenant (lessee) agrees to make rent payments to the property owner (lessor) in exchange for the use of some asset. **Operating leases** are usually short-term or cancelable. To account for an operating lease, the lessee debits Rent Expense (Lease Expense) and credits Cash for the amount of the lease payment.

**Capital leases** are long-term and noncancelable. Accounting for capital leases is similar to accounting for the purchase of an asset. Debit the asset leased, credit Cash for the initial payment, and credit Lease Liability for the present value of future lease payments. Because the leased asset is capitalized, it must be depreciated. Leased assets are usually depreciated over the term of the lease. Debit Depreciation Expense and credit the asset's Accumulated Depreciation account.

At year end, interest is accrued on the lease liability. Debit Interest Expense and credit Lease Liability. Lease payments are recorded with a debit to Lease Liability and a credit to Cash.

FASB Statement 13 sets the **guidelines for capital leases**. Only one of the following criteria is required to be present to classify the lease as capital:

1. The lease transfers title (ownership) to the lessee at the end of the lease term.
2. The lease contains a bargain purchase option.
3. The term of the lease is 75% or more of the estimated useful life of the asset.
4. The present value of the lease payments is 90% or more of the market value of the leased asset.

Operating leases are defined by exception: i.e., operating leases are only those which fail to meet all four of these criteria.

In the past, companies were attracted to operating leases because they were not required to list the lease as a liability on the balance sheet—in other words, the company had the use of an asset (or service) without the related debt showing (called **off-balance-sheet financing**). This practice has been curtailed as a result of reporting requirements in FASB Statement 13.

**Pensions** and **post-retirement benefits** are other types of liabilities found on balance sheets. **Pensions** are compensation paid to employees after retirement, usually based on a variety of factors including length of service. Companies are required to report the present value of promised future pension payments to retirees. If the plan assets exceed this amount, the plan is overfunded. Conversely, the fund could be underfunded if assets are less.

In addition to pensions, companies are required to report the present value of future payments to retirees for other benefits. The largest of these is health care. At the end of each period, companies accrue the expense and the liability of post-retirement benefits based on information about the current work force.

Recall from Chapter 14 that stockholders' equity transactions are summarized in the financing activities section of the cash flows statement. This section will also include information about the company's borrowing activities, both short and long term. Acquiring cash by issuing notes or bonds payable is reported as a cash inflow while the repayment of debt represents cash outflow.

# Appendix: Future Value and Present Value

### Objective A1 - Compute the future value of an investment made in a single amount.

Because you can earn interest on your money over time, the value of invested funds is greater in the future than it is today. This refers to the **time value of money**. To determine what a **future value** will be you simply apply an interest rate to the amount of your investment and calculate the amount of interest. Add this result to your original amount and the sum becomes the future value at the end of one interest period. Repeat this process for additional interest periods, remembering to add in the interest each time. Therefore there are three factors involved in determining a future value: 1) the amount of the original investment, 2) the length of time and 3) the interest rate. Obviously the longer the time, the more calculations are involved. Fortunately mathematical tables are available to ease your task. Review exhibit 15A-2 carefully. This is the table used to determine a future value of a single investment, again assuming time and interest rate.

### Objective A2 - Compute the future value of annuity-type investment.

Instead of investing a single amount for a specific period, you might wish to invest multiple amounts over time. This is an example of an **annuity-type investment**. In other words, you invest identical amounts for several years—what will the future value of these multiple investments be? Of course, you could calculate each individually and add the results, or you can consult mathematical tables which do the multiple calculations for you. Review Exhibit 15A-3 carefully. This is the table used to determine a future value of multiple investments, again assuming time and interest rate. This table is used to answer questions like "If I start setting aside (investing) $500 each year for the next ten years, what will it be worth assuming I can invest this money at 8%?" Exhibit 15A-3 shows the value 14.487 at the intersection of 10 and 8%. Multiply this value by your annual investment ($500) and the result is $7,243.50.

### Objective A3 - Compute the present value of a single future amount.

Another way to look at present and future values is to begin with the future value and work backwards. In other words, in order to have X amount some time in the future, how much would one need to set aside today? Again assumptions need to be made about the time and the interest rate (this is always true).

As with the preceding discussions, you could calculate the result manually but the longer the period of time the more calculations you would have to complete. Once again, mathematical tables are available to use. Study Exhibit 15A-6 carefully. The value at the intersection of the appropriate period and rate is multiplied by the future amount to determine the present value.

## Objective A4 - Compute the present value of an annuity.

Rather than determining the present value of a single amount, you may be interested in the **present value of an annuity-type investment**. In other words, what is the present value of an investment that will give you the same fixed amount over a number of periods? As with earlier discussions, this value can be calculated manually, but it is time-consuming. Once again, tables are available to simplify the process. Study exhibit 15A-7 carefully.

> **Study Tip:** BEFORE PROCEEDING BE CERTAIN YOU UNDERSTAND IN WHICH CIRCUMSTANCES YOU USE WHICH TABLE. This is vital to understanding the topics which follow.

Chapter 15 examines long-term liabilities, primarily bonds payable. What is a bond? It is a way for a company to borrow funds. When a company issues a bond, what happens? The company promises to pay the face value of the bond at maturity and, during the life of the bond, the company also promises to pay a fixed amount of interest periodically. The face value at maturity is a single value, whereas the interest payments are like an annuity. Therefore, when a company issues bonds it needs to know what price should be asked (remember bond prices are quoted as percentages of face value) in order to attract investors. To determine this, consult the appropriate tables—in this case 15A-6 and 15A-7 in your text. Using the market rate of interest, the first table will give you the present value of a future single amount, the second the present value of an annuity. Sum the results and you have an estimate of the market price of the bonds. The market rate of interest is used because this is the rate potential investors will demand for the use of their funds. If the market rate is higher than the contract (or stated) rate of interest, the bonds will have to be sold at a discount to attract investors. Conversely, if the market rate is lower than the contract rate, the bonds will sell at a premium.

## Objective A5 - Determine the cost of an asset acquired through a capital lease.

Earlier you learned about capital leases. When a company acquires an asset with a capital lease, the company needs to record the asset at "cost." What is the cost when the lease requires payments over the life of the lease? Using present value tables, specifically Exhibit 15A-7, you can value the asset because the fixed payments over the life of the lease are like annuities and you want to determine the present value (i.e., cost) of all those payments.

# TEST YOURSELF

All the self-testing materials in this chapter focus on information and procedures that your instructor is likely to test in quizzes and examinations. *Questions followed by the letter "A" refer to topics in the chapter appendix.*

**I. Matching**   Match each numbered term with its lettered definition.

    ____  1.  bond discount
    ____  2.  bond premium
    ____  3.  callable bonds
    ____  4.  contract interest rate
    ____  5.  debentures
    ____  6.  lessee
    ____  7.  stated interest rate
    ____  8.  market interest rate
    ____  9.  registered bonds
    ____ 10.  trading on the equity
    ____ 11.  off-balance-sheet financing
    ____ 12.  bond indenture
    ____ 13.  bonds payable
    ____ 14.  capital lease
    ____ 15.  convertible bonds
    ____ 16.  lease
    ____ 17.  lessor
    ____ 18.  mortgage
    ____ 19.  operating lease
    ____ 20.  serial bonds
    ____ 21.  term bonds
    ____ 22.  underwriter
    ____ 23A. annuity

A. a rental agreement in which the tenant agrees to make rent payments to the property owner in exchange for the use of the asset
B. another name for the contract interest rate
C. acquisition of assets or services with debt that is not reported on the balance sheet
D. bonds for which the owners receive interest checks from the issuing company
E. bonds that may be exchanged for the common stock of the issuing company at the option of the investor
F. bonds that mature in installments over a period of time
G. bonds that the issuer may pay off at a specified price whenever the issuer desires
H. bonds that all mature at the same time for a particular issue
I. borrower's promise to transfer the legal title to certain assets to the lender if the debt is not paid on schedule
J. contract under which bonds are issued
K. earning more income than the interest on the borrowed amount
L. excess of a bond's maturity (par) value over its issue price
M. excess of a bond's issue price over its maturity (par) value
N. groups of notes payable issued to multiple lenders, called bondholders
O. interest rate that investors demand in order to lend their money
P. a lease agreement that meets any one of four special criteria
Q. organization that purchases bonds from an issuing company and resells them to clients, or sells the bonds for a commission and agrees to buy all unsold bonds
R. the property owner in a lease agreement
S. the tenant in a lease agreement
T. the interest rate that determines the amount of cash interest the borrower pays
U. unsecured bonds backed only by the good faith of the borrower
V. usually a short-term or cancelable rental agreement
W. a fixed amount paid (or received) over a number of periods

## II. Multiple Choice  *Circle the best answer.*

1. A $10,000 bond quoted at 96 5/8 has a market price of:

   A. $10,000
   B. $9,662.50
   C. $9,658.00
   D. $9,606.25

2. All of the following affect the market price of bonds except:

   A. bond holder's credit rating
   B. bond issuer's credit rating
   C. market interest rate
   D. length of time to maturity

3A. The present value of a future amount does not depend on the:

   A. interest rate
   B. convertibility of a bond
   C. amount of the future payment
   D. length of time until the future payment is made

4. The interest rate demanded by investors in order to lend their money is the:

   A. contract rate
   B. issue rate
   C. effective rate
   D. stated rate

5. The premium on a bond payable:

   A. increases the interest expense only in the year the bonds are sold
   B. increases the interest expense over the life of the bonds
   C. reduces interest expense only in the year the bonds mature
   D. is a liability account that is amortized (to expense) over the life of the bonds

6. The book value of Bonds Payable on the balance sheet equals:

   A. Bonds Payable + Discount on Bonds Payable or + Premium on Bonds Payable
   B. Bonds Payable - Discount on Bonds Payable or - Premium on Bonds Payable
   C. Bonds Payable + Discount on Bonds Payable or - Premium on Bonds Payable
   D. Bonds Payable - Discount on Bonds Payable or + Premium on Bonds Payable

7. When bonds are issued at a premium, their carrying amount:

   A. decreases from issuance to maturity
   B. increases from issuance to maturity
   C. remains constant over the life of the bonds
   D. decreases when the market interest rate increases

8. Gains and losses from the early conversion of debt to equity are:

   A. reported as operating gains and losses on the income statement
   B. reported as increases or decreases to Retained Earnings on the statement of retained earnings
   C. reported as extraordinary items on the income statement
   D. not reported

9. When a convertible bond is exchanged for common stock:

   A. stockholders' equity increases
   B. liabilities increase
   C. revenues increase
   D. expenses increase

10. Which of the following is not reported on the balance sheet?

    A. capital leases
    B. pension liabilities
    C. post-retirement benefit liabilities
    D. operating leases

### III. Completion   *Complete each of the following statements.*

1. When the market interest rate is _____ than the stated rate, bonds will sell at a premium.
2. When the premium on bonds payable is reduced, the book value of bonds payable _____.
3. Gains or losses on early retirement of debt is _____ and reported separately on the income statement.
4. The liability to make _____ lease payments is not reported on the balance sheet.
5. If a lease transfers ownership of assets at the end of the lease term, the lease is a(n) _____ lease.
6. The _____ method of interest amortization results in the same amount of discount/premium amortization for identical periods of time.
7. Accruing pension and post-retirement benefit liabilities is an example of the _____ principle.
8. When the market interest rate is greater than the stated rate, the bonds will sell at a _____.
9. Convertible bonds give the _____ the right to convert the bonds to common stock.
10. When the _____ method of amortization is used, the total amount of interest expense over the life of the bonds is a constant percentage.
11A. A(n) _____ is a fixed sum of money received over a number of periods.

### IV. Daily Exercises

1. Calculate the cash proceeds when a $10,000, 6% bond is sold at 98 ½ on December 15, assuming interest is paid on October 15 and April 15.

398   Chapter 15

2. Refer to the facts in Daily Exercise 1 above and record the necessary journal entry on December 15.

|   |   |   |
|---|---|---|
|   |   |   |
|   |   |   |
|   |   |   |
|   |   |   |

3. On December 31, the following information appears on the balance sheet:

    Bonds Payable                                            1,000,000
    Less: Discount on Bonds Payable           24,800           975,200

Assuming the interest has been paid through December 31, journalize the entry to convert the bonds into 180,000 shares of $0.50 par common stock.

|   |   |   |
|---|---|---|
|   |   |   |
|   |   |   |
|   |   |   |
|   |   |   |
|   |   |   |

4. Assume the same information in Daily Exercise 3, but the bonds are called at 101 ½. Record the entry to retire the bonds.

|   |   |   |
|---|---|---|
|   |   |   |
|   |   |   |
|   |   |   |
|   |   |   |
|   |   |   |

5. Soundtronics Corporation signs a 20-year lease for a new manufacturing facility. The agreement requirements a $500,000 payment upon signing plus annual payments of $100,000 at the end of each year for the life of the lease. Assuming an implied interest rate of 8%, present the journal entry upon signing the lease.

|   |   |   |
|---|---|---|
|   |   |   |
|   |   |   |
|   |   |   |
|   |   |   |

6. Review the information in Daily Exercise 5A above and record the first $100,000 annual payment on the lease.

|   |   |   |
|---|---|---|
|   |   |   |
|   |   |   |
|   |   |   |
|   |   |   |

## V. Exercises

1. Complex Communications issued $5,000,000 in 20-year bonds with a stated interest rate of 7%. The bonds were issued at par on April 1, 1999. Interest is paid October 1 and April 1.

   Give the journal entries for:

   A. Issuance of the bonds on April 1, 1999.
   B. Payment of interest on October 1, 1999.
   C. Maturity payment of bonds on April 1, 2019.

   |    | Date | Account and Explanation | Debit | Credit |
   |----|------|-------------------------|-------|--------|
   | A. |      |                         |       |        |
   |    |      |                         |       |        |
   |    |      |                         |       |        |
   | B. |      |                         |       |        |
   |    |      |                         |       |        |
   |    |      |                         |       |        |
   | C. |      |                         |       |        |
   |    |      |                         |       |        |
   |    |      |                         |       |        |

2. Maxwell Corporation issued $500,000 in 7-year bonds with a stated interest rate of 8%. The bonds were sold on January 1, 1999, for $477,956 to yield 9%. Interest is paid July 1 and January 1. Maxwell uses the effective interest method to amortize Discount on Bonds Payable. (Assume a December 31 year end.)

   Record the journal entries for:

   A. Issuance of bonds on January 1, 1999.
   B. Payment of interest on July 1, 1999.
   C. Accrual of interest and related amortization on December 31, 1999 (year end).
   D. Payment of interest on January 1, 2000.
   E. Maturity payment of bonds on January 1, 2006.

|   | Date | Account and Explanation | Debit | Credit |
|---|------|------------------------|-------|--------|
| A. |   |   |   |   |
| B. |   |   |   |   |
| C. |   |   |   |   |
| D. |   |   |   |   |
| E. |   |   |   |   |

3. Crawford Corporation issued $500,000 in 7-year bonds with a stated interest rate of 8%. The bonds were sold on January 1, 1999, for $477,956 to yield 9%. Interest is paid July 1 and January 1. Crawford uses the straight-line method to amortize Discount on Bonds Payable. (Assume an October 31 year end.)

Record the journal entries for:

A. Issuance of bonds on January 1, 1999.
B. Payment of interest on July 1, 1999.
C. Accrual of interest and related amortization on October 31, 1999 (year end)
D. Payment of interest on January 1, 2000
E. Maturity payment of bonds on January 1, 2006.

|   | Date | Account and Explanation | Debit | Credit |
|---|------|------------------------|-------|--------|
| A. |   |   |   |   |
| B. |   |   |   |   |

|   | C. | | | |
|---|---|---|---|---|
|   |   |   |   |   |
|   | D. |   |   |   |
|   |   |   |   |   |
|   | E. |   |   |   |
|   |   |   |   |   |

4. Feldman Corporation issued $500,000 in 7-year bonds with a stated interest rate of 8%. The bonds were sold on January 1, 1999, for $558,420 to yield 6%. Interest is paid July 1 and January 1. Feldman uses the effective interest method to amortize Premium on Bonds Payable. (Assume a December 31 year end.)

Record the journal entries for:

A. Issuance of bonds on January 1, 1999.
B. Payment of interest on July 1, 1999.
C. Accrual of interest and related amortization on December 31, 1999 (year end)
D. Payment of interest on January 1, 2000
E. Maturity payment of bonds on January 1, 2006.

|   | Date | Account and Explanation | Debit | Credit |
|---|---|---|---|---|
| A. |   |   |   |   |
| B. |   |   |   |   |
| C. |   |   |   |   |
| D. |   |   |   |   |
| E. |   |   |   |   |

402   Chapter 15

5A. The board of directors for J. Morel, Inc., has approved a financial package to raise additional capital for expansion purposes. Included in the package are debentures for $22,500,000. The interest rate for the bonds approved by the board is 7%, per annum, paid semiannually. When the bonds are finally placed with an underwriter, the market rate of interest is 8%. Determine the price at which the bonds should be sold.

## VI. Beyond the Numbers

Review the information in Exercise 3 and 4 above and assume, in each case, that each $1,000 bond is convertible, at the option of the holder, into 31.25 shares of the corporation's common stock. Determine when an investor should seriously consider exercising the option to convert the bonds to stock.

## VII. Demonstration Problems

### Demonstration Problem #1

On February 1, 1999, Speed-Pak, Inc., issued $20,000,000 of 7% bonds at 97 ½. The market rate on that date was approximately 8%. The bonds mature in 10 years. Interest is paid each July 31 and January 31.

### Required:

1. Record the issuance of the bonds.
2. Record the July 31, 1999, interest payment and straight-line amortization on premium or discount.
3. Accrued interest and amortize premium or discount as of December 31, 1999, the last day of the reporting year for Speed-Pak, Inc., Use straight line amortization.
4. Show how the bonds would be reported on the balance sheet at the year end, 1999.
5. Record the payment of interest and amortization of the premium or discount on January 31, 2000. Use straight line amortization.
6. On February 1, 2001, bondholders convert $5,000,000 of the bonds into 350,000 shares of $1 par value common stock. Record the transaction.
7. On February 1, 2002, the remaining $15,000,000 of bonds are called by the corporation at a call price of 102. Record the retirement of the bonds.

| Date | Account and Explanation | Debit | Credit |
|---|---|---|---|
| 1. | | | |
| | | | |
| | | | |
| | | | |
| 2. | | | |
| | | | |
| | | | |
| | | | |
| | | | |
| 3. | | | |
| | | | |
| | | | |
| | | | |

| | | | |
|---|---|---|---|
| 4. | | | |
| | | | |
| | | | |
| | | | |
| | | | |

| Date | Accounts and Explanation | Debit | Credit |
|---|---|---|---|
| 5. | | | |
| | | | |
| | | | |
| | | | |
| | | | |
| | | | |
| 6. | | | |
| | | | |
| | | | |
| | | | |
| 7. | | | |
| | | | |
| | | | |
| | | | |
| | | | |
| | | | |

# Demonstration Problem #2

McCall-Carlton Corporation has outstanding an issue of 10% callable bonds that mature in 2013. The bonds were dated January 1, 1998, and pay interest each July 1 and January 1. Additional bond data:

a. Fiscal year end for McCall-Carlton Corporation: September 30.
b. Maturity value of the bonds: $2,000,000.
c. Issue price: 106.
d. Market interest rate at time of issue: 9%

**Required:**

1. Complete the effective interest method amortization table through January 1, 2001. Round pennies to the nearest dollar. You may use the Summary Problem in Chapter 15 of the text as a guide.

2. Using the amortization table that you have completed, record the following transactions:
   a. Issuance of the bonds on January 1, 1998.
   b. Payment of interest and amortization of premium on July 1, 1998.
   c. Accrued interest and amortization of premium as of September 30, 1998.
   d. Payment of interest and amortization of premium on January 1, 1999.
   e. Retirement of the bonds on January 2, 2000. Callable price of bonds was 102.

## Requirement 1

| Semi-annual Interest Date | A<br>Interest Payment | B<br>Interest Expense | C<br>Premium Amortization | D<br>Premium Account Balance | E<br>Bond Carrying Value |
|---|---|---|---|---|---|
| 1/1/98 | | | | 120,000 | 2,120,000 |
| 1/1/98 | | | | | |
| 1/1/99 | | | | | |
| 1/1/99 | | | | | |
| 1/1/00 | | | | | |
| 1/1/00 | | | | | |
| 1/1/01 | | | | | |

**Requirement 2**

| | Date | Account and Explanation | Debit | Credit |
|---|---|---|---|---|
| a. | | | | |
| b. | | | | |
| c. | | | | |
| d. | | | | |
| e. | | | | |

# SOLUTIONS

## I. Matching

| | | | | | |
|---|---|---|---|---|---|
| 1. L | 5. U | 9. D | 13. N | 17. R | 21. H |
| 2. M | 6. S | 10. K | 14. P | 18. I | 22. Q |
| 3. G | 7. B | 11. C | 15. E | 19. V | 23A. W |
| 4. T | 8. O | 12. J | 16. A | 20. F | |

## II. Multiple Choice

1. B   The number 96 5/8 means 96.625% (or .96625) of the face value: $10,000 × 96.625% = $9,662.50.

2. A   Since anyone may be a bondholder, it does not make sense that a bondholder's credit rating would affect the market price of the bond. All the other listed items do affect the market price of the bond.

3. B   Interest rate, amount of payment, and length of time until payment all affect present value whether or not the bond is convertible will not.

4. C   Effective rate of interest and market rate of interest are synonymous.

5. D   Amortization of the premium on bonds payable serves to reduce the recorded amount of interest expense over the life of the bonds.

6. D   The book value or carrying amount of a bond is equal to the face amount of the bond minus the unamortized discount or plus the unamortized premium.

7. A   The carrying amount of a bond is the face amount of the bond plus (minus) unamortized premium (discount). Since the balance of the premium (discount) account is amortized over the life of the bond, it moves towards zero. Accordingly, the carrying amount of bonds issued at a premium (discount) decreases (increases) over time.

8. D   GAAP identifies gains and losses on early retirement of debt as an extraordinary item. However, when debt is converted to equity no gain or loss results. The carrying value of the debt is converted into paid-in capital.

9. A   The conversion of a bond to common stock converts a liability to stockholders' equity, which increases stockholders' equity.

10. D  Of the items listed, only "operating lease" is not reported on the balance sheet. Operating leases are generally short-term rental agreements that transfer none of the rights of ownership.

## III. Completion

1. lower

> **Study Tip:** When market rate > stated rate, then discount; when market rate < stated rate, then premium.

2. decreases (The book value or carrying value amount of a bond is equal to the face amount of the bond plus (minus) the unamortized premium (discount).)
3. extraordinary (Though not meeting the normal "infrequent and unusual" requirement for other extraordinary items, GAAP specifies that such gains and losses are extraordinary items.)
4. operating (Operating leases are normally short term and transfer none of the rights of ownership to the lessee. Accordingly, neither an asset nor a liability is recorded for such leases.)
5. capital (Capital leases require that the lessee record the leased property as an asset and the obligation to make future lease payments as a liability.)
6. straight-line (This method divides the amount of the discount/premium by the number of time periods resulting in the same figure each period.)
7. matching
8. discount (because the lender expects a greater return on the loan than the stated rate provides)
9. lender (not the borrower; convertibility make the bonds more attractive to prospective lenders because of the potential for greater returns)
10. effective interest (as compared with the straight-line method where the amount of discount/premium is constant). The effective rate is required, although the straight line method can be used if the difference between the two is not material.
11A. annuity

## IV. Daily Exercises

1. $10,000 × 98 ½ % = $9,850.00

   In addition, interest must be accrued from 10/15 to 12/15 (the sale date). Interest = $10,000 × 6% × 2/12 = $100.00.

   Proceeds = $9,850.00 + 100.00 = $9,950.00

2.

| 12/15 Cash | 9,950 | |
|---|---|---|
| Discount on Bonds Payable | 150 | |
| Bonds Payable | | 10,000 |
| Interest Payable | | 100 |

3.

| Bonds Payable | 1,000,000 | |
|---|---|---|
| Discount on Bonds Payable | | 24,800 |
| Common Stock | | 90,000 |
| Paid-in Capital in Excess of Par - Common | | 885,200 |

On the date of conversion, the carrying value of the bonds is $975,200 ($1,000,000 principle less $24,800 discount.) The carrying value, not the principle is the amount being converted. The credit to the Common

Stock account = 180,000 shares × $0.50 per share (from Chapter 13). The difference of $885,200 ($975,000 - $90,000) is credited to the paid-in capital account.

> **Study Tip:** Gains or losses NEVER arise when debt is converted to equity.

4.

| Bonds Payable | 1,000,000 | |
| Loss on Retirement of Bonds | 39,800 | |
| Discount on Bonds Payable | | 24,800 |
| Cash | | 1,015,000 |

The loss of $39,800 is the difference between the cash paid and carrying value of the bonds ($1,015,000 - $975,000 = $39,800). Remember, when carrying value > call price, difference = gain; when carrying value < call price, difference = loss.

Gains or losses on retirement of bonds are extraordinary items, reported on the income statement net of tax.

> **Study Tip:** A gain or loss on the retirement of bonds will always occur unless call price equals carrying value.

5A.

| Building | 1,381,800 | |
| Cash | | 500,000 |
| Lease Liability | | 981,800 |

The "cost" of the building is the sum of the initial payment ($500,000) plus the present value of the lease liability. While the lease requires annual payments totaling $2,000,000 ($100,000 × 20 years), the present value of the payment is $981,800 (based on Exhibit 15A-7 in your text: 20 and 8% intersect at 9.818 multiplied by $100,000 = $981,800).

6A.

| Interest Expense | 78,544 | |
| Lease Liability | 21,456 | |
| Cash | | 100,000 |

Interest Expense = $981,800 × 8% = $78,544.
$78,544 is interest, then the difference of $21,456 ($100,000 - $78,544) is applied to the Lease. Alternatively, you could first accrue the interest

| Interest Expense | 78,544 | |
| Lease Liability | | 78,544 |

then record the payment

| Lease Liability | 100,000 | |
| Cash | | 100,000 |

Long-Term Liabilities 409

Either approach ends with the same result. The Lease Liability account is reduced by $21,456, the amount of the $100,000 payment in excess of the interest.

## V. Exercises

1. A.   Cash                                                5,000,000
          Bonds Payable                                                                  5,000,000

   B.   Interest Expense ($5,000,000 × .07 × 6/12)      175,000
          Cash                                                                             175,000

   C.   Bonds Payable                                      5,000,000
          Cash                                                                    5,000,000

2. A.   Cash                                                       477,956
         Discount on Bonds Payable                 22,044
           Bonds Payable                                           500,000

   B.   Interest Expense (477,956 ×.09 × 6/12)        21,508
          Cash (500,000 ×.08 × 6/12)                          20,000
          Discount on Bonds Payable                       1,508

   New book value of bonds = Bonds Payable - Discount on Bonds Payable = 500,000 - (22,044 - 1,508) = 479,464

   C.   Interest Expense (479,464 ×.09 × 6/12)        21,576
          Interest Payable (500,000 ×.08 × 6/12)             20,000
          Discount on Bonds Payable                       1,576

   New book value of bonds = Bonds Payable - Discount on Bonds Payable = 500,000 - (20,536 - 1,576) = 481,040

   D.   Interest Payable                                20,000
          Cash                                                                     20,000

   E.   Bonds Payable                                    500,000
          Cash                                                              500,000

   Note that after the last interest payment, the account Discount on Bonds Payable has a zero balance.

3. A.   Cash                                                       477,956
         Discount on Bonds Payable                 22,044
           Bonds Payable                                           500,000

B. Interest Expense (20,000 + 1,575)     21,575
      Cash (500,000 ×.08 × 6/12)     20,000
      Discount on Bonds Payable     1,575
        (22,044 / 14 interest payments)

C. Interest Expense (13,333 + 1,050)     14,383
      Interest Payable (500,000 × .08 × 4/12)     13,333
      Discount on Bonds Payable (22,044/14 × 2/3)     1,050
   Note: In this exercise, the year end is October 31, not December 31.

D. Interest Expense [(20,000 - 13,333) + 525]     7,192
   Interest Payable     13,333
      Cash (500,000 × .08 × 6/12)     20,000
      Discount on Bonds Payable (22,044/14 × 1/3)     525

E. Bonds Payable     500,000
      Cash     500,000

4. A. Cash     558,420
      Bonds Payable     500,000
      Premium on Bonds Payable     58,240

  B. Interest Expense (558,420 × .06 × 6/12)     16,753
    Premium on Bonds Payable     3,247
      Cash (500,000 × .08 × 6/12)     20,000

   New book value of bonds = Bonds Payable + Premium on Bonds Payable = 500,000 + (58,240 - 3,247) = 555,173

  C. Interest Expense (555,173 × .06 × 6/12)     16,655
    Premium on Bonds Payable     3,345
      Cash (500,000 × .08 × 6/12)     20,000

   New book value of bonds = 500,000 + (55,173 - 3,345) = 551,828

  D. Interest Payable     20,000
      Cash     20,000

  E. Bonds Payable     500,000
      Cash     500,000

Note that after the last interest payment, the account Premium on Bonds Payable has a zero balance.

5A.

To determine the selling price of the bonds (expressed as a percentage of their face value), two calculations are required, both using present value tables. First we calculate the present value of the bonds, using table 15A-6 in your text.

PV of $22,500,000 at 4% for 20 periods = $22,500,000 × 0.456 = $10,260,000

Second, we determine the present value of the periods interest payments over the life of the bond. Each interest payment equals $22,500,000 × 7% × 6/12 or $787,500. Remember, the interest payments are like an annuity—a fixed amount paid periodically. Therefore, we use Table 15A-7 in the text and find the intersection of 4% and 20 periods; 4% because the market rate of interest is 8%, but paid semiannually.

PV of $787,500 for the life of the bonds is therefore $787,500 × 13.590, or $10,702,125.

Now, sum the two results, $10,260,000 + $10,702,215 = $20,962,215

Given that the market rate of interest is higher than the stated rate, the bonds will have to be sold at a discount (i.e., less than face value). Other things being equal (which, of course, they never are) the selling price of the bonds should be 93.1655%.

## VI. Beyond the Numbers

If each $1,000 bond can be converted into 31.25 shares of common stock, then a quick calculation indicates an investor should seriously think about converting when the market price of the stock reaches $32 per share ($1,000 divided by 31.25 shares). However, this assumes the investor paid face value for the bonds. In Exercise 3, investors purchased the bonds at a discount of 89.55% of face value or $895.50 for each $1,000 bond. Therefore, investors in Crawford's bonds could consider converting at a lower price of approximately $28.66 per share ($895.50 divided by 31.25). In Exercise 4 the investors paid a premium for the bonds because they were purchased at 111.68% of face value ($558,420 divided by $500,000). These investors would not be interested in converting until the price rose to $35.74 ($1,116.80 divided by 31.25 shares).

## VII. Demonstration Problems

### Demonstration Problem #1 Solved and Explained

(Amounts rounded to nearest dollar)

**Requirement 1**

| 2/1/1999 | Discount on Bonds Payable | 500,000 | |
| | Cash | 19,500,000 | |
| |    Bonds Payable | | 20,000,000 |
| | (Selling price = 97 ½% × $20,000,000 = $19,500,000) | | |

## Requirement 2

| 7/31/1999 | Interest Expense | 725,000 | |
| --- | --- | --- | --- |
| | Discount on Bonds Payable | | 25,000 |
| | Cash | | 700,000 |
| | (Interest = $20,000,000 × 7% × 6/12 = $700,000) | | |

The straight-line method of interest amortization ignores the market rate of interest at the time the bonds are sold. To amortize you divide the amount of the premium (or discount) by the total number of interest payments ($500,000 / 20 = $25,000).

## Requirement 3

| 12/31/1999 | Interest Expense | 604,166 | |
| --- | --- | --- | --- |
| | Discount on Bonds Payable | | 20,833 |
| | Interest Payable | | 583,333 |
| | (Interest Payable = $20,000,000 × .07 × 5/12 = $583,333) | | |
| | (Discount on Bonds Payable = $500,000 / 10 × 5/12 = $20,833) | | |

## Requirement 4

Bonds Payable               $20,000,000
Less Discount on Bonds Payable    454,167        19,545,833
(Discount on Bonds Payable = $800,000 - $25,000 - $20,833 = $454,167)

> **Study Tip:** When bonds are sold at a discount, their carrying value INCREASES over time; when sold at a premium, their carrying value DECREASE over time.

## Requirement 5

| 1/31/2000 | Interest Expense | 120,834 | |
| --- | --- | --- | --- |
| | Interest Payable | 583,333 | |
| | Cash | | 700,000 |
| | Discount on Bonds Payable | | 4,167 |

This may seem a difficult transaction but it is not if you separate it and THINK. The bondholders are owed $700,000. This is your credit to cash ($20,000,000 × .07 × 6/12). In Requirement 3 you accrued $583,333 as Interest Payable. This is your debit to the same account. Also in Requirement 3 you recorded five months of discount amortization ($20,833). You now need to amortize one additional month, or $4,167 (six months' amortization is $25,000 - see Requirement 2; therefore, one month's amortization is $25,000 / 6 = $4,167). The debit to Interest Expense reconciles the entry.

## Requirement 6

| 2/1/2001 | Bonds Payable | 5,000,000 | |
| --- | --- | --- | --- |
| | Discount on Bonds Payable | | 100,000 |
| | Common Stock | | 350,000 |
| | Paid-in Capital in Excess of Par – Common | | 4,550,000 |

$5,000,000 equals one-fourth of the bond issue. Therefore, one-fourth of the original discount, or $125,000 ($500,000 × ¼) applies to the bonds. Two years have passed since the bonds were issued, one-fifth of the discount, or $25,000 ($125,000 × 1/5) has already been amortized. The amount of remaining discount attached to the $5,000,000 is $100,000 ($125,000 - $25,000). Therefore, the carrying value of the bonds on date of conversion is $4,900,000. This is the amount credited to the Common Stock and Paid-in Capital in Excess accounts. The Common Stock account credited for the number of shares × par value (350,000 × $1.00) while the difference is credited to the Paid-in Capital in Excess account.

**Requirement 7**

| 2/1/2002 | Bonds Payable | 15,000,000 | |
| | Loss on Retirement Bonds Payable | 562,500 | |
| | Discount on Bonds Payable | | 262,500 |
| | Cash | | 15,300,000 |

The carrying value of the bonds on the call date is $14,737,500 ($15,000,000 - $262,500). The cost of calling the bonds is $15,300,000 ($15,000,000 × 102%). Therefore, a loss of $562,500 ($15,300,000 - $14,737,500) results. Of the original $500,000 discount, three-fourth or $375,000, applies to the $15,000,000. Three years have passed since they were originally issued, so 3/10 of the discount, or $112,500 (3/10 × $375,000) has already been amortized. Therefore, $262,500 ($375,000 - $112,500) remains.

# Demonstration Problem #2 Solved and Explained

## Requirement 1

| | A | B | C | D | E |
|---|---|---|---|---|---|
| Semi-annual Interest Date | Interest Payment | Interest Expense | Premium Amortization | Premium Account Balance | Bond Carrying Value |
| 1/1/98 | | | | 120,000 | 2,120,000 |
| 7/1/98 | 100,000 | 95,400 | 4,600 | 115,400 | 2,115,400 |
| 1/1/99 | 100,000 | 95,193 | 4,807 | 110,593 | 2,110,593 |
| 7/1/99 | 100,000 | 94,977 | 5,023 | 105,570 | 2,105,570 |
| 1/1/00 | 100,000 | 94,751 | 5,249 | 100,321 | 2,100,321 |
| 7/1/00 | 100,000 | 94,514 | 5,486 | 94,835 | 2,094,835 |
| 1/1/01 | 100,000 | 94,268 | 5,732 | 89,103 | 2,089,103 |

**Study Tip:** As the premium is amortized, the carrying amount moves toward the maturity value.

## Requirement 2

a. 1/1/98
    Cash ($2,000,000 × 106/100)      2,120,000
        Premium on Bonds Payable      120,000
        Bonds Payable      2,000,000
    To issue 10%, 15-year bonds at premium.

The bonds were sold at 106, indicating that investors were willing to pay a premium of $120,000 to earn 10% of interest on $2,000,000 of principal over a 15-year period. This is to be expected because the bond is paying 10% annual interest at a time when the market rate of interest is only 9%.

b. 7/1/98
    Interest Expense ($100,000 - $4,600 amortization)      95,400
    Premium on Bonds Payable      4,600
        Cash      100,000
    To pay interest and amortize bond premium for six months.

Note that the amortization of the premium has the effect of reducing interest expense from the stated rate ($100,000) to the market rate ($95,400). If the bond is sold at a discount, the interest expense is increased from the stated rate to the market rate.

c. 9/30/98
    Interest Expense ($50,000 - $2,404 amortization)      47,596
    Premium on Bonds Payable ($4,807 × 3/6)      2,404
        Interest Payable      50,000
    To accrue three months' interest and amortize three months' premium.

d. 1/1/99  Interest Expense ($50,000 - $2,403 amortization)      47,597
           Interest Payable                                      50,000
           Premium on Bonds Payable ($4,807 × 3/6)                2,403
               Cash                                                        100,000
           To pay semiannual interest, part of which was accrued, and amortize three months' premium on bonds payable.

In this entry, six months of interest is actually paid to the bondholders on January 1. Note, however, only half (three months' worth) of the interest is current accounting period expense; the remaining amount represents the payment of the September 30 accrual of three months' interest.

e. 1/2/00  Bonds Payable                                      2,000,000
           Premium on Bonds Payable                              94,835
               Gain on Retirement on Bonds                                  54,835
               Cash ($2,000,000 × 102/100)                               2,040,000
           To record the retirement of bonds payable at 102, retired before maturity.

This entry removes the bonds payable and related premium account from the corporate records, and records the gain on retirement. The carrying value of the bonds ($2,094,835) is greater than the cost to call the bonds ($2,040,000) resulting in the $54,835 gain. Had the price paid to call the bonds been greater than the carrying value, the entry would have recorded an extraordinary loss. Extraordinary gains and losses are reported separately on the income statement.

The interest rate stated on a debt instrument such as a corporate bond will typically differ from the actual market rate of interest when the bond is ultimately issued to the public. This occurs because of the lag in time that frequently occurs between the approval of the bond by the corporation (and regulatory agencies), its actual printings and finally, its issuance to the public. Rather than reprint the bond and potentially miss the rapidly changing market interest rate again, bonds are sold at a discount or premium. Occasionally, bonds are sold at face amount.

> **Study Tip:** A bond is sold at a discount when the stated interest rate of the bond is below the current market rate. A premium is paid when the contract rate is higher than interest rates paid by comparable investments.

Premiums and discounts are, in effect, an adjustment to the interest rates. Thus, premiums and discounts should be amortized over the life of the bond. A few things should be noted:

1. A good rule to remember is that Bonds Payable are always recorded at the face amount of the bond. Premiums and discounts are recorded in separate accounts.

2. The actual interest paid to the bondholders at the periodic payment dates (generally semiannually) will always be the face value of the bond multiplied by the stated interest rate. A discount or premium will not affect these periodic cash payments.

3. The carrying amount (or book value) of a bond is conceptually similar to the book value of a fixed asset. Premiums are added to the face amount of bonds payable, and discounts are subtracted.

|   | Bonds Payable |
|---|---|
| + | Bond Premiums or |
| - | Bond Discount |
| = | Carrying Value |

**Study Tip:** Bonds sold at a premium will have a carrying amount greater than the face amount owed and discounted bonds will have a smaller value. In both cases, the carrying value will always move toward the face amount of the bond as the discount or premium is amortized. (Because of this, it is possible to quickly double-check your amortization entries—be sure the bond carrying value is moving in the right direction.)

# Chapter 16 - Accounting for Investments and International Operations

## CHAPTER OVERVIEW

In Chapters 13 and 14, you learned about capital stock from the perspective of the issuing corporation. In Chapter 15 we examined long-term liabilities and how corporations account for bonds payable and other obligations. Now we expand these topics but change the perspective. Corporations frequently purchase stocks and bonds as investments. In addition, we learn about parent and subsidiary relationships and foreign currency transactions. The learning objectives for this chapter are to

1. Account for trading investments.
2. Account for available-for-sale investments.
3. Use the equity method for investments.
4. Understand consolidated financial statements.
5. Account for long-term investments in bonds.
6. Account for transactions stated in foreign currency.
7. Report investing transactions on the statement of cash flows.

## CHAPTER REVIEW

Stocks are traded in markets. Prices are quoted in dollars and one-eighth fractions of a dollar (occasionally you will see quotes in 1/16 and even 1/32 of a dollar). The owner of a stock is the investor. The corporation that issues the stock is the investee.

**Stock investments** are assets to the investor. **Short-term investments** are 1) liquid (readily convertible to cash) and 2) expected to be converted to cash within one year. **Long-term investments** are 1) expected to be held for longer than one year or 2) not readily marketable. Stock investments fall into two categories: 1) trading securities or 2) available-for-sale securities. It is important your understand the distinction between the two types! **Trading securities** are always classified as current assets because the investor's intent is to hold them for only a short time in the hopes of earning profits on price changes. When a stock investment is acquired but the intent is not to capture profits from price changes immediately, the investment is classified as an **available-for-sale security**. Trading securities, by definition, are always current assets whereas available-for-sale securities could be either current or long term.

### Objective 1 - Account for trading investments.

Because trading securities will be sold in the near future at their current market value, the **market-value method** is used to account for all trading investments. When acquired, trading investments are debited to a Short-Term Investment account at their cost (price per share × number of shares acquired, plus any associated costs), as follows:

| | | |
|---|---|---|
| Short-Term Investments | XX | |
|     Cash | | XX |

As dividends are received, the transaction is

| | | |
|---|---|---|
| Cash | XX | |
|     Dividend Revenue | | XX |

On the balance sheet date, all trading investments are reported at their current market value, which is likely to be different from their original cost. If the current market value of the investment is greater than the cost, the following adjustment is recorded:

| | | |
|---|---|---|
| Short-Term Investment | XX | |
|     Unrealized Gain on Investment | | XX |

The amount of the entry is the difference between the current market value and the original cost. If the current market value is lower than original cost the adjustment is:

| | | |
|---|---|---|
| Unrealized Loss on Investments | XX | |
|     Allowance to Adjust Investment to Market | | XX |

Either way, the effect of the adjustment is to report the trading investment on the balance sheet as its current market value. Unrealized Gains and Losses are reported on the Income Statement in the "other gains/losses" section.

When a trading investment is sold, the proceeds is compared with the current carrying value (NOT THE ORIGINAL COST) to determine whether a gain or loss results. Gains and losses on the sale of trading securities are also reported in the "other gains/losses" section of the Income Statement.

## Objective 2 - Account for available-for-sale investments.

As with all assets, available-for-sale securities are recorded at cost. Thereafter, however, they are reported at their current market value. Any cash dividends received are credited to an appropriate revenue account. Stock dividends do not trigger an entry. Rather, the portfolio is updated to reflect the additional shares. At the end of the accounting period, the market value of the securities is determined and compared with the balance in the investments accounts. If the market value is greater, the following adjusting entry is recorded for the difference:

| | | |
|---|---|---|
| Allowance to Adjust Investment to Market | XX | |
|     Unrealized Gain on Investments | | XX |

When the market value of the available-for-sale security is less than the balance in the account, the adjustment is:

| | | |
|---|---|---|
| Unrealized Loss on Investments | XX | |
|     Allowance to Adjust Investment to Market | | XX |

The Allowance to Adjust Investment to Market account is a companion account to the Investment account. Recall that a companion account is added to (or subtracted from) a related account. With available-for-sale securities, the Allowance account increases/decreases the Investment account depending on its balance. If the Allowance account has a debit balance the effect is to increase the Investment account. If the Allowance account has a credit balance the effect is to decrease the Investment account.

Unrealized Gains/Losses are reported in the stockholders' equity section of the balance sheet. Gains are an addition to equity, losses are a reduction.

> **Study Tip**: The Allowance to Adjust Investment to Market account is used regardless of an increase or decrease in the market value. Compare the current market value with the carrying value of the investment and adjust accordingly, always using the Allowance account.

When an available-for-sale investment is sold, a gain or loss on sale will result when the proceeds are greater than (a gain) or less than (a loss) the carrying value of the investment. These gains and losses are realized and therefore reported on the income statement as "Other Revenue and Expense" after the operating income.

## Objective 3 - Use the equity method for investments.

The **equity method** is used when an investor holds between 20% and 50% of an investee's voting stock because the investor may exert significant influence on the investee's business decisions.

The investment is recorded at cost. Debit Long-Term Investment and credit Cash.

The investor records his proportionate ownership of the investee's net income and dividends. If the investor owns 40% of the voting stock, the investor will record 40% of the net income as revenue and will receive 40% of the dividends. The share of income is recorded with a debit to the Long-Term Investment account and a credit to Equity Method Investment Revenue. The receipt of cash dividends reduces the investment. Therefore, the dividend is recorded with a debit to Cash and a credit to the Long-Term Investment account. Equity Method Investment Revenue is reported as "Other Revenue" on the income statement.

When the equity method is used and an investment is sold, the gain (or loss) on sale is the difference between the proceeds and the balance in the investment account.

**Joint ventures**, regardless of the percentage owned, also use the equity method.

## Objective 4 - Understand consolidated financial statements.

An investor who owns more than 50% of an investee's voting stock has a controlling (majority) interest. The investor is called the **parent company**, and the investee is called the **subsidiary**. See Exhibits 16-3 and 16-4 in your text. Parent-subsidiary relationships are very common.

**Consolidation accounting** combines the financial statements of two or more companies that are controlled by the same owners. The assets, liabilities, revenues, and expenses of the subsidiary are added to the parent's accounts.

A separate set of books for the consolidated entity does not exist. The consolidation is accomplished by the use of a work sheet. **Goodwill** is recorded during the consolidation process if the parent buys the subsidiary for a price above book value.

A **minority interest** will appear on the consolidated balance sheet when the parent company owns more than 50% but less than 100% of the subsidiary's stock. Minority interest usually is recorded as a liability on the consolidated balance sheet.

**Consolidated income** is equal to the net income of the parent plus the parent's proportionate interest in the subsidiary's net income.

## Objective 6 - Account for Long-Term Investment in Bonds.

Investors purchase bonds issued by corporations. The investor can purchase short-term (current asset) or long-term (long-term investment) bonds.

Short-term investments in bonds are rare. More commonly, companies purchase bonds as long-term investments, known as **held-to-maturity securities**. When acquired, these held-to-maturity bonds are recorded at cost. Thereafter they are reported on the balance sheet at their **amortized cost**. This means the balance in the Long-Term Investment account reflects both the initial cost of the bond plus or minus a portion of the discount (an addition to the account) or premium (a reduction to the account) on the bond. No Discount or Premium account is used. If the bonds were initially purchased at a discount, the balance in the Long-Term Investment account increases as the bonds approach maturity. If the bonds were initially purchased at a premium, the balance in the Long-Term Investment account decreases as the bonds approach maturity. The amortization of the bond discount would appear as follows:

| | | |
|---|---|---|
| Long-Term Investment in Bonds | XX | |
|     Interest Revenue | | XX |

The amortization of a bond premium would be recorded as follows:

| | | |
|---|---|---|
| Interest Revenue | XX | |
|     Long-Term Investment in Bonds | | XX |

> **Study Tip**: From the buyer's perspective, a discount means additional interest revenue while a premium means less interest revenue. This effect is exactly the opposite from the perspective of the issuer.

Carefully review the Decision Guideline in your text. It presents an excellent summary of the rules governing stock and bond investments.

## Objective 6 - Account for transactions stated in a foreign currency.

**International accounting** deals with business activities that cross national boundaries. Each country uses its own national currency; therefore, a step has been added to the transaction—one currency must be converted into another.

The price of one nation's currency stated in terms of another country's currency is called the **foreign currency exchange rate**. The conversion of one currency into another currency is called **translation**. Exchange rates are determined by supply and demand.

A **strong currency** is rising relative to other nations' currencies and a **weak currency** is falling relative to other currencies.

When Company A in Country A purchases goods from Company B in Country B, the transaction price may be stated in the currency of either country. Suppose the transaction is stated in Country A's currency. The transaction requires two steps:

Accounting for Investments and International Operations 421

1. The transaction price must be translated for recording in the accounting records of Company B.
2. When payment is made, Company B may experience a foreign-currency translation gain or loss. This gain or loss results when there is a change in the exchange rate between the date of the purchase on account and the date of the subsequent payment of cash.

Note that there will be no foreign-currency gain or loss for Company A because the transaction price was stated in the currency of Country A.

The net amount of Foreign Currency Transaction Gains and Losses are combined for each accounting period and reported on the income statement as Other Revenue and Expense.

**Hedging** is a means of protecting the company from foreign currency transaction losses by purchasing a **futures contract**, the right to receive a certain amount of foreign currency on a particular date.

United States companies with foreign subsidiaries must consolidate the subsidiary financial statements into their own for external reporting. This can cause two problems:

1. GAAP may be different in the foreign country. (See Exhibit 16-8.)
2. When the foreign subsidiary's financial statements are translated into dollars, there may be a translation adjustment.

A **foreign currency translation adjustment** arises because of changes in exchange rates over time. Assets and liabilities are translated using exchange rates as of the balance sheet date. Stockholders' equity, including revenues and expenses, are translated using the exchange rates that were in effect when those transactions were executed (this results in shareholders' equity not equaling assets minus liabilities). The adjustment necessary to bring the subsidiary's balance sheet back into balance ("translation adjustment") is reported as part of stockholders' equity on the consolidated balance sheet. The translation adjustment will be positive when the book value of the investment in the foreign subsidiary has increased. A negative amount reflects a reduction.

Unrealized gains and losses on available-for-sale investments and foreign-currency translation adjustments are two of the main elements of comprehensive income (you were introduced to comprehensive income in Chapter 14). These are reported on the income statement as "other comprehensive income" and on the balance sheet within stockholders' equity. (Review Exhibit 16-9 in your text.)

## Objective 7 - Report investing transactions on the statement of cash flows.

The purchase and sale of stock and bond investments are reported on the statement of cash flows in the investing activities section. Revenues from Dividends and Interest Revenue (from bonds) are operating activities because they are reported on the income statement. However, the actual purchase of investments is listed as a cash outflow in the investing activities section of the cash flow statement while the proceeds from the sale of investments will appear as a cash inflow. Carefully review the financial statements for Campbell Soup Company (Exhibit 16-10) in your text.

# Appendix - Preparing Consolidated Financial Statements

When consolidating financial statements, the individual amounts (cash, payables, investments, etc.) from the subsidiaries must be added to those amounts of the parent. Each entity has a set of books; however, the consolidated entity does not keep a separate set of books. Instead, the combining process is accomplished with a work sheet. Exhibits 16-A1 and 16-A2 in you text illustrates work sheets for consolidated balance sheets.

An important consideration is the elimination of activity occurring between the two entities. If not eliminated, the effect would be double counting the activity. Examples of such activity are loans between the parent and the subsidiary. When the parent owns 100% of the subsidiary, the parent's Investment in Subsidiary account must be eliminated against the subsidiary's stockholders' equity accounts (common stock and retained earnings). Any excess is recorded as goodwill on the consolidated balance sheet. When the parent owns less than 100% of the subsidiary, a Minority Interest account will appear on the consolidated balance sheet.

# TEST YOURSELF

All the self-testing materials in this chapter focus on information and procedures that your instructor is likely to test in quizzes and examinations. Items with an *A* refer to information in the chapter appendix.

## I. Matching   *Match each numbered term with its lettered definition.*

\_\_\_\_\_ 1A.  consolidated statements
\_\_\_\_\_ 2.  joint ventures
\_\_\_\_\_ 3.  controlling interest
\_\_\_\_\_ 4.  held-to-maturity investments
\_\_\_\_\_ 5.  equity method for investments
\_\_\_\_\_ 6.  foreign currency exchange rate
\_\_\_\_\_ 7.  short-term investments
\_\_\_\_\_ 8.  hedging
\_\_\_\_\_ 9.  long-term investment
\_\_\_\_\_ 10.  trading securities
\_\_\_\_\_ 11.  minority interest
\_\_\_\_\_ 12.  parent company
\_\_\_\_\_ 13.  available-for-sale securities
\_\_\_\_\_ 14.  strong currency
\_\_\_\_\_ 15.  subsidiary company
\_\_\_\_\_ 16.  foreign currency translation adjustment
\_\_\_\_\_ 17.  weak currency
\_\_\_\_\_ 18.  market value method

A. a separate entity or project owned and operated by a small group of businesses
B. the balancing figure that brings the dollar amount of the total liabilities and stockholders' equity of a foreign subsidiary into agreement with the dollar amount of total assets
C. stocks and bonds held for the short term with the intent of realizing profits from increases in prices
D. combine the balance sheets, income statements, and other financial statements of the parent with those of the majority-owned subsidiaries into an overall set as if the separate entities were one
E. currency whose exchange rate is rising relative to other nations' currencies
F. investee company in which a parent owns more than 50% of the voting stock
G. investor company that owns more than 50% of the voting stock of a subsidiary company
H. stocks and bonds not held with the intent of realizing profits from increases in prices
I. method used to account for investments in which the investor can significantly influence the decisions of the investee
J. bonds and notes that investors intend to hold to maturity
K. ownership of more than 50% of an investee company's voting stock
L. an investment that is readily convertible to cash and that the investor intends to convert to cash within one year or to use to pay a current liability
M. separate asset category reported on the balance sheet between current assets and plant assets
N. strategy to avoid foreign currency transaction losses
O. subsidiary company's equity that is held by stockholders other than the parent company
P. the price of one country's currency stated in terms of another country's monetary unit
Q. currency whose exchange rate is decreasing relative to other nations' currencies
R. used to account for all available-for-sale securities

## II. Multiple Choice  *Circle the best answer.*

1. A stock is listed in the Wall Street Journal as having a High of 45 1/4, a Low of 43, a Close of 43 1/2, and a Net Change of +1 1/4. What was the previous day's closing price?

   A. $46.50
   B. $41.75
   C. $44.75
   D. $42.25

2. Assets listed as Short-term Investments on the balance sheet are

   A. only liquid
   B. listed on a national stock exchange
   C. only intended to be converted to cash within one year
   D. liquid and intended to be converted to cash within one year

3. Available-for-sale securities are reported on the balance sheet at

   A. current cost
   B. historical cost
   C. lower of cost or market
   D. market value

4A. Intercompany payables and receivables are eliminated in the consolidated entries so that

   A. assets will not be overstated
   B. liabilities will not be understated
   C. stockholders' equity will not be understated
   D. net income will not be overstated

5A. All of the following accounts are eliminated in the consolidated work sheet entries *except*

   A. investment in subsidiary
   B. subsidiary's cash
   C. subsidiary's common stock
   D. subsidiary's retained earnings

6A. The minority interest account is usually classified as a(n)

   A. revenue
   B. expense
   C. liability
   D. asset

7. The rate at which one unit of a currency can be converted into another currency is called the foreign currency:

   A. market rate
   B. interest rate
   C. exchange rate
   D. conversion rate

8. A strong currency has an exchange rate that is

   A. inelastic with respect to other nations' currencies
   B. inelastic with respect to its balance of trade
   C. increasing relative to other nations' currencies
   D. decreasing relative to other nations' currencies

9. Available-for-sale securities are

   A. stock investments only
   B. bond investments only
   C. the same as held-to-maturity investments
   D. those other than trading securities

10. An unrealized gain (or loss) results from

    A. available-for-sale securities
    B. trading securities
    C. held-to-maturity securities
    D. all of the above

## III. Completion   *Complete each of the following statements.*

1. The price at which stock changes hands is determined by the _____.
2. Unrealized gains and losses on trading securities are reported on the _____ in the _____.
3. Investments in stock are initially recorded at _____.
4. The _____ method is used to account for investments when the investor can significantly influence the actions of the investee.
5. A(n) _____ is ownership of at least 50% of the voting stock of a company.
6. Goodwill is a(n) _____ asset.
7. A change in the currency exchange rates between the date of purchase and the date of payment will result in a(n) _____.
8. Cash used to purchase bonds is reported on the statement of cash flows as a(n) _____ activity.
9. When a parent owns less than 100% of a subsidiary, the other owners are called the _____.
10. Unrealized gains and losses on Available-for-Sale investments are reported on the _____ in the _____ section.

## IV. Daily Exercises

1. Parent, Inc., owns 100% of Subsidiary Corp. Parent's Investment in Subsidiary account shows a balance of $1,230,000, while Subsidiary's Common Stock account has a balance of $150,000 and Subsidiary's Retained Earnings account has a balance of $950,000. In the space below, make the journal entry to eliminate the appropriate accounts.

2. On October 20 of the current year, Miller Corporation purchases 1,000 shares of Webster Company for 18 3/8 a share, plus a broker's commission of $55. On December 15, Miller receives a cash dividend of $0.50 a share. Assuming Miller's investment is not significant, what is the balance in Miller's Investment account immediately after receipt of the cash dividend?

3. Review the information in Daily Exercise #2 and assume the Webster shares are trading at 20 ¾ on December 31, the end of Miller's fiscal year. Assuming this investment is classified as a trading security, prepare the necessary adjusting entry.

4. Review the same facts in Daily Exercise #2 and #3, but assume the shares are classified as an available-for-sale security. Prepare the necessary adjusting entry on December 31.

5. When a company purchases equity securities as an investment, what determines whether the investment is classified as a trading security or an available-for-sale security?

6. On October 1 of the current year, Long Company purchased a $100,000, 8%, 10-year bond at 98. Interest is payable on October 1 and April 1 each year. Long's intent is to hold the bond to maturity. Prepare the entry to record the purchase of the bond.

7. Review the information in Daily Exercise #6 and prepare the necessary adjusting entry on December 31, the end of Long's fiscal period.

## V. Exercises

1. Polly Company purchased 85,000 shares of Cracker Corporation on January 1, 19X9, for $425,000. Cracker Corporation has 850,000 shares outstanding. Cracker earned income of $240,000 and paid dividends of $80,000 during 19X9. Cracker Corporation stock was trading at 6 1/8 on December 31, 19X9.

    A. What method should be used to account for the investment in Cracker?

    B. How much revenue will be recorded by Polly in 19X9 from the investment in Cracker?

    C. What is the balance in Polly's Investment account at the end of 19X9?

2. King Company purchased 40% of Prince Corporation on January 1, 19X9, for $6,750,000. Prince Corporation earned income of $1,800,000 and paid dividends of $700,000 during 19X9.

    A. What method should be used to account for the investment in Prince Corporation?

    B. How much revenue will be recorded by King Co. in 19X9 from the investment in Prince Corporation?

    C. What is the balance in the Investment account at the end of 19X9?

3. Golden Company invested in Gate Corporation on January 1, 19X9, by purchasing 70% of the total stock of Gate Corporation for $787,500. Gate Corporation had common stock of $400,000 and retained earnings of $725,000.

    A. What amount of Minority Interest will appear on a consolidated balance sheet prepared on January 1, 19X9?

B. If Golden Company owes Gate Corporation $85,000 on a note payable, prepare the two elimination entries in general journal form.

| Date | Account and Explanation | Debit | Credit |
|------|-------------------------|-------|--------|
|      |                         |       |        |
|      |                         |       |        |
|      |                         |       |        |
|      |                         |       |        |
|      |                         |       |        |
|      |                         |       |        |
|      |                         |       |        |

4. Hunter Company purchased 100% of the common stock of Prey Corporation for $1,315,000. Prey Corporation showed Common Stock of $280,000 and Retained Earnings of $510,000. Compute the amount of goodwill resulting from the purchase.

5. Prepare journal entries for the following available-for-sale stock investment:

6/10   Purchased 1,000 shares of Micro-Tech Corporation common stock at 35 1/4, plus a broker's commission of $205.
10/2   Received a $1.50 per share cash dividend.
11/15  Sold 400 shares at 40 1/4 per share, less a commission of $80.
12/31  Micro-Tech Corporation stock closed at $39 1/8.

| Date | Account and Explanation | Debit | Credit |
|------|-------------------------|-------|--------|
|      |                         |       |        |
|      |                         |       |        |
|      |                         |       |        |
|      |                         |       |        |
|      |                         |       |        |
|      |                         |       |        |
|      |                         |       |        |
|      |                         |       |        |
|      |                         |       |        |
|      |                         |       |        |
|      |                         |       |        |
|      |                         |       |        |
|      |                         |       |        |
|      |                         |       |        |
|      |                         |       |        |
|      |                         |       |        |

6. Prepare journal entries for the following foreign currency transactions.

   1/5   Purchased 5,000 cases of dry cider from a British wholesaler for 4.55 pounds sterling per case. Today's exchange rate is $1.62 = 1 pound sterling.
   1/20  Purchased 2,000 cases of red wine from a cooperative in Coustouge, France. The price was 64 francs per case. Today's exchange rate is $1.00 = 6.10 French francs.
   2/10  Paid the British wholesaler. Today's exchange rate is $1.59 = 1 pound sterling.
   3/20  Paid for the French wine. Today's exchange rate is $1.00 = 5.90 French francs.

| Date | Account and Explanation | Debit | Credit |
| --- | --- | --- | --- |
|  |  |  |  |

## VI. Beyond the Numbers

Review the information in Exercise 5 and change the 10/2 entry to the following:

10/2 Received a 15% stock dividend. The stock was trading at $38 per share.

Prepare journal entries for 10/2, 11/15 and 12/31

| Date | Account and Explanation | Debit | Credit |
| --- | --- | --- | --- |
|  |  |  |  |

## VII. Demonstration Problems

### Demonstration Problem #1A

Parent Corporation paid $375,000 for 90% of the common stock of Subsidiary Corporation. Subsidiary owes Parent $60,000 on an intercompany note payable. Complete the following work sheet:

|  | Parent Company | Subsidiary Company | Eliminations Debit | Eliminations Credit | Consolidated Amounts |
|---|---|---|---|---|---|
| Assets: |  |  |  |  |  |
| Cash | 58,000 | 26,000 |  |  |  |
| Note receivable from Subsidiary | 60,000 | - |  |  |  |
| Investment in Subsidiary | 375,000 | - |  |  |  |
| Goodwill | - | - |  |  |  |
| Plant & equipment, net | 218,000 | 328,000 |  |  |  |
| Other assets | 37,000 | 92,000 |  |  |  |
| Total | 748,000 | 446,000 |  |  |  |
|  |  |  |  |  |  |
| Liabilities and Stockholders' equity: |  |  |  |  |  |
| Accounts payable | 38,000 | 41,000 |  |  |  |
| Notes payable | 170,000 | 125,000 |  |  |  |
| Minority interest |  |  |  |  |  |
| Common stock | 500,000 | 110,000 |  |  |  |
| Retained earnings | 40,000 | 170,000 |  |  |  |
| Total | 748,000 | 446,000 |  |  |  |

## Demonstration Problem #2

At 12/31/99, Knox Corporation had the following long-term investments in its portfolio:

|  | Cost | Market Value |
|---|---|---|
| **Available-for-sale securities** |  |  |
| 2,500 shares Bibtech, Inc. | $25 1/5 | $28 |
| 6,000 shares FFA Industries | 10 3/8 | 18 1/2 |
| 3,800 shares Globex | 48 | 37 3/4 |
| 1,400 shares Textronics | 63 1/2 | 66 7/8 |
| **Held-to-maturity bonds** |  |  |
| $100,000, 9% NatSci, Inc., due 10/1/2009 | $100,000 | $100,000 |

### Requirement 1

In the space below, present the long-term investments as they would appear on Knox Corporation's 12/31/99 balance sheet. None of the stock investments are influential. The bonds pay interest semiannually on 4/1 and 10/1.

|  |  |  |
|---|---|---|
|  |  |  |
|  |  |  |
|  |  |  |
|  |  |  |
|  |  |  |
|  |  |  |
|  |  |  |

### Requirement 2

Record the following 2000 events related to Knox Corporation's long-term investments:

Bibtech, Inc.—these shares paid quarterly dividends of $.15/share on 2/10 and 5/10. The shares were sold on 7/2 for $32/share less a broker's commission of $185.

FFA Industries—these shares pay no cash dividends; however, a 10% stock dividend was received on 8/10. The investment remained in the portfolio at the end of the year, at which time its market value was $24 1/4 per share.

Globex—these shares continued to decline in value throughout January and management decided to sell them on 2/8 for $31/share, less a commission of $205.

Textronics—these shares remained in the portfolio throughout the year. On 9/15 the stock split 3 for 2. At year end, the shares were trading for $55/share.

NatSci, Inc.—Checks for interest were received 4/1 and 10/1. The bonds remained in the portfolio at year end.

On 11/1/2000 Knox Corporation purchased $250,000, 10-year, 6% bonds from Wood, Inc., for 97. The bonds pay semiannual interest on 5/1 and 11/1.

| Date | Account and Explanation | Debit | Credit |
|------|-------------------------|-------|--------|
|      |                         |       |        |

**Requirement 3**

Record the necessary adjusting entries.

| Date | Account and Explanation | Debit | Credit |
|------|------------------------|-------|--------|
|      |                        |       |        |
|      |                        |       |        |
|      |                        |       |        |
|      |                        |       |        |
|      |                        |       |        |
|      |                        |       |        |
|      |                        |       |        |
|      |                        |       |        |
|      |                        |       |        |
|      |                        |       |        |
|      |                        |       |        |
|      |                        |       |        |
|      |                        |       |        |
|      |                        |       |        |

**Requirement 4**

Present the long-term investments as they would appear on Knox Corporation's 12/31/2000 balance sheet, taking into consideration the events described in Requirement 2 above.

|   |   |   |
|---|---|---|
|   |   |   |
|   |   |   |
|   |   |   |
|   |   |   |
|   |   |   |
|   |   |   |
|   |   |   |

# SOLUTIONS

## I. Matching

| | | | | |
|---|---|---|---|---|
| 1. D | 5. I | 9. M | 13. H | 17. Q |
| 2. A | 6. P | 10. C | 14. E | 18. R |
| 3. K | 7. L | 11. O | 15. F | |
| 4. J | 8. N | 12. G | 16. B | |

## II. Multiple Choice

1. **D** The High is the previous day's highest price, the Low is the lowest price of the previous day. The Close is the last price at which the stock traded yesterday. Net Change is the increase (+) or decrease (-) in the Close compared to the previous day. The previous day's close is 43 1/2 - 1 1/4 or $43.50 - $1.25 = $42.25.

2. **D** Note that besides the determinable liquidity of the investment, the intent of management determines an investment's classification as a Short-Term Investment.

3. **D** GAAP requires trading securities to be reported on the balance sheet at market value.

4. **A** Failure to eliminate intercompany payables and receivables would result in the overstatement of both assets and liabilities of the consolidated entity. Accordingly, of the items listed, only A is correct.

5. **B** Elimination is not intended to remove the assets and liabilities of the subsidiary. The intent of elimination is to remove only those things that would double up or be counted twice if not eliminated, such as intercompany payables and receivables and the investment in subsidiary and subsidiary stockholders' equity.

6. **C** The Minority Interest account represents the ownership interest of parties outside of the Parent-Subsidiary relationship. In actual practice it is most often reported as part of the liability section on the balance sheet.

7. **C** The exchange rate is used to convert one currency into another.

8. **C** Strong currencies are those that increase relative to other currencies.

9. **D** Available-for-sale securities are stock investments other than trading securities and bond investments other than trading securities and held-to-maturity securities.

10. **A** Unrealized gains (or losses) are a result of the market value method applied to available-for-sale securities.

## III. Completion

1. market (The market allows buyers and sellers with opposing interests to arrive at a price acceptable to both.)
2. income statement, other gains and losses
3. cost

4. equity
5. controlling interest
6. intangible
7. foreign-currency transaction gain or loss
8. investing
9. minority interest
10. balance sheet; stockholders' equity

## IV. Daily Exercises

1.
|  |  |  |
|---|---|---|
| Common Stock | 150,000 |  |
| Retained Earnings | 950,000 |  |
| Goodwill | 130,000 |  |
|     Investments in Subsidiary |  | 1,230,000 |

Goodwill is the difference between the Investment in Subsidiary account balance and the combined balance of the Subsidiary's Stockholders' equity.

2. $18,430 (1,000 × $18 3/8 = $18,375 + $55) The dividends would be credited to a Dividend Revenue Account.

3.
|  |  |  |
|---|---|---|
| Short-term Investment | 2,320 |  |
|     Unrealized Gain on Investment |  | 2,320 |

The market value method requires trading securities to be listed on the balance sheet at their current market value. The shares are currently worth $20,750 (1,000 × $20 ¾) but listed in the account at $18,430. The difference, $2,320, is an unrealized gain on short-term investment.

> **Study Tip:** Unrealized Gains and Losses on trading securities are reported on the income statement under "other gains and losses."

4.
|  |  |  |
|---|---|---|
| Allowance to Adjust Investment to Market | 2,320 |  |
|     Unrealized Gain on Investment |  | 2,320 |

5. Available-for-sale securities are defined by exception. In other words, if the investment is not a trading investment, then it is classified as an available-for-sale investment.

6.
|  |  |  |
|---|---|---|
| Long-term Investment | 98,000 |  |
|     Cash |  | 98,000 |

The discount is not recorded on the books of the purchaser, only on the books of the selling corporation.

7.
　　　　Interest Receivable　　　　　　　　　　　　　　2,000
　　　　　　Interest Revenue　　　　　　　　　　　　　　　　　　　　2,000
　　　　($100,000 × 8% × 3/12)

　　　　Long-term Investment　　　　　　　　　　　　　　50
　　　　　　Interest Revenue　　　　　　　　　　　　　　　　　　　　50
　　　　($2,000 ÷ 10 years × 3/12)

## V. Exercises

1. A. market value
   B. 10% of $80,000 = $8,000 dividend revenue
   C. $520,625 ($425,000 balance in the Investment account plus $95,625 (1 1/8 per share gain × 85,000 shares) in the Allowance to Adjust Investment account)

2. A. equity method
   B. .40 × $1,800,000 = $720,000
   C. $6,750,000 + $720,000 - (.40 × $700,000) = $7,190,000

3. A. .30 × ($400,000 + $725,000) = $337,500
   B. (1) Note Payable to Gate　　　　　　85,000
　　　　　　　Note Receivable from Golden　　　　　　　　85,000
　　　　　(2) Common stock (Gate)　　　　　400,000
　　　　　　　Retained earnings (Gate)　　　　725,000
　　　　　　　　Investment in Gate　　　　　　　　　　　787,500
　　　　　　　　Minority Interest　　　　　　　　　　　　337,500
   (Note: Refer to Exhibit 16-A1 in your text.)

4. $1,315,000 - ($280,000 + $510,000) = $525,000

5.
　　6/10　　Investment—Micro-Tech　　　　　　35,455
　　　　　　　　Cash　　　　　　　　　　　　　　　　　　　35,455
　　　　　　(1,000 shares × $35.25 plus $205)
　　　　　　Actual cost/share is 35,455 / 1000 = $35.455

　　10/2　　Cash　　　　　　　　　　　　　　　　1,500
　　　　　　　　Dividend Revenue　　　　　　　　　　　　　1,500

　　11/15　　Cash　　　　　　　　　　　　　　　　16,020
　　　　　　　　Investment—Micro-Tech　　　　　　　　　　14,182
　　　　　　　　Gain on Sale of Investment　　　　　　　　　1,838
　　　　　　The gain is the difference between the proceeds and our cost. Our cost is 400 shares × $35.455/share (see 6/10)

　　12/31　　Allowance to Adjust Investment to Market　　2,202
　　　　　　　　Unrealized Gain on Investment　　　　　　　2,202
　　　　　　Our cost basis was $35.455/share and we have 600 shares for a total of $21,273. The current market value is 600 × $39 1/8 = $23,475. Therefore, $2,202 is needed to adjust the Investment

to market. Since the $2,202 represents an increase in value, it represents an unrealized gain on the investment.

6.

| | | | | |
|---|---|---|---|---|
| 1/5 | Inventory | | 36,855.00 | |
| |     Accounts Payable | | | 36,855.00 |
| | (5,000 cases × 4.55 pounds sterling × $1.62) | | | |
| | | | | |
| 1/20 | Inventory | | 20,983.61 | |
| |     Accounts Payable | | | 20,983.61 |
| | (2,000 cases × 64 francs / 6.10) | | | |
| | | | | |
| 2/10 | Accounts Payable | | 36,855.00 | |
| |     Foreign Currency Transaction Gain | | | 682.50 |
| |     Cash | | | 36,172.50 |
| | (5,000 cases × 4.55 pounds sterling × $1.59) | | | |
| | | | | |
| 3/20 | Accounts Payable | | 20,983.61 | |
| | Foreign Currency Transaction Loss | | 711.31 | |
| |     Cash | | | 21,694.92 |
| | (2,000 cases × 64 francs / $5.90) | | | |

Because the dollar strengthened relative to the British pound (on 1/5 it took $1.62 to purchase 1 pound sterling - a month later the same pound would only cost $1.59) a foreign currency transaction gain was realized when we paid the bill. Conversely, the dollar weakened relative to the French franc, so we realized a foreign currency transaction loss. Foreign currency transaction gains and losses are reported on the income statement as "Other Revenues and Expenses."

## VI. Beyond the Numbers

| | | | |
|---|---|---|---|
| 6/10 | Investment - Micro-Tech | 35,455 | |
| |     Cash | | 35,455 |
| | (1,000 shares × $35.25 plus $205) | | |

10/2     No entry - however we need to note the receipt of the additional 150 shares. We now own 1,150 shares which cost us $35,455, or $30.83 (rounded) per share.

> **Study Tip:** the current trading value of the shares is irrelevant from our perspective. It is only relevant to Micro-Tech. They used it to record the charge against Retained Earnings when the dividend was declared.

| | | | |
|---|---|---|---|
| 11/15 | Cash | 16,020 | |
| |     Investment— Micro-Tech | | 12,332 |
| |     Gain on Sale of Investment | | 3,688 |

Our cost per share was $30.83 (rounded)—see 10/2 details. We sold 400 shares at $40.25/share, less the $80 commission. The gain is the difference between our proceeds (400 shares × $40.25 less $80) and the cost basis of those shares, $30.83 × 400.

| | | | |
|---|---|---|---|
| 12/31 | Allowance to Adjust Investment to Market | 6,229 | |
| | Unrealized Gain on Investment | | 6,229 |

You need to give some thought to this adjustment. Remember our adjusted cost per share is $30.83 and we have 750 shares (the original 1,000 plus the 150 share dividend less the 400 shares sold on 11/15). Therefore, our cost basis for those remaining shares is $23,115 (750 shares × $30.83/share). On 12/31 the shares were trading at $39 1/8 ($39.125), so their market value is $29,344 (rounded); the Unrealized Gain is the difference between $29,344 and $23,115, or $6,229. Available-for-sale stock securities are reported on the balance sheet at their market value. The amount in the Allowance to Adjust account will be added to the balance in the Investment account, thereby reporting the investment in stock at the market value.

## VII. Demonstration Problems

### Demonstration Problem #1A Solved and Explained

|  | Parent Company | Subsidiary Company | Eliminations Debit | Eliminations Credit | Consolidated Amounts |
|---|---|---|---|---|---|
| **Assets:** |  |  |  |  |  |
| Cash | 58,000 | 26,000 |  |  | 84,000 |
| Note receivable from Subsidiary | 60,000 | - |  | (a) 60,000 |  |
| Investment in Subsidiary | 375,000 | - |  | (b) 375,000 |  |
| Goodwill | - | - | (b) 123,000 |  | 123,000 |
| Plant & equipment, net | 218,000 | 328,000 |  |  | 546,000 |
| Other assets | 37,000 | 92,000 |  |  | 129,000 |
| Total | 748,000 | 446,000 |  |  | 882,000 |
| **Liabilities and Stockholders' equity:** |  |  |  |  |  |
| Accounts payable | 38,000 | 41,000 |  |  | 79,000 |
| Notes payable | 170,000 | 125,000 | (a) 60,000 |  | 235,000 |
| Minority interest |  |  |  | 28,000 | 28,000 |
| Common stock | 500,000 | 110,000 | (b) 110,000 |  | 500,000 |
| Retained earnings | 40,000 | 170,000 | (b) 170,000 |  | 40,000 |
| Total | 748,000 | 446,000 | 463,000 | 463,000 | 882,000 |

Entry (a) eliminated Parent's $60,000 intercompany note receivable against the note payable owed by the Subsidiary. Note that the consolidated total represents the amount owed to outside creditors ($170,000 owed by Parent + $125,000 owed by Subsidiary less $60,000 intercompany debt = $235,000).

Entry (b) eliminates Parent's $375,000 investment balance against the $280,000 in Subsidiary's equity. Parent acquired a 90% interest, so the minority interest is $28,000 (10% × $280,000). Goodwill is the difference between the investment ($375,000) and 90% of the Subsidiary's Common Stock and Retained Earnings, or $123,000 ($375,000 - 90% × $280,000).

### Demonstration Problem #2 Solved and Explained

**Requirement 1**

    Long-Term Investments (at market value)         $518,075

The cost of the combined long-term investments (both equity and debt) is $496,675, while the 12/31/99 market value of the portfolio is $518,075. Recall that long-term investments are reported on the balance sheet at market value. Prior to the preparation of the balance sheet, an adjusting entry would have been recorded, as follows:

    Allowance to Adjust Investment to Market     21,400
        Unrealized Gain on Long-Term Investments         21,400

The effect of this adjustment is to increase the Investments to their market value. Most companies would report the Investments at market value, then report the cost in a footnote. The Unrealized Gain would be added into the stockholders' equity section. Knox would also have adjusted for the accrued interest on the NatSci bond; however, the amount ($2,250) is NOT included with the Long-Term Investments, but reported separately as Interest Receivable in the current asset section.

**Requirement 2**

Bibtech, Inc.

| | | | |
|---|---|---|---|
| 2/10 | Cash | 375 | |
| | Dividend Revenue | | 375 |
| 5/10 | Cash | 375 | |
| | Dividend Revenue | | 375 |
| 7/2 | Cash | 79,815 | |
| | Long-Term Investment | | 63,125 |
| | Gain on Sale of Investment | | 16,690 |

The gain is the difference between the proceeds (2,500 shares × $32/share less the $185 commission) and the cost (2,500 shares × $25 1/4).

FFA Industries

    8/10    no entry—memo only reflecting 6,600 shares now in the portfolio

Globex

| | | | |
|---|---|---|---|
| 2/8 | Cash | 117,595 | |
| | Loss on Sale of Investment | 64,805 | |
| | Long-Term Investment | | 182,400 |

The loss is the difference between the cost (3,800 × $48) and the proceeds (3,800 × $31 less the $205 commission).

Textronics

    9/15    no entry—memo only reflecting 2,100 shares now in the portfolio

NatSci

| | | | |
|---|---|---|---|
| 4/1 | Cash | 4,500 | |
| | Interest Receivable | | 2,250 |
| | Interest Revenue | | 2,250 |

| | | | |
|---|---|---|---|
| 10/1 | Cash | 4,500 | |
| | Interest Revenue | | 4,500 |

**Wood, Inc.**

| | | | |
|---|---|---|---|
| 11/1 | Long-Term Investment | 242,500 | |
| | Cash | | 242,500 |

As the purchaser of the bonds, we do not record the $7,500 discount in a contra account.

**Requirement 3 (adjusting entries)**

| | | | |
|---|---|---|---|
| 12/31 | Allowance to Adjust Investments to Market | 103,000 | |
| | Unrealized Gain on Long-Term Investments | | 103,000 |

As of the end of 1999, the Allowance to Adjust account has a debit balance of $21,400 (see Requirement 1 Solution). At the end of 2000, the cost and market values of the remaining available-for-sale equity securities are as follows:

| | Cost | Market |
|---|---|---|
| FFA Industries | $62,250 | $160,050 |
| Textronics | 88,900 | 115,500 |
| Totals | $151,150 | $275,550 |

These totals reflect a difference of $124,400. Given the existing debit balance of $21,400, we need to adjust for $103,000 to increase the Allowance account to the desired $124,400 figure.

| | | | |
|---|---|---|---|
| 12/31 | Interest Receivable | 2,250 | |
| | Interest Revenue | | 2,250 |
| | To adjust accrued interest ($100,000 × .09 × 3/12) on NatSci bonds | | |

| | | | |
|---|---|---|---|
| 12/31 | Interest Receivable | 2,500 | |
| | Long-Term Investment | 125 | |
| | Interest Revenue | | 2,625 |
| | To adjust for accrued interest ($250,000 × .06 × 2/12) and amortize the discount ($7,500/10 years × 2/12). | | |

Recall that long-term investments in bonds must be reported on the balance sheet at their fully amortized cost. When bonds are purchased at a discount, the amortized cost will increase over the life of the bonds. At maturity, the amortized cost will equal the bond's face value.

**Requirement 4**

Long-Term Investments (at market)    $618, 175

The balance in the Long-Term Investments account consists of the following:

| | |
|---|---|
| Stocks  ($151,150 cost + $124,400 Allowance) | $275,550 |
| Bonds  NatSci | 100,000 |
| Wood, Inc. ($242,500 + $125) | 242,625 |
| Total | $618,175 |

Interest Receivable will be listed among the current assets, Interest Revenue under "Other Revenues" on the Income Statement, and the Unrealized Gain with stockholders' equity on the balance sheet.

# Chapter 17 - Preparing and Using the Statement of Cash Flows

## CHAPTER OVERVIEW

In most of the preceding chapters, reference has been made to the statement of cash flows and the cash flow effects of selected transactions. Many people think the cash flows statement is more important than the income statement and the balance sheet, as demonstrated by the opening vignette to this chapter in your text. It is certainly the most complex of the published financial statements. The learning objectives for this chapter are to

1. Identify the purposes of the statement of cash flows.
2. Distinguish among operating, investing, and financing activities.
3. Prepare a statement of cash flows by the direct method.
4. Use the financial statements to compute the cash effects of a wide variety of business transactions.
5. Prepare a statement of cash flows by the indirect method.

A1. Prepare a work sheet for the statement of cash flows - direct method.
A2. Prepare a work sheet for the statement of cash flows - indirect method.

## CHAPTER REVIEW

### Objective 1 - Identify the purposes of the statement of cash flows.

**Cash flows** are cash receipts and cash payments. The **statement of cash flows** reports all these receipts and disbursements under three categories (operating, investing, and financing) and shows the reasons for changes in the cash balance. The statement is used to:

1. Predict future cash flows
2. Evaluate management decisions
3. Determine the company's ability to pay dividends to stockholders and interest and principal to creditors
4. Show the relationship of net income to changes in the business's cash

The term cash is used to include **cash equivalents** which are highly liquid short-term investments (such as T-bills and money market accounts).

### Objective 2 - Distinguish among operating, investing, and financing activities.

**Operating activities** create revenues and expenses in the entity's major line of business. Therefore, operating activities are related to the transactions that make up net income. Operating activities include:

1. Collections from customers
2. Payments to suppliers and employees
3. Interest revenue and expense
4. Taxes
5. Dividends received on investments

Operating activities are always listed first because they are the largest and most important source of cash for a business.

**Investing activities** increase and decrease the assets with which the business works. Investing activities require analysis of the long-term asset accounts and include:

1. Buying and selling plant assets and investments
2. Lending money to others and collecting principal repayments

Investing activities are critical because they help determine the future course of the business.

**Financing activities** obtain the funds from investors and creditors needed to launch and sustain the business. Financing activities require analysis of the long-term liability accounts and the owners' equity accounts and include:

1. Issuing stock
2. Treasury stock transactions
3. Paying dividends
4. Borrowing money and repaying the principal

> **Study Tip:** While principal payments on notes and bonds payable are a financing activity, the interest payments are classified as an operating activity.

Review Exhibit 17-2 in your text and become familiar with both the format and content of a cash flow statement.

## Objective 3 - Prepare a statement of cash flows by the direct method.

The statement of cash flows reports cash flows from operating activities, investing activities, and financing activities, calculates the net increase or decrease in cash over the year, and adds that to the previous year's cash balance in order to arrive at the current year's cash balance. It shows where cash came from and how it was spent.

Preparing the statement of cash flows requires these steps:

1. Identify items that affect cash
2. Classify the items as operating activities, investing, or financing activities
3. Determine the increase or decrease in cash for each item

## Objective 4 - Use the financial statements to compute the cash effects of a wide variety of business transactions.

Accounts may be analyzed for the cash effects of various transactions using the income statement amounts in conjunction with changes in the balance sheet amounts.

To determine cash flow amounts from operating activities, keep the following in mind:

Revenue/expense from the income statement  →  Adjust for the change in related balance sheet accounts  →  Amount for the cash flows statement

**Cash collections from customers** can be computed using Sales Revenue from the income statement and the changes in Accounts Receivable from the balance sheet:

$$\text{COLLECTIONS FROM CUSTOMERS} = \text{SALES REVENUE} \begin{bmatrix} + \text{ DECREASES IN ACCOUNTS RECEIVABLE} \\ \text{or} \\ - \text{ INCREASES IN ACCOUNTS RECEIVABLE} \end{bmatrix}$$

**Payments to suppliers** computation:

$$\text{PAYMENTS FOR INVENTORY} = \text{COST OF GOODS SOLD} \begin{bmatrix} + \text{ INCREASE IN INVENTORY} \\ \text{or} \\ - \text{ DECREASE IN INVENTORY} \end{bmatrix} \text{ and } \begin{bmatrix} + \text{ DECREASE IN ACCOUNTS PAYABLE} \\ \text{or} \\ - \text{ INCREASE IN ACCOUNTS PAYABLE} \end{bmatrix}$$

**Payments for operating expenses** computation:

$$\text{PAYMENTS FOR OPERATING EXPENSES} = \text{OPERATING EXPENSES OTHER THAN SALARIES, WAGES, AND DEPRECIATION} \begin{bmatrix} + \text{ INCREASE IN PREPAID EXPENSES} \\ \text{or} \\ - \text{ DECREASE IN PREPAID EXPENSE} \end{bmatrix} \text{ and } \begin{bmatrix} + \text{ DECREASE IN ACCRUED LIABILITIES} \\ \text{or} \\ - \text{ INCREASE IN ACCRUED LIABILITIES} \end{bmatrix}$$

Remember that depreciation is not included in operating expenses because depreciation is a noncash expense.

**Payments to employees** computation:

$$\text{PAYMENTS TO EMPLOYEES} = \text{SALARY AND WAGE EXPENSE} \begin{bmatrix} + \text{ DECREASES IN SALARY AND WAGE PAYABLE} \\ \text{or} \\ - \text{ INCREASES IN SALARY AND WAGE PAYABLE} \end{bmatrix}$$

**Payments of interest and taxes** follow the pattern for payments to employees. Exhibit 17-8 summarizes this discussion.

For investing activities we look to the asset accounts (Plant assets, Investments, Notes receivable).

**Plant asset transactions** can be analyzed by first determining book value:

$$\text{BEGINNING PLANT ASSET BALANCE (NET)} + \text{ACQUISITIONS} - \text{DEPRECIATION} - \text{BOOK VALUE OF PLANT ASSETS SOLD} = \text{ENDING PLANT ASSET BALANCE (NET)}$$

In order to compute sale proceeds:

$$\text{SALE PROCEEDS} = \text{BOOK VALUE SOLD} + \text{GAIN} - \text{LOSS}$$

Acquisitions will decrease cash, while sale proceeds will increase cash.

Investments and Loans and Notes Receivable are analyzed in a manner similar to plant assets; however, there is no depreciation to account for. Review Exhibit 17-9 for a summary of this discussion.

Financing activities affect liability and stockholders' equity accounts.

**Long-term debt** can be analyzed with this equation:

$$\text{BEGINNING LONG-TERM DEBT BALANCE} + \text{ISSUANCE OF NEW DEBT} - \text{PAYMENTS} = \text{ENDING LONG-TERM DEBT BALANCE}$$

**Stock transactions** (other than treasury stock) can be analyzed using this equation:

$$\text{BEGINNING STOCK BALANCE} + \text{ISSUANCE OF NEW STOCK} - \text{RETIREMENTS} = \text{ENDING STOCK BALANCE}$$

Issuances increase cash, while retirements decrease cash.

**Treasury stock** can be analyzed with this equation:

$$\text{BEGINNING TREASURY STOCK BALANCE} + \text{PURCHASES} - \text{COST OF TREASURY STOCK SOLD} = \text{ENDING TREASURY STOCK BALANCE}$$

Purchases will decrease cash. Remember that cash is increased by the proceeds of treasury stock sold. These proceeds may differ from the cost of treasury stocks sold.

**Dividend payments** can be computed by analyzing Retained Earnings:

BEGINNING RETAINED EARNINGS BALANCE + NET INCOME - DIVIDENDS DECLARATIONS = ENDING RETAINED EARNINGS BALANCE

Remember that stock dividends must be separated from cash dividends. Also, a change in the Dividends Payable account will affect the actual cash dividends paid. Review Exhibit 17-10 in your text.

**Noncash investing and financing activities**

Some investing and financing activities are noncash. Some typical noncash investing and financing activities include:

1. Acquisition of assets by issuing stock
2. Acquisition of assets by issuing debt
3. Payment of long-term debt by transferring investment assets to the creditor

Noncash activities are included in a schedule or a note to the statement of cash flows.

When the direct method of computing operating cash flows is used, FASB requires companies to include a reconciliation from net income to net cash flows. This reconciliation is identical to the indirect method.

## Objective 5 - Prepare a statement of cash flows by the indirect method.

The **indirect** or **(reconciliation) method** reconciles net income to cash flows and affects only the operating activities section of the statement. The investing activities and financing activities sections are identical to the sections prepared using the direct method.

To prepare the operating activities section using the indirect method, we must add and subtract items that affect net income and cash flows differently. Begin with net income from the income statement.

1. Depreciation, amortization, and depletion are noncash expenses which reduce net income. Therefore, we add them back to net income as part of our effort to arrive at cash flow from operations.
2. Gains and losses from the sale of plant assets are reported as part of net income, and the proceeds are reported in the investing activities section. To avoid counting gains and losses twice, we must remove their effect from net income. Therefore, gains are subtracted from net income and losses are added to net income.
3. Changes in current assets and current liabilities:
   a. Increases in current assets, other than cash, are subtracted from net income.
   b. Decreases in current assets, other than cash, are added to net income.
   c. Decreases in current liabilities, other than dividends payable, are subtracted from net income.
   d. Increases in current liabilities are added to net income.

**Study Tip:** Under the indirect method, only changes in current assets and current liabilities are used.

Review Exhibit 17-16 in your text.

Cash flows are only one source of information creditors and investors use to evaluate a company. The Decision Guidelines in your text provide an excellent summary of questions, factors to consider, and financial statement predictors from both a creditor's and an investor's perspective.

Free cash flows refers to the amount of cash flow that a company could access quickly should a need/opportunity arise. **Free cash flow** is defined as the amount of cash available from operations after paying for planned investments in plant, equipment, and other long-term assets. When net cash flows from operations exceed the amount of cash required for investments in long-term assets, the excess is available for additional investments. Obviously, a positive free cash flow is preferable to a negative amount. Free cash flow is yet another tool to be used in evaluating a company's performance.

Work sheets are frequently used as an aid in preparing the statement of cash flows. Regardless of approach (direct or indirect), the format is the same. The work sheet has four columns, with the upper half labeled as follows:

| (1) | (2) | (3) | (4) |
|---|---|---|---|
|  | Transaction Analysis |  |  |
| Beginning Balance Sheet Amounts | Debit | Credit | Ending Balance Sheet Amounts |
|  |  |  |  |

The lower half of the work sheet uses only the two analysis columns and provides the amounts needed to present the statement of cash flows. For both the direct and indirect method, cash flows from investing and financing activities are analyzed in the same manner. (Remember, the two methods differ only in the presentation of cash flows from operating activities.)

## Objective A1 - Prepare a work sheet for the statement of cash flows - direct method.

For the direct method, cash flows from operating activities are divided into cash receipts and cash payments on the lower half of the work sheet. Amounts listed as debits represent cash receipts; amounts listed as credits represent cash payments. The statement of cash flows can then be prepared directly from the lower half of the transaction analysis columns after adding in (or subtracting) the net increase (or decrease) in cash during the period. Review Exhibit 17A-2 in your text.

## Objective A2 - Prepare a work sheet for the statement of cash flows - indirect method.

To use the work sheet for the indirect method, start by entering beginning and ending balance sheet amounts on the upper half of the work sheet, with the transaction analysis columns in the middle. However, the lower half of the work sheet starts with net income (listed as a debit with an offsetting credit to Retained Earnings). Increases and decreases in current assets and current liabilities are reconciled as changes to net income. For example, an increase in accounts receivable is analyzed with a debit to accounts receivable and a credit to net income. After all the balance sheet changes have been reconciled to changes in net income, the net increase (or decrease) in cash during the period is listed. Review Exhibit 17A-3 in your text.

# TEST YOURSELF

All the self-testing materials in this chapter focus on information and procedures that your instructor is likely to test in quizzes and examinations.

## I. Matching  *Match each numbered term with its lettered definition.*

_____ 1. cash equivalents
_____ 2. direct method
_____ 3. indirect method
_____ 4. operating activity
_____ 5. cash flows
_____ 6. financing activity
_____ 7. investing activity
_____ 8. statement of cash flows
_____ 9. work sheet
_____ 10. free cash flow

A. a report of cash receipts and cash disbursements classified according to the entity's major activities: operating, investing, and financing
B. activity that creates revenue or expense in the entity's major line of business
C. activity that increases or decreases the assets with which the business has to work
D. activity that obtains from creditors the funds needed to launch and sustain the business or repays such funds
E. cash receipts and cash disbursements
F. format of the operating activities section of the statement of cash flows that lists the major categories of operating cash receipts and cash disbursements
G. format of the operating activities section of the statement of cash flows that starts with net income and shows the reconciliation from net income to operating cash flows
H. highly liquid short-term investments that can be converted into cash with little delay
I. a columnar tool used to analyze changes in account balances to derive the amounts for the cash flows statement
J. the amount of cash available from operations after paying for planned investments in plant, equipment, and other long-term assets

## II. Multiple Choice  *Circle the best answer.*

1. All of the following are uses of the statement of cash flows except

   A. evaluate employee performance
   B. evaluate management decisions
   C. predict future cash flows
   D. relate net income to changes in cash

2. Activities which increase or decrease business assets such as machinery are called

   A. financing activities
   B. investing activities
   C. operating activities
   D. reporting activities

3. Transactions involving capital or debt activities are called

   A. financing activities
   B. investing activities
   C. operating activities
   D. reporting activities

4. Which of the following is considered a cash equivalent?

   A. accounts receivable
   B. inventory
   C. supplies
   D. treasury bills

5. The receipt of cash dividend revenues would be reported on the

   A. balance sheet
   B. income statement
   C. statement of cash flows only
   D. both the income statement and the statement of cash flows

6. All of the following are examples of operating activities except

   A. purchases from suppliers
   B. sales to customers
   C. sales of equipment
   D. recording rent expense

7. All of the following are examples of investing activities except

   A. sale of building
   B. payment of dividends
   C. purchase of equipment
   D. receipt of cash from sale of California State bonds

8. All of the following are financing activities except

   A. issuing stock
   B. paying dividends
   C. selling equipment
   D. long-term borrowing

9. Cash collections from customers are computed by

   A. Sales Revenue + Increase in Accounts Receivable
   B. Sales Revenue - Increase in Accounts Receivable
   C. Sales Revenues - Decrease in Accounts Receivable
   D. Sales Revenue + Decrease in Accounts Receivable
   E. Either B or D.

10. When using a work sheet to prepare the statement of cash flows, the account balances to analyze come from the

    A. income statement
    B. retained earnings statement
    C. balance sheet
    D. all of the above

## III. Completion  *Complete each of the following statements.*

1. The _____ is the only financial statement that is dated as of the end of the period.
2. The largest cash inflow from operations is _____.
3. Both the _____ method and the _____ method of preparing the statements of cash flows are permitted by the FASB.
4. Payments of dividends is a(n) _____ activity on the statement of cash flows.
5. Making loans is a(n) _____ activity on the statement of cash flows.

Preparing and Using the Statement of Cash Flows   451

6. Depreciation is included in the _____ activity section on the statement of cash flows when using the indirect method.
7. The purchase of equipment is a(n) _____ activity on the statement of cash flows.
8. While permitting both methods, FASB recommends the _____ method.
9. The _____ method begins with net income.
10. The difference between the direct and indirect method is found in the _____ section of the statement of cash flows.

## IV. Daily Exercises

1. Classify each of the following as an operating, investing, or financing activity.

   **Item**　　　　　　　　　　　　　　　　　　　　　　**Classification**

   a) payment to employees　　　　　　　　　　　　_____
   b) lending money　　　　　　　　　　　　　　　　_____
   c) receiving dividends on investments　　　　　　　_____
   d) selling treasury stock　　　　　　　　　　　　　_____
   e) raising funds by selling bonds　　　　　　　　　_____
   f) receiving cash from customers　　　　　　　　　_____
   g) paying taxes　　　　　　　　　　　　　　　　　_____
   h) purchasing equipment by paying cash　　　　　　_____
   i) purchasing equipment and signing a note payable　_____
   j) purchasing inventory on account　　　　　　　　_____
   k) receiving interest revenue　　　　　　　　　　　_____
   l) paying dividends to stockholders　　　　　　　　_____
   m) selling short-term investments　　　　　　　　　_____
   n) selling shares of common stock　　　　　　　　　_____

2. For each of the following income statement accounts, indicate the related balance sheet accounts to analyze when using the direct method.

   a. operating expenses　　_____
   b. sales　　　　　　　　　_____
   c. income tax expense　　 _____
   d. cost of goods sold　　　_____
   e. salary expense　　　　　_____
   f. dividend revenue　　　　_____
   g. interest expense　　　　 _____
   h. interest revenue　　　　 _____

3. When using the direct method and analyzing changes in balance sheet accounts, how do you treat (add or deduct) each of the following specific changes:

   a. _____ increase in interest payable
   b. _____ increase in dividends receivable
   c. _____ decrease in salary payable
   d. _____ increase in accounts receivable
   e. _____ decrease in prepaid expenses
   f. _____ decrease in inventory
   g. _____ decrease in accrued liabilities
   h. _____ increase in income tax payable
   i. _____ decrease in interest receivable
   j. _____ decrease in accounts payable

4. When preparing the operating activities section of a cash flows statement using the indirect method, indicate (using a + or -) the effect on net income of each of the following items:

   a. _____ amortization expense
   b. _____ gain on sale of equipment
   c. _____ increase in prepaid expenses
   d. _____ depreciation expense
   e. _____ loss on sale of building
   f. _____ increase in accrued liabilities
   g. _____ depletion expense
   h. _____ decrease in inventory
   i. _____ decrease in accounts payable
   j. _____ decrease in accounts receivable

5. Depreciation expense is ignored when preparing the operating activities section using the direct method, but needs to be considered when using the indirect method. Why?

## V. Exercises

1. Crandall Company had tax expense of $36,000 in 19X9. The balance in Taxes Payable was $1,400 at the beginning of the year and $2,400 at the end of the year. How much cash was paid for taxes during 19X9?

2. Shimer Company had cost of goods sold of $400,000, an increase in inventory of $10,000, and an increase in Accounts Payable of $18,000 in 19X9. How much cash was paid to suppliers?

3. Mancuzo Company had sales of $1,250,000 in 19X9. Eighty percent of sales are on credit. During the year, Accounts Receivable increased from $35,000 to $81,000. How much cash was received from customers during 19X9?

4. Saephan Company purchased machinery for $91,000, loaned $14,000 to a customer, borrowed $12,000, and sold securities that were not cash equivalents for $42,000. What was the net cash flow from investing activities?

5. From the following list of cash receipts and payments, present the cash flows from the operating activities section of the cash flows statement, using the direct method.

| | |
|---|---:|
| Cash receipts from interest revenues | $ 2,440 |
| Cash paid for taxes | 32,855 |
| Cash payments to suppliers | 287,990 |
| Cash receipts from customers | 451,385 |
| Cash paid for dividends | 4,660 |
| Cash payments to employees | 61,075 |
| Cash receipts from dividend revenues | 1,565 |
| Cash payments for interest | 1,010 |

| | | |
|---|---|---|
| Receipts: | | |
| collection from customers | 451,385 | |
| interest revenues | 2,440 | |
| dividends revenues | 1,565 | |

## VI. Beyond the Numbers

Review the information in Exercises 1 and 3. Calculate the same answer using a different approach.

## VII. Demonstration Problems

### Demonstration Problem #1

The income statement, schedule of current account changes, and additional data for Johnson Jones Corporation follows:

Johnson Jones Corporation<br>Income Statement<br>For the Year Ended December 31, 19X9

| | | |
|---|---:|---:|
| Revenues: | | |
|     Net sales revenue | $1,405,000 | |
|     Dividend revenue | 27,000 | $1,432,000 |
| Expenses: | | |
|     Cost of goods sold | 1,081,000 | |
|     Salary expense | 129,000 | |
|     Other operating expense | 31,000 | |
|     Depreciation expense | 55,000 | |
|     Interest expense | 65,000 | |
|     Amortization expense-patents | 5,000 | 1,366,000 |
| Net income | | $ 66,000 |

Additional data:

a. Collections exceeded sales by $7,000.
b. Dividend revenue equaled cash amounts received, $27,000.
c. Payments to suppliers were $18,000 less than cost of goods sold. Payments for other operating expense and interest expense were the same as Other Operating Expenses.
d. Payments to employees were less than salary expense by $4,000.
e. Acquisition of plant assets totaled $130,000. Of this amount, $20,000 was paid in cash and the balance was financed by signing a note payable.
f. Proceeds from the sale of land were $85,000.
g. Proceeds from the issuance of common stock were $50,000.
h. Full payment was made on a long-term note payable, $40,000.
i. Dividends were paid in the amount of $16,000.
j. A small parcel of land located in an industrial park was purchased for $74,000.
k. Current asset and liability activity changes were as follows:

|  | December 31 | |
| --- | --- | --- |
|  | 19X9 | 19X8 |
| Cash and cash equivalents | 232,000 | 92,000 |
| Accounts receivable | 236,000 | 243,000 |
| Inventory | 378,000 | 384,000 |
| Prepaid expense | 12,000 | 12,000 |
| Accounts payable | 214,000 | 202,000 |
| Salary payable | 11,000 | 7,000 |
| Income tax payable | 3,200 | 3,200 |

**Required**
1. Using the direct method, prepare the December 31, 19X9, statement of cash flows and accompanying schedule of noncash investing and financing activities for Johnson Jones Corporation.
2. Calculate the corporation's free cash flow.

**Requirement 1 (statement of cash flows—direct method)**

| Johnson Jones | | |
| --- | --- | --- |
| Statement of Cash Flows | | |
| For the Year Ended December 31, 19X9 | | |
|  |  |  |

456   Chapter 17

**Requirement 2 (free cash flow)**

**Demonstration Problem #2**

Using the information in Problem 1, prepare a statement of cash flows and accompanying schedule of noncash investing and financing activities using the indirect method.

**Indirect Method**

Johnson Jones
Statement of Cash Flows
For the Year Ended December 31, 19X9

# SOLUTIONS

## I. Matching

1. H
2. F
3. G
4. B
5. E
6. D
7. C
8. A
9. I
10. J

## II. Multiple Choice

1.   A  Replace A with "to determine ability to pay dividends and interest" and you have a list of all the purposes for the statement of cash flows.

2.   B  Changes in property, plant, and equipment are investing activities.

3.   A  Changes in capital and debt are financing activities.

4.   D  Cash and cash equivalents are highly liquid, short-term investments that can be converted into cash with little delay and include money market investments and investments in T-bills.

5.   D  Recall that the receipt of a dividend from an investment accounted for under the cost method is treated as income and accordingly will be included in the income statement. For cash flow statement purposes, the receipt of dividends is considered an operating activity and will be reflected in that portion of the statement.

6.   C  Operating activities create revenues and expenses in the entity's major line of business. Equipment sales are assumed not to be this entity's major line of business.

7.   B  Investing activities increase and decrease the assets the business has to work with. Payment of a dividend is a financing activity. Note that while the receipt of interest on a bond is an operating activity, buying and selling bonds is an investing activity.

8.   C  Financing activities include transactions with investors and creditors needed to obtain funds to launch and sustain the business. Of the items listed, only C, an investing activity, does not fit that definition.

9.   E  Sales revenue is recorded on the accrual basis. To convert this to a cash flow, the net change in accounts receivable must be considered. A decrease in accounts receivable indicates that customers have paid more than they purchased and should be added to sales. An increase in accounts receivable indicates that customers have purchased more than they paid and should be subtracted from sales.

10.   C  Regardless of method, changes in balance sheet accounts are analyzed.

## III. Completion

1. balance sheet (The income statement, statement of retained earnings, and statement of cash flows all cover a period of time. Only the balance sheet is as of a particular date.)
2. collections of cash from customers
3. direct, indirect (order not important)
4. financing

5. investing
6. operating (Recall from our previous discussion that depreciation is a noncash expense.)
7. investing
8. direct
9. indirect
10. operating activities

## IV. Daily Exercises

1.
   a) operating activity
   b) investing activity
   c) operating activity
   d) financing activity
   e) financing activity
   f) operating activity
   g) operating activity
   h) investing activity
   i) none (this is a noncash investing activity)
   j) operating activity
   k) operating activity
   l) financing activity
   m) investing activity
   n) financing activity

**Study Tip:** Remember, operating activities relate to the income statement, investing activities to long-term assets, and financing activities to long-term liabilities and owners' equity.

2.
   a. prepaid expenses and accrued liabilities
   b. accounts receivable
   c. income tax payable
   d. inventory and accounts payable
   e. salaries payable
   f. dividends receivable
   g. interest payable
   h. interest receivable

3.
   a. deduct
   b. deduct
   c. add
   d. deduct
   e. deduct
   f. deduct
   g. add
   h. deduct
   i. add
   j. add

4.
    a.   +
    b.   -
    c.   -
    d.   +
    e.   +
    f.   +
    g.   +
    h.   +
    i.   -
    j.   +

5. The direct method ignores net income; therefore, the operating activities lists cash receipts and payments. Since depreciation expense is a non cash item, it can be ignored. The indirect method begins with net income, which includes a deduction for depreciation expense. Since the latter is a non cash item, it needs to be added back to net income.

## V. Exercises

1. Note that this exercise and the next ones may be solved using what you learned in earlier chapters:

|   | Taxes Payable (beginning) | $1,400 |
|---|---|---|
| + | Taxes Expense | 36,000 |
| = | Subtotal | 37,400 |
| - | Cash Payments | ? |
| = | Taxes Payable (ending) | $2,400 |

$1,400 + $36,000 - x = $2,400
x = $35,000

2.
|   | Cost of Goods Sold | $400,000 |
|---|---|---|
| + | Increase in Inventory | 10,000 |
| = | Subtotal | 410,000 |
| - | Increase in Accounts Payable | 18,000 |
| = | Cash paid to suppliers | $392,000 |

3. Cash received from credit sales:

|   | Accounts Receivable (beginning) | $35,000 |
|---|---|---|
| + | Credit sales (80% × 1,250,000) | 1,000,000 |
| = | Subtotal | 1,035,000 |
| - | Cash collected from customers | ? |
| = | Accounts Receivable (ending) | $81,000 |

Cash received from credit sales ($1,035,000 - $81,000)   $ 954,000
Cash collected from cash sales (20% × 1,250,000)      250,000
= Total cash collected from customers                   $1,204,000

4.  Purchase of machinery                    $(91,000)
    Loan made to customer                    (14,000)
    Sale of securities                       42,000
    Net cash flow from investing activities  $(63,000)

Borrowing $12,000 is not an investing activity. It is a financing activity.

5.
    Cash flows from operating activities:
| | |
|---|---:|
| Cash receipts from customers | 451,385 |
| Cash receipts from dividends | 1,565 |
| Cash receipts from interest | 2,440 |
| Cash payments to suppliers | (287,990) |
| Cash payments to employees | (61,075) |
| Cash paid for taxes | (32,855) |
| Cash payments for interest | (1,010) |
| Net cash inflow from operating activities | $72,460 |

The cash paid for dividends is not an operating activity. Dividends paid to shareholders relate to owners' equity on the balance sheet and are, therefore, a financing activity.

## VI. Beyond the Numbers

Exercise 1    Tax Expense    $36,000
                 * Less increase in Taxes Payable    1,000
                 Payments for taxes    $35,000

*The increase in the related liability is deducted because it represents an expense which has not been paid. Similarly, a decrease in the related liability would be added. Remember we are concerned with cash payments.

Exercise 3    Sales    $1,250,000
                ** Less increase in Accounts Receivable    46,000
                Cash received from customers    $1,204,000

**The increase in Accounts Receivable is deducted because it represents credit sales which have not been collected. Similarly a decrease in Accounts Receivable would be added because it represents additional credit sales collected. Remember we are concerned with cash receipts.

## VII. Demonstration Problems

### Demonstration Problem #1 Solved and Explained

**Requirement 1 (direct method)**

Johnson Jones<br>
Statement of Cash Flows<br>
For the Year Ended December 31, 19X9

| | | |
|---|---:|---:|
| Cash flows from operating activities: | | |
|   Receipts: | | |
|     Collections from customers | $1,412,000 (A) | |
|     Dividends received on investments in stock | 27,000 (B) | |
|     Total cash receipts | | $1,439,000 |
|   Payments: | | |
|     To suppliers | 1,094,000 (C) | |
|     To employees | 125,000 (D) | |
|     For interest | 65,000 (C) | |
|     Total cash payments | | 1,284,000 |
|     Net cash inflow from operating activities | | 155,000 |
| Cash flows from investing activities: | | |
|   Acquisition of plant assets | (20,000) (E) | |
|   Proceeds from sale of land | 85,000 (F) | |
|   Acquisition of industrial park land | (74,000) (E) | |
|   Net cash outflow from investing activities | | (9,000) |
| Cash flows from financing activities: | | |
|   Proceeds from common stock issuance | 50,000 (G) | |
|   Payment of long-term note payable | (40,000) (G) | |
|   Dividends | (16,000) (G) | |
|   Net cash outflow from financing activities | | (6,000) |
| Net increase in cash | | 140,000 |
| Cash balance beginning of year | | 92,000 |
| Cash balance end of year | | 232,000 |
| Noncash investing and financing activities: | | |
|   Acquisition of plant assets by issuing note payable | | $ 110,000 (E) |

### Computations and Explanations

(A) The largest cash inflow from operations will almost always be the collection of cash from customers. Cash sales obviously will bring in cash immediately. Since sales on account increase Accounts Receivable (not Cash), companies need to know the actual collections from customers. Item (a) of the additional data indicates that collections from customers were more than sales by $7,000. Thus, collections must have been $1,412,000 ($1,405,000 sales plus $7,000).

(B) Dividends do not accrue with the passage of time, but rather are recorded when received. Item (b) of the additional data states that $27,000 was received, the identical amount shown in the income statement. Thus, no adjustment is necessary. Note that dividends received result in a cash inflow reported as an operating activity. Although the origin of the dividend was from an investment activity, in accordance with the FASB, dividends received were accounted for as part of operating activities because they have a direct impact on net income.

(C) Payments to suppliers is a broad category which includes all cash payments for inventory and all operating expenses except disbursements for:

1. employee compensation expense
2. interest expense
3. income tax expense

A review of Item (c) indicates that payments to suppliers were $1,094,000 ($1,063,000 + $31,000) as follows:

| | |
|---|---:|
| Cost of goods sold | $1,081,000 |
| Less: Additional amounts owed to suppliers | 18,000 |
| Payments for inventory | $1,063,000 |
| | |
| Payments for Operating expense | $31,000 |

Payments to suppliers include all payments (except those listed above as exceptions) to those who supply the business with its inventory and essential services. Note that interest payment equals interest expense, an item that is separately disclosed in the statement of cash flows.

(D) Payments to employees include all forms of employee compensation. The income statement reports the expense (including accrued amounts), whereas the statement of cash flows reports only the payments. Item (d) indicates that actual payments were $125,000, which is $4,000 less than the $129,000 reported in the income statement as salary expense.

(E) The purchase of $130,000 in plant assets used $20,000 in cash. The balance was financed with a $110,000 promissory note. Because the note is not an outflow of cash, it is separately disclosed as a noncash investing activity at the bottom of the statement of cash flows.

The $74,000 industrial park land (Item j) used $74,000 cash and is shown as a cash outflow or "use." A firm's investment in income-producing assets often signals to investors the direction that the firm is taking.

(F) The receipt of $85,000 from the land sale (Item f) is essentially the opposite of the acquisition of a plant asset, and should be reported as a cash inflow from an investment transaction.

(G) Investors and other financial statement users want to know how an entity obtains its financing. The financing activities section of the cash flow statement for Johnson Jones Corporation discloses the effect of the sale of common stock (inflow of $50,000, Item g), payment of a long-term note (outflow of $40,000, Item h), and payment of cash dividends (outflow of $16,000, Item i).

## Requirement 2 (free cash flow)

$146,000

Free cash flow is the difference between cash flows from operating activities and cash flows from investing activities. A review of the cash flow statement shows cash inflows from operating activities of $155,000 and net cash outflows from investing activities of $9,000. Therefore, free cash flows are $155,000 - $9,000 = $146,000.

## Demonstration Problem #2 Solved and Explained

### Indirect Method

Johnson Jones Corporation<br>
Statement of Cash Flows<br>
For the Year Ended December 31, 19X9

| | | |
|---|---:|---:|
| Cash flows from operating activities: | | |
| Net income (from income statement): | | $ 66,000 |
| Add (subtract) items that affect net income and cash flow differently: | | |
|    Depreciation | 55,000 | |
|    Amortization | 5,000 | |
|    Decrease in accounts receivable | 7,000 | |
|    Decrease in inventory | 6,000 | |
|    Increase in accounts payable | 12,000 | |
|    Increase in salary payable | 4,000 | 89,000 |
|    Net cash inflow from operating activities | | 155,000 |
| | | |
| Cash flows from investing activities: | | |
|    Acquisition of plant assets | (20,000) | |
|    Proceeds from sale of land | 85,000 | |
|    Acquisition of industrial park land | (74,000) | |
|    Net cash outflow from investing activities | | (9,000) |
| | | |
| Cash flows from financing activities: | | |
|    Proceeds from common stock issuance | 50,000 | |
|    Payment of long-term note payable | (40,000) | |
|    Dividends | (16,000) | |
|    Net cash outflow from financing activities | | (6,000) |
| Net increase in cash | | $140,000 |
| Cash balance beginning of year | | 92,000 |
| Cash balance end of year | | $232,000 |
| Noncash investing and financing activities: | | |
|    Acquisition of plant assets by issuing note payable | | $110,000 |

As emphasized many times in this chapter, the difference between the direct method and the indirect method appears only in the presentation of the cash flows from operating activities section of the statement. The indirect method begins with net income, then 'adjusts' the net income figure in order to convert it to a cash based value. Regardless of method, the presentation of cash flows from investing activities and financing activities are the same. FASB Statement No. 95 permits either method, but recommends the direct method because it is thought to be more "user friendly."

# Chapter 18 - Financial Statement Analysis

## CHAPTER OVERVIEW

Financial statements are the primary means an outsider uses to evaluate a particular company. Once completed, the results can be compared with other companies. There are a variety of tools used to evaluate performance. In this chapter you are introduced to some of these techniques. The learning objectives for the chapter are to

1. Perform a horizontal analysis of comparative financial statements.
2. Perform a vertical analysis of financial statements.
3. Prepare common-size financial statements for benchmarking against the industry average and key competitors.
4. Compute the standard financial ratios used for decision making.
5. Use ratios in decision making.
6. Measure economic value added by a company's operations.

## CHAPTER REVIEW

**Financial statement analysis** is based on information taken from the annual report, SEC reports, articles in the business press, and so on. The objective of financial statement analysis is to provide information to creditors and investors to help them 1) predict future returns and 2) assess the risk of those returns. Past performance is often a good indicator of future performance. Three categories of financial statement analysis are: horizontal, vertical, and ratio analysis.

## Objective 1 - Perform a horizontal analysis of comparative financial statements.

The study of percentage changes in comparative statements is called **horizontal analysis**. Horizontal analysis highlights changes over time. Computing a percentage change in comparative statements requires two steps: 1) compute the dollar amount of the change from the base period to the later period, and 2) divide the dollar amount of the change by the base period amount.

The **base period** for horizontal analysis is the year prior to the year being considered. Suppose there are three years of data. The change from Year 1 to Year 2 is:

$$\frac{\$ \text{YEAR 2} - \$ \text{YEAR 1}}{\$ \text{YEAR 1}}$$

and the change from Year 2 to Year 3 is:

$$\frac{\$ \text{YEAR 3} - \$ \text{YEAR 2}}{\$ \text{YEAR 2}}$$

No percentage changes are computed if the base-year amount is zero or negative. Exhibits 18-2 and 18-3 illustrate horizontal analysis on an income statement and balance sheet.

**Trend percentages** are a form of horizontal analysis. They indicate the direction of business activities by comparing numbers over a span of several years. Trend percentages are computed by selecting a base and expressing the amount of each item for each of the following years as a percentage of the base year's amount for that item.

## Objective 2 - Perform a vertical analysis of financial statements.

**Vertical analysis** of a financial statement reveals the percentage of the total that each statement item represents. Percentages on the comparative income statement are computed by dividing all amounts by net sales. Percentages on the comparative balance sheet are shown as either 1) a percentage of total assets or 2) a percentage of total liabilities and stockholders' equity.

Vertical analysis of the income statement highlights changes in such items as the gross profit percentage and net income.

Vertical analysis of the balance sheet shows the composition of balance sheet items. Trend analysis can be used to highlight year-to-year percentage changes.

(Review Exhibits 18-4 and 18-5 in your text.)

## Objective 3 - Prepare common-size financial statements for benchmarking against the industry average and key competitors.

**Common-size statements** report amounts in percentages only. The common-size statement is a form of vertical analysis. On a common-size income statement, each item is expressed as a percentage of the net sales amount. In the balance sheet, the common-size is the total on each side of the accounting equation. Note that common-size percentages are the same percentages shown on financial statements using vertical analysis. (Review Exhibit 18-6 in your text).

Benchmarking is the practice of comparing a company to a standard set by other companies. Benchmarking is used to compare a company's results with the average for their industry. In addition, common-size statements can be compared with those of specific competitors within the industry. Exhibits 18-7 and 18-8 in your text illustrate these two uses of benchmarking.

Common-size percentages can be used to compare financial statements of different companies or to compare one company's financial statements to industry averages.

## Objective 4 - Compute the standard financial ratios used for decision making.

There are many, many different ratios used in financial analysis. Sometimes a ratio is used alone but more frequently a group of ratios are calculated and used to analyze a particular issue. The ratios discussed in this section are grouped as follows:

1. Ratios that measure the company's ability to pay current liabilities
2. Ratios that measure the company's ability to sell inventory and collect receivables
3. Ratios that measure the company's ability to pay short-term and long-term debt
4. Ratios that measure the company's profitability
5. Ratios used to analyze the company's stock as an investment

1. **Ratios that measure the company's ability to pay current liabilities**

**Working capital** is used to measure a business's ability to meet its short-term obligations with its current assets.

$$\text{WORKING CAPITAL} = \text{CURRENT ASSETS} - \text{CURRENT LIABILITIES}$$

The **current ratio** is used to measure the availability of sufficient current assets to maintain normal business operations.

$$\text{CURRENT RATIO} = \frac{\text{CURRENT ASSETS}}{\text{CURRENT LIABILITIES}}$$

The **acid-test (or quick) ratio** measures the ability of a business to pay all of its current liabilities if they came due immediately.

$$\text{ACID-TEST RATIO} = \frac{\text{CASH} + \text{SHORT-TERM INVESTMENTS} + \text{NET CURRENT RECEIVABLES}}{\text{CURRENT LIABILITIES}}$$

> **Study Tip:** Inventory and prepaid expenses are not used to compute the acid-test ratio.

2. **Ratios that measure the company's ability to sell inventory and collect receivables**

**Inventory turnover** is a measure of the number of times a company sells an average level of inventory during a year.

$$\text{INVENTORY TURNOVER} = \frac{\text{COST OF GOODS SOLD}}{\text{AVERAGE INVENTORY}}$$

$$\text{AVERAGE INVENTORY} = \frac{\text{BEGINNING INVENTORY} + \text{ENDING INVENTORY}}{2}$$

**Accounts receivable turnover** measures the ability of a company to collect cash from its credit customers.

$$\text{ACCOUNTS RECEIVABLE TURNOVER} = \frac{\text{NET CREDIT SALES}}{\text{AVERAGE NET ACCOUNTS RECEIVABLE}}$$

$$\text{AVERAGE NET ACCOUNTS RECEIVABLE} = \frac{\text{BEGINNING ACCOUNTS RECEIVABLE} + \text{ENDING ACCOUNTS RECEIVABLE}}{2}$$

**Days' sales in receivables** measures in sales days the value of accounts receivable; it tells how many days' sales remain uncollected (in accounts receivable).

$$\text{ONE DAY'S SALES} = \frac{\text{NET SALES}}{365}$$

$$\text{DAYS' SALES IN ACCOUNTS RECEIVABLE} = \frac{\text{AVERAGE NET ACCOUNTS RECEIVABLE}}{\text{ONE DAY'S SALES}}$$

To compute the ratio for the beginning of the year, substitute beginning net Accounts Receivable for average net Accounts Receivable. To compute the ratio for the end of the year, substitute ending net Accounts Receivable for average net Accounts Receivable.

3. **Ratios that measure the company's ability to pay long-term debt**

The **debt ratio** measures the relationship between total liabilities and total assets.

$$\text{DEBT RATIO} = \frac{\text{TOTAL LIABILITIES}}{\text{TOTAL ASSETS}}$$

The **times-interest-earned ratio** measures the ability of a business to pay interest expense.

$$\text{TIMES-INTEREST-EARNED RATIO} = \frac{\text{INCOME FROM OPERATIONS}}{\text{INTEREST EXPENSE}}$$

Remember that income from operations does not include interest revenue, interest expense, or income tax expense.

4. **Ratios that measure the company's profitability**

**Rate of return on net sales** measures the relationship between net income and sales.

$$\text{RATE OF RETURN ON NET SALES} = \frac{\text{NET INCOME}}{\text{NET SALES}}$$

**Rate of return on total assets** measures the success a company has in using its assets to earn a profit.

$$\text{RATE OF RETURN ON TOTAL ASSETS} = \frac{\text{NET INCOME} + \text{INTEREST EXPENSE}}{\text{AVERAGE TOTAL ASSETS}}$$

$$\text{AVERAGE TOTAL ASSETS} = \frac{\text{BEGINNING TOTAL ASSETS} + \text{ENDING TOTAL ASSETS}}{2}$$

Financial Statement Analysis

The **rate of return on common stockholders' equity** shows the relationship between net income and the common stockholders' investment in the company.

$$\text{RATE OF RETURN ON COMMON STOCKHOLDERS' EQUITY} = \frac{\text{NET INCOME - PREFERRED DIVIDENDS}}{\text{AVERAGE COMMON STOCKHOLDERS' EQUITY}}$$

$$\text{AVERAGE COMMON STOCKHOLDERS' EQUITY} = \frac{\text{BEGINNING + ENDING COMMON STOCKHOLDERS' EQUITY}}{2}$$

**Earnings per share (EPS)** is the amount of net income per share of the company's common stock.

$$\text{EPS} = \frac{\text{NET INCOME - PREFERRED DIVIDENDS}}{\text{NUMBER OF SHARES OF COMMON STOCK OUTSTANDING}}$$

**Study Tip:** Remember, if the number of shares outstanding has changed during the year, the denominator is changed to reflect the **weighted average** number of shares outstanding.

5. **Ratios used to analyze the company's stock as an investment**

The **price/earnings (P/E) ratio** is the ratio of the market price of a share of common stock to the company's EPS.

$$\text{PRICE/EARNINGS RATIO} = \frac{\text{MARKET PRICE PER SHARE OF COMMON STOCK}}{\text{EARNINGS PER SHARE}}$$

**Dividend yield** is the ratio of dividends per share of stock to the stock's market price per share.

$$\text{DIVIDENDS YIELD ON COMMON STOCK} = \frac{\text{DIVIDENDS PER SHARE OF COMMON STOCK}}{\text{MARKET PRICE PER SHARE OF COMMON STOCK}}$$

The formula for calculating **book value per share of common stock** is:

$$\text{BOOK VALUE PER SHARE OF COMMON STOCK} = \frac{\text{TOTAL STOCKHOLDERS' EQUITY - PREFERRED EQUITY}}{\text{NUMBER OF SHARES OF COMMON STOCK OUTSTANDING}}$$

## Objective 5 - Use ratios in decision making.

Ratios should be 1) evaluated over a period of years, and 2) compared with industry standards.

When a problem is found, the items used to compute the ratio should be analyzed to determine the nature of the problem. At that time, possible solutions to the problem can be suggested.

In an efficient capital market, stock prices reflect all information that is available to the public. Financial statement analysis helps to identify and evaluate the inherent risks in potential investments.

## Objective 6 - Measure economic value added by a company's operations.

**Economic value added (EVA)** is one measure many companies use to evaluate whether the company has increased stockholder wealth from operations. The formula for EVA is

**Net income + interest expense - capital charge × cost of capital**

**Capital charge** is notes payable plus loans payable plus long-term debt and stockholders' equity. The **cost of capital** is the weighted average of the returns demanded by the company's stockholders and lenders. Newer companies, because of the added risk, have a higher cost of capital compared with older, more established companies. The underlying assumption behind EVA is that returns to both stockholders and lenders should be greater than the company's capital charge. If the calculation results in a positive value, the result indicates an increase in stockholder wealth. If negative, stockholders may consider selling the stock which, if done in large enough amounts, could lower the price of the stock. Obviously, companies who use this measure strive to achieve a positive result.

# TEST YOURSELF

All the self-testing materials in this chapter focus on information and procedures that your instructor is likely to test in quizzes and examinations.

**I. Matching** *Match each numbered term with its lettered definition.*

_____ 1. accounts receivable turnover
_____ 2. working capital
_____ 3. common-size statements
_____ 4. days' sales in receivables
_____ 5. dividend yield
_____ 6. inventory turnover
_____ 7. return on total assets
_____ 8. times-interest-earned ratio
_____ 9. vertical analysis
_____ 10. acid-test ratio
_____ 11. current ratio
_____ 12. debt ratio
_____ 13. horizontal analysis
_____ 14. price/earnings ratio
_____ 15. return on net sales
_____ 16. book value per share of common stock
_____ 17. return on common stockholders' equity
_____ 18. benchmarking
_____ 19. cost of capital
_____ 20. economic value added

A. analysis of a financial statement that reveals the relationship of each statement item to the total which is the 100% figure
B. common stockholders' equity divided by the number of shares of common stock outstanding
C. current assets divided by current liabilities
D. current assets minus current liabilities
E. financial statements that report only percentages (no dollar amounts)
F. measures the number of times that operating income can cover interest expense
G. measures the number of times a company sells its average level of inventory during a year
H. ratio of the market price of a share of common stock to the company's earnings per share
I. measures the success a company has in using its assets to earn a profit
J. net income minus preferred dividends, divided by average common stockholders' equity; a measure of profitability
K. ratio of average net accounts receivable to one day's sales
L. ratio of dividends per share to the stock's market price per share
M. ratio of net income to net sales; a measure of profitability
N. study of percentage changes in comparative financial statements
O. tells the proportion of a company's assets that it has financed with debt
P. tells whether an entity could pay all its current liabilities if they came due immediately
Q. the ratio of net credit sales to average net accounts receivable; it measures ability to collect cash from credit customers
R. used to measure if a company has increased shareholder wealth from operations
S. the practice of comparing a company with other companies with a view toward improvement
T. a weighted average of the returns demanded by the company's stockholders and lenders

## II. Multiple Choice  *Circle the best answer.*

1. In vertical analysis the relationship between net income and net sales is shown by the

   A. income from operations percentage
   B. net income percentage
   C. rate of return on sales
   D. gross profit percentage

2. Which of the following measures profitability?

   A. debt ratio
   B. current ratio
   C. dividend yield
   D. earnings per share common stock

3. Which of the following current assets is not used to compute the acid-test ratio?

   A. accounts receivable
   B. cash
   C. prepaid expenses
   D. short-term investments

4. Which of the following is a common measure of a firm's ability to meet short-term obligations?

   A. working capital
   B. rate of return on sales
   C. net assets
   D. price/earnings ratio

5. The times-interest-earned ratio measures

   A. profitability
   B. ability to pay interest expense on debt
   C. ability to pay current liabilities
   D. ability to collect receivables

6. The proportion of a firm's assets financed by debt is measured by the

   A. current ratio
   B. debt ratio
   C. debt yield ratio
   D. times-interest-earned ratio

7. Assume that a company's current ratio is greater than one. If the company pays current liabilities with cash, the new current ratio will

   A. increase
   B. decrease
   C. remain unchanged
   D. cannot be determined

8. The dividend yield evaluates

   A. the ability to pay current debt
   B. profitability
   C. stock as an investment
   D. ability to pay long-term debt

9. The excess of current assets less current liabilities is

   A. a measure of profitability
   B. economic value added
   C. a measure of short-term liquidity
   D. a measure of long-term debt paying ability

10. Book value measures

   A. profitability
   B. short-term liquidity
   C. long-term debt paying ability
   D. stock as an investment

## III. Completion  *Complete each of the following statements.*

1. The study of percentage changes in comparative financial statements is called _____ analysis.
2. Vertical analysis percentages on the income statement are computed by dividing all amounts by _____.
3. Vertical analysis percentages on the balance sheet are computed by dividing all amounts by _____.
4. Working capital is _____.
5. _____ and _____ are the two most common measures of firm size.
6. Leverage _____ the risk to common stockholders.
7. The _____ ratio indicates the market price of one dollar of earnings.
8. The rate of return on total assets equals _____.
9. The most widely quoted of all financial statistics is _____.
10. The _____ is the recorded accounting value of each share of common stock outstanding.

## IV. Daily Exercises

1. Net income was $300,000 in Year 1, $400,000 in Year 2, and $320,000 in Year 3. What were the percentage changes in net income?

2. A company had 300,000 shares of common stock outstanding at the beginning of the year. On March 1, 200,000 additional shares were sold and on June 30, 150,000 shares were exchanged when bonds were converted. On November 1, the company purchased 100,000 of common stock for the treasury. Net income for the year was $1,570,000. Calculate earnings per share.

3. Refer to The Complex Corporation income statement in Demonstration Problem #1 and complete a vertical analysis.

|  | Amount | % |
|---|---|---|
| Net sales |  |  |
| Cost of products sold |  |  |
| Selling, delivery, and administration |  |  |
| Advertising |  |  |
| Research and development |  |  |
| Interest expense |  |  |
| Other (income) expense, net |  |  |
| Total costs and expenses |  |  |
| Earnings before income taxes |  |  |
| Income Taxes |  |  |
| Net earnings |  |  |

4. Examine your results in Daily Exercise #3, and calculate Complex's gross profit rate for 1997.

5. Presented below are The Complex Corporation's net sales (in thousands) and net earnings (in thousands) for the past five years. Calculate trend percentages.

|  | 1997 | 1996 | 1995 | 1994 | 1993 |
|---|---|---|---|---|---|
| Net Sales | 2,532,651 | 2,217,843 | 1,984,170 | 1,836,949 | 1,634,171 |
| Net Earnings | 249,442 | 222,092 | 200,832 | 212,057 | 167,051 |

## V. Exercises

1. Hoffman Industries had the following information for 19X9:

| | |
|---|---|
| Cost of goods sold | $400,000 |
| Beginning inventory | 30,000 |
| Ending inventory | 60,000 |
| Net credit sales | 725,000 |
| Beginning accounts receivable | 75,000 |
| Ending accounts receivable | 85,000 |

A. What is inventory turnover?

B. What is the accounts receivable turnover?

C. What is the days' sales in average receivable?

2. The following information is given for Ramirez Corporation for 19X9:

| | |
|---|---|
| Net sales | $825,000 |
| Net income | 60,000 |
| Average common stockholders' equity | 3,150,000 |
| Average total assets | 4,225,000 |
| Interest expense | 75,000 |
| Preferred dividends | 20,000 |
| Common dividends | 55,000 |
| Common stock outstanding | 240,000 shares |

A. What is the rate of return on net sales?

B. What is the rate of return on total assets?

C. What is the rate of return on common stockholders' equity?

3. The following information is given for Williams Corporation:

Assets:
| | |
|---|---|
| Cash | $ 60,000 |
| Marketable securities | 118,000 |
| Accounts receivable | 214,000 |
| Inventory | 141,000 |
| Equipment | 420,000 |
| Total assets | $953,000 |

Liabilities and Stockholders' equity:
| | |
|---|---|
| Accounts payable | $105,000 |
| Salary payable | 17,000 |
| Long-term bonds payable | 165,000 |
| Common stock | 200,000 |
| Retained earnings | 466,000 |
| Total liabilities and stockholders' equity | $953,000 |

A. What is the current ratio?

B. What is the acid-test (quick) ratio?

C. What is the debt ratio?

4. Calvin Lauren, Inc., has a price/earnings ratio of 19, dividends of $1.50 per share, and earnings per share of $1.28.

   A. What is the market price per share?

   B. What is the dividend yield?

## VI. Beyond the Numbers

The operating cycle is the length of time between the purchase of merchandise and its conversion to cash following the sale and receipt of payment (you were introduced to the operating cycle in Chapter 5). Using the information in Exercise 1 above, calculate the operating cycle for Hoffman Industries.

# VII. Demonstration Problems

## Demonstration Problem #1

The Complex Company, headquartered in San Jose, California, manufactures household products. Figures from their 1997 annual report (slightly modified for ease of presentation) follow:

The Complex Company
Statement of Consolidated Earnings
For Year Ended June 30, 1997

|  | (In thousands) |
|---|---:|
| Net sales | $2,532,651 |
|  |  |
| Cost and expenses |  |
|    Cost of products sold | 1,123,459 |
|    Selling, delivery, and administration | 543,804 |
|    Advertising | 348,521 |
|    Research and development | 50,489 |
|    Interest expense | 55,623 |
|    Other (income) expense, net | (5,260) |
|      Total costs and expenses | 2,116,636 |
| Earnings before income taxes | 416,015 |
| Income Taxes | 166,573 |
| Net earnings | $ 249,442 |
| Weighted average shares outstanding | 103,292 |

The Complex Company
Consolidated Balance Sheet
June 30, 1997

|  | (In thousands) | |
|---|---|---|
|  | 1997 | 1996 |
| **Assets** | | |
| Current assets: | | |
| Cash and short-term investments | 101,046 | 90,828 |
| Accounts receivable, less allowance | 356,996 | 315,106 |
| Inventories | 170,340 | 138,848 |
| Prepaid expenses | 22,534 | 18,076 |
| Deferred income taxes | 22,581 | 10,987 |
| Total current assets | 673,497 | 573,845 |
| Property, plant, and equipment—net | 570,645 | 551,437 |
| Brands, trademarks, patents and other intangibles—net | 1,186,951 | 704,669 |
| Investment in affiliates | 93,004 | 99,033 |
| Other assets | 253,855 | 249,910 |
| Total | $2,777,952 | $2,178,894 |
| | | |
| **Liabilities and Stockholders' Equity** | | |
| Current liabilities: | | |
| Accounts payable | $ 143,360 | $ 155,366 |
| Accrued liabilities | 358,785 | 266,192 |
| Short-term debt | 369,973 | 192,683 |
| Income tax payable | 17,049 | 9,354 |
| Current maturity of long-term debt | 3,551 | 291 |
| Total current liabilities | 892,718 | 623,886 |
| Long-term debt | 565,926 | 356,267 |
| Other obligations | 112,539 | 100,246 |
| Deferred income taxes | 170,723 | 148,408 |
| Stockholders' equity | | |
| Common stock - authorized, 375,000,000 shares, $1 par value; issued: 110,844,594 shares | 110,844 | 110,844 |
| Additional paid-in capital | 66,803 | 56,360 |
| Retained earnings | 1,207,524 | 1,078,789 |
| Treasury shares, at cost: 1997, 7,680,056 shares; 1996, 7,848,942 shares | (289,075) | (251,393) |
| Cumulative translation adjustments | (60,050) | (44,513) |
| Total Stockholders' equity | 1,036,046 | 950,087 |
| Total liabilities and stockholders' equity | $2,777,952 | $2,178,894 |

**Required:**

Assume annual dividends of $1.16 and a market price of 79 5/16 per share. Compute the following for 1997:

A) working capital

B) current ratio

C) acid-test (quick) ratio

D) inventory turnover

E) accounts receivable turnover

F) days' sales in receivables

G) debt ratio

H) times-interest-earned ratio

I) rate of return on sales

J) rate of return on total assets

K) rate of return on common stockholders' equity

L) earnings per share

M) price/earnings ratio

N) dividend yield


O) book value per share of common stock


**Demonstration Problem #2**

Chris Daniel Corporation's balance sheets and income statements are presented below:

Chris Daniel Corporation
Balance Sheet
Years 19X9 and 19X8

|  | 19X9 | 19X8 |
|---|---|---|
| **Assets** |  |  |
| Current assets: |  |  |
| Cash | $ 13,300 | $ 20,350 |
| Short-term investments | 8,200 | 8,000 |
| Receivables, net | 26,000 | 24,000 |
| Inventories | 45,000 | 40,000 |
| Prepaid expenses | 2,500 | 4,650 |
| Total current assets | 95,000 | 97,000 |
| Property, plant, and equipment—net | 185,680 | 196,500 |
| Land | 40,000 | 35,000 |
| Intangibles and other assets | 2,400 | 2,400 |
| Total assets | $323,080 | $330,900 |
| **Liabilities and Stockholders' Equity** |  |  |
| Current liabilities: |  |  |
| Notes payable | $ 10,000 | $ 10,500 |
| Current installments of long-term debt | 3,550 | 3,445 |
| Accounts payable-trade | 14,447 | 18,500 |
| Accrued liabilities | 3,670 | 1,605 |
| Total current liabilities | 31,667 | 34,050 |
| Long-term debt, less current installments | 95,500 | 93,330 |
| Capital lease obligations, less current portion | 1,100 | 2,150 |
| Deferred income and deferred income taxes | 4,813 | 4,370 |
| Total common stockholders' equity | 190,000 | 197,000 |
| Total liabilities and stockholders' equity | $323,080 | $330,900 |

Chris Daniel Corporation
Income Statements
Years 19X9 and 19X8

|  | 19X9 | 19X8 |
|---|---|---|
| Net sales | $416,500 | $406,316 |
| Cost and expenses: |  |  |
|   Cost of goods sold | 322,593 | 315,812 |
|   Operating expenses | 41,219 | 43,200 |
|  | 363,812 | 359,012 |
| Income from operations | 52,688 | 47,304 |
| Interest expense | 3,251 | 3,150 |
| Earnings before income taxes | 49,437 | 44,154 |
| Income taxes | 7,437 | 6,554 |
| Net income | $ 42,000 | $ 37,600 |

**Required:**

1. Prepare a horizontal analysis for 19X9 of the balance sheet, using the 19X8 amounts as the base.

| Chris Daniel Corporation ||||||
|---|---|---|---|---|---|
| Balance Sheet ||||||
| Years 19X9 and 19X8 ||||||
|  | 19X9 | 19X8 | Amount Increase (Decrease) | % Change ||
| Assets |  |  |  |  ||
| Current assets: |  |  |  |  ||
|   Cash | $ 13,300 | $ 20,350 |  |  ||
|   Short-term investments | 8,200 | 8,000 |  |  ||
|   Receivables, net | 26,000 | 24,000 |  |  ||
|   Inventories | 45,000 | 40,000 |  |  ||
|   Prepaid expenses | 2,500 | 4,650 |  |  ||
|   Total current assets | 95,000 | 97,000 |  |  ||
| Property, plant, and equipment—net | 185,680 | 196,500 |  |  ||
| Land | 40,000 | 35,000 |  |  ||
| Intangibles and other assets | 2,400 | 2,400 |  |  ||
|   Total assets | $323,080 | $330,900 |  |  ||

| Liabilities and stockholders' equity | | | | |
|---|---|---|---|---|
| Current liabilities: | | | | |
|   Notes payable | $ 10,000 | $ 10,500 | | |
|   Current installments of long-term debt | 3,550 | 3,445 | | |
|   Accounts payable-trade | 14,447 | 18,500 | | |
|   Accrued liabilities | 3,670 | 1,605 | | |
|     Total current liabilities | 31,667 | 34,050 | | |
| Long-term debt, less current installments | 95,500 | 93,330 | | |
| Capital lease obligations, less current portion | 1,100 | 2,150 | | |
| Deferred income and deferred income taxes | 4,813 | 4,370 | | |
| Total common stockholders' equity | 190,000 | 197,000 | | |
|     Total liabilities and stockholders' equity | $323,080 | $330,900 | | |

2. Convert the 19X9 and 19X8 Income Statements to common-size statements, using net sales as the base figures.

<table>
<tr><td colspan="5" align="center">Chris Daniel Corporation</td></tr>
<tr><td colspan="5" align="center">Income Statements</td></tr>
<tr><td colspan="5" align="center">Years 19X9 and 19X8</td></tr>
<tr><td></td><td colspan="2">19X9</td><td colspan="2">19X8</td></tr>
<tr><td></td><td>Amount</td><td>%</td><td>Amount</td><td>%</td></tr>
<tr><td>Net sales</td><td>$416,500</td><td></td><td>$406,316</td><td></td></tr>
<tr><td>Cost and expenses:</td><td></td><td></td><td></td><td></td></tr>
<tr><td>  Cost of goods sold</td><td>322,593</td><td></td><td>315,812</td><td></td></tr>
<tr><td>  Operating expenses</td><td>41,219</td><td></td><td>43,200</td><td></td></tr>
<tr><td>  Total costs and expenses</td><td>363,812</td><td></td><td>359,012</td><td></td></tr>
<tr><td>Income from operations</td><td>52,688</td><td></td><td>47,304</td><td></td></tr>
<tr><td>Interest expense</td><td>3,251</td><td></td><td>3,150</td><td></td></tr>
<tr><td>Earnings before income taxes</td><td>49,437</td><td></td><td>44,154</td><td></td></tr>
<tr><td>Income taxes</td><td>7,437</td><td></td><td>6,554</td><td></td></tr>
<tr><td>Net income</td><td>$ 42,000</td><td></td><td>$ 37,600</td><td></td></tr>
</table>

# SOLUTIONS

## I. Matching

| | | | | |
|---|---|---|---|---|
| 1. Q | 5. L | 9. A | 13. N | 17. J |
| 2. D | 6. G | 10. P | 14. H | 18. S |
| 3. E | 7. I | 11. C | 15. M | 19. T |
| 4. K | 8. F | 12. O | 16. B | 20. R |

## II. Multiple Choice

1. C   The rate of return on sale is net income / net sales.

2. D   Debt ratio measures the ability to pay long-term debts. Current ratio measures ability to pay current liabilities. Dividend yield is used in analyzing stock as an investment.

3. C   Only the most liquid current assets are used to calculate the acid-test ratio.

4. A   Working capital is current assets less current liabilities. It measures a firm's ability to meet short-term obligations.

5. B   Times-interest-earned measures how many times operating income is greater than interest expense.

6. B   Current ratio measures the ability to pay current liabilities. Debt yield ratio has no meaning. Times-interest-earned ratio measures ability to pay interest on debt. The debt ratio is total liabilities / total assets.

7. A   Let CA = current assets, CL = current liabilities, and X = the amount of cash paid on current liabilities. Then given that CA > CL (or CL < CA), show that:

$$(CA - X) / (CL - X) > CA / CL$$
$$CL(CA - X) > CA(CL - X)$$
$$CL(CA) - CL(X) > CA(CL) - CA(X)$$
$$-CL(X) > -CA(X)$$

dividing by -X:   CL < CA

> **Study Tip:** In a firm with current assets greater than current liabilities, the current ratio can be improved by using cash to pay current liabilities.

8. C   Dividend yield compares the amount of dividend per share with the current market price and therefore is one way to evaluate a stock as a potential investment.

9. C   Working capital (the excess of current assets over current liabilities) measures short-term liquidity.

10. D   Book value indicates the value of each share of common stock outstanding and is one way to analyze a stock investment.

## III. Completion

1. horizontal
2. net sales
3. total assets (or total liabilities plus stockholders' equity)
4. current assets minus current liabilities
5. Net sales, total assets
6. increases (Leverage is the practice of increasing the debt financing of an entity with respect to owner financing. Leverage is a two-edged sword, increasing profits (and returns to stockholders') during good times but compounding losses during bad times.)
7. price/earnings
8. (net income plus interest expense) / average total assets
9. earnings per share
10. book value per share of common stock

## IV. Daily Exercises

1. Year 2 = $100,000 / $300,000 = 33.33%
   Year 3 = ($80,000) / $400,000 = (20%)

2.
   | | | |
   |---|---|---|
   | 300,000 × 2/12 | = | 50,000 |
   | 500,000 × 4/12 | = | 166,667 |
   | 650,000 × 4/12 | = | 216,667 |
   | 550,000 × 2/12 | = | 91,667 |
   | | | 427,001 |

   $1,570,000 ÷ 427,001 = $3.68 (rounded)

   **Study Tip:** When the number of outstanding shares has changed during the year, the denominator must reflect the weighted-average number of shares.

3.
   | | Amount | % |
   |---|---:|---:|
   | Net sales | $2,532,651 | 100% |
   | Cost of products sold | 1,123,459 | 44.4% |
   | Selling, delivery, and administration | 543,804 | 21.5% |
   | Advertising | 348,521 | 13.8% |
   | Research and development | 50,489 | 2.0% |
   | Interest expense | 55,623 | 2.2% |
   | Other (income) expense, net | (5,260) | (.2%) |
   | Total costs and expenses | 2,116,636 | 83.6% |
   | Earnings before income taxes | 416,015 | 16.4% |
   | Income Taxes | 166,573 | 6.6% |
   | Net earnings | $ 249,442 | 9.8% |

4. If Cost of products sold is 44.4% of net sales, the gross profit (gross profit = net sales - cost of products sold) must be 55.6% (100% - 44.4%).

5.

|  | 1997 | 1996 | 1995 | 1994 | 1993 |
|---|---|---|---|---|---|
| Net Sales | 155% | 136% | 121% | 112% | 100% |
| Net Earnings | 149% | 133% | 120% | 127% | 100% |

## V. Exercises

1.  A.  Cost of goods / Average inventory = [$400,000 / ($30,000 + $60,000) / 2] = 8.89
    B.  Net credit sales / Average accounts receivable = [$725,000 / ($75,000 + $85,000) / 2] = 9.06
    C.  Average accounts receivable / One day's sales = [($75,000 + $85,000) / 2] / ($725,000 / 365) = 40.3 days

2.  A.  Net income / Net sales = $60,000 / $825,000 = .073 = 7.3%
    B.  (Net income + Interest expense) / Average total assets = ($60,000 + $75,000) / $4,225,000 = .032 = 3.2%
    C.  (Net income - Preferred dividends) / Average common stockholders' equity = ($60,000 - $20,000) / $3,150,000 = .013 = 1.3%

3.  A.  Current assets / Current liabilities = ($60,000 + $118,000 + $214,000 + $141,000) / ($105,000 + $17,000) = 4.4 (rounded)
    B.  (Cash + Short-term investments + Net current receivables) / Current liabilities = ($60,000 + $118,000 + $214,000) / ( $105,000 + $17,000) = 3.2

**Study Tip:** Remember only the assets that will convert to cash "quickly" are called quick assets. Inventory does not do this.

    C.  Total liabilities / Total assets = ($105,000 + $17,000 + $165,000) / $953,000 = .301 = 30.1%

4.  A.  Market price per share of common stock / Earnings per share = P / $1.28 = 19; P = $24.32 or $24 1/3.

    B.  Dividends per share of common stock / Market price per share of common stock = $1.50 / $24.32 = .06 = 6%

## VI. Beyond the Numbers

The operating cycle for Hoffman Industries is 81 days (rounded). Instruction (C) in the exercise asked you to calculate the days' sales in average receivables. The correct figure was 40.3 days. Another way of characterizing this result is to say that it takes approximately 40 days to collect an average account receivable. Instruction (A) asked you to calculate inventory turnover. The correct amount was 8.89—in other words, inventory "turns" slightly less than 9 times each year. Divide this result into 365 to convert it to days, or 41 days. In other words, on average it takes 41 days for an item to sell and 40 days on average to collect a receivable. Therefore, the operating cycle is 81 days.

# VII. Demonstration Problems

**Demonstration Problem #1 Solved and Explained**

A) working capital = current assets - current liabilities = $673,497 - 892,718 = ($219,221)

> **Study Tip:** When current liabilities exceed current assets, the result is negative working capital. Negative working capital always exists when the current ratio is less than 1.

B) current ratio = current assets ÷ current liabilities = $673,497 ÷ $892,718 = .75 (rounded)

C) acid-test (quick) = quick assets ÷ current liabilities
   = ($101,046 + $356,996) ÷ $892,718 = 0.51 (rounded)

This means Complex has 51 cents of quick assets (cash and short-term investment plus net accounts receivable) for every dollar of current liability.

D) inventory turnover = cost of goods sold / average inventory
   = $1,123,459 ÷ [($138,848 + $170,340) ÷ 2] = 7.27 times

Complex "turns" its inventory 7.27 times each year. Another way of stating this ratio is to convert it to days by dividing the "turn" into 365. For Complex, the turnover averages 50 days (365 ÷ 7.27).

E) accounts receivable turnover = net credit sales ÷ average accounts receivable
   = $2,532,651 ÷ [($315,106 + $356,996) ÷ 2] = 7.54 times

F) days' sales in receivables = average net accounts receivable ÷ one day's sales
   = $336,051 ÷ ($2,532,651 ÷ 365) = 48.4 days

The numerator for this ratio was the denominator for the previous ratio.

G) debt ratio = total liabilities ÷ total assets
   = $1,741,906 ÷ $2,777,952
   = 0.627 or 62.7%

This means that 62.7% of the Complex assets were financed with debt. Notice the numerator (total liabilities) was not presented on the balance sheet but had to be calculated by adding together total current liabilities, long-term debt, other obligations, and deferred income taxes.

H) times-interest-earned = income from operations / interest expense
   = $471,638 ÷ $55,623
   = 8.48 times

Note we used earnings before income taxes plus interest expense as the numerator because interest expense had already been deducted from the earnings before income taxes amount.

I) rate of return on sales = net income ÷ net sales
   = $249,442 ÷ $2,532,651
   = 0.098 0r 9.8%

J)  rate of return on total assets = (net income + interest expense) / average total assets
   = ($249,442 + $55,623) ÷ [($2,178,894 + $2,777,952) ÷ 2]
   = 0.123 or 12.3%

This ratio measures the return on assets generated by this year's operations.

K)  rate of return on common stockholders' equity = (net income - preferred dividends) ÷ average common stockholders' equity
   = ($249,442 - 0) ÷ [($950,087 + $1,036,046) ÷ 2]
   = 0.251 or 25.1%

Complex does not have preferred stock outstanding, so the numerator is the same as net earnings.

L)  earnings per share = (net income - preferred dividends) ÷ weighted average number of common stock outstanding
   = $249,442 ÷ 103,292
   = $2.41 (rounded)

This should be calculated for each "net earnings" amount. Companies are required to include these per share amounts on the income statement, not in the footnotes.

M)  price/earnings ratio = market price per share of common stock ÷ earnings per share
   = $79.3125 ÷ $2.41 = 33 (rounded)

N)  dividend yield = dividend per share of common stock ÷ market price of common stock
   = $1.16 ÷ $79.3125
   = 0.0146 or 1.46%

O)  book value per share of common stock = (total stockholders' equity - preferred equity) ÷ number of shares of common stock outstanding
   = 1,036,046 ÷ 103,164,538
   = $10.04 per share

The dollars are presented "in thousands," so you must add three zeroes to the total stockholders' equity amount. To determine the number of shares outstanding, deduct the treasury shares (7,680,056) from the issued shares (110,844,594). As emphasized in your text, these ratios would have more meaning if you did them over consecutive years. In addition, to properly evaluate a company you would also want to compare the ratios with those of competitors and with the industry as a whole.

**Demonstration Problem #2 Solved and Explained**

1.

<table>
<tr><td colspan="5">Chris Daniel Corporation<br>Balance Sheet<br>Years 19X9 and 19X8</td></tr>
<tr><td></td><td>19X9</td><td>19X8</td><td>Amount Increase (Decrease)</td><td>% Change</td></tr>
<tr><td>Assets</td><td></td><td></td><td></td><td></td></tr>
<tr><td>Current assets:</td><td></td><td></td><td></td><td></td></tr>
<tr><td>Cash</td><td>$ 13,300</td><td>$ 20,350</td><td>$(7,050)</td><td>(34.6)</td></tr>
<tr><td>Short-term investments</td><td>8,200</td><td>8,000</td><td>200</td><td>2.5</td></tr>
<tr><td>Receivables, net</td><td>26,000</td><td>24,000</td><td>2,000</td><td>8.3</td></tr>
<tr><td>Inventories</td><td>45,000</td><td>40,000</td><td>5,000</td><td>12.5</td></tr>
<tr><td>Prepaid expenses</td><td>2,500</td><td>4,650</td><td>(2,150)</td><td>(46.2)</td></tr>
<tr><td>Total current assets</td><td>95,000</td><td>97,000</td><td>(2,000)</td><td>(2.1)</td></tr>
<tr><td>Property, plant, and equipment—net</td><td>185,680</td><td>196,500</td><td>(10,820)</td><td>(5.5)</td></tr>
<tr><td>Land</td><td>40,000</td><td>35,000</td><td>5,000</td><td>14.3</td></tr>
<tr><td>Intangibles and other assets</td><td>2,400</td><td>2,400</td><td>0</td><td>0</td></tr>
<tr><td></td><td>$323,080</td><td>$330,900</td><td>$(7,820)</td><td>(2.4)</td></tr>
<tr><td>Liabilities and stockholders' equity</td><td></td><td></td><td></td><td></td></tr>
<tr><td>Current liabilities:</td><td></td><td></td><td></td><td></td></tr>
<tr><td>Notes payable</td><td>$ 10,000</td><td>$ 10,500</td><td>$ (500)</td><td>(5.0)</td></tr>
<tr><td>Current installments of long-term debt</td><td>3,550</td><td>3,445</td><td>105</td><td>3.0</td></tr>
<tr><td>Accounts payable-trade</td><td>14,447</td><td>18,500</td><td>(4,053)</td><td>(21.9)</td></tr>
<tr><td>Accrued liabilities</td><td>3,670</td><td>1,605</td><td>2,065</td><td>128.7</td></tr>
<tr><td>Total current liabilities</td><td>31,667</td><td>34,050</td><td>(2,383)</td><td>(7.0)</td></tr>
<tr><td>Long-term debt, less current installments</td><td>95,500</td><td>93,330</td><td>2,170</td><td>2.3</td></tr>
<tr><td>Capital lease obligations, less current portion</td><td>1,100</td><td>2,150</td><td>(1,050)</td><td>(48.9)</td></tr>
<tr><td>Deferred income and deferred income taxes</td><td>4,813</td><td>4,370</td><td>443</td><td>10.1</td></tr>
<tr><td>Total common stockholders' equity</td><td>190,000</td><td>197,000</td><td>(7,000)</td><td>(3.6)</td></tr>
<tr><td></td><td>$323,080</td><td>$330,900</td><td>$(7,820)</td><td>(2.4)</td></tr>
</table>

2.

| Chris Daniel Corporation |||||
| Income Statements |||||
| Years 19X9 and 19X8 |||||
| | 19X9 || 19X8 ||
| | Amount | % | Amount | % |
| Net sales | $416,500 | 100.0 | $406,316 | 100.0 |
| Cost and expenses: | | | | |
| Cost of goods sold | 322,593 | 77.5 | 315,812 | 77.7 |
| Operating expenses | 41,219 | 9.9 | 43,200 | 10.6 |
| | 363,812 | | 359,012 | |
| Income from operations | 52,688 | 12.7 | 47,304 | 11.6 |
| Interest expense | 3,251 | 0.8 | 3,150 | .8 |
| Earnings before income taxes | 49,437 | 11.9 | 44,154 | 10.8 |
| Income taxes | 7,437 | 1.8 | 6,554 | 1.6 |
| Net income | $42,000 | 10.1 | $37,600 | 9.3 |

Points to remember:

1. When presenting horizontal analysis, each year's change is divided by the base-year amount (in this case 19X8) and converted to a percentage. While the change in any single item in any single year may not be significant, applying horizontal analysis over a number of years may highlight significant changes.

2. Common-size statements for a single year are only meaningful when the results are compared to other companies or industry data. However, common-size statements covering two or more years permit analysis of the particular company being examined. In this case, we see that 19X9 results improved over 19X8 due to lower cost of goods sold and lower operating expenses.

3. Financial ratios are mathematical formulas that quantify the relationship between two or more items reported in the financial statements. Ratios are used to assess and compare a firm's liquidity, profitability, rate of return, and ability to meet debt obligations.

**Study Tip:** One of the most common mistakes students make is forgetting to use the average amount of inventory, accounts receivable, or shares outstanding in some of the formulas. It is important that an average be used to reduce distortions that might occur if only year-end balances were used.

# Chapter 19 - Introduction to Management Accounting

## CHAPTER OVERVIEW

This chapter is the first of eight introducing you to management accounting. Very few of the topics covered in these chapters result in information available to individuals outside a business. Instead, you will learn about techniques businesses use to assist them in planning and controlling activities. In this chapter you are introduced to management accounting. The learning objectives for the chapter are to

1. Distinguish between financial accounting and management accounting, and use management accounting information for decision making.
2. Describe the value chain and classify costs by value-chain function.
3. Distinguish direct costs from indirect costs.
4. Distinguish among full product costs, inventoriable product costs, and period costs.
5. Prepare the financial statements of a manufacturing company.
6. Identify major trends in the business environment, and use cost-benefit analysis to make business decisions.
7. Use reasonable standards to make ethical judgments.

## CHAPTER REVIEW

### Objective 1 - Distinguish between financial accounting and management accounting, and use management accounting information for decision making.

**Financial accounting** refers to accounting that reports to parties outside a business. This reporting is summarized in the income statement, balance sheet, and cash flows statement. **Management accounting** provides information to individuals inside a business (called managers). This information helps managers to plan and control the business, allocate resources in the organization, and make strategic decisions. Review Exhibit 19-2 in your textbook for a concise summary of the differences between financial and management accounting.

The weighing of costs against benefits to aid decision making is called **cost-benefit analysis**. For planning and control purposes, managers must know the costs of the products and services provided. For service businesses, the most significant cost is labor. For merchandising companies, the most significant cost will be inventory. For manufacturers, the cost of the finished product will include raw materials, labor, and all the costs related to the conversion of the raw materials into a finished good. (See Exhibit 19-3 in your text.)

Manufacturers have three kinds of inventory; materials inventory, work in process inventory, and finished goods inventory. **Materials inventory** consists of the basic materials required to produce a finished good. **Work in process inventory** consists of those goods which have begun the manufacturing process, but are still being converted to a finished good. **Finished goods inventory** refers to those products that have been completed and are ready for sale.

## Objective 2 - Describe the value chain and classify costs by value-chain function.

The **value chain** refers to those business activities that result in value being added to a company's product. Some examples are research and development, manufacturing and marketing. Controlling costs throughout the entire chain is of primary importance to managers. In manufacturing, the term "cost" has a variety of meanings, determined by the context in which it is used. Carefully review Exhibit 19-4 in your text to become familiar with the term "value chain."

## Objective 3 - Distinguish direct costs from indirect costs.

**Direct costs** are costs which can be traced to cost objects, whereas **indirect costs** are costs which cannot be traced to cost objects. A **cost object** can be anything for which a measurement of cost is desired. Therefore, the important consideration in distinguishing direct from indirect costs is the specific cost object. Consider the calculator you use in this accounting course. If it is the cost object, then some of the direct costs will be its plastic casing, the container and packing material in which it was sold, the components inside which make it work, and batteries (if they were included when you purchased it). In other words, each of the costs mentioned can be traced directly to the calculator. However, these are not the only costs involved in the calculator's manufacture. For instance, the building in which the calculator was produced is also a cost, but its cost cannot be traced directly to the calculator. Therefore, the building is an indirect cost. Obviously, if the cost object changes, the assignment of costs as direct or indirect will also change.

## Objective 4 - Distinguish among full product costs, inventoriable product costs, and period costs.

The term **product costs** refers to the costs of producing (if a manufacturer) or purchasing (if a merchandiser) goods intended for sale. The two types of product costs are full product costs and inventoriable product costs. **Full product costs** include all those used throughout the value chain and are used internally as the basis for decision making concerning those products. **Inventoriable product costs** refer to only those product costs regarded as assets for external reporting purposes. Full product costs do not conform to GAAP while inventoriable product costs must conform to GAAP.

For a merchandiser, inventoriable product costs are only those included as Inventory (an asset) until the product is sold, at which time they become part of Cost of Goods Sold. Therefore, inventoriable product costs for a merchandiser would include the actual price paid for the product plus the freight costs. Any other related costs (advertising, sales salaries, etc.) are not inventoriable. These "other" related costs are classified as **period costs**—ones which appear on the income statement in the period in which they are incurred. They never become part of the asset account Inventory.

For a manufacturing company, the inventoriable product costs are more complex. This is due to the manufacturing process (raw materials are combined to create a finished product).

**Manufacturing costs:**

   **Direct materials** 1) become a physical part of the finished product and 2) are separately and conveniently traceable to finished goods.

   **Direct labor** is the cost of salaries and wages of the employees who physically convert materials into finished goods.

**Manufacturing overhead** includes all manufacturing costs other than direct materials and direct labor.

**Indirect materials** are materials used to manufacture a product that are not conveniently traceable to specific finished products. The cost of indirect materials is accounted for as part of manufacturing overhead.

**Indirect labor** consists of the wages and salaries of all factory workers who are not directly involved in converting material into finished goods. The cost of indirect labor is accounted for as part of manufacturing overhead.

**Prime costs** are the sum of direct materials plus direct labor.

**Conversion costs** are the sum of direct labor plus manufacturing overhead.

(Review carefully Exhibit 19-6 in your text.)

## Objective 5 - Prepare the financial statements of a manufacturing company.

### Computing cost of goods manufactured:

1) Cost of goods manufactured = Beginning work in process inventory + Total manufacturing costs - Ending work in process

2) Total manufacturing costs = Direct materials used + Direct labor + Manufacturing overhead

3) Direct materials used = Beginning materials inventory + Purchases - Ending materials inventory

Familiarize yourself with Exhibit 19-10 to be sure you understand how to compute cost of goods manufactured. Study the diagram below. It will help you to understand the flow of inventory costs through a manufacturing company.

| DIRECT MATERIALS | WORK IN PROCESS | FINISHED GOODS |
|---|---|---|
| Beginning inventory<br>+ Purchases | Beginning inventory<br>+ Direct material used<br>   Direct labor<br>   Manufacturing overhead | Beginning inventory<br>+ Cost of goods manufactured |
| Direct materials<br>  available for use<br>- Ending inventory | Total manufacturing costs<br>  to account for<br>- Ending inventory | Goods available for sale<br>- Ending inventory |
| Direct materials<br>  used | Cost of goods<br>  manufactured | Cost of goods sold |

All of the costs that flow through manufacturing inventories are **inventoriable costs**. **Period costs** are not traced through the inventory accounts. They are accounted for as operating expenses and include selling expenses and general and administrative expenses.

## Objective 6 - Identify major trends in the business environment, and use cost-benefit analysis to make business decisions.

Business operations and management accounting are being influenced by several trends in the business environment. Among these are:

1. a shift towards a service economy
2. competing in the global marketplace
3. the just-in-time management philosophy
4. quality

As the economy becomes more service oriented, managers will need increasing amounts of information about the costs of providing services thereby enabling the companies to more competitively price those services.

As the marketplace becomes more global, competition becomes greater so companies will need even more information about costs to make accurate decisions. Relatedly, companies need to consider the costs of domestic manufacture versus the costs of manufacturing elsewhere.

The **just-in-time (JIT) management philosophy** has been adopted by many companies. Originally developed in Japan by Toyota, JIT emphasizes the cost benefits of scheduling production precisely to meet demands thereby eliminating the costs associated with excess raw materials and finished goods inventory. Doing so means the **throughput time** (the length of time from the purchase of raw materials to the actual sale of a finish product) is drastically reduced. Obviously, the shorter the time commitment, the lower the costs. Careful analysis, frequently using present value tables, can assist managers in analyzing the costs-benefits of adopting JIT.

As competition becomes global, customers will be attracted to those products providing the highest quality. **Total quality management** is a philosophy whereby employees not only strive for top quality, but attempt to insure their success through a program of continuous improvement. Ethical behavior is a key indicator of quality.

## Objective 7 – Use reasonable standards to make ethical judgments.

Everyone is faced with ethical dilemmas. Occasionally the correct decision (i.e., the ethical decision) is not always clear cut, particularly when there might be adverse consequences to your decisions. Both the Institute of Management Accountants (IMA) and the American Institute of Certified Public Accountants (AICPA) have adopted Standards of Ethical Conduct which serves as guides. To resolve ethical dilemmas, the IMA suggest discussing ethical situations with a supervisor, or with an objective advisor.

# TEST YOURSELF

All the self-testing materials in this chapter focus on information and procedures that your instructor is likely to test in quizzes and examinations.

**I. Matching** *Match each numbered term with its lettered definition.*

_____ 1. budget
_____ 2. direct labor
_____ 3. direct materials
_____ 4. manufacturing overhead
_____ 5. indirect materials
_____ 6. indirect labor
_____ 7. continuous improvement
_____ 8. cost-benefit analysis
_____ 9. period costs
_____ 10. inventoriable product cost
_____ 11. throughput time
_____ 12. materials inventory
_____ 13. conversion costs
_____ 14. just-in-time
_____ 15. total quality management
_____ 16. value chain
_____ 17. work in process inventory
_____ 18. finished goods inventory
_____ 19. prime costs
_____ 20. cost object

A. the time between buying raw materials and selling the finished products
B. sequence that adds value to a firm's products or services
C. direct labor plus manufacturing overhead
D. the weighing of costs against benefits to aid in decision making
E. all manufacturing costs other than direct materials and direct labor
F. a philosophy requiring employees to continually look for ways to improve performance
G. all costs of a product that are regarded as an asset for financial reporting
H. quantitative expression of a plan of action that helps managers to coordinate and implement that plan
I. completed goods that have not yet been sold
J. cost of salaries and wages for the employees who physically convert materials into the company's products
K. costs that are never traced through the inventory accounts
L. manufacturing labor costs which are difficult to trace to specific products
M. goods that are in production but not complete at the end of the period
N. manufacturing materials whose costs cannot easily be traced to a particular finished product
O. material that becomes a physical part of a finished product and whose cost is separately and conveniently traceable through the manufacturing process to finished goods
P. materials on hand to be used in the manufacturing process
Q. a system in which a company schedules production just in time to satisfy needs
R. a philosophy of satisfying customers by providing them with superior products and services
S. anything for which a separate measurement of costs is desired
T. direct materials plus direct labor

**II. Multiple Choice** *Circle the best answer.*

1. If cost of goods manufactured exceeds total manufacturing costs, which of the following must be true?

   A. finished goods inventory has increased
   B. finished goods inventory has decreased
   C. work in process inventory has decreased
   D. work in process inventory has increased

2. If finished goods inventory has increased, which of the following must be true?

   A. total manufacturing costs are more than cost of goods manufactured
   B. total manufacturing costs are less than cost of goods manufactured
   C. cost of goods sold is less than cost of goods manufactured
   D. cost of goods sold is more than cost of goods manufactured

3. All of the following are period costs except:

   A. office supplies expense
   B. factory supervisor's salary
   C. advertising expense
   D. delivery expense

4. Total manufacturing costs equals:

   A. direct materials plus direct labor plus manufacturing overhead
   B. beginning finished goods inventory plus cost of goods manufactured
   C. beginning work in process plus direct materials plus direct labor plus manufacture overhead
   D. beginning finished goods plus cost of goods manufactured less ending finished goods inventory

5. Which of the following would not be included in manufacturing overhead?

   A. factory utilities
   B. repairs to manufacturing equipment
   C. property taxes on the factory
   D. supplies used in the warehouse

6. If beginning finished goods inventory is $55,000, ending finished goods inventory is $40,000, and cost of goods sold is $385,000, then cost of goods manufactured must be:

   A. $480,000
   B. $400,000
   C. $370,000
   D. cannot be determined

7. Which of the following is not an inventoriable product cost?

   A. indirect labor
   B. direct labor
   C. sales commissions
   D. direct materials

8. Which of the following accounts would not be found in a merchandiser's records?

   A. Supplies
   B. Merchandise Inventory
   C. Work in Process Inventory
   D. Finished Goods Inventory

9. Which of the following is a period cost?

   A. materials used
   B. office salary expense
   C. depreciation expense - manufacturing
   D. manufacturing wages expense

10. Throughput time refers to:

    A. the time between selling a product and collecting the receivable
    B. the time between purchasing raw materials and completing the finished product
    C. the time between purchasing raw materials and placing those materials into production
    D. the time between purchasing raw materials and selling the finished product

## III. Completion   *Complete each of the following.*

1. The dual objectives of a cost accounting system are _____ and _____.
2. The inventory accounts of a manufacturing firm will include _____, _____, and _____ inventories.
3. _____ are a physical part of the finished product and their cost is separately and conveniently traceable through the manufacturing process.
4. Indirect materials and indirect labor are part of _____.
5. _____ are also called inventoriable costs.
6. _____ are never traced through the inventory accounts.
7. A reduction in throughput time is a feature of _____ management philosophy.
8. Prime costs include _____ and _____.
9. Conversion costs include _____ and _____.
10. Educating, training, and cross-training employees are all features of _____.

## IV. Daily Exercises

1. If cost of goods manufactured was $240,000, and beginning and ending Work in Process Inventories were $18,000 and $21,000 respectively, what were total manufacturing costs?

2. Work in Process Inventory increased $4,000 during the year for a manufacturing company. Total manufacturing costs were $305,000. What was Cost of Goods Manufactured?

3. Given the following information, calculate total Manufacturing Overhead:

| | |
|---|---:|
| Factory Building Depreciation | $ 50,000 |
| Sales Office Expense | 4,400 |
| Factory Equipment Depreciation | 21,900 |
| Advertising Expense | 51,000 |
| Administrative Salaries | 202,000 |
| Property Taxes - Manufacturing | 42,000 |
| Depreciation on Delivery Equipment | 17,000 |
| Office Utilities Expense | 8,200 |
| Indirect Materials | 2,700 |
| Factory Equipment Repair Expense | 6,600 |
| Indirect Labor | 12,500 |
| Utilities Expense - Manufacturing | 9,100 |

4. Given the following information, determine the amount of direct materials used.

| | |
|---|---:|
| Raw Material Inventory, 12/31 | $ 15,000 |
| Freight-In | 1,200 |
| Materials Returns | 10,300 |
| Raw Materials Inventory, 1/1 | 17,800 |
| Discounts on Materials Purchases | 3,480 |
| Raw Material Purchases | 109,740 |

5. Review the information in Daily Exercise #4 above and calculate total manufacturing costs, assuming direct labor was $67,580 and manufacturing overhead was $71,065.

6. Review the information in Daily Exercises #4 and #5 above and calculate cost of goods manufactured assuming Beginning Work in Process was $23,810 and Ending Work in Process was $19,770.

## V. Exercises

1. The following information pertains to Ace Manufacturing, Inc., for 19X9:

   | | |
   |---|---|
   | Cost of Goods Sold | $425,000 |
   | Direct Materials Purchased | 170,000 |
   | Direct Materials Used | 158,000 |
   | Ending Work in Process Inventory Less Beginning Work in Process Inventory | 18,000 |

   Finished Goods Inventory did not change.
   Manufacturing Overhead is twice direct labor cost.
   Beginning Work in Process Inventory is 25% of Ending Work in Process Inventory.

   A. Compute Beginning and Ending Work in Process Inventories.

   B. Compute Cost of Goods Manufactured.

   C. Compute Total Manufacturing Costs.

D. Compute Direct Labor and Manufacturing Overhead.

2. Using a check mark, indicate if the following list of accounts would appear in the records of a service, merchandising, or manufacturing business. Some of the accounts may appear in more than one business.

| Accounts | Service | Merchandising | Manufacturing |
|---|---|---|---|
| Fees Earned | | | |
| Cost of Goods Sold | | | |
| Merchandise Inventory | | | |
| Freight-In | | | |
| Sales Discounts | | | |
| Advertising Expense | | | |
| Raw Materials Inventory | | | |
| Purchase Discounts | | | |
| Factory Wages | | | |
| Insurance Expense | | | |
| Prepaid Rent | | | |
| Work in Process Inventory | | | |
| Sales Returns | | | |
| Finished Goods Inventory | | | |
| Office Salary Expense | | | |
| Payroll Tax Expense | | | |
| Purchase Discounts | | | |
| Manufacturing Overhead | | | |

3. Novis Company wants to adopt a Just-in-Time (JIT) system for manufacturing their electrical components. A review of their current traditional system compared with a JIT system indicates Novis would incur the following additional costs:

| | |
|---|---|
| Cost to remodel the raw materials warehouse | $450,000 |
| Cost to re-configure the manufacturing facility | $670,000 |
| Cost to train workforce | $140,000 |
| Lost sales during changeover | $850,000 |

Novis estimates a change to the JIT system will result in an annual reduction in overall operating expenses of $385,000 for the next eight years. Assuming a 10% discount rate (use Exhibit 15A-7 in your text), analyze the costs and benefits if JIT is adopted.

4. Review the information in Exercise #3 above and assume the following additional facts:

Further analysis indicates the $385,000 cost reduction has a 70% probability of resulting while a lesser cost savings of $260,000 has a 30% probability of occurring. However, management will be able to rent out the excess space in the raw materials warehouse for $8,000 per month ($96,000 annually). Given this additional information, what are the costs and benefits of adopting JIT?

## VI. Beyond the Numbers

When would the use of direct labor costs not be an appropriate base for allocating manufacturing overhead?

## VII. Demonstration Problems

### Demonstration Problem #1

Lifestyle Liquids manufactures a variety of organic vegetable and fruit juice blends, all sold exclusively in health-food stores. During the current period, the following amounts were recorded:

| | |
|---|---:|
| Freight-In | $ 650 |
| Insurance Expense – Delivery Trucks | 1,400 |
| Depreciation Expense – Manufacturing Equipment | 2,770 |
| Payroll Tax Expense – Manufacturing Wages | 14,215 |
| Utilities Expense – Manufacturing | 9,970 |
| Sales Salaries Expense | 124,000 |
| Advertising Expense | 72,440 |
| Fresh Organic Vegetables | 189,600 |
| Manufacturing Wage Expense – Direct | 204,114 |
| Research and Development Expenses | 71,265 |
| Miscellaneous Selling Expense | 820 |
| Fresh Organic Fruits | 161,970 |
| Sales Discounts | 2,775 |
| Fresh Vegetable/Fruit Returns | 3,545 |
| Manufacturing Supervisor Salaries | 51,150 |
| Product Design Expenses | 81,735 |
| Consumer Hotline Expense | 36,000 |
| Sales | 1,937,400 |
| Purchase Discounts | 2,030 |
| Sales Returns/Allowances | 8,990 |
| Fresh Herbs/Spices/Flavoring | 810 |
| Maintenance Expense – Manufacturing | 14,930 |
| Property Tax Expense – Manufacturing | 28,790 |
| Container Expense | 104,720 |
| Delivery Wages Expense | 80,205 |

**Requirement 1** - Using the format which follows, classify the above costs according to their place in the value chain. When you have finished, total each column.

|  | Research | Design | Production |  |  | Marketing | Distribution | Customer Service |
|---|---|---|---|---|---|---|---|---|
|  |  |  | DM | DL | MO |  |  |  |
| Freight-In |  |  |  |  |  |  |  |  |
| Insurance Expense – Delivery Trucks |  |  |  |  |  |  |  |  |
| Depreciation Expense – Manufacturing Equipment |  |  |  |  |  |  |  |  |
| Payroll Tax Expense – Manufacturing Wages |  |  |  |  |  |  |  |  |
| Utilities Expense – Manufacturing |  |  |  |  |  |  |  |  |
| Sales Salaries Expense |  |  |  |  |  |  |  |  |
| Advertising Expense |  |  |  |  |  |  |  |  |
| Fresh Organic Vegetables |  |  |  |  |  |  |  |  |
| Manufacturing Wage Expense – Direct |  |  |  |  |  |  |  |  |
| Research and Development Expenses |  |  |  |  |  |  |  |  |
| Miscellaneous Selling Expense |  |  |  |  |  |  |  |  |
| Fresh Organic Fruits |  |  |  |  |  |  |  |  |
| Sales Discounts |  |  |  |  |  |  |  |  |
| Fresh Vegetable/Fruit Returns |  |  |  |  |  |  |  |  |
| Manufacturing Supervisor Salaries |  |  |  |  |  |  |  |  |
| Product Design Expenses |  |  |  |  |  |  |  |  |
| Consumer Hotline Expense |  |  |  |  |  |  |  |  |
| Sales |  |  |  |  |  |  |  |  |
| Purchase Discounts |  |  |  |  |  |  |  |  |
| Sales Returns/Allowances |  |  |  |  |  |  |  |  |
| Fresh Herbs/Spices/Flavoring |  |  |  |  |  |  |  |  |
| Maintenance Expense – Manufacturing |  |  |  |  |  |  |  |  |
| Property Tax Expense – Manufacturing |  |  |  |  |  |  |  |  |
| Container Expense |  |  |  |  |  |  |  |  |
| Delivery Wages Expense |  |  |  |  |  |  |  |  |
| Totals |  |  |  |  |  |  |  |  |

## Requirement 2 – Calculate the following

a. total full product costs

b. total inventoriable product costs

c. total prime costs

d. total conversion costs

e. total period costs

## Demonstration Problem #2

Lifestyle Liquids had the following inventories for the current period:

| | |
|---|---|
| Raw Materials, 1/1 | $18,680 |
| Work in Process, 1/1 | 8,225 |
| Finished Goods, 1/1 | 30,005 |
| | |
| Raw Materials, 12/31 | 14,130 |
| Work in Process, 12/31 | 7,830 |
| Finished Goods, 12/31 | 34,375 |

**Requirement 1** – In the space provided, present the annual Schedule of Cost of Goods Manufactured for Lifestyle Liquids using the appropriate amounts from both Demonstration Problem #1 and the inventory values listed above.

**Requirement 2** – In the space provided, present the annual Income Statement for Lifestyle Liquids using the appropriate amounts above and from Demonstration Problem #1.

# SOLUTIONS

## I. Matching

| | | | | |
|---|---|---|---|---|
| 1. H | 5. N | 9. K | 13. C | 17. M |
| 2. J | 6. L | 10. G | 14. Q | 18. I |
| 3. O | 7. F | 11. A | 15. R | 19. T |
| 4. E | 8. D | 12. P | 16. B | 20. S |

## II. Multiple Choice

1. **C** Recall:
   Beginning Work in Process Inventory
   + Total Manufacturing Costs
   − Ending Work in Process Inventory
   = Cost of Goods Manufactured
   
   If cost of goods manufactured exceeds total manufacturing costs, then the effect on WIP inventory must be positive. Accordingly, beginning WIP must be greater than ending WIP inventory. If the ending balance is smaller than the beginning balance, the inventory has decreased.

2. **C** Recall:
   Beginning Finished Goods Inventory
   + Cost of Goods Manufactured
   = Goods Available for Sale
   − Ending Finished Goods Inventory
   = Cost of Goods Sold
   
   If finished goods inventory has increased, the net effect of finished goods on the above formula is negative. Accordingly, Cost of Goods Sold would be less than Cost of Goods Manufactured. Answers A and B are incorrect because they do not relate to the finished goods account.

3. **B** The factory supervisor's salary is a component of manufacturing overhead and therefore an inventoriable product cost, not a period cost.

4. **A** Manufacturing costs is synonymous with inventoriable costs, i.e., direct materials, direct labor plus manufacturing overhead.

5. **D** Warehouse supplies are a cost incurred after the product has been manufactured and would not be included in manufacturing overhead.

6. **C** The formula is beginning finished goods inventory + cost of goods manufactured − ending finished goods inventory = cost of goods sold. $55,000 + X − $40,000 = $385,000; so X = $370,000.

7. **C** Inventoriable product costs = direct materials + direct labor + manufacturing overhead. Indirect labor is a component of manufacturing overhead. Sales commissions are a period cost, not a product cost.

8. C  The Work in Process Inventory account relates to a manufacturer, not a merchandiser. Finished Goods Inventory is synonymous with Merchandise Inventory.

9. B  Of those listed, only office salaries is a period cost. Materials, manufacturing depreciation, and manufacturing wages are all inventoriable costs.

10. D

## III. Completion

1. cost control, product costing
2. materials, work in process, finished goods
3. Direct materials
4. manufacturing overhead
5. Products costs
6. Period costs
7. just-in-time (JIT)
8. direct materials, direct labor
9. direct labor, manufacturing overhead
10. total quality management (TQM)

## IV. Daily Exercises

1.  
|   | | |
|---|---|---|
| | Beginning Work in Process | $ 18,000 |
| + | Total Manufacturing Costs | ? |
| − | Ending Work in Process | 21,000 |
| = | Cost of Goods Manufactured | $240,000 |

Total Manufacturing Costs = $243,000

2.  
|   | | |
|---|---|---|
| | Beginning Work in Process | $ X |
| + | Total Manufacturing Costs | 305,000 |
| − | Ending Work in Process | X + 4,000 |
| = | Cost of Goods Manufactured | $ ? |

X + $305,000 − (X + $4,000) = $301,000

3.  
| | |
|---|---|
| Factory Building Depreciation | $ 50,000 |
| Factory Equipment Depreciation | 21,900 |
| Property Taxes – Manufacturing | 42,000 |
| Indirect Materials | 2,700 |
| Factory Equipment Repair Expense | 6,600 |
| Indirect Labor | 12,500 |
| Utilities Expense – Manufacturing | 9,100 |
| Total Manufacturing Overhead | $144,800 |

4.

| | | |
|---|---|---|
| Beginning Raw Materials Inventory | | $17,800 |
| Add: Raw Materials Purchases | 109,740 | |
| Freight-In | 1,200 | |
| | 110,940 | |
| Less: Returns | 10,300 | |
| Discounts | 3,480 | 13,780 |
| Net Raw Materials Purchases | | 97,160 |
| Raw Materials Available for Use | | 114,960 |
| Less: Ending Raw Materials Inventory | | 15,000 |
| Raw Materials Used | | $99,960 |

**Study Tip:** This format is identical to the one you learned in the Chapter 5 Appendix for cost of goods sold.

5. Total Manufacturing Costs = Direct Materials + Direct Labor + Manufacturing Overhead

| | |
|---|---|
| Direct Materials | $ 99,960 |
| Direct Labor | 67,580 |
| Manufacturing Overhead | 71,065 |
| Total Manufacturing Costs | $238,605 |

6. Cost of Goods Manufactured = Beginning Work in Process + Total Manufacturing Costs - Ending Work in Process

| | |
|---|---|
| Beginning Work in Process | $ 23,810 |
| Total Manufacturing Costs | 238,605 |
| | 261,415 |
| Less: Ending Work in Process | 19,770 |
| Cost of Goods Manufactured | $241,645 |

**Study Tip:** Remember, "Total Manufacturing Costs" and "Costs of Goods Manufactured" are NOT synonymous terms.

## V. Exercises

1.
  A.
  Beginning Work in Process = .25 × Ending Work in Process
  Ending Work in Process - .25 × Ending Work in Process = $18,000
  Ending Work in Process = $24,000
  Beginning Work in Process = .25 × $24,000 = $6,000

  B. Beginning FG + Cost of Goods Manufactured - Ending FG = COGS
  Beginning FG = Ending FG
  Cost of Goods Manufactured = COGS = $425,000

C. 
|   |   |   |
|---|---|---|
|   | Beginning Work in Process | $ 6,000 |
| + | Total Manufacturing Costs | X |
| − | Ending Work in Process | 24,000 |
| = | Cost of Goods Manufactured | $425,000 |

Total Manufacturing Costs = $443,000

D.

|   |   |   |
|---|---|---|
|   | Direct Materials Used | $158,000 |
| + | Direct Labor | X |
| + | Manufacturing Overhead | 2X |
| = | Total Manufacturing Costs | $443,000 |

3X = $285,000
X = $95,000 (Direct Labor)
2X = $190,000 (Manufacturing Overhead)

2.

| Accounts | Service | Merchandising | Manufacturing |
|---|---|---|---|
| Fees Earned | √ |   |   |
| Cost of Goods Sold |   | √ | √ |
| Merchandise Inventory |   | √ |   |
| Freight-In |   | √ | √ |
| Sales Discounts |   | √ | √ |
| Advertising Expense | √ | √ | √ |
| Raw Materials Inventory |   |   | √ |
| Purchase Discounts |   | √ | √ |
| Factory Wages |   |   | √ |
| Insurance Expense | √ | √ | √ |
| Prepaid Rent | √ | √ | √ |
| Work in Process Inventory |   |   | √ |
| Sales Returns |   | √ | √ |
| Finished Goods Inventory |   |   | √ |
| Office Salary Expense | √ | √ | √ |
| Payroll Tax Expense | √ | √ | √ |
| Purchase Discounts |   | √ | √ |
| Manufacturing Overhead |   |   | √ |

3. Costs to adopt JIT:

| | |
|---|---|
| Raw Materials Warehouse | $ 450,000 |
| Manufacturing Facility | 670,000 |
| Training | 140,000 |
| Lost Sales | 850,000 |
| | $2,110,000 |

Benefits: $385,000 \times 5.335^* = \underline{\$1,867,250}$
*From Exhibit 15A-7, 10% for 8 periods = 5.335

4. The costs do not change, only the benefits, as follows:

$385,000 \times 5.335 = \$1,867,250 \times .7 = 1,307,075$
$260,000 \times 5.335 = \$1,387,100 \times .3 = 416,130$
$\$ 96,000 \times 5.335 = \phantom{xxxxxxxxxxxxxxxxx} 512,160$
$\phantom{xxxxxxxxxxxxxxxxxxxxxxxxxxxxxxxxxxxxxxxxxxxx} \$2,235,365$

Obviously, this additional information makes the proposal more attractive.

## VI. Beyond the Numbers

Direct labor costs should not be used to allocate manufacturing overhead when direct labor is not the cost driver for overhead. For instance, with the increasing use of robots in manufacturing, direct labor costs are minor (or nonexistent). In this case, machine hours (or the total machine costs) might be a more appropriate base for allocating overhead.

## VII. Demonstration Problems

### Demonstration Problem #1 Solved and Explained

**Requirement 1**

| Item | Research | Design | Production DM | Production DL | Production MO | Marketing | Distribution | Customer Service |
|---|---|---|---|---|---|---|---|---|
| Freight-In | | | $ 650 | | | | | |
| Insurance Expense – Delivery Trucks | | | | | | | $ 1,400 | |
| Depreciation Expense – Manufacturing Equipment | | | | | $ 2,770 | | | |
| Payroll Tax Expense – Manufacturing Wages | | | | $ 14,215 | | | | |
| Utilities Expense – Manufacturing | | | | | 9,970 | | | |
| Sales Salaries Expense | | | | | | $124,000 | | |
| Advertising Expense | | | | | | 72,440 | | |
| Fresh Organic Vegetables | | | 189,600 | | | | | |
| Manufacturing Wage Expense – Direct | | | | 204,114 | | | | |
| Research and Development Expenses | $71,265 | | | | | | | |
| Miscellaneous Selling Expense | | | | | | 820 | | |
| Fresh Organic Fruits | | | 161,970 | | | | | |
| Sales Discounts | | | | | | | | |
| Fresh Vegetable/Fruit Returns | | | (3,545) | | | | | |
| Manufacturing Supervisor Salaries | | | | | 51,150 | | | |
| Product Design Expenses | | $81,735 | | | | | | |
| Consumer Hotline Expense | | | | | | | | $36,000 |
| Sales | | | | | | | | |
| Purchase Discounts | | | (2,030) | | | | | |
| Sales Returns/Allowances | | | | | | | | |
| Fresh Herbs/Spices/Flavoring | | | 810 | | | | | |
| Maintenance Expense – Manufacturing | | | | | 14,930 | | | |
| Property Tax Expense – Manufacturing | | | | | 28,790 | | | |
| Container Expense | | | 104,720 | | | | | |
| Delivery Wages Expense | | | | | | | 80,205 | |
| Totals | $71,265 | $81,735 | $452,175 | $218,329 | $107,610 | $197,260 | $81,605 | $36,000 |

> **Study Tip:** Sales, Sales Discounts, and Sales Returns/Allowance are not listed because they are not "costs."

## Requirement 2

a. total full product costs = all costs associated with the value chain

| | |
|---|---:|
| Research | $ 71,265 |
| Design | 81,735 |
| Production – DM | 452,175 |
| Production – DL | 218,329 |
| Production – MO | 107,610 |
| Marketing | 197,260 |
| Distribution | 81,605 |
| Customer Service | 36,000 |
| Total Full Product Costs | $1,245,979 |

b. total inventoriable product costs = total production costs

| | |
|---|---:|
| Direct Materials | $452,175 |
| Direct Labor | 218,329 |
| Manufacturing Overhead | 107,610 |
| | $778,114 |

c. total prime costs = direct materials + direct labor

| | |
|---|---:|
| Direct Materials | $452,175 |
| Direct Labor | 218,329 |
| Total | $670,504 |

d. total conversion costs = direct labor + manufacturing overhead

| | |
|---|---:|
| Direct Labor | $218,329 |
| Manufacturing Overhead | 107,610 |
| Total | $325,939 |

e. total period costs = total full product costs less total inventoriable product costs

| | | |
|---|---|---|
| total full product costs | = | $1,245,979 (from (a) above) |
| total inventoriable product costs | = | 778,114 (from (b) above) |
| total period costs | = | $ 467,865 |

Introduction to Management Accounting 513

**Demonstration Problem #2 Solved**

**Requirement 1**

Lifestyle Liquids<br>
Schedule of Cost of Goods Manufactured<br>
1/1 – 12/31

| | | | | |
|---|---|---|---|---|
| Beginning Work in Process | | | | $ 8,225 |
| Add: Direct Materials | | | | |
|   Beginning Inventory | | $ 18,680 | | |
|   Add: Purchases | | 457,100 | | |
|     Freight-In | | 650 | | |
|     Total | | 476,430 | | |
|     Less: Discounts | $2,030 | | | |
|       Returns | 3,545 | 5,575 | | |
|     Net Direct Material Available | | 470,855 | | |
|     Less: Ending Direct Material Inventory | | 14,130 | | |
|   Direct Material Used | | | 456,725 | |
|   Direct Labor | | | 218,329 | |
| Manufacturing Overhead: | | | | |
|   Depreciation Expense – Manufacturing Equipment | | 2,770 | | |
|   Utilities Expense | | 9,970 | | |
|   Supervisor Salaries | | 51,150 | | |
|   Maintenance Expense | | 14,930 | | |
|   Property Taxes | | 28,790 | 107,610 | |
|   Total Manufacturing Costs Incurred | | | | 782,664 |
|   Total Manufacturing Costs to Account for | | | | 790,889 |
|   Less: Ending Work in Process Inventory | | | | 7,820 |
| Cost of Goods Manufactured | | | | $783,069 |

**Requirement 2**

Lifestyle Liquids  
Income Statement  
1/1 – 12/31

| | | |
|---|---:|---:|
| Revenues: | | |
|   Sales | | $ 1,937,400 |
|   Less: Sales Discounts | $ 2,775 | |
|     Sales Returns/Allowance | 8,990 | 11,765 |
|   Net Sales | | 1,925,635 |
| Cost of Goods Sold: | | |
|   Beginning Inventory | 30,005 | |
|   Add: Cost of Goods Manufactured | 783,069 | |
|   Goods Available for Sale | 813,074 | |
|   Less: Ending Inventory | 34,375 | |
|   Cost of Goods Sold | | 778,699 |
| Gross Profit | | 1,146,936 |
| Less: Operating Expenses | | |
|   Research | 71,265 | |
|   Design | 81,735 | |
|   Marketing | 197,260 | |
|   Distribution | 81,605 | |
|   Customer Service | 36,000 | |
|     Total Operating Expenses | | 467,865 |
| Net Income | | $ 679,071 |

# Chapter 20 - Job Costing

## CHAPTER OVERVIEW

In Chapter 19, you were introduced to Management Accounting and some topics unique to manufacturing operations. We now apply that information to one specific type of cost accounting system—job costing. This chapter is followed by a second type of cost accounting system—process costing. The learning objectives for this chapter are to

1. Distinguish between job costing and process costing.
2. Account for materials and labor in a manufacturer's job costing system.
3. Account for manufacturing overhead, including underallocated and overallocated overhead in a manufacturer's job costing system.
4. Account for non-inventoriable costs using job costing.

## CHAPTER REVIEW

### Objective 1 – Distinguish between job costing and process costing.

The two major types of costing systems are **job costing and process costing**. Both types share common characteristics. For instance, both accumulate the same type of costs – direct materials, direct labor, and manufacturing overhead. Also, both systems average these accumulated costs over the number of units produced. The major distinguishing characteristic between the two is the cost object. As the names imply, the cost object in job costing is a job (from raw materials to finished good) whereas the cost object in process costing is a specific process (blending, baking, finishing, packaging, for instance) Review Exhibit 20-2 in your text for a comparison between the two. Generally, job costing requires less averaging because the output is usually less – frequently only a single unit (a large construction project, for instance) or a small number of units. Process costing, in contrast, usually results in a high number of units being "processed" so costs are averaged over a larger base. In both systems, the per unit cost is calculated the same, as follows:

$$\frac{\text{Total Costs}}{\text{Total Units}} = \text{Cost per unit}$$

Also, both job and process costing can be found in service and merchandising businesses, in addition to manufacturers. Review Exhibit 20-1 in your text which presents a matrix comparing job and process costing in service, merchandising, and manufacturing businesses.

In job costing, a job cost record is used to accumulate costs for each job. Remember that manufacturing "costs" include direct materials, direct labor, and manufacturing overhead. The job cost record continues to accumulate direct materials and direct labor until the job is complete, at which time manufacturing overhead is allocated. Exhibit 20-3 in your text is an example of a job cost record.

### Objective 2 – Account for materials and labor in a manufacturer's job costing system.

A manufacturer acquires materials by sending a purchase order to a supplier. When the materials are received, a receiving report is prepared and a journal entry is recorded:

| | | |
|---|---|---|
| Materials Inventory | XX | |
|     Accounts Payable | | XX |

A **subsidiary materials ledger** is maintained which tracks the receipt, usage, and the balance of each materials inventory item. See Exhibit 20-4.

When a job is entered into production, a **materials requisition** is prepared to have materials transferred from inventory storage to the factory floor. See Exhibit 20-6.

The cost of direct materials is debited to Work in Process Inventory, while the cost of any indirect materials is debited to Manufacturing Overhead:

| | | |
|---|---|---|
| Work in Process Inventory | XX | |
| Manufacturing Overhead | XX | |
|     Materials Inventory | | XX |

This entry records the transfer of materials from inventory to the manufacturing process. At the same time, the cost of the direct materials is entered on the job cost record.

A **labor time ticket** (Exhibit 20-8 in your text) is used to accumulate the time spent on a job and the labor cost associated with the job.

Manufacturing wages are recorded with this entry:

| | | |
|---|---|---|
| Manufacturing Wages | XX | |
|     Wages Payable | | XX |

Based on the information from the labor time tickets, the balance in the Manufacturing Wages account is allocated to direct labor and indirect labor, and recorded with this entry:

| | | |
|---|---|---|
| Work in Process Inventory | XX | |
| Manufacturing Overhead | XX | |
|     Manufacturing Wages | | XX |

The direct labor costs associated with each job are posted to the appropriate job cost records.

Exhibit 20-10 in your text summarizes accounting for materials and labor in job costing.

## Objective 3 - Account for manufacturing overhead in a manufacturer's job costing system.

During the year, overhead costs are debited to Manufacturing Overhead as they are incurred:

| | | |
|---|---|---|
| Manufacturing Overhead | XX | |
|     Various Accounts | | XX |

At year end, Manufacturing Overhead contains all the actual overhead costs of the period. Our task now is to determine how to apply these overhead costs to the products that were produced. However, applying overhead costs to production cannot wait until the end of each year. Accountants usually compute a **predetermined manufacturing overhead rate** so that overhead can be applied during the year:

$$\text{Predetermined manufacturing overhead rate} = \frac{\text{Estimated manufacturing overhead costs}}{\text{Estimated quantity of the manufacturing overhead allocation base}}$$

To accurately allocate manufacturing overhead, the allocation base should the primary cost driver of those overhead costs. Historically, direct labor (expressed as either dollars or hours) has been the primary cost driver in many manufacturing operations. While this remains the case in some industries, increasingly some other cost driver becomes primary, particularly in highly automated processes. Obviously, selecting the primary cost driver accurately will insure the most realistic total cost for each job. To develop a predetermined rate and allocate overhead:

1. Select a cost allocation base
2. Estimate the total overhead cost for the planning period
3. Estimate the total quantity of the overhead allocation base
4. Compute the predetermined manufacturing overhead rate
5. Obtain actual quantities of the overhead allocation base used by individual jobs
6. Allocate manufacturing overhead jobs

The entry to record the allocation of overhead is:

| | | |
|---|---|---|
| Work in Process Inventory | XX | |
| Manufacturing Overhead | | XX |

Once overhead is allocated to a job, we can compute unit cost:

$$\text{unit cost} = \frac{\text{direct materials + direct labor + overhead allocated}}{\text{number of units produced}}$$

As jobs are completed, they are transferred to finished goods:

| | | |
|---|---|---|
| Finished Goods Inventory | XX | |
| Work in Process Inventory | | XX |

When goods are sold, these two entries are recorded:

| | | |
|---|---|---|
| Accounts Receivable | XX | |
| Sales Revenue (Retail selling price) | | XX |

| | | |
|---|---|---|
| Cost of Goods Sold (Cost) | XX | |
| Finished Goods Inventory | | XX |

Note: The difference in these two entries represents gross profit.

Consider this T-account:

| Manufacturing Overhead | |
|---|---|
| Actual | Allocated |

If allocated overhead is less than actual overhead (a debit balance remains), then overhead is **underallocated**. If allocated overhead is greater than actual overhead (a credit balance remains), then overhead is **overallocated**.

Insignificant amounts of over- or underallocated overhead are closed to Cost of Goods Sold at year end. Significant amounts of over- or underallocated overhead are distributed to Work in Process, Finished Goods, and Cost of Goods Sold.

The process for distributing a significant amount of over- or under allocated overhead is called **proration**. Proration spreads the remaining debit balance (representing an under-allocation) or credit balance (representing an over-allocation) to the three accounts in proportion to the balance in each.

Whether significant or insignificant, the balance of the Manufacturing Overhead account should be zero at the end.

Review Exhibit 20-12 in your text for a summary of job costing.

## Objective 4 – Account for non-inventoriable costs using job costing.

Recall from Chapter 19 that inventoriable costs refer to only manufacturing costs (direct materials, direct labor, and manufacturing overhead) and not to the costs incurred in other elements of the value chain. However, these non-inventoriable costs can also be traced and allocated using the same principles introduced in the preceding sections of this chapter. However, non-inventoriable costs will not result in journal entries because GAAP only allows inventoriable costs to be reflected in the accounting records.

As illustrated in Exhibit 20-1, both job and process costing systems can also be used by service and merchandising businesses.

Obviously, a service business will not have any direct materials assigned to particular jobs (a lawyer advising a client, a CPA preparing a tax return, a physician examining a patient, etc.); however, direct labor can constitute a significant portion of the fee charged for the service. In addition, every service business will incur many indirect costs (rent, utilities, insurance, salaries for support staff, etc.) and these costs need to be accurately allocated to jobs if the business owner is going to have a realistic picture of business operations. In order to allocate these direct costs, follow the same six steps listed earlier for manufacturers:

1. Select a cost allocation base – in most cases this will be direct labor
2. Estimate the total indirect costs – last year's costs, adjusted for anticipated increases, will provide a reasonable basis for the estimate
3. Estimate the total quantity of the cost allocation base – as in #2 above, last year's figures could be the basis for a reasonable estimate for the current year
4. Compute the predetermined indirect cost allocation rate (step 2 divided by step 3)
5. Obtain the actual quantity of the indirect cost allocation base used by individual jobs – this should occur through normal business operation as individual jobs are completed
6. Allocate indirect costs to jobs by multiplying the predetermined indirect cost rate by the actual quantity of the allocation base pertaining to each job (step 4 times step 5)

# TEST YOURSELF

All the self-testing materials in this chapter focus on information and procedures that your instructor is likely to test in quizzes and examinations.

**I. Matching**   *Match each numbered term with its lettered definition.*

_____ 1. predetermined manufacturing overhead rate
_____ 2. job cost record
_____ 3. cost driver
_____ 4. cost allocation base
_____ 5. cost allocation
_____ 6. cost assignment
_____ 7. labor time ticket
_____ 8. materials requisition
_____ 9. overallocated overhead
_____ 10. underallocated overhead
_____ 11. cost tracing
_____ 12. job costing
_____ 13. process costing
_____ 14. time record

A. a common denominator for systematically linking indirect costs to products
B. any factor that affects costs
C. document used to accumulate the costs of a job
D. request for materials, prepared by manufacturing personnel
E. source document used primarily by employees engaging in service activities, to trace direct labor to specific costs
F. a credit balance in manufacturing overhead after overhead has been allocated to jobs
G. system for assigning costs to large numbers of identical units that usually proceed in a continuos fashion through a series of uniform production processes
H. estimated manufacturing overhead rate computed at the beginning of the year
I. source document manufacturing firms commonly use to trace direct labor to specific job cost records
J. assigning indirect costs to cost objects
K. assigning direct costs to cost objects
L. a general term that covers both tracing direct costs and allocating indirect costs
M. a remaining debit balance in manufacturing overhead after overhead has been allocated to jobs
N. a system for assigning costs to specific units or to a small batch of products

**II. Multiple Choice**   *Circle the best answer.*

1. When manufacturing labor costs are incurred, that amount credited is:

   A. Manufacturing Wages
   B. Wages Payable
   C. Manufacturing Overhead
   D. Work In Process Inventory

2. Which of the following is not an inventoriable cost?

   A. Manufacturing Overhead
   B. Indirect Materials
   C. Delivery Materials
   D. Delivery Expense

3. Which of the following manufacturers would be most likely to use process costing?

   A. oil refinery
   B. contractors
   C. aircraft
   D. furniture

520   Chapter 20

4. When indirect materials are used in production:

   A. Work In Process Inventory is debited
   B. Manufacturing Overhead is credited
   C. Manufacturing Overhead is debited
   D. Materials Inventory is debited

5. When direct materials are used in production:

   A. Work In Process Inventory is credited
   B. Manufacturing Overhead is debited
   C. Materials Inventory is debited
   D. Work In Process Inventory is debited

6. When manufacturing wages are allocated, indirect labor is:

   A. Debited to Work In Process Inventory
   B. Debited to Manufacturing Overhead
   C. Credited to Manufacturing Overhead
   D. Credited to Work In Process Inventory

7. The entry to debit Cost of Goods Sold and credit Finished Goods Inventory as sales are made is recorded in:

   A. a periodic inventory system
   B. a perpetual inventory system
   C. both a periodic inventory system and a perpetual inventory system
   D. neither a periodic inventory system nor a perpetual inventory system

8. Underallocated overhead implies:

   A. a credit balance in the Manufacturing Overhead account
   B. a debit balance in the Manufacturing Overhead account
   C. too much overhead was applied
   D. Cost of Goods Sold is overstated

9. In a service business, which of the following is an appropriate allocation base for indirect costs?

   A. time record
   B. labor time ticket
   C. direct materials
   D. none of the above

10. A significant amount of under/over allocated manufacturing overhead should be:

    A. carried forward to the next accounting period
    B. closed to Cost of Goods Sold
    C. reported as an "Other expenses and revenues" on the income statement
    D. allocated proportionately to Work In Process, Finished Goods, and Cost of Goods Sold

## III. Completion   *Complete each of the following.*

1. In a job costing system, unit cost is determined by dividing _____ by _____.
2. The document used to accumulate all the costs for each job is the _____.
3. _____ are a physical part of the finished product and their cost is separately and conveniently traceable through the manufacturing process.
4. Indirect materials and indirect labor are part of _____.
5. _____ are also called inventoriable costs.

Job Costing   521

6. _____ are never traced through the inventory accounts.
7. There are two main types of accounting systems for product costing: _____ and _____.
8. The purpose of a Materials Ledger is to _____.
9. Generally, the difference between direct and indirect labor is _____.
10. Job costing is used by companies that manufacture products _____.

## IV. Daily Exercises

1. Place the following in correct sequence (use 1 through 6).

    _____ A. Compute the predetermined manufacturing overhead rate
    _____ B. Estimate the total overhead cost for the planning period
    _____ C. Obtain actual quantities of the overhead allocation base used by individual jobs
    _____ D. Select a cost allocation base
    _____ E. Allocate manufacturing overhead to jobs
    _____ F. Estimate the total quantity of the overhead allocation base

2. Raw Material XX had a balance of $56,500. During November, the following requisitions were processed for XX:

    | | |
    |---|---|
    | Job 243 | $11,550 |
    | Job 256 | 8,210 |
    | Job 261 | 14,925 |
    | Factory Maintenance | 775 |

    Record the entry assigning Raw Material XX.

3. During November, the following manufacturing labor costs were incurred and the following time tickets were assigned:

    | | |
    |---|---|
    | Job 243 | $ 6,250 |
    | Job 256 | 2,340 |
    | Job 261 | 5,980 |
    | Factory Maintenance | 16,810 |

    Record the entry to assign November's labor costs.

4. Review the information in Daily Exercises #2 and #3 above and assume $53,200 in manufacturing overhead costs have been recorded, exclusive of indirect materials and indirect labor. If direct materials are selected as the overhead cost allocation base, allocate manufacturing overhead to Jobs 243, 256, and 261.

5. Review the information in Daily Exercises #2, #3, and #4 above but assume overhead is allocated at the rate of 450% direct labor costs. Determine the amount of overhead to allocate to Jobs 243, 256, and 261.

Job Costing    523

## V. Exercises

1. Review the information in Daily Exercises #2, #3 and #4, assuming the number of units produced for each job were:

    Job 243         200 units
    Job 256         120 units
    Job 261         350 units

    A. Calculate the total cost and the per unit cost for each job.

    B. Record the journal entry for the completed jobs.

    |  |  |  |
    |---|---|---|
    |  |  |  |
    |  |  |  |
    |  |  |  |
    |  |  |  |
    |  |  |  |
    |  |  |  |

2. At the end of the year, the Manufacturing Overhead account appears as follows:

    ```
              Manufacturing Overhead
              280,000    |   292,000
                         |
    ```

    A. Was overhead under or overallocated for the year?

    B. Assuming the balance in the overhead account is not significant, record the journal entry to close the account.

    |  |  |  |
    |---|---|---|
    |  |  |  |
    |  |  |  |
    |  |  |  |

C. If the balance in the overhead account is significant, record the entry to close the account, assuming the balances in the three related accounts are as follows:

| | | |
|---|---|---|
| Work In Process | $ 52,000 | |
| Finished Goods | 80,000 | |
| Cost of Goods Sold | 668,000 | |

| | | |
|---|---|---|
| | | |
| | | |
| | | |
| | | |
| | | |

3. Given the following information, calculate total Manufacturing Overhead:

| | |
|---|---:|
| Factory Building Depreciation | $ 50,000 |
| Sales Office Expense | 4,400 |
| Factory Equipment Depreciation | 21,900 |
| Advertising Expense | 51,000 |
| Administrative Salaries | 202,000 |
| Property Taxes - Manufacturing | 42,000 |
| Depreciation on Delivery Equipment | 17,000 |
| Office Utilities Expense | 8,200 |
| Indirect Materials | 2,700 |
| Factory Equipment Repair Expense | 6,600 |
| Indirect Labor | 12,500 |
| Utilities Expense - Manufacturing | 9,100 |

4. The following information pertains to Ace Manufacturing, Inc., for 19X9:

| | |
|---|---:|
| Cost of Goods Sold | $425,000 |
| Direct Materials Purchased | 170,000 |
| Direct Materials Used | 158,000 |
| Ending Work in Process Inventory Less Beginning Work in Process Inventory | 18,000 |

Finished Goods Inventory did not change.
Manufacturing Overhead is twice direct labor cost.
Beginning Work in Process Inventory is 25% of Ending Work in Process Inventory.

A. Compute Beginning and Ending Work in Process Inventories.




B. Compute Cost of Goods Manufactured.




C. Compute Total Manufacturing Costs.




D. Compute Direct Labor and Manufacturing Overhead.




## VI. Beyond the Numbers

Review the information in Daily Exercises #2 though #5 and comment on the appropriateness of direct materials or direct labor as the manufacturing overhead cost allocation base.

## VII. Demonstration Problems

### Demonstration Problem #1

Pat's Pottery had the following inventory balances on January 1, 19X9:

| | |
|---|---:|
| Materials | $28,000 |
| Work in Process | 41,250 |
| Finished Goods | 62,425 |

During the month of January 19X9, the following transactions occurred:

A. Pat purchased 900 tons of clay (materials) for $35 per ton.

B. His workers requisitioned $38,000 of direct materials.

C. $4,050 of indirect materials were used.

D. He incurred $9,000 in manufacturing wages (90% was direct labor). (2 entries)

E. He incurred the following additional overhead costs: $1,600 in depreciation on manufacturing equipment and $3,765 in miscellaneous other costs (credit Accounts Payable).

F. Overhead is allocated to production at the rate of 30% of direct materials cost.

G. Five orders were completed. The total cost of these orders was $71,215.

H. Pat sold six orders on account. The total cost of these orders was $124,000. The total sales price for the orders was $186,000.

I. The balance in Manufacturing Overhead was considered significant and allocated to Work in Process, Finished Goods, and Cost of Goods Sold.

Required:

1. Record the transactions in the general journal.

2. What were the ending balances in the inventory accounts?

3. Was Manufacturing Overhead overallocated or underallocated?

4. What will be the amount of Cost of Goods Sold on the January income statement?

## Requirement 1 (record transactions)

| Date | Accounts and Explanation | PR | Debit | Credit |
|------|--------------------------|----|-------|--------|
|      |                          |    |       |        |

Manufacturing Overhead account:

## Manufacturing Overhead

**Requirement 2 (inventory balances)**

| Materials | Work in Process | Finished Goods |

**Requirement 3 (overhead)**

Manufacturing overhead is _____.

**Requirement 4 (cost of goods sold)**

## Cost of Goods Sold

## Demonstration Problem #2

Review your solution to Demonstration Problem #1 and present a Schedule of Cost of Goods Manufactured for Pat's Pottery for January, 19X9.

# SOLUTIONS

## I. Matching

1. H
2. C
3. B
4. A
5. J
6. L
7. I
8. D
9. F
10. M
11. K
12. N
13. G
14. E

## II. Multiple Choice

1. B  Manufacturing Wages is credited when direct labor is assigned to jobs, Manufacturing Overhead is credited when overhead is allocated to jobs, and Work in Process is credited when a job is completed

2. D  Delivery Expense is a non-inventoriable cost.

3. A  Process costing is used by manufacturers producing a continuous flow of the same product. Of the manufacturers listed, the oil refinery is most likely to produce the same product in a continuous flow.

4. C  The use of indirect materials requires Materials Inventory to be reduced and Manufacturing Overhead to be increased. The journal entry is:
   Manufacturing Overhead         XX
        Materials Inventory                    XX

5. D  The journal entry for the use of direct materials is:
   Work in Process Inventory       XX
        Materials Inventory                    XX

6. B  Recall that manufacturing wages are cleared through a clearing account so that direct labor and indirect labor can be allocated properly. In recording the payroll allocation, Work in Process Inventory is debited for direct labor and Manufacturing Overhead is debited for indirect labor.

7. B  Only a perpetual inventory system has a Cost of Goods Sold account.

8. B  If overhead is underallocated, actual overhead costs were greater than overhead allocated to Work in Process Inventory. Accordingly, the debits to Manufacturing Overhead are greater than the credits, and Manufacturing Overhead will have a debit balance.

9. A  Labor time tickets are used in manufacturing businesses and service businesses rarely have significant direct materials.

10. D  When the amount of under/overallocated overhead is significant it is allocated to Work in Process, Finished Goods, and Cost of Goods Sold.

## III. Completion

1. total costs assigned to a job, number of units completed (order important)

2. job cost record
3. direct materials
4. manufacturing overhead
5. Product costs
6. Period costs
7. job costing, process costing
8. maintain accurate records for each raw material
9. direct labor can be traced directly to the units being manufactured
10. as individual units or in small batches

## IV. Daily Exercises

1. 4 A
   2 B
   5 C
   1 D
   6 E
   3 F

2. Work in Process Inventory    34,685
   Manufacturing Overhead      775
       Raw Materials                35,460

3. Work in Process Inventory    14,570
   Manufacturing Overhead    16,810
       Manufacturing Wages        31,380

4. 
   Total overhead  =  $53,200 + $775 (from Daily Exercise #2) + $16,810 (from Daily Exercise #3) = $70,785

   Total Direct Materials = $34,685 (from Daily Exercise #2)

   Job 243  =  $11,550/$34,685 × $70,785 = $23,571
   Job 256  =  $8,210/$34,685 × $70,785 = $16,755
   Job 261  =  $14,925/$34,685 × $70,785 = $30,459

5. Total overhead = $70,785 (from Daily Exercise #4)
   Job 243  =  $6,250 × 450% = $28,125
   Job 256  =  $2,340 × 450% = $10,530
   Job 261  =  $5,980 × 450% = $26,910

## V. Exercises

1. A.

|  | Job 243 | Job 256 | Job 261 |
|---|---|---|---|
| Direct Materials | $11,550 | $8,210 | $14,925 |
| Direct Labor | 6,250 | 2,340 | 5,980 |
| Manufacturing Overhead | 23,571 | 16,755 | 30,459 |
| Total Costs | $41,371 | $27,305 | $51,364 |
| Divided by units | 200 | 120 | 350 |
| Unit Cost | $206.86 | $227.54 | $146.75 |

B. Finished Goods Inventory    120,040
    Work in Process Inventory    120,040

This could also be recorded as separate entries for each of the three jobs.

2. A. Over-allocated

> **Study Tip:** debit balance = under-allocated
> credit balance = over-allocated

B. Manufacturing Overhead    12,000
    Cost of Goods Sold    12,000

> **Study Tip:** Because too much overhead was allocated to jobs throughout the year, the cost of goods sold account contains more overhead there was actually incurred. Therefore, it needs to be reduced by the amount of the overallocation.

C.
Manufacturing Overhead    12,000
    Work in Process    780
    Finished Goods Inventory    1,200
    Cost of Goods Sold    10,020

Calculations:
| | | |
|---|---|---|
| Work in Process: | $52,000 / $800,000 × $12,000 = | $780 |
| Finished Goods: | $80,000 / $800,000 × $12,000 = | $1,200 |
| Cost of Goods Sold: | $668,000 / $800,000 × $12,000 = | $10,020 |

3.

| | |
|---|---|
| Factory Building Depreciation | $ 50,000 |
| Factory Equipment Depreciation | 21,900 |
| Property Taxes - Manufacturing | 42,000 |
| Indirect Materials | 2,700 |
| Factory Equipment Repair Expense | 6,600 |
| Indirect Labor | 12,500 |
| Utilities Expense - Manufacturing | 9,100 |
| Total Manufacturing Overhead | $144,800 |

4.
   A. Ending Work in Process - Beginning Work in Process = $18,000
      Beginning Work in Process = .25 × Ending Work in Process
      Ending Work in Process - .25 × Ending Work in Process = $18,000
      Ending Work in Process = $24,000
      Beginning Work in Process = .25 × $24,000 = $6,000

   B. Beginning FG + Cost of Goods Manufactured - Ending FG = COGS
      Beginning FG = Ending FG
      Cost of Goods Manufactured = COGS = $425,000

   C.
   |   | | |
   |---|---|---|
   |   | Beginning Work in Process | $ 6,000 |
   | + | Total Manufacturing Costs | X |
   | - | Ending Work in Process | 24,000 |
   | = | Cost of Goods Manufactured | $425,000 |

   Total Manufacturing Costs = $443,000

   D.
   |   | | |
   |---|---|---|
   |   | Direct Materials Used | $158,000 |
   | + | Direct Labor | X |
   | + | Manufacturing Overhead | 2X |
   | = | Total Manufacturing Costs | $443,000 |

   3X = $285,000
   X = $95,000 (Direct Labor)
   2X = $190,000 (Manufacturing Overhead)

## VI. Beyond the Numbers

In many respects, the question is unfair because one would need a great deal of additional information before one could determine if direct materials or direct labor are the appropriate cost drivers to use as the manufacturing overhead allocation base. However, as you were given just the two choices, it should be apparent that direct materials is the more appropriate of the two. Why? First, a comparison of the two total amounts reveals the cost of direct materials is over twice the amount of direct labor. Second, the total direct labor charged to the jobs is even less than the indirect labor charged to manufacturing overhead. Therefore, between the two, direct materials would appear to be the more appropriate cost driver.

## VII. Demonstration Problems

### Demonstration Problem #1 Solved and Explained

**Requirement 1 (record transactions)**

|   | Accounts and Explanation | PR | Debit | Credit |
|---|---|---|---|---|
|   |   |   |   |   |
| A. | Material Inventory |   | 31,500 |   |
|   | Accounts Payable |   |   | 31,500 |
|   |   |   |   |   |

| | | | | |
|---|---|---|---|---|
| B. | Work in Process | | 38,000 | |
| |    Materials Inventory | | | 38,000 |
| | | | | |
| C. | Manufacturing Overhead | | 4,050 | |
| |    Materials Inventory | | | 4,050 |
| | | | | |
| D. | Manufacturing Wages | | 9,000 | |
| |    Wages Payable | | | 9,000 |
| | | | | |
| | Work in Process (.90 × $9,000) | | 8,100 | |
| | Manufacturing Overhead (.10 × $9,000) | | 900 | |
| |    Manufacturing Wages | | | 9,000 |
| | | | | |
| E. | Manufacturing Overhead | | 5,365 | |
| |    Accumulated Depreciation | | | 1,600 |
| |    Accounts Payable | | | 3,765 |
| | | | | |
| F. | Work in Process (.30 × $38,000) | | 11,400 | |
| |    Manufacturing Overhead | | | 11,400 |
| | | | | |
| G. | Finished Goods Inventory | | 71,215 | |
| |    Work in Process | | | 71,215 |
| | | | | |
| H. | Accounts Receivable | | 186,000 | |
| |    Sales Revenue | | | 186,000 |
| | | | | |
| | Cost of Goods Sold | | 124,000 | |
| |    Finished Goods Inventory | | | 124,000 |
| | | | | |
| I. | Manufacturing Overhead | | 1,085 | |
| |    Work in Process (27,535 / 161,175 × 1,085) | | | 185 |
| |    Finished Goods (9,640 / 161,175 × 1,085) | | | 65 |
| |    Cost of Goods Sold (124,000 / 161,175 × 1,085) | | | 835 |

### Points to Remember

In transaction D, it is important to distinguish between direct labor and indirect labor. Direct labor is 90% of the total manufacturing wages of $9,000, or $8,100. The remaining is indirect labor.

In transaction F, it is important to note that overhead is allocated based on *direct materials*. The only direct materials in this problem are the $38,000 of direct materials in transaction B.

To prepare the entry for item I, it is necessary to know the balance in the Manufacturing Overhead account:

| Manufacturing Overhead ||
|---|---|
| (C) 4,050 | |
| (D) 900 | |
| (E) 5,365 | (F) 11,400 |
| (I) 1,085 | Bal. 1,085 |
| Bal. 0 | |

Since the account has a credit balance, we debit it in order to bring its balance to zero, and distribute the balance among Work in Process, Finished Goods, and Cost of Goods Sold. If the balance was not significant, it would be closed to Cost of Goods Sold.

### Requirement 2 (inventory balances)

| Materials || Work in Process || Finished Goods ||
|---|---|---|---|---|---|
| Beg. 28,000 | (B) 38,000 | Beg. 41,250 | | Beg. 62,425 | |
| (A) 31,500 | (C) 4,050 | (B) 38,000 | (G) 71,215 | (G) 71,215 | |
| Bal. 17,450 | | (D) 8,100 | | | (H) 124,000 |
| | | (F) 11,400 | | Bal. 9,640 | (I) 65 |
| | | Bal. 27,535 | (I) 185 | Bal. 9,575 | |
| | | Bal. 27,350 | | | |

### Requirement 3 (overhead)

A credit balance in the Manufacturing Overhead account indicates that Manufacturing Overhead is overallocated. The T-account in requirement 1 indicates that Manufacturing Overhead had a credit balance of $1,085 prior to closing the account.

### Requirement 4 (cost of goods sold)

| Cost of Goods Sold ||
|---|---|
| (H) 124,000 | (I) 835 |
| Bal. 123,165 | |

## Demonstration Problem #2 Solved and Explained

Pat's Pottery<br>
Schedule of Cost of Goods Manufactured<br>
Month Ended January 31, 19X9

|     |                                              |          |          |          |
|-----|----------------------------------------------|----------|----------|----------|
|     | Beginning work in process inventory          |          |          | $41,250  |
|     | Direct materials                             |          |          |          |
|     |   Beginning inventory              | $28,000  |          |          |
| (A) |   Purchases of direct materials    | 27,450   |          |          |
|     |   Materials available for use      | 55,450   |          |          |
|     |   Less: Ending inventory           | 17,450   |          |          |
|     |   Direct materials used            |          | $38,000  |          |
|     | Direct labor                                 |          | 8,100    |          |
|     | Manufacturing overhead                       |          |          |          |
|     |   Indirect materials               | 4,050    |          |          |
|     |   Indirect labor                   | 900      |          |          |
|     |   Depreciation - factory equipment | 1,600    |          |          |
|     |   Miscellaneous                    | 3,765    |          |          |
| (B) |   Total manufacturing overhead     |          | 10,315   |          |
|     | Total manufacturing costs incurred           |          |          | 56,415   |
|     | Total manufacturing costs to account for     |          |          | 97,665   |
|     | Less: Ending work in process inventory       |          |          | 27,350   |
| (C) | Cost of goods manufactured                   |          |          | $70,315  |

A. Because we only include 'direct materials purchased' in this section, the total materials purchased ($31,500) has been reduced by the amount of indirect materials used ($4,050).

B. Total manufacturing overhead includes the actual costs *incurred*, not the actual amount allocated.

C. The cost of goods manufactured shown on the schedule ($70,315) differs from the amount recorded in entry (G) ($71,215) for the following reasons:

$71,215 is the amount which includes the *allocated* manufacturing overhead, not the actual overhead incurred. After entry (I) is recorded and posted, the three related accounts (work in process, finished goods, cost of goods sold) are reduced proportionately because manufacturing overhead was overallocated (i.e., too much was allocated). The ending work in process balance ($27,350) has already been reduced by $185. The remainder ($65 to finished goods and $835 to cost of goods sold for a total of $900) reconciles the $71,215 from entry (G) with the $70,315 reported on the schedule ($71,215 - $70,315 = $900).

**Study Tip:** Remember, Finished Goods do not appear on this schedule. They are reported on the Income Statement and used to calculate Cost of Goods Sold.

# Chapter 21 - Process Costing

## CHAPTER OVERVIEW

In Chapter 20 you were introduced to job costing. In this chapter we turn our attention to a second system found in many manufacturing operations—process costing. Process costing is more complex than job costing, and both systems assume an understanding of manufacturing accounting. Therefore, it is important that you are familiar with the material in Chapters 19 and 20 in order to master these concepts. The learning objectives for this chapter are to

1. Distinguish between the flow of costs in process costing and job costing.
2. Record process costing transactions.
3. Compute equivalent units of production.
4. Apply costs to units completed and to units in ending work in process inventory.
5. Account for a second processing department by the FIFO method.
6. Account for a second processing department by the weighted-average method.

## CHAPTER REVIEW

### Objective 1 - Distinguish between the flow of costs in process costing and job costing.

**Process costing** assigns costs to goods produced in a continuous sequence of steps called processes. With process costing, costs are accumulated for a period of time, such as a week or a month. This contrasts with a **job cost system**, which accounts for costs of specific batches of product.

With process costing, a product typically passes through several departments. For each department, there is a separate Work in Process Inventory account. (In a job costing system, there is one Work in Process Inventory account supported by job cost records for the various jobs.) Review Panels A and B in Exhibit 21-1 for a summary of the differences between the two systems. Exhibit 21-3 illustrates the flow of costs in a process costing system.

### Objective 2 - Record process costing transactions.

Process costing typically accounts for **direct materials** and **conversion costs**. Recall that conversion costs represent the sum of direct labor plus manufacturing overhead. The journal entries used for process costing are very similar to those used for job costing.

To record current period costs:

| | | |
|---|---|---|
| Work in Process Inventory - Dept. 1 | XX | |
|     Materials Inventory | | XX |
| | | |
| Work in Process Inventory - Dept. 1 | XX | |
|     Manufacturing Wages | | XX |
| | | |
| Work in Process Inventory - Dept. 1 | XX | |
|     Manufacturing Overhead | | XX |

To record the transfer to the next department:

    Work in Process Inventory - Dept. 2        XX
        Work in Process Inventory - Dept. 1               XX

Additional materials and conversion costs may be added in subsequent departments.

## Objective 3 - Compute equivalent units of production.

The task in process costing is to account for both the cost of goods that have been completed as well as the cost of incomplete units.

**Equivalent units of production** is a measure of the amount of work done during a production period, expressed in terms of fully complete units of output.

To calculate equivalent units, multiply the number of partially completed units by their percentage of completion. The result is the number of conversion equivalent units. For instance, if 5,000 units are 40% complete, the number of conversion equivalent units is 2,000 (5,000 × 40%).

The **steps in process costing accounting** may be summarized as follows:

**Step 1: Summarize the flow of production in physical units.**

Total **physical units to account for** = beginning Work in Process + production started during the period.

Total **physical units accounted for** = units completed and transferred out during the period + ending Work in Process.

Units to account for must equal units accounted for.

**Step 2: Compute output in terms of equivalent units.**

Compute equivalent units separately for direct materials and conversion costs. Remember that this is necessary because the percentage of completion may be different for materials and conversion costs. Exhibit 21-5 in your text reviews Steps 1 and 2.

**Step 3: Summarize total costs to account for.**

**Total costs to account for** = cost of Beginning work in process + Direct materials + Direct labor + Manufacturing overhead. This is equal to the sum of the debit entries in the Work in Process account for the department. Review Exhibit 21-6.

# Objective 4 - Apply costs to units completed and to units in ending work in process inventory.

### Step 4: Compute the cost per equivalent unit.

Compute separate unit costs for direct materials and conversion costs: (i.e., make two separate calculations):

$$\text{UNIT COSTS} = \frac{\text{COSTS ADDED DURING THE PERIOD}}{\text{EQUIVALENT UNITS}}$$

$$\text{TOTAL COST PER UNIT} = \text{UNIT COST FOR DIRECT MATERIALS} + \text{UNIT COST FOR CONVERSION COSTS}$$

Review Exhibit 21-7.

### Step 5: Assign costs to units completed and to units in ending Work in Process Inventory.

The unit costs from Step 4 are applied to units completed and to units in ending Work in Process. Cost of units completed and transferred out = units completed and transferred out times total unit costs.

Cost of ending work in process = (equivalent units of ending work in process for direct materials × unit cost for direct materials) + (equivalent units of ending work in process for conversion costs × unit cost for conversion costs).

Review Exhibit 21-8. Note that the total costs accounted for in Step 5 must agree with the total costs from Step 3.

Exhibit 21-9 in your text summarizes these five steps. It is important you understand both the correct order and the meaning of each. (Helpful hint: you may find it helpful to trace through the middle chapter review problem in your text.)

# Objective 5 - Account for a second processing department by the FIFO method.

When working with multiple departments, it is important to distinguish between costs from the prior department and costs in the current department. Remember that the costs follow the units from department to department.

All costs in a department which were incurred in prior department are called **transferred-in costs**. Only costs in the current department are accounted for as material or conversion costs in that department.

When beginning Work in Process Inventory exists and the FIFO (first-in, first-out) method is used, certain changes occur in the five steps used in the application of process costing:

**Step 1: Flow of production in physical units.**

With a second department, units started are replaced by units transferred in. This follows the flow of production in physical units.

Total units to account for = beginning Work in Process + units transferred in.

Total units accounted for = units from beginning Work in Process completed and transferred out + units transferred in, completed and transferred out during the current period + ending Work in Process.

Note that total units to account for must equal total units accounted for. Note also that the FIFO method requires the separation of completed units into units from beginning inventory and units started and completed during the period.

**Step 2: Equivalent units of production.**

When computing equivalent units, there are three categories: transferred-in equivalent units, direct materials equivalent units, and conversion costs equivalent units. For each category, equivalent units are computed for 1) units from beginning inventory that were completed and transferred out, 2) units started (transferred in) and completed during the period, and 3) units in ending inventory.

Note that equivalent units for units completed from beginning inventory is equal to the percentage of work done during the current month (subtract the percentage completed during the prior month from 100%).

Study Exhibits 21-11 and 21-12 in your text to be sure you understand equivalent unit computations using FIFO in a multiple department process costing system.

**Step 3 and 4: Summarize total costs to account for and compute cost per equivalent unit.**

These steps are similar to what is done for a single department with no beginning inventory. When performing Step 4, remember that costs associated with beginning Work in Process are NOT included in the unit cost calculation.

Review Exhibit 21-13.

**Step 5: Assign costs to units completed and to units in ending work in process.**

The journal entries to record costs in a second department are:

| | | |
|---|---|---|
| Work in Process Inventory - Dept. 2 | XX | |
|     Materials Inventory | | XX |
| Work in Process Inventory - Dept. 2 | XX | |
|     Manufacturing Wages | | XX |
| Work in Process Inventory - Dept. 2 | XX | |
|     Manufacturing Overhead | | XX |

The entry to record the transfer of completed units to Finished Goods Inventory (or to a subsequent department) is:

Finished Goods Inventory (or Work in Process Inventory - Dept. 3)     XX
    Work in Process Inventory - Dept. 2                               XX

Review Exhibit 21-14.

A **production cost report** summarizes the operations in a department during the period. Exhibit 21-15 in your text presents a production cost report incorporating all the information contained in the five steps outlined above. Study it carefully.

## Objective 6 - Account for a second processing department by the weighted-average method.

When applying the **weighted-average cost assumption**, consideration is given to both the current period's costs and those from the preceding period. Review each of the five steps in process costing and note the differences between weighted-average and FIFO.

### Step 1: Summarize the flow of production in physical units.

Same as FIFO! Why? Because the cost flow assumption applied only affects costs, not physical units.

### Step 2: Compute output in terms of equivalent units.

With weighted-average, no distinction is made between those units transferred out from beginning Work in Process and those units transferred out that were also transferred in during the period. The key numbers are simply those units transferred out and those units still in process at period's end. For those units transferred out, the equivalent unit is the same as the number transferred out. Those units still in process at the end need to be converted to equivalent units. (Helpful hint: compare Exhibit 21-12 with 21-17 in your text.)

### Step 3: Summarize total costs to account for.

Under weighted-average the total costs to account for include both the beginning work in process costs and those costs added during the current period. This is consistent with the equivalent unit calculation discussed in Step 2.

### Step 4: Compute the cost per equivalent unit.

This step integrates the information from Steps 2 and 3. Using the equivalent unit calculation from Step 2, the equivalent unit costs are quickly determined by dividing the amount from Step 2 into the totals obtained in Step 3. (Helpful hint: carefully review and compare exhibit 21-13 with exhibit 21-18 in your text.)

**Step 5: Assign total cost to units completed and to units in ending work in process inventory.**

Weighted-average does not distinguish between those units in process at the beginning of the period and those units transferred in and completed during the period. Instead, weighted-average uses the total number of units transferred out, assigning to this total the amounts calculated in Step 4. Thereafter, the ending work in process inventory is calculated, once again using the unit costs determined in Step 4. (Helpful hint: compare exhibits 21-14 with 21-19 to clarify this distinction.)

The Production Cost Report is identical in format to the one illustrated with FIFO. Comparing Exhibit 21-15 with 21-20 (the condensed version) demonstrates this. Remember, this report is a summary of the information obtained in the five steps detailed above.

Regardless of cost assumption applied (FIFO or weighted-average), the journal entries are identical, only the amounts differ.

BY THIS POINT IN YOUR STUDY OF THIS CHAPTER YOU SHOULD HAVE THE FIVE STEPS COMMITTED TO MEMORY:

Step 1: Compute physical units.

Step 2: Compute equivalent units.

Step 3: Summarize total costs.

Step 4: Compute equivalent unit cost.

Step 5: Assign total cost to units completed and units in ending inventory.

# TEST YOURSELF

All the self-testing materials in this chapter focus on information and procedures that your instructor is likely to test in quizzes and examinations.

## I. Matching  *Match each numbered term with its lettered definition.*

_____ 1. FIFO
_____ 2. equivalent units
_____ 3. process costing
_____ 4. weighted-average
_____ 5. conversion cost
_____ 6. physical units
_____ 7. production cost report
_____ 8. equivalent costs per unit
_____ 9. transferred-in costs

A. a costing method which considers both the current and previous period's cost
B. measure of the number of complete units that could have been manufactured from start to finish using the costs incurred during the period
C. a costing method which considers only the current period's costs
D. the actual number of units processed without regard to their percent of completion
E. summary of the activity in a processing department for a period
F. the sum of direct labor and manufacturing overhead
G. used to account for the manufacture of goods that are mass-produced in a continuous sequence of steps
H. the result of dividing equivalent units into total costs
I. costs incurred in a previous process that are carried forward as part of the product's cost when it moves to the next department

## II. Multiple Choice  *Circle the best answer.*

1. The journal entry to assign manufacturing overhead in a process costing system would:

   A. debit Work in Process Inventory
   B. debit Manufacturing Overhead
   C. credit Work in Process Inventory
   D. debit Finished Goods

2. All of the following businesses are likely to use a process costing system except:

   A. industrial chemicals
   B. paint
   C. residential construction
   D. soft drinks

3. The journal entry to assign direct labor costs in a process costing system would:

   A. credit Manufacturing Wages
   B. credit Work in Process Inventory
   C. credit Wages Payable
   D. debit Manufacturing Wages

4. The journal entry transferring costs from Department A to Department B in a process costing system would:

   A. debit Work in Process - Department A
   B. credit Work in Process - Department B
   C. debit Work in Process - Department B and credit Work in Process - Department A
   D. debit Work in Process - Department A and credit Work in Process - Department B

5. Which of the following systems will usually have more than one Work in Process Inventory account?

   A. job costing
   B. process costing
   C. both job costing and process costing
   D. job costing and process costing both have only one Work in Process Inventory account

6. Direct materials in the second department refer to:

   A. materials added in the first department
   B. materials added in the second department
   C. materials added in both departments
   D. materials added in departments other than the first or second

7. As manufacturing overhead costs are incurred in a process costing system:

   A. Work in Process Inventory is debited
   B. Work in Process Inventory is credited
   C. Manufacturing Overhead is credited
   D. Manufacturing Overhead is debited

8. The first step in process cost accounting is:

   A. the production cost report
   B. determining physical units
   C. determining equivalent units
   D. determining equivalent unit costs

9. In process cost accounting when the last process is complete and goods are transferred out:

   A. Work in Process Inventory is debited
   B. Finished Goods is credited
   C. Finished Goods is debited
   D. Individual credits are recorded to Materials, Manufacturing Wages, and Manufacturing Overhead

10. The final step in process cost accounting is:

    A. the production cost report
    B. determining physical units
    C. determining equivalent units
    D. determining equivalent unit costs

## III. Completion   *Complete each of the following.*

1. A manufacturer who produces custom goods uses a _____ cost system.
2. A manufacturer with a continuous mass production of identical units through a sequence of steps uses a _____ cost system.
3. Conversion costs refer to _____ and _____.
4. Ending Work in Process of 5,000 units one-fourth complete would represent _____ equivalent units.
5. If the beginning Work in Process of 8,000 units is one-fifth complete, the amount of work left to complete would represent _____ equivalent units.
6. After the physical units have been determined, the next step in process cost accounting is _____.
7. The 'Costs to be accounted for' are on the (debit or credit) _____ side of the Work in Process account.
8. Costs that flow with the goods from one department to another are called _____ cost.
9. Under the _____ cost flow assumption, units transferred out from beginning inventory are treated differently from those units transferred in and out when calculating equivalent units.
10. The last step in process cost accounting is the _____.

## IV. Daily Exercises

1. Using the numbers 1 to 6, place the following steps in correct sequence.

    _____ A.   Determine equivalent units

    _____ B.   Determine equivalent unit costs

    _____ C.   Determine the costs to be accounted for

    _____ D.   Determine physical units

    _____ E.   Production Cost Report

    _____ F.   Apply total cost to units completed and units in ending inventory

2. An assembly department has no units in process at the beginning of the current period. During the period, 25,000 units were added to production. At the end of the current period, 4,500 units remained in the assembly department. Calculate the physical units for the assembly department for the current period.

3. Using the information in Daily Exercise 2 above, calculate the equivalent units assuming the units remaining in work in process are 40% complete.

4. A processing department has the following amounts charged to it during the current period:

   | | |
   |---|---|
   | Beginning work in progress | $ 12,000 |
   | Direct Materials | 109,000 |
   | Direct Labor | 45,000 |
   | Manufacturing Overhead | 60,000 |

   Assuming the Work in Progress account has an ending balance of $27,500, determine the amount transferred out to the next department.

5. Using the information in Daily Exercise 4 above, present the journal entry assuming (a) the units were transferred to the packing department or (b) the units were transferred to finished goods

   | a) | | |
   |---|---|---|
   | | | |
   | | | |
   | b) | | |
   | | | |
   | | | |
   | | | |

## V. Exercises

1. The following information is for Department 2 of Atlas Electroplating Co. for the month of April:

   | | |
   |---|---|
   | Beginning Work in Process Inventory (40% complete as to conversion costs) | 10,000 |
   | Units completed and transferred to Department 3 | 60,000 |
   | Units in ending Work in Process Inventory (20% complete as to conversion costs) | 15,000 |

   All materials are added at the beginning of Department 2

   A. Assuming FIFO, determine:

      1. The number of units started into production in April.

      2. The number of units started and completed in April.

   B. Assuming weighted-average, determine:

      1. The number of units started into production in April.

      2. The number of units started and completed in April.

2. Refer to the information in Exercise 1 and:

   A. Assuming FIFO, determine:

      1. The number of equivalent units for materials for April.

      2. The number of equivalent units for conversion costs for April.

   B. Assuming weighted-average, determine:

      1. The number of equivalent units for materials for April.

      2. The number of equivalent units for conversion costs for April.

3. Marliss Corporation prepared the following production cost report for Department A for September:

|  | Physical Units | Total Costs |
|---|---|---|
| Work in Process Sept. 1 (100% complete as to materials and 20% complete as to conversion) | 2,000 | $ 11,150 |
| Started into production in September (costs include $102,000 for materials and $82,350 for conversion) | 24,000 | 184,350 |
| Total to account for | 26,000 | $195,500 |
| Completed and transferred to Department B during September | 20,000 | ? |
| Work in Process, Sept. 30 (100% complete as to materials and 40% complete as to conversion) | 6,000 | ? |
|  | 26,000 | $195,500 |

Process Costing 549

Assuming FIFO, answer the following:

   A. What is the cost per equivalent unit for materials?

   B. What is the cost per equivalent unit for conversion costs?

   C. What costs are transferred to Department B at the end of September?

   D. What costs remain in Ending Work in Process Inventory - Department A?

4. Review the information in Exercise 3 for Marliss Corporation, adding the following assumption: The $11,150 balance in beginning work in process consists of $9,540 in materials cost and $1,610 in conversion costs.

   A. Assuming weighted-average, what is the cost per equivalent unit for materials?

   B. What is the cost per equivalent unit for conversion?

## VI. Beyond the Numbers

Compare your answers in Exercise 3 (A and B) with your answers in Exercise 4 (A and B). What conclusions can you draw concerning the direction of both materials and conversion costs from August to September?

_____
_____
_____
_____
_____

## VII. Demonstration Problems

### Demonstration Problem #1 (FIFO)

Flush Manufacturing Corporation produces plumbing fixtures. The following is a summary of activity and costs for the enameling department for the month of November:

Enameling Department
For the Month Ended November 30, 19XX

| | |
|---|---:|
| **Units:** | |
| Beginning Work in Process Inventory | |
| (20% complete as to materials; 40% complete as to conversion) | 22,500 |
| Transferred in from the Fabricating Department | 105,000 |
| Total units completed | 90,000 |
| Ending Work in Process Inventory | |
| (40% complete as to materials; 50% complete as to conversion) | 37,500 |
| | |
| **Costs:** | |
| Beginning Work in Process | $ 54,000 |
| Transferred in costs from the Fabricating Department | 157,500 |
| Materials added | 14,070 |
| Conversion costs added | $205,485 |

**Required:**

Show the application of total cost to units completed and units in ending Work in Process Inventory for the Enameling Department for the month of November, assuming a first-in, first-out (FIFO) cost flow assumption.

Steps 1 & 2

| Flow of Production in Physical Units and Equivalent Units of Production Enameling Department For the Month Ended November 30, 19XX ||||| 
|---|---|---|---|---|
| Flow of Production | Flow of Physical Units | Equivalent Units |||
| ^ | ^ | Transferred In | Materials | Conversion |
|  |  |  |  |  |
|  |  |  |  |  |
|  |  |  |  |  |
|  |  |  |  |  |
|  |  |  |  |  |
|  |  |  |  |  |
|  |  |  |  |  |
|  |  |  |  |  |
|  |  |  |  |  |
|  |  |  |  |  |
|  |  |  |  |  |
|  |  |  |  |  |

Steps 3 & 4

| Computation of Unit Cost Enameling Department For the Month Ended November 30, 19XX |||||
|---|---|---|---|---|
|  | Transferred In | Materials | Conversion | Total |
|  |  |  |  |  |
|  |  |  |  |  |
|  |  |  |  |  |
|  |  |  |  |  |
|  |  |  |  |  |
|  |  |  |  |  |
|  |  |  |  |  |
|  |  |  |  |  |
|  |  |  |  |  |

Step 5

| | Transferred In | Materials | Conversion | Total |
|---|---|---|---|---|
| Application of Total Cost to Units Completed and Units in Ending Work in Process — Enameling Department — For the Month Ended November 30, 19XX | | | | |
| | | | | |
| | | | | |
| | | | | |
| | | | | |
| | | | | |
| | | | | |
| | | | | |
| | | | | |
| | | | | |
| | | | | |
| | | | | |
| | | | | |
| | | | | |
| | | | | |
| | | | | |
| | | | | |
| | | | | |

**Demonstration Problem #2 (Weighted-Average)**

Flush Manufacturing Corporation produces plumbing fixtures. The following is a summary of activity and costs for the enameling department for the month of November:

Enameling Department
For the Month Ended November 30, 19XX

| | |
|---|---:|
| Units: | |
| Beginning Work in Process Inventory | |
| (20% complete as to materials; 40% complete as to conversion) | 22,500 |
| Transferred in from the Fabricating Department | 105,000 |
| Total units completed | 90,000 |
| Ending Work in Process Inventory | |
| (40% complete as to materials; 50% complete as to conversion) | 37,500 |
| | |
| Costs: | |
| Beginning Work in Process (Transferred in cost, $34,800; Materials cost, $650; Conversion cost, $18,550) | $ 54,000 |
| Transferred in costs from the Fabricating Department | 157,500 |
| Materials added | 14,070 |
| Conversion costs added | $205,485 |

**Required:**

Show the application of total cost to units completed and units in ending Work in Process Inventory for the Enameling Department for the month of November, assuming a weighted-average cost flow assumption.

Steps 1 & 2

| Flow of Production in Physical Units and Equivalent Units of Production Enameling Department For the Month Ended November 30, 19XX ||||| 
|---|---|---|---|---|
| Flow of Production | Flow of Physical Units | Equivalent Units |||
| ^ | ^ | Transferred In | Materials | Conversion |
|  |  |  |  |  |
|  |  |  |  |  |
|  |  |  |  |  |
|  |  |  |  |  |
|  |  |  |  |  |
|  |  |  |  |  |
|  |  |  |  |  |
|  |  |  |  |  |
|  |  |  |  |  |
|  |  |  |  |  |
|  |  |  |  |  |

Steps 3 & 4

| Computation of Unit Cost Enameling Department For the Month Ended November 30, 19XX |||||
|---|---|---|---|---|
|  | Transferred In | Materials | Conversion | Total |
|  |  |  |  |  |
|  |  |  |  |  |
|  |  |  |  |  |
|  |  |  |  |  |
|  |  |  |  |  |
|  |  |  |  |  |
|  |  |  |  |  |
|  |  |  |  |  |
|  |  |  |  |  |

Step 5

| | Application of Total Cost to Units Completed and Units in Ending Work in Process Enameling Department For the Month Ended November 30, 19XX ||||
| --- | --- | --- | --- | --- |
| | Transferred In | Materials | Conversion | Total |
| | | | | |
| | | | | |
| | | | | |
| | | | | |
| | | | | |
| | | | | |
| | | | | |
| | | | | |
| | | | | |
| | | | | |
| | | | | |
| | | | | |
| | | | | |
| | | | | |
| | | | | |
| | | | | |
| | | | | |

# SOLUTIONS

## I. Matching

1. C    2. B    3. G    4. A    5. F    6. D    7. E    8. H    9. I

## II. Multiple Choice

1. A   A debit to Work in Process assigns overhead to a department. Manufacturing overhead is debited as overhead is incurred, Work in Process is credited only when goods are transferred out and Finished Goods is debited only when items are completed and ready for sale.

2. C   Since residential construction tends to be of identifiable units, job costing would be appropriate for it. Process costing is appropriate for the others listed.

3. A   The entry to assign direct labor costs in a process costing system would be:
   Work in Process Inventory - Dept. C         XX
       Manufacturing Wages                              XX

4. C   The materials, labor and overhead costs accumulated as Work in Process Inventory in Dept. A would be transferred to Dept. B with the following journal entry:
   Work in Process Inventory - Dept. B.       XX
       Work in Process Inventory - Dept. A.          XX

5. B   Job cost systems maintain only one Work in Process Inventory account. The job cost record for each incomplete job in such a system comprises the job cost or work in process subsidiary ledger for the control account. In a process cost system, with more than one department, each department has its own Work in Process Inventory account.

6. B   Materials added in the first department and transferred to the second department are referred to as Transferred-in Costs. Accordingly, only materials added in the current department are called direct materials.

7. D   Manufacturing overhead is debited as overhead is incurred. Work in Process in process is debited when costs are added to a department and credited when goods are transferred out. Manufacturing overhead is credited when overhead is assigned to departments.

8. B   The first of the five steps in process cost accounting is determining physical units.

9. C   Finished Goods is debited when goods are ready to sell. Work in Process is debited when goods are transferred in and when additional costs are added. Finished Goods is only credited when goods are sold. Materials, Manufacturing Wages, and Manufacturing Overhead are credited as costs are assigned to Work in Process.

10. A   The last of the five steps in process costing accounting is the production cost report. Choices B, C, and D must be completed before the production cost report can be organized.

## III. Completion

1. job
2. process
3. direct labor, manufacturing overhead
4. 1/4 × 5,000 units = 1,250
5. (1 - 1/5) × 8,000 units = 6,400
6. calculating equivalent units
7. debit
8. transferred in
9. FIFO
10. production cost report

## IV. Daily Exercises

1. A. 2    B. 4    C. 3    D. 1    E. 6    F. 5

2. Units to be accounted for = Beginning work in process + units added to production
   = 0 + 25,000 = 25,000

   Units accounted for = units completed + ending work in progress
   = 20,500 + 4,500 = 25,000

3.

| | | |
|---|---|---|
| Beginning work in process | = | 0 |
| Units began and completed | = | 20,500 |
| Ending work in process | = | 1,800 * |
| Equivalent units | | 22,300 |

*4500 units × 40% complete

4.

Processing Department

| | | | |
|---|---|---|---|
| Bal. | 12,000 | | |
| | 109,000 | 198,500 | |
| | 45,000 | | |
| | 60,000 | | |
| | 27,500 | | |

5.

| | | |
|---|---|---|
| a) Work in Process- Packing | 198,500 | |
|     Work in Process- Processing | | 198,500 |
| | | |
| b) Finished Goods | 198,500 | |
|     Work in Process- Processing | | 198,500 |

## V. Exercises

1. The figures for FIFO and weighted-average are the same (remember these assumptions concern the flow of costs, not the actual physical flow).

    A.  1.  Units transferred out + Ending inventory = Units accounted for
            60,000 + 15,000 = 75,000
            Beginning inventory - Units started = Units to account for
            10,000 - X = 75,000
            Units started = 65,000
        2.  If 65,000 units were started and 15,000 are in process at the end of April, then 50,000 (65,000 -15,000) must have been started and completed. Alternatively, units completed (60,000) less units completed from beginning Work in Process (10,000) equals units started and completed (60,000 - 10,000 = 50,000).

    B.  1.  Same as above

        2.  Same as above

2.  A.  1.  Equivalent units for materials = units started = 65,000

        2.  
            |  |  |
            |---|---:|
            | From Beginning Inventory (10,000 ×.60) | 6,000 |
            | + Started and completed | 50,000 |
            | + Ending Inventory (.20 × 15,000) | 3,000 |
            | Equivalent units for conversion costs | 59,000 |

    B.  1.  
            |  |  |
            |---|---:|
            | Completed and transferred out | 60,000 |
            | In process, 4/30 (100% complete) | 15,000 |
            | Equivalent units for materials | 75,000 |

        2.  
            |  |  |
            |---|---:|
            | Completed and transferred out | 60,000 |
            | In process, 4/30 (20% complete) | 3,000 |
            | Equivalent units for materials | 63,000 |

3.  A.  Equivalent units for materials = 24,000
        Cost per equivalent unit for materials = $102,000/24,000 = $4.25

    B.  Equivalent units for conversion = (2,000 ×.80) + 18,000 + (6,000 ×.40) = 22,000
        Cost per equivalent unit = $82,350/22,000 = $3.743 (rounded)

C.

| | |
|---|---:|
| Cost of beginning Work in Process | $11,150 |
| Cost to complete (2,000 × 80% × $3.743) | 5,989 |
| Units started and finished | |
| [18,000 × ($4.25 + $3.743)] | 143,874 |
| Cost transferred out | $161,023 |

D.

| | |
|---|---:|
| Materials (6,000 × 100% × 4.25) | $25,500 |
| Conversion (6,000 × 40% × $3.743) | 8,983 |
| Cost of ending Work in Process | $34,483 |

4. A. Equivalent units for materials = 26,000 (20,000 + 6,000)
   Cost per equivalent unit for materials:
   $9,540 + $102,000 = $111,540/26,000 = $4.29

   B. Equivalent units for conversion = 22,400 (20,000 + 2,400)
   Cost per equivalent unit for conversion:
   $1,610 + $82,350 = $83,960/22,400 = $3.748 (rounded)

## VI. Beyond the Numbers

The cost of materials appears to be falling whereas the conversion costs (direct labor and overhead) are stable. Since the FIFO assumption only considers current (September) costs while the weighted-average assumption includes both August and September costs, the larger equivalent unit cost for materials under weighted-average ($4.29 vs. $4.25 under FIFO) means that August's material costs were higher than September's. However, the equivalent unit cost for conversion was almost identical under the two assumptions ($3.748 vs. $3.743 under FIFO).

## VII. Demonstration Problems

**Demonstration Problem #1 Solved and Explained**

Steps 1 & 2

Flow of Production in Physical Units
and Equivalent Units of Production
Enameling Department
For the Month Ended November 30, 19XX

| Flow of Production | Flow of Physical Units | Transferred In | Materials | Conversion |
|---|---|---|---|---|
| Units to account for: | | | | |
|   Work in process, October 31 | 22,500 | | | |
|   Transferred in | 105,000 | | | |
| Total units to account for | 127,500 | | | |
| | | | | |
| Units accounted for: | | | | |
| Completed and transferred out in November: | | | | |
|   From beginning inventory | 22,500 | | 18,000[2] | 13,500[3] |
|   Transferred-in and completed | 67,500[1] | 67,500 | 67,500 | 67,500 |
| Total transferred out | 90,000 | | | |
| Ending inventory | 37,500 | 37,500 | 15,000[4] | 18,750[5] |
| Total units accounted for | 127,500 | 105,000 | 100,500 | 99,750 |

[1] A total of 90,000 units were transferred out according to the problem. Since 22,500 of those units were from beginning inventory, the balance of 67,500 was transferred-in and completed during the period. Since these are completed units, each completed unit equals one equivalent unit, and the completed units are carried across to the equivalent unit computation.

    Total transferred out  -  Beginning inventory  =  Transferred in and completed
          90,000          -         22,500       =        67,500 units

[2] The Beginning Work in Process Inventory was 20% complete with respect to direct materials. Therefore, 80% of the direct materials were added during November to the physical units in beginning inventory (100% - 20%).

$$.80 \times 22,500 = 18,000 \text{ equivalent units}$$

[3] The Beginning Work in Process Inventory was 40% complete with respect to conversion. Therefore, 60% of the conversion was performed on Beginning Work in Process Inventory during November (100% - 40%).

$$.60 \times 22{,}500 = 13{,}500 \text{ equivalent units}$$

4  The problem states that 40% of the direct materials had been added during November to the physical units remaining in ending inventory.

$$.40 \times 37{,}500 = 15{,}000 \text{ equivalent units}$$

5  The problem states that 50% of the conversion had been performed during November to the physical units remaining in ending inventory.

$$.50 \times 37{,}500 = 18{,}750 \text{ equivalent units}$$

Steps 3 & 4

### Computation of Unit Cost
### Enameling Department
### For the Month Ended November 30, 19XX

|  | Transferred In | Materials | Conversion | Total |
|---|---|---|---|---|
| Work in process, October 31 (costs for work done before November) |  |  |  | $ 54,000 |
| Costs added in November | $157,500 | $14,070 | $205,485 | 377,055 |
| Divide by equivalent units | 105,000 | 100,500 | 99,750 |  |
| Cost per equivalent unit | $1.50 | $0.14 | $2.06 |  |
| Total cost to account for: |  |  |  | $431,055 |

*Points to Remember:*

When computing unit costs, the costs from the prior period are *not included* in the computation of unit costs. The unit cost for each cost category is equal to the costs added to that category during the period divided by the equivalent units for that category, which were computed in Step 2.

Step 5

## Application of Total Cost to Units Completed and Units in Ending Work in Process
### Enameling Department
### For the Month Ended November 30, 19XX

|  | Transferred In | Materials | Conversion | Total |
|---|---|---|---|---|
| Units completed and transferred out to Finished Goods Inventory: |  |  |  |  |
| From work in process, October 31 |  |  |  | $ 54,000 |
| Costs added during November |  |  |  |  |
| Direct materials |  | 18,000 × $0.14 |  | 2,520 |
| Conversion costs |  |  | 13,500 × $2.06 | 27,810 |
| Total completed from beginning inventory |  |  |  | 84,330 |
| Units transferred in and completed during November | 67,500 × ($1.50 + $0.14 + $2.06) |  |  | 249,750 |
| Total costs transferred out |  |  |  | $334,080 |
|  |  |  |  |  |
| Work in process, November 30: |  |  |  |  |
| Transferred-in costs | 37,500 × $1.50 |  |  | $ 56,250 |
| Direct materials |  | 15,000 × $0.14 |  | 2,100 |
| Conversion costs |  |  | 18,750 × $2.06 | 38,625 |
| Total work in process, |  |  |  | 96,975 |
| Total costs accounted for |  |  |  | $431,055 |

*Points to Remember:*

Units Completed and Transferred Out

*Units from Work in Process, October 31:*

The problem states that $54,000 of cost was associated with the October 31 work in process balance. The FIFO process costing method *always* assumes that costs associated with beginning work in process are the *first* costs to be transferred out in the next period.

*Costs added during November:*

Whenever beginning work in process exists, it is necessary to compute the balance of costs incurred to complete the work. According to the problem, additional materials and conversion were needed to complete the beginning work in process. The equivalent units were computed in Step 2, and the units costs for each category were determined in Step 3. The amount of cost to complete beginning work in process is the equivalent units times the unit cost. A separate computation is made for (1) direct materials and (2) conversion costs.

*Units Transferred-In and Completed during November:*

Since transferred-in and completed units are 100% complete, separate computations for each of the cost categories are not necessary. The cost associated with units transferred-in and completed in the same period will equal the number of units times the sum of the unit costs of 1) transferred-in costs, 2) direct materials, and 3) conversion.

*Ending Work in Process, November 30:*

To compute the balance of ending work in process, it is necessary to make a separate computation for 1) transferred-in costs, 2) direct materials, and 3) conversion. For each of the costs, the balance in ending work in process will equal the equivalent units of production from Step 2 times the unit cost from Step 3.

Once the costs have been applied, you should compare the total costs accounted for in Step 5 with the total cost to account for from Step 4. In both cases the amount in this problem is $431,055.

**Demonstration Problem #2 Solved and Explained**

Steps 1 & 2

Flow of Production in Physical Units
and Equivalent Units of Production
Enameling Department
For the Month Ended November 30, 19XX

| Flow of Production | Flow of Physical Units | Transferred In | Materials | Conversion |
|---|---|---|---|---|
| Units to account for: | | | | |
| Work in process, October 31 | 22,500 | | | |
| Transferred in | 105,000 | | | |
| Total units to account for | 127,500 | | | |
| | | | | |
| Units accounted for: | | | | |
| Completed and transferred out in November | 90,000[1] | 90,000 | 90,000 | 90,000 |
| Ending inventory | 37,500 | 37,500 | 15,000[2] | 18,750[3] |
| Total units accounted for | 127,500 | 127,500 | 105,000 | 108,750 |

[1] A total of 90,000 units were transferred out according to the problem. Since these are completed units, each completed unit equals one equivalent unit, and the completed units are carried across to the equivalent unit computation.

[2] The problem states that 40% of the direct materials had been added during November to the physical units remaining in ending inventory.

564 Chapter 21

$$.40 \times 37{,}500 = 15{,}000 \text{ equivalent units}$$

3. The problem states that 50% of the conversion had been performed during November to the physical units remaining in ending inventory.

$$.50 \times 37{,}500 = 18{,}750 \text{ equivalent units}$$

Steps 3 & 4

### Computation of Unit Cost
### Enameling Department
### For the Month Ended November 30, 19XX

|  | Transferred In | Materials | Conversion | Total |
|---|---|---|---|---|
| Work in process, October 31 | $34,800 | $650 | $18,550 | $ 54,000 |
| Costs added in November | 157,500 | 14,070 | 205,485 | 377,055 |
| Total cost | 192,300 | 14,720 | 224,035 | 431,055 |
| Divide by equivalent units | 127,500 | 105,000 | 108,750 |  |
| Cost per equivalent unit | $1.508235 | $0.14019 | $2.06001 |  |

Total cost to account for:                                                                $431,055

*Points to Remember:*

When computing unit costs using the weighted-average method, the costs from the prior period are included in the computation of unit costs. The unit cost for each cost category is the sum of the current period's cost plus the amounts incurred last period and carried into the current period as beginning inventory.

Step 5

Application of Total Cost to Units Completed
and Units in Ending Work in Process
Enameling Department
For the Month Ended November 30, 19XX

|  | Transferred In | Materials | Conversion | Total |
|---|---|---|---|---|
| Units completed and transferred out to Finished Goods Inventory: 90,000 × (1.5008235 + 0.14019 + 2.06001) |  |  |  | $333,768† |
| Work in process, November 30: |  |  |  |  |
|   Transferred-in costs | 37,500 × $1.508235 |  |  | $56,559 |
|   Direct materials |  | 15,000 × $0.14019 |  | 2,103 |
|   Conversion costs |  |  | 18,750 × $2.06001 | 38,625 |
| Total work in process, |  |  |  | 97,287 |
| Total costs accounted for |  |  |  | $431,055 |

†Adjusted for rounding

*Points to Remember:*

The Step 5 procedure above is less complicated using weighted-average because all 90,000 units transferred out are assigned the unit cost amounts calculated in Step 4. Unlike the FIFO method, there is no need to distinguish between those units in process at the beginning of the period and those units transferred-in and completed during the period.

Like the FIFO method however, the ending work in process amounts are determined by multiplying equivalent units (from Step 2) times unit cost (Step 4).

Once the costs have been applied, you should compare total costs accounted for in Step 5 with the total cost to account for from Step 4. In both cases the amount in this problem is $431,055.

# Chapter 22 - Cost-Volume-Profit Analysis and the Contribution Margin Approach to Decision Making

## CHAPTER OVERVIEW

In Chapters 20 and 21 you learned about a particular type of management accounting concerned with manufacturing businesses wherein direct materials are converted into finished goods. We now turn our attention to a closer examination of "costs" and how costs change relative to changes in output. The interaction of cost and volume results in changes in profits (or losses). The learning objectives for this chapter are to

1. Identify different cost behavior patterns.
2. Use a contribution margin income statement to make business decisions.
3. Compute breakeven sales.
4. Compute the sales level needed to earn a target operating income.
5. Graph a set of cost-volume-profit relationships.
6. Compute a margin of safety.
7. Use the sales mix in CVP analysis.
8. Compute income using variable costing and absorption costing

## CHAPTER REVIEW

### Objective 1 - Identify different cost behavior patterns.

**Cost behavior** is the way that costs change in response to changes in business activity. A **cost driver** is any factor that affects costs. You were introduced to cost drivers in Chapter 19. The three patterns of cost behavior are variable, fixed, and mixed.

**Variable costs** change in direct proportion to changes in volume or level of activity. Examples of variable costs include direct materials, sales commissions, and delivery expense. Suppose CDs have a cost of $6 per disk when purchased for resale. If a retailer sells 1,000 CDs, costs of goods sold will be $6,000. However, if 2,000 CDs are sold, costs of goods sold will be $12,000. Thus, the more CDs the retailer sells, the higher the cost of goods sold will be since the $6 variable cost per unit is constant.

**Fixed costs** do not change as volume changes. Examples of fixed costs include expenses such as rent and depreciation. Suppose the rent for a store is $5,000 per month. The store owner will pay $5,000 per month whether sales increase, decrease, or remain the same.

**Mixed costs** (also called **semivariable costs**) are part variable and part fixed. The monthly telephone bill, for example, is based both on local service and long distance service. The amount for local (unlimited) service is a fixed cost, while the amount for long distance service is a variable cost. Therefore, the total telephone bill is a mixed cost.

Study the graphs in your text which illustrate cost behavior patterns (Exhibits 22-1, 22-2, and 22-3). The variable cost graph begins at the origin (zero volume, zero cost). Variable cost increases in a straight line, whose slope equals the variable cost per unit. As the slope of the line gets steeper, the more the variable cost per unit increases. The fixed cost graph is a horizontal line that intersects the cost (vertical) axis at fixed cost level. The mixed cost graph intersects the cost axis at the level of the fixed cost component, and its slope equals the variable cost per unit.

When budgeting costs, companies use the **relevant range concept**. Relevant range is the band of activity or volume of operations within which relationships between costs and volume can be predicted. These relationships will be different in other ranges. See Exhibit 22-4 in your text.

The conventional income statement focuses on the perspective of external users of financial statements. It has the format:

```
      Sales
   -  Cost of Goods Sold
   =  Gross Margin
   -  Operating Expenses
   =  Income from Operations
```

Note that the conventional income statement classifies expenses according to the value chain, such as cost of goods sold or operating expenses.

The **contribution margin income statement** focuses on the **contribution margin**, the excess of sales over variable expenses. It classifies expenses according to cost behavior, which will be either variable or fixed. It has the format:

```
      Sales
   -  Variable Expenses
   =  Contribution Margin
   -  Fixed Expenses
   =  Income from Operations
```

Exhibit 22-5 presents the two formats. Note the end result "operating income" is the same in both.

### Objective 2 - Use a contribution margin income statement to make business decisions.

The contribution margin income statement is a useful management tool. Once fixed expenses are covered, the balance of the contribution margin "contributes" to income. Since fixed expenses remain constant, when the contribution margin changes, income will change by the same amount. Remember that, in general, variable expenses will change proportionately with sales. Thus, if sales increase by 10 percent, variable expenses will increase by 10 percent, and the contribution margin will increase by 10 percent.

Using the contribution margin income statement, it is possible to calculate exactly how a change in sales will affect profit. Similar analysis using the conventional income statement is not possible.

# Objective 3 - Compute breakeven sales.

**Cost-volume-profit analysis** is often called **breakeven analysis**. The **breakeven point** is the sales level at which operating income is zero. If sales are below the breakeven point, the result is a loss. If sales are above the breakeven point, the result is a profit.

Decision makers use cost-volume-profit analysis to answer questions such as, "How much do we need to sell to break even?" or "If our sales are some specific amount, what will our profit be?"

Two approaches used in cost-volume-profit (or CVP) analysis are the equation approach and the contribution margin approach. With either approach, start by separating total expenses into variable expenses and fixed expenses.

The **equation approach** is:

$$\text{Sales} - \text{Variable Expenses} - \text{Fixed Expenses} = \text{Operating Income}$$

Operating income is zero at breakeven. The equation shows how many units must be sold (and the total dollar amount of the sales) in order to break even.

The **contribution margin approach** is:

$$\text{Contribution Margin} = \text{Sales} - \text{Variable Costs}$$

The contribution margin receives its name because it contributes to the payment of fixed costs and operating income.

The contribution margin may be expressed on a per-unit basis, or as a percentage or ratio:

$$\text{Contribution Margin Per Unit} = \text{Sales Price Per Unit} - \text{Variable Expense Per Unit}$$

$$\text{Contribution Margin Percentage or Ratio} = \frac{\text{Contribution Margin}}{\text{Selling Price}}$$

**Breakeven sales in units** is computed by dividing fixed expenses by the contribution margin per unit:

$$\text{Breakeven Sales in Units} = \frac{\text{Fixed Expenses in Units}}{\text{Contribution Margin Per Unit}}$$

**Breakeven sales in dollars** is computed by dividing fixed expenses by the contribution margin ratio:

$$\text{Breakeven Sales in Dollars} = \frac{\text{Fixed Expenses}}{\text{Contribution Margin Ratio}}$$

Review the examples in the text so that you know what will happen to the breakeven point if a fixed cost is changed, if the sale price is changed, or if the variable cost per unit is changed. If fixed costs or variable cost increase, breakeven increases. If the sale price increases, breakeven decreases.

## Objective 4 - Compute the sales level needed to earn a target operating income.

The profit that a business wishes to earn is called the **target operating income**.

$$\text{Target Sales In Units} = \frac{\text{Fixed Expenses} + \text{Target Operating Income}}{\text{Contribution Margin Per Unit}}$$

$$\text{Target Sales In Dollars} = \frac{\text{Fixed Expenses} + \text{Target Operating Income}}{\text{Contribution Margin Ratio}}$$

Notice that the only difference between computing breakeven sales and target sales is that with target sales, the target operating income amount is added to fixed expenses.

## Objective 5 - Graph a set of cost-volume-profit relationships.

Often, a business is interested in knowing the amount of operating income or operating loss to expect at various levels of sales. One convenient way to provide this information is to prepare a **cost-volume-profit graph**.

In order to familiarize yourself with the components of the CVP graph, study these steps and review Exhibit 22-7 in your text:

- Step 1: Draw a sales line from the origin through a preselected sales volume.
- Step 2: Draw the fixed expense line.
- Step 3: Draw the total expense line by computing the variable expenses at your preselected sales volume (Step 1) then plot them beginning at your fixed expense line.
- Step 4: Identify the breakeven point (where sales and total expenses intersect).
- Step 5: Identify the operating income and operating loss areas.

## Objective 6 - Compute a margin of safety.

The **margin of safety** is the excess of expected or actual sales over breakeven sales. It tells a business how much sales can drop before an operating loss is incurred. The margin of safety may be computed in terms of either dollars or units:

$$\text{Margin of Safety} = \text{Expected Sales} - \text{Breakeven Sales}$$

The following assumptions underlie CVP analysis:

1. Expenses can be classified as either variable or fixed.
2. Cost-volume-profit relationships are linear over a wide range of production and sales.
3. Sales prices, unit variable costs, and total fixed expenses are constant.
4. Volume is the only cost driver.
5. The relevant range of volume is specified.
6. Inventory levels will be unchanged.
7. The sales mix of products will not change during the period.

## Objective 7 – Use the sales mix in CVP analysis.

One of the basic assumptions underlying CVP analysis is that the **sales mix**, the combination of products that make up total sales, does not change.

Breakeven questions involving multiple products can be answered using either the contribution margin approach or the equation approach.

Regardless of approach, you begin by establishing the sales mix (for instance 3 units of one product for every 2 of a second product, or 3:2). The sales mix is then 5 units, the total of 3 and 2. Determine the contribution margin for this mix then divide the result into total fixed expenses. The result is breakeven for the "mix" (3 of one product and 2 of a second). Multiply the breakeven by each component in the mix for breakeven in sales units.

## Objective 8 – Compute income using variable costing and absorption costing.

**Absorption costing** assigns both variable and fixed manufacturing costs to products (the term refers to the products absorbing the costs). Absorption costing has been assumed in the financial statements presented throughout this discussion because it conforms to GAAP requirements. However, there is an alternative approach called **variable costing**, although it can only be used for internal purposes. Variable costing assigns variable manufacturing costs to products, but fixed manufacturing costs (property taxes on the factory, depreciation on the building, etc.) are treated as period costs and reported on the income statement when incurred. The argument for the variable costing approach is that fixed manufacturing costs will be incurred regardless of production levels and should therefore be treated as period costs.

Carefully review Exhibit 22-9 in your text. Notice that the only difference between these two approaches is the treatment of fixed manufacturing costs. However, this difference will affect net income, as illustrated in Exhibit 22-10 in your text. Because absorption costing assigns fixed manufacturing costs to inventory, these costs will not appear on the income statement until the units are actually sold, whereas under variable costing all fixed manufacturing costs are included on the income statement when they are incurred. The general rule is that when inventories are increasing, absorption costing income will be higher than variable costing income. The reverse is true when inventories are declining.

> **Study Tip:** Review the Decision Guidelines comparing absorption and variable costing in your text. Remember, variable costing is only used internally—external reports and statements use absorption costing.

# TEST YOURSELF

All the self-testing materials in this chapter focus on information and procedures that your instructor is likely to test in quizzes and examinations.

**Matching**  *Match each numbered term with its lettered definition.*

_____ 1. cost behavior
_____ 2. variable cost
_____ 3. fixed cost
_____ 4. mixed cost
_____ 5. breakeven point
_____ 6. contribution margin
_____ 7. target operating income
_____ 8. margin of safety
_____ 9. relevant range
_____ 10. variable costing
_____ 11. sales mix
_____ 12. CVP analysis
_____ 13. absorption costing
_____ 14. period costs

A. The amount of unit sales or dollar sales at which revenues equal expenses
B. A costing method that assigns only variable manufacturing costs to products
C. The description of how costs change in response to a shift in the volume of business activity
D. The excess of sales price over variable expenses
E. A band of activity or volume in which actual operations are likely to occur
F. A cost that does not change in total as volume changes
G. The excess of expected (or actual) sales over breakeven sales
H. A cost that is part variable and part fixed
I. A cost that changes in total in direct proportion to changes in volume or activity
J. The desired income a business wishes to earn
K. Costs reported on the income statement as incurred
L. The combination of products that make up total sales
M. A costing method that assigns all manufacturing costs to products
N. A part of the budgeting system that helps managers predict the outcome of their decisions by analyzing relationships among costs, volume, and profit or loss.

## II. Multiple Choice  *Circle the best answer.*

Use the following information for Questions 1 through 4:

Video Point sells VCR tapes. Last year Video Point sold 5,500 cases at $24 per case. The variable cost per case was $14.40 and fixed costs amounted to $28,800.

1. The breakeven point in cases of tapes was:

   A. 1,200
   B. 2,000
   C. 3,000
   D. 5,500

2. The breakeven point in sales dollars was:

   A. $66,000
   B. $72,000
   C. $24,000
   D. $14,400

3. The margin of safety in dollars was:

   A. $60,000
   B. $48,000
   C. $51,000
   D. $-0-

4. If Video Point wished to earn an operating income of $34,800, how many cases of tapes would have to be sold?

   A. 3,600
   B. 4,400
   C. 5,500
   D. 6,625

5. Dividing breakeven sales dollars by the unit selling price results in the:

   A. variable cost per unit
   B. breakeven point in dollars
   C. breakeven point in units
   D. variable cost ratio

6. Which of the following will decrease the breakeven point?

   A. decreasing fixed costs
   B. increasing fixed costs
   C. increasing variable costs per unit
   D. decreasing selling price

7. Which of the following will increase the breakeven point?

   A. Decreasing fixed costs
   B. Increasing fixed costs
   C. Decreasing variable cost per unit
   D. Decreasing selling price

Use the following graph to answer questions 8 through 10:

8. Line D must be:

   A. the sales line
   B. total expense line
   C. fixed expense line
   D. cannot be determined

9. If E is the total expense line then I must be:

   A. operating income area
   B. variable expense area
   C. operating loss area
   D. cannot be determined

10. If C is the sales line and E is the total expense line then F must be:

   A. breakeven point
   B. total units
   C. total dollars
   D. cannot be determined

## III. Completion  *Complete each of the following.*

1. The _____ is equal to the selling price per unit minus the variable expenses per unit.
2. A convenient way to determine operating income or loss at various levels of sales is to prepare a _____.
3. _____ and _____ are examples of costs that change proportionately with sales.
4. The _____ is the combination of products that make up total sales.
5. Two approaches used in CVP analysis are the _____ approach and the _____ approach.
6. _____ tells a decision maker how much sales can drop before an operating loss is incurred.

For questions 7 through 10, complete the sentence with **increase, decrease,** or **not affect**.

7. An increase in direct material cost will _____ the contribution margin.
8. An increase in direct labor cost will _____ the breakeven point.
9. A decrease in direct materials costs will _____ the breakeven point.
10. An increase in fixed plant insurance will _____ the breakeven point.
11. Absorption costing reports all _____ costs as _____ costs on the income statement.
12. Variable costing reports only _____ costs as _____ costs on the income statement.

## IV. Daily Exercises

1. Classify each of the following costs as fixed, variable, or mixed (assume a relevant range and current period).

| Cost | Classification |
|---|---|
| a) property taxes | _____ |
| b) direct materials | _____ |
| c) depreciation on office equipment | _____ |
| d) advertising expense | _____ |
| e) office salaries expense | _____ |
| f) direct labor | _____ |
| g) manufacturing overhead | _____ |
| h) rent expense | _____ |
| i) insurance expense | _____ |
| j) supplies expense | _____ |

2. Bola's Basketry has fixed costs of $420,000. Variable costs are 30% of sales. Assuming each basket sells for $10, what is their breakeven point in unit sales?

3. Manuel's Manufacturing sells a product for $8 per unit. If the variable cost is $4.25 per unit, and breakeven is 48,000 units, what are Manuel's fixed costs?

4. If variable costs are 60% of sales and fixed costs are $230,000 what is the breakeven point in sales dollars?

5. Gayle's Greetings sells boxes of greeting cards and packages of gift wrap. Boxes sell for $5.00 and packages sell for $1.75. Variable costs are $2.50 for boxes and $1.00 for packages. Gayle expects to sell 1,500 boxes of greeting cards and 750 packages of gift wraps. Fixed costs are $2,350. What is the breakeven point?

## V. Exercises

1. A monthly income statement for Bijan's Burritos appears as follows:

   | | | |
   |---|---:|---:|
   | Sales | | $280,000 |
   | Cost of Goods Sold | | 120,000 |
   | Gross Margin | | 160,000 |
   | Operating Expenses: | | |
   |   Marketing Expense | $35,000 | |
   |   General Expense | 70,000 | 105,000 |
   | Operating Income | | $ 55,000 |

   Cost of Goods Sold is a variable expense. Marketing expense is 70% variable and 30% fixed. General Expense is half fixed and half variable. In the space below, present a contribution margin income statement for the month.

2. Review the information in Exercise 1 above, and calculate the following:

   a. contribution margin ratio

   b. breakeven point in sales

   c. If the frozen burritos sell for $2 per package, what is the breakeven point in units?

d. By what amount would operating income decrease if sales dropped by 20%?

3. Using the form below and the information in Exercise 1 above, graph Bijan's Burritos total expense (both fixed and variable) and sales, showing clearly the breakeven point calculated in Exercise 2 above.

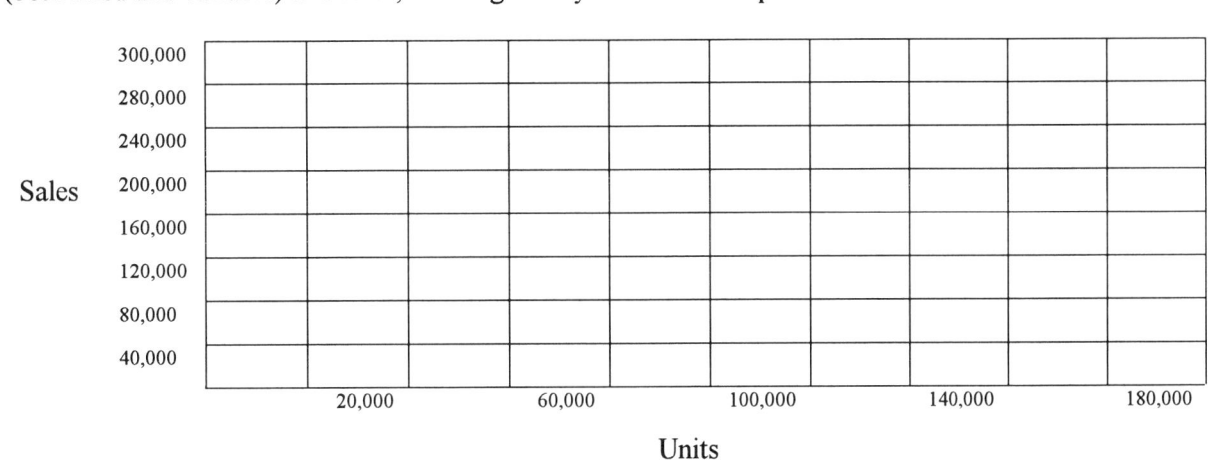

Sales (y-axis): 40,000; 80,000; 120,000; 160,000; 200,000; 240,000; 280,000; 300,000
Units (x-axis): 20,000; 60,000; 100,000; 140,000; 180,000

4. A manufacturer of rubber exercise balls provides the following cost information:

| | |
|---|---|
| Variable cost per ball | $ 9.50 |
| Fixed monthly expenses | $15,000 |
| Selling price per ball | $ 20.00 |

a. What is the manufacturer's contribution margin per ball and contribution margin ratio?

b. What is the manufacturer's breakeven point in units and dollars?

c. Prove the accuracy of your answers in (b) above by presenting an income statement at breakeven.

|  |  |  |
|--|--|--|
|  |  |  |
|  |  |  |
|  |  |  |
|  |  |  |
|  |  |  |
|  |  |  |
|  |  |  |
|  |  |  |

d. Assuming the manufacturer's targeted net income is $12,000 per month, and the company is subject to a 40% tax rate, calculate the sales necessary to achieve the targeted net income (after tax).

5. Review the information in Exercise 4 above, assuming the manufacturer achieves the $10,000 targeted net income, after tax. The owner is considering an advertising campaign to increase sales. The cost of the ads would be $5,000 per month. By what amount, expressed in units and dollars, would sales need to increase to justify the advertising expenditure?

## VI. Beyond the Numbers

Review Daily Exercise 1. How would your answers change if output remains within the relevant range but the costs listed are classified over a long period?

| Cost | Classification |
|------|----------------|
| a) property taxes |  |
| b) direct materials |  |
| c) depreciation on office equipment |  |
| d) advertising expense |  |
| e) office salaries expense |  |
| f) direct labor |  |
| g) manufacturing overhead |  |
| h) rent expense |  |
| i) insurance expense |  |
| j) supplies expense |  |

# VII. Demonstration Problems

## Demonstration Problem #1

The Ganji Game Corporation is planning to introduce a new table game. The relevant range of output is between 10,000 and 40,000 units. Within this range, fixed expenses are estimated to be $325,000 and variable expenses are estimated at 35% of the $30 selling price.

### Required:

1. Using the contribution margin approach, calculate breakeven sales in units and in dollars.

2. If targeted net income (pretax) is $120,000, how many games must be sold?

3. Prepare a graph showing operating income and operating loss areas from 0 to 40,000 games, assuming a selling price of $30. Identify the breakeven sales level and the sales level needed to earn operating income of $120,000.

4. If the corporation increases the selling price to $36, how many games must be sold to earn operating income of $60,000?

### Requirement 1 (Breakeven sales in units and dollars)

### Requirement 2 (Targeted operating income)

**Requirement 3 (Graph)**

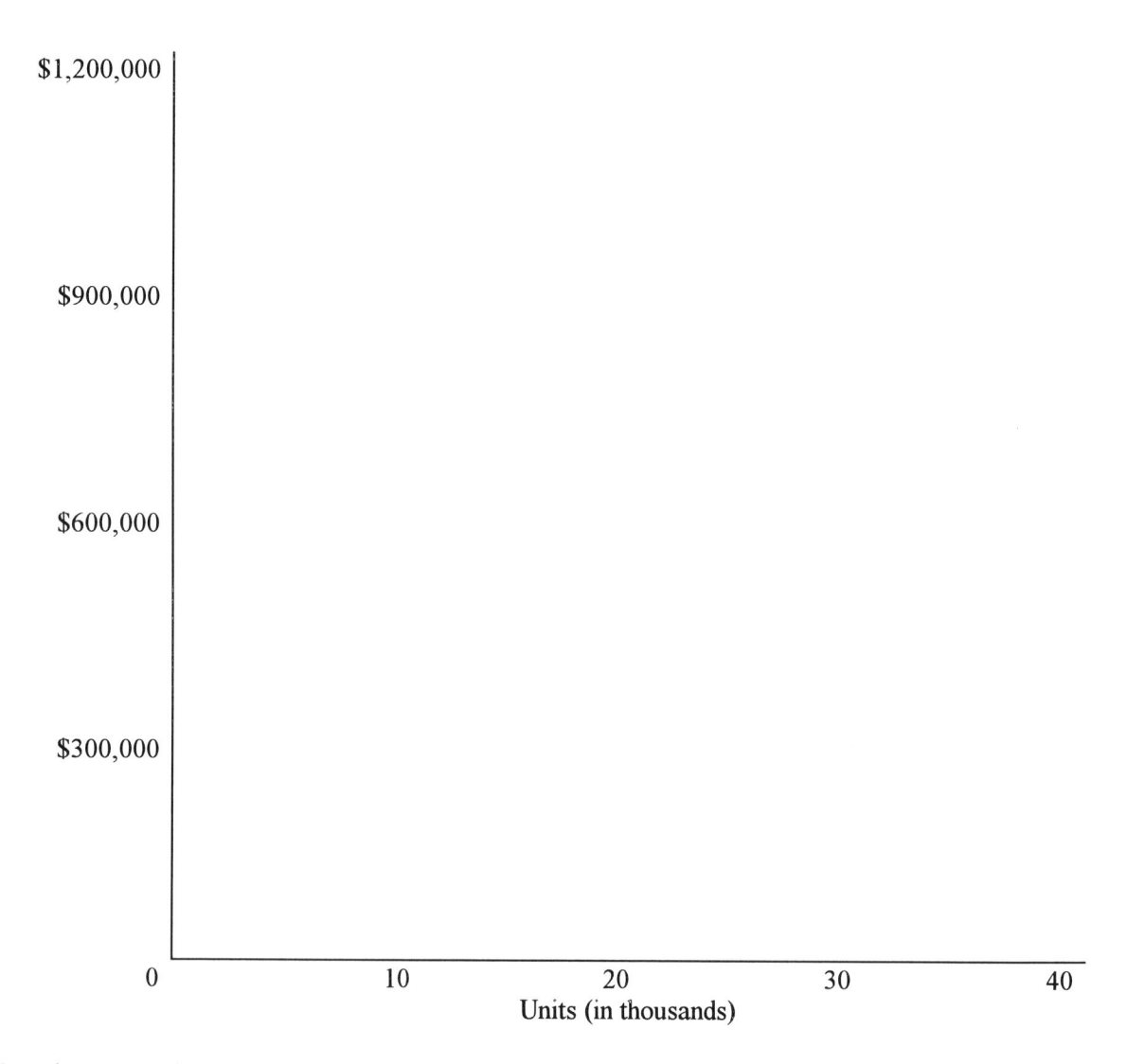

$1,200,000

$900,000

$600,000

$300,000

0          10          20          30          40
              Units (in thousands)

**Requirement 4 (Effect of change in selling price)**

## Demonstration Problem #2

Will and Daniel's Deluxe Ice Cream Company manufactures top of the line premium ice cream. The product, in a variety of styles, is available in pints, quarts and half-gallons. Past experience has shown that 4 quarts are sold for each half-gallon and 5 pints are sold for each quart. Selling prices and variable costs for the product line are as follows:

|  | Pints | Quarts | Half-gallons |
|---|---|---|---|
| Selling price | $1.50 | $2.75 | $5.25 |
| Variable cost | $0.60 | $1.15 | $2.25 |

Fixed costs average $900,000 per month. Of this amount, approximately 2/3 is manufacturing overhead and 1/3 is operating expense. Variable costs consist entirely of direct materials (ingredients and packaging) and direct labor.

### Part A

1. Determine the sales mix.
2. Calculate breakeven in units and sales.
3. Assuming the company pays taxes at the rate of 40% of pretax operating income, calculate the sales needed to earn after-tax operating income of $1,200,000 annually.

### Part B

The company is considering an increase in price and, at the same time, eliminating the manufacture of the half-gallon size. Research indicates the elimination of the half gallon would result in a 25% increase in quart sales but have no impact on pint sales. Assuming the decision is made to eliminate the half-gallons and increase the selling price of pints and quarts to $1.75 and $3.00 respectively, answer the following:

1. Which variable and fixed costs are likely to change as a result of this decision?
2. What is the new sales mix?
3. Assuming variable and fixed costs remain the same, what is the new breakeven point in units and sales?
4. Assuming variable costs remain the same but the elimination of half-gallons results in a one-time restructuring charge of $750,000 and a 20% reduction in fixed manufacturing costs, what is the effect on operating income?

Part A

1. Determine the sales mix.

2. Calculate breakeven in units and sales.

3. Targeted operating income

Part B

1. Effects on variable and fixed costs

2. New sales mix

3. New breakeven point in units and dollars

4. Effect on operating income

# SOLUTIONS

## I. Matching

| | | | | | | |
|---|---|---|---|---|---|---|
| 1. C | 3. F | 5. A | 7. J | 9. E | 11. L | 13. M |
| 2. I | 4. H | 6. D | 8. G | 10. B | 12. N | 14. K |

## II. Multiple Choice

1. C   $28,800 / ($24.00 - $14.40) = 3,000

2. B   $28,800 / [($24.00 - $14.40) / $24.00] = $72,000

3. A   (5,500 boxes - 3,000 boxes) × $24.00 = $60,000

4. D   ($28,800 + $34,800) / [($24.00 - $14.40) / $24.00] = $159,000 / $24 = 6,625

5. C   BE$ = Breakeven sales dollars.  BEu = Breakeven in units.
       $Pu = unit selling price.
       BE$ = BEu × $Pu
       BE$ / $Pu = BEu

6. A   BE$ = Breakeven sales dollars. BEu = Breakeven in units.
       $Pu = unit selling price. FC = Fixed Cost
       VCu = Variable cost per unit.

       Recall that BEu = FC /($Pu - VCu)

       Of the answers listed, only A "Decreasing fixed costs" will decrease the breakeven point.

7. D   Refer to 6 above. Note that answer D, "Decreasing selling price," will decrease the
   or  contribution margin and increase the breakeven point.
   B

**Study tip:** If you have difficulty with 5 through 7, consider the formula for the breakeven point in units:

Fixed Expenses / Contribution Margin Per Unit = Breakeven in Units

If the numerator increases, or the denominator decreases, the breakeven point increases. If the numerator decreases, or the denominator increases, the breakeven point decreases.

8. C   The sales and total expense line slope upward; only the fixed expense line is flat.

9. B   The variable expense area is the difference between the total expense line and the fixed expense line.

10. A  Total units and total dollars are the A and B axis. F is the breakeven point where sales intersect total expenses.

## III. Completion

1. contribution margin per unit
2. cost-volume-profit graph
3. Cost of goods sold, selling commission (other answers may be acceptable)
4. sales mix
5. equation, contribution margin
6. The margin of safety
7. decrease (An increase in direct materials is an increase in the variable cost per unit. This decreases the contribution margin.)
8. increase (An increase in direct labor cost is an increase in the variable cost per unit. This decreases the contribution margin. As the contribution margin decreases, the breakeven point increases.)
9. decrease (A decrease in direct materials cost is a decrease in variable cost per unit. This increases the contribution margin. As the contribution margin increases, the breakeven point decreases. Contrast with #8.)
10. increase (An increase in plant insurance is an increase in fixed costs. An increase in fixed costs increases the breakeven point.)
11. manufacturing, product (order important)
12. variable, product (order important)

## IV. Daily Exercises

1.

| Cost | Classification |
| --- | --- |
| a) property taxes | fixed |
| b) direct materials | variable |
| c) depreciation on office equipment | fixed |
| d) advertising expense | fixed |
| e) office salaries expense | fixed |
| f) direct labor | variable |
| g) manufacturing overhead | mixed (because some are fixed, such as rent, depreciation, etc., whereas others are variable—indirect materials, utilities, for instance) |
| h) rent expense | fixed |
| i) insurance expense | fixed |
| j) supplies expense | variable |

2. If VC = 30% of sales, then CM = 70% of sales, or $7 per unit.

$$\frac{\text{Fixed expenses}}{\text{Contribution margin}} = \text{Breakeven point}$$

$$\frac{\$420,000}{\$7} = 60,000 \text{ units}$$

3.

$$\frac{\text{Fixed expenses}}{\text{Contribution margin}} = \text{Breakeven point}$$

$$\frac{FE}{\$3.75} = 48{,}000$$

$$FE = \$180{,}000$$

4. If VC = 60% of sales, then CM = 40% of sales.

$$\frac{\text{Fixed costs}}{\text{Contribution margin ratio}} = \text{Breakeven in sales}$$

$$\frac{\$230{,}000}{40\%} = \$575{,}000$$

5.

|  | Boxes - greeting cards | Packages - gift wrap | Total |
|---|---|---|---|
| Sales price per unit | $5.00 | $1.75 |  |
| Variable expense per unit | $2.50 | $1.00 |  |
| Contribution margin per unit | $2.50 | $0.75 |  |
| Estimated sales in units | × 1,500 | × 750 | 2,250 |
| Estimated contribution margin per unit | $3,750 + | $562.50 = | $4,312.50 |
| Weighted-average contribution margin per unit ($4,312.50/2,250) |  |  | $1.92 (rounded) |

$$\text{Breakeven sales in units} = \frac{\text{Fixed expenses}}{\text{Weighted-average contribution margin}} = \frac{\$2{,}350}{\$1.92} = 1{,}224$$

Breakeven sales of boxes of greeting cards = 1,224 × (1,500 / 2,250) = 816 boxes

Breakeven sales of packages of gift wraps = 1,224 × (750 / 2,250) = 408 packages

## V. Exercises

1.

| | | |
|---|---:|---:|
| Sales | | $280,000 |
| Less: Variable Expenses | | |
|     Cost of Goods Sold | $120,000 | |
|     Marketing Expense | 24,500 | |
|     General Expense | 35,000 | 179,500 |
| Contribution Margin | | 100,500 |
| Less: Fixed Expenses | | |
|     Marketing Expense | 10,500 | |
|     General Expense | 35,000 | 45,500 |
| Operating Income | | $ 55,000 |

2.

  a.  contribution margin ratio  =  contribution margin / sales
                                              =  100,500 / 280,000 = 35.9% (rounded)

  b.  breakeven point in sales   =  $0 operating income
                                                =  fixed expense / contribution margin ratio
                                                =  $45,500 / 35.9% = $126,741

  c.  $126,741 / $2 each = 63,371 packages

  d.

| | | |
|---|---:|---:|
| Sales [($280,000 – 20%($280,000)] | | $224,000 |
| Less: Variable Expenses | | |
|     Cost of Goods Sold | $96,000 | |
|     Marketing Expense | 19,600 | |
|     General Expense | 28,000 | 143,600 |
| Contribution Margin | | 80,400 |
| Less: Fixed Expenses | | 45,500* |
| Operating Income | | $ 34,900 |

*Fixed expenses remain the same, regardless of sales level (assuming no change in the relevant range).

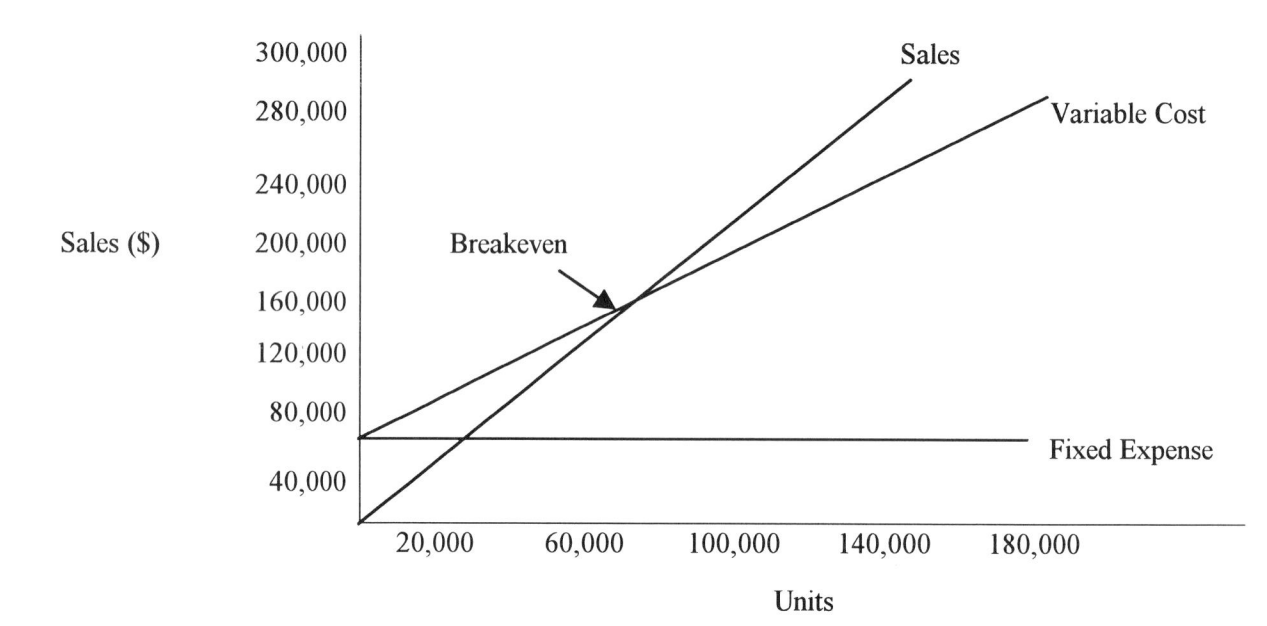

3.

Sales ($) chart showing Sales line, Variable Cost line, Fixed Expense line, with Breakeven point marked. Y-axis: 40,000 to 300,000. X-axis (Units): 20,000 to 180,000.

4.
- a. contribution margin = sales − variable costs
  = $20 - $9.50 = $10.50

  contribution ratio = contribution margin / sales
  = $10.50 / $20.00 = 52.5%

- b. breakeven (units) = fixed expenses / contribution margin
  = $15,000 / $10.50 = 1,429 units (rounded)

  breakeven (sales) = fixed expenses / contribution margin ratio
  = $15,000 / 52.5% = $28,572 (rounded)

- c.

  | | |
  |---|---|
  | Sales | $28,572 |
  | Less: Variable Costs (1,429 units × $9.50 ea) | 13,576 (rounded) |
  | Contribution Margin | 15,000 (rounded) |
  | Less: Fixed Expenses | 15,000 |
  | Operating Income | -0- |

- d. Since the targeted net income ($12,000) is after-tax, first we have to calculate the pre-tax target income.

  pre-tax income = $12,000 / 60% = $20,000
  targeted sales = (fixed expenses + net income) / contribution margin
  = ($15,000 + $20,000) / 52.5%
  = $35,000 / 52.5% = $66,667 (rounded)

5. The advertising cost is a fixed expense so replace the $15,000 amount with $20,000, then solve as follows:

target sales (dollars) = ($20,000 + $20,000) / 52.5% = $76,190 (rounded)

target sales (units) = ($20,000 + $20,000) / $10.50 = 3,810 units

# VI. Beyond the Numbers

a) fixed (while property taxes will probably rise over the long run, they still are a fixed cost)
b) variable
c) fixed
d) mixed (the business will always advertise, but the amount will vary over the long run)
e) fixed
f) variable
g) variable
h) mixed
i) possibly mixed (a portion fixed regardless of output with add-ons to reflect changes in output)
j) variable

# VII. Demonstration Problems

### Demonstration Problem #1 Solved and Explained

**Requirement 1**

To compute breakeven in dollars and in units, we need to find the contribution margin per unit and the contribution margin ratio:

Contribution Margin Per Unit = Sales Price Per Unit - Variable Cost Per Unit

Contribution Margin Percentage or Ratio = Contribution Margin / Sales Price Per Unit

Since the variable costs are 35% (0.35) of sales, the contribution margin per unit is:

$30 - (.35 × 30) = $30 - $10.50 = $19.50

The contribution margin ratio is:

$19.50 / 30 = .65

The computation of breakeven sales in units is:

$$\text{Breakeven Sales in Units} = \frac{\text{Fixed Expenses}}{\text{Contribution Margin Per Unit}}$$

$$\$325,000 / \$19.50 = 16,667 \text{ games}$$

The breakeven point in units is 16,667 games.

The computation of breakeven sales in dollars is:

$$\text{Breakeven Sales in Dollars} = \frac{\text{Fixed Expenses}}{\text{Contribution Margin Percentage}}$$

$$\$325,000 / .65 = \$500,000$$

The breakeven point in dollars is $500,000.

**Requirement 2**

The target operating income is given as $120,000. The number of games that must be sold to earn a target income of $120,000 is:

$$\text{Target Sales in Units} = \frac{\text{Fixed Expenses} + \text{Target Operating Income}}{\text{Contribution Margin Per Unit}}$$

$$(\$325,000 + \$120,000) / \$19.50 = 22,821 \text{ games}$$

To achieve the target operating income of $120,000, 22,821 games must be sold.

**Requirement 3 (Graph)**

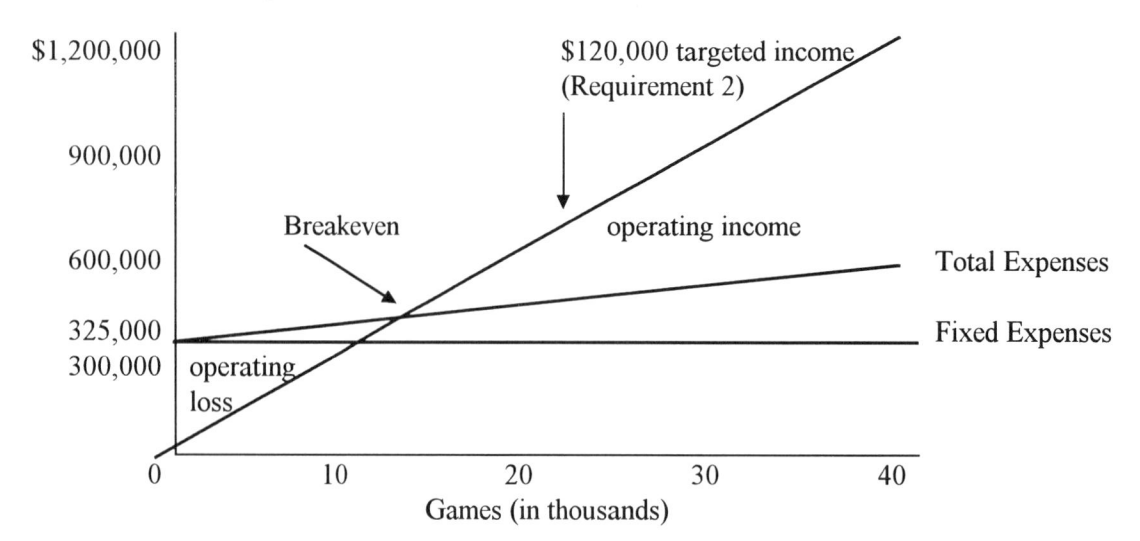

## Requirement 4

To find the solution to Requirement 4, you must first determine exactly what item changes. No change in fixed expenses is indicated, and the target operating income of $120,000 remains the same. However, the selling price increases from $30 to $36, an increase of $6. Since variable expenses are 35% of the selling price, the new variable costs is $12.60 (35% × $36). Since the selling price of the game has changed, we must find the new contribution margin per unit in order to use the formula for target sales in using in Requirement 2. The new contribution margin per unit is:

$$\$36 - \$12.60 = \$23.40$$

Since the contribution margin per unit has increased to $23.40, the new target sales in units will be:

$$(\$325{,}000 + \$60{,}000) / \$23.40 = 16{,}453 \text{ games}$$

Target sales in units has decreased to 16,453 units. This is due to the increase in the selling price and the resulting increase in the contribution margin per unit.

## Demonstration Problem #2 Solved and Explained

### Part A

1. Determine the sales mix.

The sales mix is the combination of products that make up total sales. In this problem the sales mix is:

one half-gallon = 4 quarts = 20 pints (5 pints are sold for each <u>quart</u>).

Another way of expressing this relationship is to convert the "mix" to percentages. Doing so results in

| | |
|---|---|
| 4% | half-gallons (1/25) |
| 16% | quarts (4/25) |
| 80% | pints (20/25) |
| 100% | |

2. Calculate breakeven in units and sales.

To do this, we first calculate the weighted-average contribution margin, as follows:

| | Half-gallons | Quarts | Pints | |
|---|---|---|---|---|
| Selling price | $5.25 | $2.75 | $1.50 | |
| Less variable cost | 2.25 | 1.15 | 0.60 | |
| Contribution margin | 3.00 | 1.60 | 0.90 | |
| × weight | × 1 | × 4 | × 20 | |
| Weighted-average contribution margin | $3.00 | $6.40 | $18.00 | = $27.40 |

| | | | | | | |
|---|---|---|---|---|---|---|
| Breakeven Sales in Units | = | Fixed Expenses / Weighted-average Contribution Margin | = | $900,000 / $27.40 | = | 32,847 units |

or

|  | Half-gallons | Quarts | Pints |
|---|---|---|---|
|  | 32,847 | 32,847 | 32,847 |
|  | × 1 | × 4 | × 20 |
|  | 32,847 | 131,388 | 656,940 |

Now apply the unit selling price to each result to obtain breakeven sales (or convert the weighted-average contribution margin to a ratio).

|  | Half-gallons | Quarts | Pints |
|---|---|---|---|
|  | 32,847 | 131,388 | 656,940 |
|  | × $5.25 | × $2.75 | × $1.50 |
| Total breakeven sales $1,519,174 = | $172,447 + | $361,317 + | $985,410 |

Remember, fixed expenses were given as monthly, so both of the above results are monthly.

3. Targeted operating income

$$\text{Sales} = \frac{\text{Fixed Expenses} + \text{Target Operating Income}}{\text{Contribution Margin Ratio}}$$

$$\text{Sales} = \frac{\$10,800,000^* + \$2,000,000^{**}}{59.3\% \text{ (rounded)}}$$

[*] If fixed expenses are $900,000 monthly, then they are $10,800,000 ($900,000 × 12) annually.

[**] If the tax rate is 40%, the pretax operating income is $2,000,000 ($1,200,000 / 0.6).

Sales needed to achieve after tax operating income of $1,200,000 are $21,585,160 annually or $1,798,763 monthly.

**Part B**

1. In the short run, neither variable nor fixed costs will change. In the longer run, variable costs will not change either (the problem states all variable costs are prime costs). However, fixed costs should decrease as facilities (equipment, etc.) needed to produce the half-gallons are eliminated (see #4 below).

2. The new sales mix is 5 quarts to 20 pints or 20% quarts and 80% pints.

3.

|  | Quarts | Pints |
|---|---|---|
| Selling price | $3.00 | $1.75 |
| Less variable cost | 1.15 | 0.60 |
| Contribution margin | 1.85 | 1.15 |
| × weight | × 5 | × 20 |
| Weighted-average contribution margin | $9.25 | + $23.00 = $32.25 |

$$\frac{\text{Fixed Expenses}}{\text{Contribution Margin}} = \frac{\$900{,}000}{\$32.25} = 27{,}907 \text{ units}$$

| Quarts | Pints |
|---|---|
| 27,907 | 27,907 |
| × 5 | × 20 |
| 139,535 units | 558,140 units |

In sales:

| Quarts | Pints | |
|---|---|---|
| 139,535 | 558,140 | |
| × $3.00 | × $1.75 | |
| $418,605 | $976,745 | = $1,395,350 |

Again, these are monthly amounts.

4. Operating income would not be affected by the $750,000 restructuring charge because it is an extraordinary item and is not listed as an operating expense (the $750,000—net of taxes—would be listed after operating income). The problem states that 2/3 of the fixed expenses are manufacturing overhead, or $600,000 (2/3 × $900,000). A 20% reduction would, therefore, result in an increase in operating income of $120,000 (20% × $600,000).

# Chapter 23 - The Master Budget and Responsibility Accounting

## CHAPTER OVERVIEW

In the last chapter you learned more about costs—specifically how CVP analysis is used to predict outcomes. We now turn our attention to some of the ways managers plan and control their organization's activities. The learning objectives for this chapter are to

1. Identify the benefits of budgeting.
2. Prepare an operating budget for a company.
3. Prepare the components of a financial budget.
4. Use sensitivity analysis in budgeting.
5. Distinguish among different types of responsibility centers.
6. Prepare a performance report for management by exception.
7. Allocate indirect costs to departments.

## CHAPTER REVIEW

### Objective 1 – Identify the benefits of budgeting.

A **budget** is a quantitative expression of a plan of action that helps managers to coordinate and implement the plan. The benefits of budgeting are:

1. Compels planning - budgets require managers to make plans, set goals, and design strategies for achieving those goals.
2. Promotes coordination and communication - since the master budget is an overall company plan, it requires managers to work with other departments to achieve organization goals.
3. Aids performance evaluation - the budget can be used to evaluate performance by comparing actual results with the budgeted ones.
4. Motivates employees - when employees participate in the budgeting process and/or accept the goals as fair, they are more likely to work towards achieving the goals.

The **performance report** compares actual figures with budgeted figures in order to identify areas that need corrective action. The performance report also serves as a guide for the next period's budget.

The **master budget** has three components: 1) the **operating budget**, 2) the **capital expenditures budget**, and 3) the **financial budget**.

You should study Exhibit 23-4 to understand the flow of information in preparation of the master budget.

## Objective 2 - Prepare an operating budget for a company.

The **operating budget** starts with preparation of the sales or revenue budget, the purchases budget, the cost of goods sold budget, the inventory budget, and the operating expenses budget and culminates with the budgeted income statement. The budgeted income statement contains budgeted amounts rather than actual amounts.

### Preparing the Budgeted Income Statement:

Step 1. Prepare the **sales budget** (Exhibit 23-7, Schedule A in your text). Remember that there is no way to accurately plan for inventory purchases or inventory levels without a sales budget. The sales budget will generally schedule sales for each month, and present a total for the entire budget period.

Step 2. Prepare a schedule of the **purchases**, **cost of goods sold**, and **inventory budgets** (Exhibit 23-8, Schedule B in your text). Remember that you need to buy enough to meet both expected sales levels and the desired ending inventory levels. If there is a beginning inventory, it reduces the amount of inventory you need to purchase.

> **Study Tip**: PURCHASES = COST OF GOODS SOLD + ENDING INVENTORY - BEGINNING INVENTORY

Step 3. Calculate **budgeted operating expenses** (Exhibit 23-9, Schedule C in your text). Remember that some expenses vary with sales, such as sales commissions, while other expenses, such as rent, are fixed amounts from month to month.

The schedules prepared for the operating budget are now used to prepare **the budgeted income statement**. Budgeted sales on the income statement were determined by preparation of the sales budget. Budgeted cost of goods sold was determined by the preparation of the purchases, cost of goods sold, and inventory budgets. The gross margin is equal to sales minus cost of goods sold. Operating expenses were scheduled on the operating expense budget. Operating income is equal to the gross margin minus the operating expenses. The one remaining part of the budgeted income statement is interest expense, which is determined from the cash budget. Remember, all of these are budgeted amounts. (Review Exhibit 23-6 in your text.)

## Objective 3 - Prepare the components of a financial budget.

Once the operating budget is complete, the second part of the master budget is the **financial budget**. The financial budget includes the **cash budget** (also called the **statement of budgeted cash receipts and disbursements**), the **budgeted balance sheet**, and the **budgeted statement of cash flows**.

**Budgeted cash collections from customers** (Exhibit 23-10, Schedule D in your text) requires that you estimate 1) cash sales and 2) cash collections from credit sales. These amounts should be determined for each period contained in the budget. **Budgeted cash disbursements** are generally divided into budgeted cash disbursements for purchases (Exhibit 23-11, Schedule E) and budgeted cash disbursements for operating expenses (Exhibit 23-12, Schedule F).

The budgeted acquisition of long-term assets appears in the **capital budget**, which is discussed in more detail in Chapter 26.

Carefully study the statement of budgeted cash receipts and disbursements in your text. To prepare a **cash budget**, perform these steps for each budget period:

1. Add cash receipts from customers (Schedule D) to the beginning cash balance to determine cash available before financing.
2. Calculate total cash disbursements. Subtract this total from the total you calculated in step 1 above. This equals the ending cash balance before financing.
3. Subtract the minimum cash balance desired to obtain the cash excess or deficiency.
4. If a cash deficiency exists, then borrowing will occur to cover the deficiency. If a cash excess exists and there was prior borrowing, there will be repayments of principal and interest expense applicable to the prior borrowing. Obtain the total effects of financing by adding cash borrowed or subtracting principal and interest payments.
5. Calculate the ending cash balance: ending cash available before financing (from step 2 above) plus the total effects of financing (from step 4 above).

The **budgeted balance sheet** is prepared using the budgeted income statement, cash budget, and schedules we have reviewed. The ending balance of some items, such as cash, is carried to the balance sheet directly from a budget or schedule. Other items, such as owners' equity, are carried from the previous balance sheet and adjusted for the activity specified in the budget. Study Exhibit 23-14 in your text.

The last step in preparing the master budget is the **budgeted statement of cash flows**. Information for the cash flow budget is obtained from the previously completed budgets; specifically the cash collections and disbursements schedules, the cash budget, and the cash beginning balance. These amounts are organized into the standard cash flow format: operating, investing, and financing activities. Review Exhibit 23-15 in your text.

## Objective 4 - Use sensitivity analysis in budgeting.

Remember that the master budget is a plan. What happens if actual results differ from the plan? **Sensitivity analysis** is a technique that addresses this dilemma. Specifically, what will happen if predicted outcomes are not achieved or if there is a change in one of the assumptions underlying the budgeting?

Computer spreadsheets are particularly useful in answering many of the questions which arise when there is a difference in an assumption or an actual result because their speed permits managers to react and adjust more quickly.

## Objective 5 - Distinguish among different types of responsibility centers.

**Responsibility accounting** is a system used to evaluate the performance of managers based on the activities they supervise.

A **responsibility center** can be any unit or subunit of an organization which management wishes to evaluate. Four common types of responsibility centers are: 1) **cost centers**, 2) **revenue centers** 3) **profit centers**, and 4) **investment centers**.

A **cost center** generates no revenue and is evaluated on cost control.

A **revenue center** exists where a manager is primarily responsible revenues, although they may also have some responsibility for costs. However, their primary responsibility is to generate revenue.

A **profit center** such as a sales department is evaluated on its revenues, expenses, and income.

An **investment center** such as a single department store in a chain is evaluated on its revenues, expenses, income, and investment needed to finance its operations. Review Exhibits 23-16 and 23-17 in your text.

## Objective 6 – Prepare a performance report for management by exception.

**Management by exception** is a strategy in which management investigates important deviations from budgeted amounts. Responsibility and authority are delegated to lower-level employees; management does not become involved unless necessary. Exhibit 23-18 in your text illustrates a **performance report** which stresses variances. The format of a performance report is a matter of personal preference of the users. Basically, the report compares actual and budgeted performance at different levels of the organization.

## Objective 7 - Allocate indirect costs to departments.

The most common responsibility center is a department. Calculating departmental operating income can be difficult because of indirect costs. **Direct costs** can be traced to a department, but **indirect costs** are not traceable to a single department.

Cost allocations assign various indirect costs to departments. An allocation base is a logical common denominator used to assign a specific cost to two or more departments. For example, heating cost allocation may be based on a department's cubic footage. Exhibit 23-19 lists typical allocation bases for various types of costs.

The general method to allocate costs is:

1. Determine the allocation base.
2. Obtain the proportion of the allocation base assigned to each department.
3. Multiply the cost by the proportion assigned to each department to obtain the cost assigned to each department.

**Study Tip:** Review the Decision Guidelines at the end of the chapter to be certain you feel comfortable with the topics in this chapter.

# TEST YOURSELF

All the self-testing materials in this chapter focus on information and procedures that your instructor is likely to test in quizzes and examinations.

**I. Matching**   *Match each numbered term with its lettered definition.*

_____ 1. master budget
_____ 2. responsibility center
_____ 3. indirect costs
_____ 4. cash budget
_____ 5. sensitivity analysis
_____ 6. operating budget
_____ 7. financial budget
_____ 8. capital expenditures budget
_____ 9. responsibility accounting
_____ 10. management by exception
_____ 11. direct costs

A. a company's plan for purchases of property, plant, equipment, and other long-term assets
B. details how the business expects to go from the beginning cash balance to the desired ending balance
C. costs that are conveniently identified with and traceable to a particular department
D. a system for evaluating the performance of each responsibility center and its managers
E. projects cash inflows and outflows and the period ending balance sheet
F. costs that cannot be traced to a single department
G. the practice of directing management attention to important deviations from budgeted amounts
H. sets the target revenues and expenses for the period
I. a part, segment, or subunit of an organization whose manager is accountable for specified activities
J. a "what if" technique that asks what a result will be if a predicted amount is not achieved or if an underlying assumption changes
K. the comprehensive budget that includes the operating budget, the capital expenditures budget, and the financial budget

**II. Multiple Choice**   *Circle the best answer.*

1. A variance occurs when

   A. actual results exceed budgeted amounts
   B. actual result is less than budgeted amounts
   C. actual results differ from budgeted amounts
   D. none of the above

2. Which of the following is a cost center?

   A. the men's department in a retail store
   B. the West coast division of a large oil refinery
   C. the administrative division of a corporation
   D. the local branch of a statewide chain store

3. When preparing the master budget, the first step is the

   A. financial budget
   B. operating budget
   C. the cash budget
   D. the capital expenditures budget

4. When preparing the operating budget, the first step is

   A. the purchase budget
   B. the sales budget
   C. the operating expense budget
   D. the inventory budget

5. An example of a profit center is:

   A. housewares department in a department store
   B. the accounting department in a hardware store
   C. both of these
   D. neither of these

6. An example of an investment center is:

   A. a department store in a chain of stores
   B. the delivery department of an auto parts store
   C. the shipping department of a manufacturer
   D. both B and C

7. Which factor is important in an effective responsibility accounting system?

   A. control over operations
   B. access to information
   C. both of these
   D. neither of these

8. Responsibility accounting systems are used for:

   A. finding fault
   B. placing blame
   C. both finding fault and placing blame
   D. determining who can explain specific variances

9. Indirect costs are:

   A. all costs other than direct costs
   B. traceable to a single department
   C. costs which cannot be allocated
   D. direct material and direct labor

10. The most logical way of allocating payroll department costs would be:

    A. square feet of space
    B. cubic feet of space
    C. number of orders in each department
    D. number of employees in each department

### III. Completion  *Complete each of the following statements.*

1. The benefits of budgeting are 1) _____
   2) _____
   3) _____
   4) _____
2. The budgeted income statement can be prepared after the _____ has been completed.
3. _____ costs are traceable to specific departments.

4. The three components of the master budget are _____, _____, and _____.
5. To determine what might happen if predicted outcomes are not achieved or underlying assumptions change, managers use _____.
6. _____ are evaluated on their ability to control costs.
7. Budgeted purchases for long-term assets are included in the _____ budget.
8. The financial budget consists of the _____ and the _____.
9. A _____ results when actual results differ from projected results.
10. The _____ compares actual results with budgeted figures.

## IV. Daily Exercises

1. Assuming Inventory increased by $9,000 during the period and Cost of Goods Sold was $245,000, what were purchases?

2. If ending Accounts Receivable is 50% greater than beginning Accounts Receivable, cash receipts from customers are $400,000 and credit sales are 75% of cash receipts, calculate the beginning and ending Accounts Receivable balances.

3. Bob and Ray's Appliance Store sells family entertainment appliances. Monthly rent is $40,000. Data for three departments for April, 19X9, follow:

| Department | Sales | Square Feet Occupied |
|---|---|---|
| Televisions | $425,000 | 7,000 |
| VCRs | 225,000 | 1,600 |
| CD players | 150,000 | 1,400 |

A. Allocate rent to each department based on sales.

B. Allocate rent to each department based on square feet occupied.

4. Susana's Shoes has three locations in Anytown, USA. The owner received the following data for the third quarter of the current year:

|  | Revenues | | Expenses | |
|---|---|---|---|---|
|  | Budget | Actual | Budget | Actual |
| West Store | $220,000 | $250,000 | $210,000 | $198,000 |
| Center Store | 187,000 | 175,000 | 146,000 | 150,000 |
| East Store | 713,000 | 874,000 | 706,000 | 696,000 |

Arrange the data in a performance report, showing third quarter results in thousands of dollars.

# V. Exercises

1. Kay's Cameras sells disposable, recyclable cameras for use underwater. The units cost $3 each and are sold for $6 a piece. At the end of the first quarter, 200 cameras were on hand. Projected sales for the next four months are 700 units, 900 units, 1,200 units, and 1,000 units, respectively. Kay wants to maintain inventory equal to 40% of the next month's sales.

   Prepare a sales budget, purchases budget, cost of goods sold, and inventory budget for the next quarter.

   Sales Budget - 2nd Quarter

   | 1st month | 2nd month | 3rd month | Total |
   |---|---|---|---|
   |   |   |   |   |

   Purchases, Cost of Goods Sold, and Inventory Budget

   |   | 1st month | 2nd month | 3rd month | Total |
   |---|---|---|---|---|
   |   |   |   |   |   |
   |   |   |   |   |   |
   |   |   |   |   |   |
   |   |   |   |   |   |
   |   |   |   |   |   |
   |   |   |   |   |   |
   |   |   |   |   |   |
   |   |   |   |   |   |
   |   |   |   |   |   |

2. Using the following information, present an income statement in the space provided.

   a) Consulting Fees Earned were $850,000.

   b) Salaries: the staff consists of two full-time consultants, one half-time consultant and an office assistant. The consultants are paid a base salary, plus a 30% commission on fees earned. The base for full-time consultants is $40,000 while the half-time consultant receives a base of $20,000. The office assistant's salary is $35,000.

   c) Office rent was $5,500/month for 1/1 – 6/30 at which time it was raised to $6,000 for the remainder of the year.

   d) Depreciation on office equipment, computed on the straight-line basis, was $15,000 for the year.

   e) Office expenses were $20,000 plus 5% of consulting fees.

   f) Travel expenses were 4% of consulting fees.

   g) Miscellaneous expenses were 1% of consulting fees.

|  |  |  |
|--|--|--|
|  |  |  |
|  |  |  |
|  |  |  |
|  |  |  |
|  |  |  |
|  |  |  |
|  |  |  |
|  |  |  |
|  |  |  |
|  |  |  |
|  |  |  |
|  |  |  |
|  |  |  |
|  |  |  |
|  |  |  |

3. Review the information in Exercise 2 above and the following information, and present a budgeted income statement in the space provided. You may want to first compare your answer for Exercise 2 with the solution.

   a) Revenues are expected to increase by 25%.
   b) The office assistant will receive a 10% salary increase at the beginning of the year.
   c) On 7/1 the lease for the office will be renewed. It is expected to increase by 15%/month.
   d) Depreciation will remain unchanged for the year.

|  |  |  |
|--|--|--|
|  |  |  |
|  |  |  |
|  |  |  |
|  |  |  |
|  |  |  |
|  |  |  |
|  |  |  |
|  |  |  |
|  |  |  |
|  |  |  |
|  |  |  |
|  |  |  |
|  |  |  |
|  |  |  |

4. Review the information from Exercise 3 above and present, in the space provided, a performance report for the year, considering the following additional information.

   a) Revenues increased by 40%.
   b) The growth in revenues required an expansion of the staff by one additional full-time consultant, who was hired on April 1. Also on April 1, base salaries for full-time consultants were increased to $50,000 while the half-time consultant's base was increased to $25,000. The commission rate remained unchanged.
   c) The July 1 rent increase was 25%.
   d) Travel expenses were 6% of revenues.

|   | Actual | Budgeted | Variance |
|---|---|---|---|
|   |   |   |   |
|   |   |   |   |
|   |   |   |   |
|   |   |   |   |
|   |   |   |   |
|   |   |   |   |
|   |   |   |   |
|   |   |   |   |
|   |   |   |   |
|   |   |   |   |
|   |   |   |   |
|   |   |   |   |
|   |   |   |   |
|   |   |   |   |

5. The Jones-Jackson Partnership owns and operates a sporting goods store specializing in trekking equipment. Sales for the first two quarters of the current year are as follows:

   | January | $343,200 |
   | February | 386,000 |
   | March | 408,000 |
   | April | 440,900 |
   | May | 501,800 |
   | June | 527,100 |

   The partnership's sales are 15% cash and 85% credit. Collections from credit customers are 20% the month of sale, 45% the month following sale, 30% two months following sale, and 4% three months after sale. 1% of credit sales become uncollectible and are written off.

   Using the following format, prepare a schedule for budgeted cash collections for April, May and June (round to the whole dollar amounts).

|  | April | May | June |
|---|---|---|---|
| Cash Sales |  |  |  |
| Collections from January |  |  |  |
| Collections from February |  |  |  |
| Collections from March |  |  |  |
| Collections from April |  |  |  |
| Collections from May |  |  |  |
| Collections from June |  |  |  |
|  |  |  |  |
| Monthly Totals |  |  |  |
| Total for the Quarter |  |  |  |

## VI. Beyond the Numbers

Review the information in Daily Exercise 3 above. How would your answers change given the following two additional assumptions?

A. In addition to the three departments, there is an administrative office using 1,000 square feet of space.

B. In addition to the three departments and the office, there is an appliance repair department using 1,500 square feet of space.

# VII. Demonstration Problems

## Demonstration Problem #1

Tele-data Communication's cash budget for the first three quarters of 19X9 is given below (note that some of the data is missing and must be calculated). The company requires a minimum cash balance of at least $40,000, and owes $4,000 on a note payable from a previous quarter. (Ignore interest.)

Tele-data Communications
Quarterly Cash Budget
19X9

|  | 1 | 2 | 3 |
|---|---|---|---|
| Beginning cash balance | $ 64,000 | $    D | $ 52,000 |
| Add collections from customers | A | 280,000 | 268,000 |
| Cash available | $    B | $    E | $320,000 |
| Deduct disbursements |  |  |  |
|    Inventory purchases | $124,000 | $    F | $ 92,000 |
|    Operating expenses | 100,000 | 88,000 | 120,000 |
|    Equipment purchases | 40,000 | 44,000 | 116,000 |
|    Dividends | 0 | 24,000 | J |
|    Total disbursements | $264,000 | $G | $    K |
| Excess (deficiency) in cash | $ 28,000 | $ 68,000 | ($ 8,000) |
|  |  |  |  |
| Financing |  |  |  |
|    Add borrowing | $    C | - | $ 48,000 |
|    Deduct repayments | - | H | 0 |
| Ending cash balance | $ 40,000 | $    I | $ 40,000 |

## Required:

Find the missing value represented by each letter. (Hint: it may not be possible to solve this problem in sequence, A first, B second, and so on.)

A.

B.

C.

D.

E.

F.

G.

H.

I.

J.

K.

## Demonstration Problem #2

The Baguette Bakery has two departments, wholesale and retail. The company's income statement for 19X9 appears as follows:

|  |  |  |
|---|---:|---:|
| Net Sales |  | $1,130,000 |
| Cost of Goods Sold |  | 548,000 |
| Gross Margin |  | 582,000 |
| Operating expenses: |  |  |
| Salaries | $310,000 |  |
| Depreciation | 45,000 |  |
| Advertising | 18,000 |  |
| Other | 30,000 | 403,000 |
| Operating income |  | $ 179,000 |

Cost of goods sold is distributed $226,000 for wholesale and $322,000 for retail. Salaries are allocated to departments based on sales: wholesale, $472,000; retail $658,000. Advertising is evenly allocated to the two departments. Depreciation is allocated based on square footage: wholesale, 4,000 square feet; retail, 6,000 square feet. Other expenses are allocated based on sales.

Prepare a departmental income statement showing revenue, expenses, and operating income for two departments.

| The Baguette Bakery<br>Departmental Income Statement<br>For the Year Ended December 31, 19X9 |||||
|---|---|---|---|---|
|  |  | Department ||
|  | Total | Wholesale | Retail ||
| Net sales | $1,130,000 |  |  |
| Cost of goods sold | 548,000 |  |  |
| Gross margin | 582,000 |  |  |
| Operating expenses: |  |  |  |
| Salaries | 310,000 |  |  |
| Depreciation | 45,000 |  |  |
| Advertising | 18,000 |  |  |
| Other | 30,000 |  |  |
| Total operating expenses | 403,000 |  |  |
| Operating income | $ 179,000 | $ | $ |

SOLUTIONS

## I. Matching

| | | | | |
|---|---|---|---|---|
| 1. K | 3. F | 5. J | 7. E | 9. D | 11. C |
| 2. I | 4. B | 6. H | 8. A | 10. G | |

## II. Multiple Choice

1.  C   A variance does not imply direction, only a difference.

2.  C   The men's department is a profit center, while choices B and D are investment centers.

3.  B   The order is operating budget, the capital expenditures budget, and financial budget (which includes the cash budget).

4.  B   The operating budget always begins with the sales budget - the others are prepared after the sales budget is completed.

5.  A   The accounting department is a cost center.

6.  A   Both choices B and C are cost centers.

7.  C   Both the control over operations and access to information are important factors in an effective responsibility accounting system.

8.  D   Responsibility accounting systems are not intended to find fault or place blame.

9.  A   Costs are either direct or indirect. Direct costs are those traceable to a single department (choice B), examples of which are direct materials and direct labor (choice D). Choice C is not appropriate because any cost can be allocated.

10. D   Since payroll costs are directly related to the number of employees, choice D is the most appropriate way of allocating the cost.

## III. Completion

1. compels planning; promotes coordination and communication; aids performance evaluation; motivates employees (order not important)
2. operating budget
3. Direct
4. operating budget, capital expenditures budget, financial budget
5. sensitivity analysis
6. cost centers
7. capital expenditures
8. cash budget, budgeted balance sheet
9. variance
10. performance report

# IV. Daily Exercises

1. Beginning inventory + Purchases − Ending inventory = Cost of goods sold
   X + Purchases − (X + $9,000) = $245,000
   Purchases   = $254,000

2.. Beginning Accounts Receivable = X
   Ending Accounts Receivable = 150%X
   Credit Sales = 75% × $400,000 = $300,000

   Beginning Accounts Receivable + Credit Sales − Receipts from customers =
   Ending Accounts Receivable
        X      + $400,000 − $300,000     = 150%X
   Beginning Accounts Receivable = $200,000
   Ending Accounts Receivable = 150% × $200,000 = $300,000

3. A. Based on sales:

   Total sales = $425,000 + $225,000 + $150,000 = $800,000
   Television department rent = ($425,000/$800,000) × $40,000 = $21,250
   VCR department rent = ($225,000/800,000) × $40,000 = $11,250
   CD player department rent = ($150,000/800,000) × $40,000 = $7,500
   (Proof: $21,250 + $11,250 + $7,500 = $40,000)

   B. Based on space occupied:

   Total square feet = 7,000 + 1,600 + 1,400 = 10,000
   Television department rent = (7,000/10,000) × $40,000 = $28,000
   VCR department rent = (1,600/10,000) × $40,000 = $6,400
   CD player department rent = (1,400/10,000) × $40,000 = $5,600
   (Proof: $28,000 + 6,400 + $5,600 = $40,000)

4.

| Operating income by location | Budget | Actual | Variance Favorable (Unfavorable) |
|---|---|---|---|
| West Store |  |  |  |
| (220-210) | 10 |  |  |
| (250-198) |  | 52 | 42 |
|  |  |  |  |
| Center Store |  |  |  |
| (187-146) | 41 |  |  |
| (175-150) |  | 25 | (16) |
|  |  |  |  |
| East Store |  |  |  |
| (713-706) | 7 |  |  |
| (874-696) |  | 178 | 171 |
|  | $58 | $255 | $197 |

## V. Exercises

1.

Sales Budget – 2nd Quarter

| 1st month | 2nd month | 3rd month | Total |
|---|---|---|---|
| $4,200 | $5,400 | $7,200 | $16,800 |

Multiply number of units by unit cost.

Purchases, Cost of Goods Sold, and Inventory Budget

|   |   | 1st month | 2nd month | 3rd month | Total |
|---|---|---|---|---|---|
|   | Cost of Goods Sold[1] | $2,100 | $2,700 | $3,600 | $8,400 |
| + | Desired Ending Inventory[2] | 1,080 | 1,440 | 1,200[5] | 1,200 |
|   | Subtotal | 3,180 | 4,140 | 4,800 | 9,600 |
| − | Beginning Inventory[3] | 600[4] | 1,080 | 1,440 | 600 |
| = | Purchases | $2,580 | $3,060 | $2,360 | $9,000 |

[1] Cost of Goods Sold is 50% of budgeted sales: $3/$6 = 50%
[2] Desired Ending Inventory is 40% of the following month's Cost of Goods Sold.
[3] Beginning Inventory is 40% of current month's Cost of Goods Sold (or simply last month's Ending Inventory!)
[4] Beginning Inventory is 200 units × $3 ea = $600
[5] The next month's projected Cost of Goods Sold = 1,000 units × $3 ea = $3,000; Ending Inventory = 40% × $3,000 = $1,200

2.

| | | |
|---|---:|---:|
| Consulting Fees Earned | | $850,000 |
| Less: Operating Expenses | | |
|     Salaries and Commissions Expense | $390,000 | |
|     Rent Expense | 69,000 | |
|     Depreciation Expense | 15,000 | |
|     Office Expense | 62,500 | |
|     Travel Expense | 34,000 | |
|     Miscellaneous Expense | 8,500 | 579,000 |
| Net Income | | $271,000 |

Calculations:

| Salaries and Commissions | |
|---|---:|
|   2 Full-time Consultants | $ 80,000 |
|   1 Half-time Consultant | 20,000 |
|   30% of Consulting Fees | 255,000 |
|   Office Assistant | 35,000 |
| Total | $390,000 |

| | | | |
|---|---|---|---|
| Rent Expense = 6 × $5,500 + 6 × $6,000 | = | 69,000 | |
| Office Expense = $20,000 + .05 × $850,000 | = | 62,500 | |
| Travel Expense = .04 × $850,000 | = | 34,000 | |
| Miscellaneous Expense = .01 × $850,000 | = | 8,500 | |

3.

### Budgeted Income Statement

| | | |
|---|---:|---:|
| Consulting Fees Earned | | $1,062,500 |
| Less: Operating Expenses | | |
|     Salaries and Commissions Expense | $457,250 | |
|     Rent Expense | 77,400 | |
|     Depreciation Expense | 15,000 | |
|     Office Expense | 73,125 | |
|     Travel Expense | 42,500 | |
|     Miscellaneous Expense | 10,625 | 675,900 |
| Net Income | | $ 386,600 |

Calculations:

| | |
|---|---:|
| Salaries and Commissions | |
|   Consultants Base | $100,000 |
|   30 % Commissions | 318,750 |
|   Office Assistant | 38,500 |
|   Total | $457,250 |

| | | | |
|---|---|---:|---|
| Rent Expense = 6 × $6,000 + 6 × $6,900 | = | 77,400 | |
| Office Expense = $20,000 + .05 × $1,062,500 | = | 73,125 | |
| Travel Expense = .04 × $1,062,500 | = | 42,500 | |
| Miscellaneous Expense = .01 × $1,062,500 | = | 10,625 | |

4.

### Performance Report

| | Actual | Budgeted | Variance |
|---|---:|---:|---:|
| Consulting Fees Earned | $1,190,000 | $1,062,500 | $127,500 |
| Salaries and Commissions | 552,750 | 457,250 | (95,500) |
| Rent Expense | 81,000 | 77,400 | (3,600) |
| Depreciation Expense | 15,000 | 15,000 | 0 |
| Office Expense | 79,500 | 73,125 | (6,375) |
| Travel Expense | 71,400 | 42,500 | (28,900) |
| Miscellaneous Expense | 11,900 | 10,625 | (1,275) |
| Net Income | $ 378,450 | $ 386,600 | $ (8,150) |

Calculations:
Salaries and Commissions
2 Full-time Consultants:
$40,000 × 2 × 3/12 = $ 20,000
$50,000 × 2 × 9/12 = 75,000
1 Full time Consultant:
$50,000 × 9/12 = 37,500
1 Half-time Consultant
$20,000 × 3/12 = 5,000
$25,000 × 9/12 = 18,750
30% Commission 357,000
Office Assistant 38,500
$552,750

Rent Expense = 6 × $6,000 + 6 × $7,500 = 81,000
Office Expense = $20,000 + .05 × $1,190,000 = 79,500
Travel Expense = .06 × $1,190,000 = 71,400
Miscellaneous Expense = .01 × $1,190,000 = 11,900

5.

|  | April | May | June |
| --- | --- | --- | --- |
| Cash Sales | $ 66,135 | $ 75,270 | $ 79,065 |
| Collections from January | 11,669 |  |  |
| Collections from February | 98,430 | 13,124 |  |
| Collections from March | 156,060 | 104,040 | 13,872 |
| Collections from April | 74,953 | 168,644 | 112,430 |
| Collections from May |  | 85,306 | 191,939 |
| Collections from June |  |  | 89,607 |
| Monthly Totals | $407247 | $446,384 | $486,913 |
|  |  |  |  |
| Total from Quarter |  |  | $1,340,544 |

## VI. Beyond the Numbers

A. Because the office is a cost center and not a profit center, whatever amount of monthly rent is allocated to the office would later have to be allocated to the three departments (along with the other expenses allocated to the office). Therefore, assuming these costs are allocated using either sales or square feet, the end result would be the same as the amounts calculated in the exercise.

B. Assuming the repair department is a profit center (i.e., it generates revenue) then the amount of rent expense allocated to the three departments in the exercise will decrease by the amount allocated to the repair department. However, if the repair department is a cost center (for instance, it may only do repairs covered by warranties) then the amounts ultimately allocated to the three departments would remain unchanged.

## VII. Demonstration Problems

### Demonstration Problem #1 Solved and Explained

The solution is given in the order in which the exercise may be worked.

B. Cash available - Total disbursements = Excess (deficiency)
   B - $264,000 = $28,000
   B = $292,000

A. Beginning cash balance + Cash collections = Cash available
   $64,000 + A = $292,000
   A = $228,000

C. Excess + Borrowing = Ending cash balance
   $28,000 + C = $40,000
   C = $12,000

D. $40,000; the beginning cash balance for any quarter is the ending cash balance from the previous quarter.

E. Beginning cash balance + Cash collections = Cash available
   $40,000 + $280,000 = E
   E = $320,000

I. $52,000; the ending cash balance for any quarter is the beginning cash balance for the next quarter.

H. Excess - Repayments = Ending cash balance
   $68,000 - H = $52,000
   H = $16,000

G. Cash available - Total disbursements = Excess
   $320,000 - G = $ 68,000
   G = $252,000

F. Inventory purchases + Operating expenses + Equipment purchases + Dividends = Total disbursements
   F + $88,000 + $44,000 + $24,000 = $252,000
   F = $96,000

K. Cash available - Total disbursements = (deficiency)
   $320,000 - L = ($8,000)
   $320,000 + $8,000 = L
   L = $328,000

J. Inventory purchases + Operating expenses + Equipment purchases + Dividends = Total disbursements
   $92,000 + $120,000 + $116,000 + K = $328,000
   $328,000 + K = $328,000
   K = $0

**Demonstration Problem #2 Solved and Explained**

<table>
<tr><td colspan="4" align="center">The Baguette Bakery<br>Departmental Income Statement<br>For the Year Ended December 31, 19X9</td></tr>
<tr><td></td><td></td><td colspan="2" align="center">Department</td></tr>
<tr><td></td><td>Total</td><td>Wholesale</td><td>Retail</td></tr>
<tr><td>Net sales</td><td>$1,130,000</td><td>$472,000</td><td>$658,000</td></tr>
<tr><td>Cost of goods sold</td><td>548,000</td><td>226,000</td><td>322,000</td></tr>
<tr><td>Gross margin</td><td>582,000</td><td>246,000</td><td>336,000</td></tr>
<tr><td>Operating expenses:</td><td></td><td></td><td></td></tr>
<tr><td>  Salaries</td><td>310,000</td><td>129,487</td><td>180,513</td></tr>
<tr><td>  Depreciation</td><td>45,000</td><td>18,000</td><td>27,000</td></tr>
<tr><td>  Advertising</td><td>18,000</td><td>9,000</td><td>9,000</td></tr>
<tr><td>  Other</td><td>30,000</td><td>12,531</td><td>17,469</td></tr>
<tr><td>  Total operating expenses</td><td>403,000</td><td>169,018</td><td>233,982</td></tr>
<tr><td>Operating income</td><td>$ 179,000</td><td>$ 76,982</td><td>$102,018</td></tr>
</table>

Calculations:

Salaries:
- Wholesale     [($472,000 ÷ $1,130,000)] × $310,000 = $129,487
- Retail         [($658,000 ÷ $1,130,000)] × $310,000 = $180,513

Depreciation:
- Wholesale     [4,000 ÷ (4,000 + 6,000)] × $45,000 = $18,000
- Retail         [6,000 ÷ (4,000 + 6,000)] × $45,000 = $27,000

Advertising:
- Wholesale     $18,000 ÷ 2 = $9,000
- Retail         $18,000 ÷ 2 = $9,000

Other:
- Wholesale     ($129,487 ÷ $310,000) × $30,000 = $12,531
- Retail         ($180,513 ÷ $310,000) × $30,000 = $17,469

# Chapter 24 - Flexible Budgets and Standard Costs

## CHAPTER OVERVIEW

In Chapter 23 you were introduced to the master budget and its components. In addition, you learned how budgeted amounts can be compared with actual results as one means of evaluating performance. The topics in the previous chapter provide a foundation for those covered in this chapter—flexible budgets and standard costs. The learning objectives for this chapter are to

1. Prepare a flexible budget for the income statement.
2. Prepare an income statement performance report.
3. Identify the benefits of standard costs.
4. Compute standard cost variances for direct materials and direct labor.
5. Analyze manufacturing overhead in a standard cost system.
6. Record transactions at standard cost.
7. Prepare a standard cost income statement for management.

## CHAPTER REVIEW

### Objective 1 – Prepare a flexible budget for the income statement.

As you learned in previous chapters, **cost behavior** may be fixed or variable. Mixed costs have both variable and fixed components. Cost behaviors are valid only for a relevant range of activity.

A **static budget** is prepared for only one level of activity. The static budget is used to budget unit costs and overhead rates. A **performance report** compares actual with budgeted results to show the **variance** (difference) and whether the variance is favorable or unfavorable.

A **flexible budget** is a set of budgets covering a range of different sales volumes. Generally, the flexible budget is prepared for actual volume achieved (that is, when actual volume is known). Review Exhibit 24-2 in your text.

To prepare a flexible budget, we use the **budget formula** to compute the budget amounts:

REVENUES - VARIABLE EXPENSES - FIXED EXPENSES = OPERATING INCOME (LOSS)

$$\begin{bmatrix} \text{UNITS SOLD} \\ \text{x UNIT} \\ \text{SALE PRICE} \end{bmatrix} - \begin{bmatrix} \text{UNITS SOLD} \\ \text{x VARIABLE} \\ \text{COST PER UNIT} \end{bmatrix} - \begin{matrix} \text{FIXED} \\ \text{EXPENSES} \end{matrix} = \begin{matrix} \text{OPERATING} \\ \text{INCOME} \\ \text{(or LOSS)} \end{matrix}$$

Note that fixed expenses remain constant. They do not change while the firm operates within the relevant range.

Study Exhibit 24-3 in your text to understand the preparation of a flexible budget income statement.

Graphing the expense formula provides a budget for any level of volume. The vertical axis of the budget expense graph shows total expenses and the horizontal axis shows the level of volume. Both budgeted and actual results can be graphed. Remember that the only valid portion of the graph is the area within the relevant range. Refer to Exhibit 24-4 and 24-5 in your text for a graph of a flexible expense budget and a graph of actual and budgeted total expenses.

## Objective 2 – Prepare an income statement performance report.

An **income statement performance report** is a five-column report:

Column 1    contains actual results at actual prices.

Column 3    contains the flexible budget for actual volume achieved (prepared using the budget formula).

Column 5    contains the static (master) budget.

Column 2    contains flexible budget variances. Flexible budget variances are differences between actual results (Column 1) and the flexible budget (Column 3).

Column 4    contains sales volume variances. Sales volume variances are the differences between the flexible budget (Column 3) and the static budget (Column 5).

See Exhibit 24-7 in your text for an income statement performance report.

## Objective 3 - Identify the benefits of standard costs.

A **standard cost** is a predetermined cost that management expects to attain. The benefits to an organization of standard costs are:

1. Providing the unit amounts needed for budgeting
2. Help management control operations by setting target levels of operating performance
3. Motivating employees by setting goals against which performance will be evaluated
4. Providing a unit cost basis for establishing selling prices
5. Reducing clerical costs

See Exhibit 24-8 in your text

## Objective 4 - Compute standard cost variances for direct materials and direct labor.

Variances between actual and standard costs are separated into **price variances** and **efficiency variances** for direct materials and direct labor.

### Direct Materials:

The total flexible budget variance for direct materials is separated into the price variance and the efficiency variance. The **direct materials price variance** measures the difference between the actual and the budgeted price of materials for the amount of materials used.

$$\text{PRICE VARIANCE} = \begin{bmatrix} \text{DIFFERENCE BETWEEN} \\ \text{ACTUAL AND STANDARD} \\ \text{UNIT PRICES OF INPUTS} \end{bmatrix} \times \begin{bmatrix} \text{QUANTITY OF ACTUAL} \\ \text{INPUT} \end{bmatrix}$$

If the actual unit price is less than the budgeted unit price, the variance is favorable. If the actual unit price is greater than the budgeted unit price, the variance is unfavorable.

$$\text{EFFICIENCY VARIANCE} = \begin{bmatrix} \text{INPUTS} \\ \text{ACTUALLY} \\ \text{USED} \end{bmatrix} - \begin{bmatrix} \text{INPUTS THAT SHOULD} \\ \text{HAVE BEEN USED} \\ \text{FOR ACTUAL OUTPUT} \end{bmatrix} \times \begin{bmatrix} \text{STANDARD} \\ \text{UNIT PRICE} \\ \text{OF INPUT} \end{bmatrix}$$

The **direct materials efficiency** (quantity or usage) **variance** measures the difference between the quantity of inputs actually used and the inputs that should have been used for the actual output achieved.

Note that INPUTS THAT SHOULD HAVE BEEN USED FOR ACTUAL OUTPUT is equal to standard input per unit times actual units produced.

If inputs actually used are less than inputs that should have been used, the variance is favorable. If inputs actually used are greater than inputs that should have been used, the variance is unfavorable.

Exhibit 24-10 in your text summarizes the direct materials variance computations.

### Direct Labor:

The **direct labor price** (rate) **variance** measures the difference between the actual rate per labor hour and the budgeted rate per labor hour.

$$\text{PRICE VARIANCE} = \begin{bmatrix} \text{DIFFERENCE BETWEEN} \\ \text{ACTUAL AND STANDARD} \\ \text{UNIT PRICES OF INPUTS} \end{bmatrix} \times \begin{bmatrix} \text{QUANTITY OF ACTUAL} \\ \text{INPUTS} \end{bmatrix}$$

The **direct labor efficiency variance** measures the difference between hours actually used and hours that should have been used for the output achieved.

$$\text{EFFICIENCY VARIANCE} = \left[ \begin{array}{c} \text{INPUTS} \\ \text{ACTUALLY} \\ \text{USED} \end{array} - \begin{array}{c} \text{INPUTS THAT SHOULD} \\ \text{HAVE BEEN USED} \\ \text{FOR ACTUAL OUTPUT} \end{array} \right] \times \begin{array}{c} \text{STANDARD} \\ \text{UNIT PRICE} \\ \text{OF INPUT} \end{array}$$

Note that these equations are identical to the direct materials variance equations. Exhibit 24-11 in your text summarizes direct labor variance computations.

The advantage to the company of calculating these variances is that management can investigate when the variances are significant.

In addition to direct materials and direct labor, variances are also calculated for manufacturing overhead as one means of evaluating performance. Some companies group individual overhead cost into a single cost pool, distinguishing between the variable and fixed amounts.

## Objective 5 – Analyze manufacturing overhead in a standard cost system.

**Overhead variances** are computed differently from material and labor variances. Manufacturing overhead variances are commonly separated into a **flexible budget variance** and a **production volume variance**.

The **overhead flexible budget variance** (also called the **overhead controllable variance**) is the difference between total overhead incurred and the flexible budget amount for actual production. The **production volume variance** is the difference between the flexible budget for actual production and standard overhead applied to production.

Exhibit 24-13 in your text summarizes this two-variance approach.

## Objective 6 - Record transactions at standard cost.

To record purchases of direct materials:

| | | | |
|---|---|---|---|
| Materials Inventory | XX | | |
| Direct Materials Price Variance | X | or | X |
|     Accounts Payable | | | XX |

To record direct materials used:

| | | | |
|---|---|---|---|
| Work in Process | XX | | |
| Direct Materials Efficiency Variance | X | or | X |
|     Materials Inventory | | | XX |

To record direct labor costs incurred:

| | | | |
|---|---|---|---|
| Manufacturing Wages | XX | | |
| Direct Labor Price Variance | X | or | X |
|     Wages Payable | | | XX |

To apply direct labor to production:

| | | | |
|---|---|---|---|
| Work in Process | XX | | |
| Direct Labor Efficiency Variance | X | or | X |
|     Manufacturing Wages | | | XX |

To record overhead incurred:

| | |
|---|---|
| Manufacturing Overhead | XX |
|     A/P, Accum. Dep., etc. | XX |

To assign Overhead

| | |
|---|---|
| Work in Process | XX |
|     Manufacturing Overhead | XX |

The overhead variance is recorded when the Overhead account is reduced to zero.

In all of these entries, credit variances are favorable, debits are unfavorable. At year end, all variance accounts are closed with a reconciling net debit (or credit) to Income Summary.

## Objective 7 - Prepare a standard cost income statement for management.

A **standard cost income statement** lists cost of goods sold at standard cost followed by the specific variances for direct materials, direct labor, and manufacturing overhead. Remember, debit variances are unfavorable (and therefore added to the cost of goods sold amount) while credit variances are favorable (and therefore deducted from the cost of goods sold amount). This format shows management what needs to be improved or corrected. See Exhibit 24-15 in your text.

# TEST YOURSELF

All the self-testing materials in this chapter focus on information and procedures that your instructor is likely to test in quizzes and examinations.

**I. Matching** *Match each numbered term with its lettered definition.*

_____ 1. price variance
_____ 2. standard cost
_____ 3. variance
_____ 4. efficiency variance
_____ 5. production volume variance
_____ 6. bench marking
_____ 7. sales volume variance
_____ 8. static budget
_____ 9. flexible budget
_____ 10. flexible budget variance
_____ 11. overhead flexible budget variance

A. A budget prepared for only one level of activity
B. The difference between an actual amount and the corresponding budgeted amount
C. The difference between the actual quantity and the standard quantity of input allowed for actual output, multiplied by the standard unit price of input
D. Difference between an amount in the flexible budget and the actual results
E. Difference between a revenue, expense, or operating income in the flexible budget, and the revenue, expense, or income amount in the master budget
F. Difference between total actual overhead (fixed and variable) and the flexible budget amount for actual production volume
G. Difference between the actual unit price of an input (materials and labor) and a standard unit price, multiplied by the actual quantity of inputs used
H. Difference between the flexible budget for actual production and standard overhead applied to production
I. Predetermined cost that management believes the business should incur in producing an item
J. Set of budgets covering a range of volume rather than a single level of volume
K. Using standards based on "best practice" level of performance

**II. Multiple Choice** *Circle the best answer.*

1. As volume decreases, which of the following is true?

   A. total variable costs decrease
   B. variable cost per unit decreases
   C. fixed cost per unit decreases
   D. total fixed costs increase

2. A budget covering a range of activity levels is a:

   A. flexible budget
   B. static budget
   C. conversion budget
   D. pliable budget

3. Flexible budgets can be used as:

   A. a planning tool
   B. a control device
   C. both a planning tool and a control device
   D. neither a planning tool nor a control device

4. One possible explanation for a favorable sales volume variance and an unfavorable flexible budget variance is:

   A. higher than expected sales and costs
   B. higher than expected sales and lower than expected costs
   C. lower than expected sales and higher than expected costs
   D. lower than expected sales and costs

5. The term standard cost usually refers to ___ cost. The term budgeted cost usually refers to ___ cost.

   A. unit, unit
   B. unit, total
   C. total, unit
   D. total, total

6. Price variances relate to:

   A. direct materials only
   B. direct labor only
   C. manufacturing overhead only
   D. both direct materials and direct labor

7. A production volume variance relates to:

   A. direct materials only
   B. direct labor only
   C. manufacturing overhead only
   D. both direct materials and direct labor

8. In a standard cost income statement, gross margin equals:

   A. net sales - cost of goods sold at standard cost
   B. net sales - operating expenses
   C. net sales - cost of goods sold at standard cost + unfavorable variances - favorable variances
   D. net sales - cost of goods sold at standard cost - unfavorable variances + favorable variances

9. At the end of the accounting period, variance account balances are:

   A. carried forward to the next accounting period
   B. closed to cost of goods sold
   C. closed to Income Summary
   D. none of the above

10. The difference between the actual overhead cost and the flexible budget for actual production is the

    A. production volume variance
    B. flexible budget variance
    C. sales volume variance
    D. overhead flexible budget variance

## III. Completion  *Complete each of the following statements.*

1. _____ are resources given up to achieve a specific objective.
2. Total _____ costs change proportionately with changes in volume or activity.
3. Total _____ costs do not change during a given time period over a wide range of volume.
4. A _____ cost has both variable and fixed components.
5. If rent expense is fixed at $1,000 per month and sales increase from 2,500 units to 10,000 units, the rent per unit is _____ as much as it originally was.
6. A(n) _____ variance for materials or labor measures whether the quantity of inputs used to make a product is within the budget.
7. A(n) _____ variance for materials or labor measures how well a business keeps unit prices of materials and labor within standards.
8. A budget prepared for only one level of volume is called a _____ budget.
9. A _____ refers to any group of individual items.
10. _____ measures the amount of inputs used to achieve a given level of output.

## IV. Daily Exercises

1. Nello's Delicatessen produces a salt-free pasta sauce, which is sold in one quart containers. The pasta is made in 10 gallon batches. Each 10 gallon batch requires the following:

   | Ingredients | Cost |
   | --- | --- |
   | 90 pounds of tomatoes | 25¢/lb |
   | 2 head of garlic | 90¢ ea. |
   | 20 pounds of onions | 15¢/lb |
   | 2 gallons red wine | $6.50/gallon |
   | 2 cups olive oil | 20¢/ounce |
   | 8 ounces fresh herbs | 10¢/ounce |

   In addition, the container in which the sauce is sold costs the business 9¢. Calculate the standard cost to produce one quart of pasta sauce.

2. To produce a 2-pound loaf of sourdough bread, the San Francisco Bakery's standard material cost is 82¢ per loaf (40¢ per pound plus the 2¢ for the package.) During the first week of March, the San Francisco Bakery purchased 120,000 pounds of ingredients costing $47,400 and paid $1,200 for 60,000 sacks. The week's production was 59,550 loaves of bread. Compute the price, efficiency, and total materials variances.

3. Review the information in Daily Exercise 2 above and journalize entries to record the materials variances.

|  |  |  |
|---|---|---|
|  |  |  |
|  |  |  |
|  |  |  |
|  |  |  |
|  |  |  |
|  |  |  |
|  |  |  |
|  |  |  |
|  |  |  |

4. Review the information in Daily Exercise 2 above. San Francisco Bakery's standard direct labor cost is 25¢ per unit of output. For the first week of March, the total direct labor cost was 14,600. Compute the price, efficiency, and total direct labor variances.

5. Review the information in Daily Exercise 4 above and journalize entries to record labor variances.

|   |   |   |
|---|---|---|
|   |   |   |
|   |   |   |
|   |   |   |
|   |   |   |
|   |   |   |
|   |   |   |
|   |   |   |
|   |   |   |

## V. Exercises

1. If variable costs are $5.00 per unit, the relevant range is 6,000 to 15,000 units, and total costs were $60,000 for 8,000 units:

   A. How much were fixed costs?

   B. What is the flexible budget formula for costs?

   C. At the 10,000 units level, what are total budgeted costs?

2.

| | | |
|---|---|---|
| Actual production | 3,300 | units |
| Actual cost (6,700 feet of direct materials) | $33,701 | |
| Standard price | $ 4.75 | per foot |
| Materials efficiency variance | $ 2,660 | F |

A. Compute the materials price variance.

B. Compute standard feet per unit.

2. Assuming 2,400 hours of direct labor were budgeted for actual output at a standard rate of $12.00 per hour and 2,500 hours were worked at a rate of $11.75 per hour,

A. Compute the labor price variance.

B. Compute the labor efficiency variance.

4. The Massimo Manufacturing Company hopes to produce 360,000 units of product during the next calendar year. Monthly production can range between 20,000 and 40,000 units. Per unit variable manufacturing cost have been budgeted as follows: direct materials, $2; direct labor, $2.50; and overhead, $1.25. Prepare a flexible budget for 20,000, 30,000, and 40,000 units of output.

## VI. Beyond the Numbers

Refer to the information (and solution) for Exercise 4 above. During June, 30,000 units were manufactured. Costs incurred were as follows: $59,000 for direct materials, $77,250 for direct labor, and $37,300 for overhead. Were the costs controlled?

_____
_____
_____
_____
_____

## VII. Demonstration Problems

### Demonstration Problem #1

A flexible budget for Miyamoto, Inc., is presented below:

Miyamoto, Inc.<br>Flexible Budget<br>For the Year 19X9

|  | Budget Formula per unit | \multicolumn{3}{c}{Various Levels of Volume} |  |  |
|---|---|---|---|---|
| Units | - | 40,000 | 48,000 | 56,000 |
| Sales | $4.75 | $190,000 | $228,000 | $266,000 |
| Variable expenses | $2.20 | 88,000 | 105,600 | 123,200 |
| Fixed expenses |  | 56,000 | 56,000 | 56,000 |
| Total expenses |  | 144,000 | 161,600 | 179,000 |
| Operating income |  | $ 46,000 | $ 66,400 | $ 86,800 |

The static (master) budget is based on volume of 48,000 units. Actual operating results for 19X9 are as follows:

| Sales (49,500 units) | $227,700 |
|---|---|
| Variable expenses | 106,920 |
| Fixed expenses | 57,570 |

**Required:**

1. Prepare an income statement performance report for 19X9.
2. Show that the total variances in operating income account for the net difference between actual operating income and the static (master) budget income.

**Requirement 1 (income statement performance report)**

Miyamoto, Inc.<br>Income Statement Performance Report<br>For the Year Ended December 31, 19X9

|  | (1)<br>Actual Results at Actual Prices | (2)<br>(1) - (3)<br>Flexible Budget Variances | (3)<br>Flexible Budget for Actual Volume Achieved | (4)<br>(3) - (5)<br>Sales Volume Variances | (5)<br>Static (Master) Budget |
|---|---|---|---|---|---|
| Units |  |  |  |  |  |
| Sales | $ | $ | $ | $ | $ |
| Variable expenses |  |  |  |  |  |
| Fixed expenses |  |  |  |  |  |
| Total expenses |  |  |  |  |  |
| Operating income | $ | $ | $ | $ | $ |

**Requirement 2 (recording variances)**

$_____

_____

$========

$_____

_____

$========

## Demonstration Problem #2

Fun Fabric uses a standard cost system. They produce specially manufactured goods in large batches for catalogue companies featuring unusual decorative household items. They have just received an order for 10,000 units of a decorative wall hanging. Their standard cost for one wall hanging is:

| | |
|---|---:|
| Direct materials - 2.5 feet @ $2/ft | $ 5.00 |
| Direct labor 1.5 hours @ $8/hr | 12.00 |
| Overhead 1.5 hours @ $6/hr | 9.00 |
| Standard cost/unit | $26.00 |

The normal capacity for the factory this period is 16,000 direct labor hours. Overhead costs are equally divided between variable and fixed expenses and are applied on the basis of direct labor hours. Janice Walters, the company president, has promised to have the wall hangings ready for shipment by the end of the month. The customer has agreed to pay $40 each.

During the month the following events occurred:

1. Purchased 27,500 feet of raw materials at $1.90/ft.
2. Received and placed into production 27,500 feet of raw materials.
3. Direct manufacturing wages incurred, 14,700 hours at $8.25/hr.
4. Assigned 14,700 direct labor hours to the job.
5. Recorded $91,600 of overhead costs.
6. Applied manufacturing overhead to the job.
7. The wall hangings were completed.
8. Shipped 10,000 units to the customer and billed the customer $400,000.

### Requirements:

1. Journalize the transactions.
2. Post your transactions to the appropriate T-accounts.
3. Record the overhead variances.
4. Prepare a standard cost income statement.

**Requirement 1 (journal entries)**

| Explanation | Debit | Credit |
|---|---|---|
| | | |

**Requirement 2 (post to T-accounts)**

| Materials Inventory | Direct Materials Price Variance | Direct Materials Efficiency Variance |
|---|---|---|
| | | |

| Manufacturing Wages | Direct Labor Price Variance | Direct Labor Efficiency Variance |
|---|---|---|
| | | |

| Manufacturing Overhead |
|---|
| |

| Work in Process | Finished Goods | Cost of Goods Sold |
|---|---|---|
| | | |

**Requirement 3 (record overhead variances)**

| Explanation | Debit | Credit |
|---|---|---|
| | | |
| | | |
| | | |

**Requirement 4**

Fun Fabric
Standard Cost Income Statement

|  |  |  |
|---|---|---|
|  |  |  |
|  |  |  |
|  |  |  |
|  |  |  |
|  |  |  |
|  |  |  |
|  |  |  |
|  |  |  |
|  |  |  |
|  |  |  |
|  |  |  |
|  |  |  |
|  |  |  |
|  |  |  |
|  |  |  |
|  |  |  |
|  |  |  |
|  |  |  |
|  |  |  |

SOLUTIONS

## I. Matching

1. G    3. B    5. H    7. E    9. J    11. F
2. I    4. C    6. K    8. A    10. D

## II. Multiple Choice

1. A    Variable costs on a per unit basis are not affected by changes in volume (B). Fixed cost per unit increases as volume decreases (C). Fixed costs do not change as a result of volume changes in the relevant range of production (D).

2. A    A static budget is prepared for only one level of activity (B). Answers C and D have no meaning.

3. C    All budgets are used for planning. Since the flexible budget is prepared for the actual level of activity achieved, it provides for precise control.

4. A    The sales volume variance measures differences between the static budget and the flexible budget for actual volume achieved. The flexible budget variance measures differences between actual results and the flexible budget for actual volume achieved. Accordingly, higher than expected sales could be expected to give a favorable sales volume variance, and actual costs above flexible budget costs could be expected to give an unfavorable flexible budget variance.

5. B    A standard cost is a carefully predetermined cost that is usually expressed on a per-unit basis. It is a target cost, a cost that should be attained. Budgeted costs are total costs. Think of a standard variable cost as a budget for a single unit.

6. D    Price variances relate to materials and labor.

7. C    Production volume variances relate to overhead. The variances relating to direct materials and direct labor are the price and efficiency variances.

8. C    Unfavorable variances are added to cost of goods sold and favorable variances are deducted.

9. C    Because the variances relate to only the current period, they are closed out to Income Summary at the end.

10. D

## III. Completion

1. Costs
2. variable
3. fixed
4. mixed
5. one-fourth (2,500 units / 10,000 units)

6. efficiency
7. price
8. static
9. cost pool
10. Efficiency

## IV. Daily Exercises

1.

| | | | |
|---|---|---|---|
| Tomatoes | 90 lbs × 25¢/lb | = | $22.50 |
| Garlic | 2 heads × 90¢ ea. | = | 1.80 |
| Onions | 20 lbs × 15¢/lb | = | 3.00 |
| Wine | 2 gallons × $6.50 ea. | = | 13.00 |
| Olive Oil | 16 oz. × 20¢/oz. | = | 3.20 |
| Herbs | 8 oz. × 10¢/oz | = | .80 |
| Total | | | $44.30 |

| | | |
|---|---|---|
| $44.30 / 40 quarts = | | $1.1075 |
| Container | | .09 |
| Total | | $1.1975 |

2.

| | | |
|---|---|---|
| Materials price variance | = | $600 F  ($48,600) – ($49,200) |
| Materials efficiency variance | = | $369 U  (60,000 × $0.82) – (59,550 × $0.82) |
| Total Materials variance | = | $231 F  ($48,600) – (59,550 × $0.82) |

3.

| | | |
|---|---|---|
| Materials Inventory | 49,200 | |
|    Direct Materials Price Variance | | 600 |
|    Accounts Payable | | 48,600 |
| | | |
| Work in Progress Inventory | 48,831 | |
| Direct Materials Efficiency Variance | 369 | |
|    Materials Inventory | | 49,200 |

4.

| | | |
|---|---|---|
| Direct labor price variance | = | $287.50 F  ($14,600) – ($59,550 × .25) |
| Direct labor efficiency variance | = | $112.50 F  ($59,550 × .25) – ($60,000 × .25) |
| Total labor variance | = | $400 F  ($14,600) – ($60,000 × .25) |

5.

| Manufacturing Wages | 14,887.50 | |
| Direct Labor Price Variance | | 287.50 |
| Wages Payable | | 14,600 |
| | | |
| Work In Process Inventory | 15,000 | |
| Direct Labor Efficiency Variance | | 112.50 |
| Manufacturing Wages | | 14,887.50 |

## V. Exercises

1. A. Total costs = Fixed costs + Variable costs
   $60,000 = X + ($5 × 8,000)
   60,000 = X + $40,000
   $20,000 = X

   Fixed costs were $20,000

   B. Total budgeted costs = ($5 × # of units produced) + $20,000

   C. Total budgeted costs = ($5 × 10,000) + $20,000 = $70,000

2. A. Actual cost                                    $33,701
   Less: Budgeted unit cost x actual usage
         ($4.75 x 6,700)                              31,825
   Materials price variance                         $ 1,876 U

   B. $2,660 F = (6,700 feet - X) × $4.75
      X = 7,260 feet = inputs that should have been used
      7,260 feet / 3,300 units = 2.2 standard feet

3. A. Actual cost (2,500 hours @ $11.75)              $29,375
   Less: Budgeted unit cost × actual usage
         (2,500 × $12.00)                              30,000
   Labor price variance                              $    675 F

   B. Budgeted costs for actual hours (see above)    $30,000
   Less: Standard cost for actual production
         (2,400 × $12.00)                              28,800
   Labor efficiency variance                         $ 1,200 U

4.

**Massimo Manufacturing Company**
**Monthly Flexible Budget Report**

| Output | 20,000 | 30,000 | 40,000 |
|---|---|---|---|
| **Variable costs** | | | |
| Direct materials ($2) | $ 40,000 | $ 60,000 | $ 80,000 |
| Direct labor ($2.50) | 50,000 | 75,000 | 100,000 |
| Overhead ($1.25) | 25,000 | 37,500 | 50,000 |
| | $115,000 | $172,500 | $230,000 |

## VI. Beyond the Numbers

To answer the question we need to compare actual results with the budget.

**Massimo Manufacturing Company**
**Budget Report**
**June 19XX**

| | Actual | Budget | Variance |
|---|---|---|---|
| Units | 30,000 | 30,000 | 0 |
| **Variable costs** | | | |
| Direct materials | $ 59,000 | $ 60,000 | $1,000 F |
| Direct labor | 77,250 | 75,000 | 2,250 U |
| Overhead | 37,300 | 37,500 | 200 F |
| Totals | $173,550 | $172,500 | $1,050 U |

Overall, costs were controlled. The unfavorable variance was less than 1% of the budgeted amount (1,050 / 172,500). However, this overall result has been adversely affected by a 3% (2,250 / 75,000) unfavorable variance in direct labor costs while both direct materials and overhead show favorable variances.

# VII. Demonstration Problems

## Demonstration Problem #1 Solved and Explained

### Requirement 1 (income statement performance report)

Miyamoto, Inc.
Income Statement Performance Report
For the Year Ended December 31, 19X9

|  | (1) | (2) (1) - (3) | (3) Flexible Budget for Actual Volume Achieved | (4) (3) - (5) | (5) |
|---|---|---|---|---|---|
|  | Actual Results at Actual Prices | Flexible Budget Variances |  | Sales Volume Variances | Static (Master) Budget |
| Units | 49,500 | 0 | 49,500 | 1,500 F | 48,000 |
| Sales | $227,700 | $7,425 U | $235,125 | $7,125 | $228,000 |
| Variable expenses | 106,920 | 1,980 F | 108,900 | 3,300 U | 105,600 |
| Fixed expenses | 57,570 | 1,570 U | 56,000 | - | 56,000 |
| Total expenses | 164,490 | 410 F | 164,900 | 3,300 U | 161,600 |
| Operating income | $ 63,210 | $7,015 U | $ 70,225 | $3,825 F | $ 66,400 |

Explanations:

Column 1 contains actual results that were presented in the problem statement.

Column 3

Column 3 contains the flexible budget for the volume actually sold. Actual sales were 49,500 units. Budgeted revenue is $235,125 ($4.75 per unit × 49,500). Budgeted variable expenses are $108,900 ($2.20 per unit × 49,500). Budgeted revenue and budgeted variable expenses may be calculated by multiplying units actually sold by the budget formula amounts in the flexible budget. Note that fixed expenses of $56,000 are constant at all the production levels presented in the flexible budget.

Column 5

The amounts in column 5 are the static, or master budget amounts. The problem notes that the static budget is based on 48,000 units, a volume level also found in the flexible budget.

Column 2

The flexible budget variances are the differences between actual results (column 1) and flexible budget amounts (column 3).

**Study Tip:** When actual revenue or income is greater than budgeted, the variance is *favorable*. When revenue or income is *less* than budgeted, the variance is *unfavorable*.

For example, the flexible budget variance for sales is $7,425 U (actual sales were less than the flexible budget amount).

**Study Tip:** When expenses are *greater* than budgeted, the variance is *unfavorable*. When expenses are *less* than budgeted, the variance is *favorable*.

For example, the flexible budget variance for variable expenses is $1,980 F (actual variable expenses were less than the flexible budget amount.) It may help to remember that spending less than planned is favorable, while spending more is unfavorable.

Column 4

Sales volume variances are the differences between flexible budget amounts for actual sales and static budget amounts. Note that no sales volume variance exists for fixed expenses, since fixed are constant within the relevant range. The criteria to determine whether the variances are favorable or unfavorable are the same as detailed in the explanation for column 2.

### Requirement 2 (reconciling variances)

Static (master) budget operating income  $66,400
Actual operating income at actual prices   63,210
 Total difference to account for      $ 3,190 U

**Study Tip:** When actual operating income is less than static budget operating income, the variance is unfavorable.

Sales volume variance          $3,825 F
Flexible budget variance        7,015 U
 Total net variance            $3,190 U

Since the unfavorable flexible budget variance is greater than the favorable sales volume variance, the overall net variance is unfavorable.

### Demonstration Problem #2 Solved and Explained

### Requirement 1 (journal entries)

| 1) | Materials Inventory (27,500 × $2) | 55,000 | |
| --- | --- | --- | --- |
| | Direct Materials Price Variance (27,500 × $.20) | | 2,750 |
| | Accounts Payable (27,500 × $1.90) | | 52,250 |
| 2) | Work in Process (25,000 × $2) | 50,000 | |
| | Materials Efficiency Variance (2,500 × $2) | 5,000 | |
| | Materials Inventory | | 55,000 |

Flexible Budgets and Standard Costs   639

| | | | |
|---|---|---|---|
| 3) | Manufacturing Wages (14,700 × $8) | 117,600 | |
| | Direct Labor Price Variance (14,700 × $.25) | 3,675 | |
| | Wages Payable (14,700 × $8.25) | | 121,275 |
| | | | |
| 4) | Work in Process (15,000 × $8) | 120,000 | |
| | Direct Labor Efficiency Variance (300 × $8) | | 2,400 |
| | Manufacturing Wages | | 117,600 |
| | | | |
| 5) | Manufacturing Overhead | 91,600 | |
| | Various accounts | | 91,600 |
| | | | |
| 6) | Work in Process (15,000 × $6) | 90,000 | |
| | Manufacturing Overhead | | 90,000 |
| | | | |
| 7) | Finished Goods (10,000 × $26) | 260,000 | |
| | Work in Process | | 260,000 |
| | | | |
| 8) | Cost of Goods Sold | 260,000 | |
| | Finished Goods | | 260,000 |
| | | | |
| | Accounts Receivable | 400,000 | |
| | Sales | | 400,000 |

**Requirement 2 (post to T-accounts)**

| Materials Inventory | | | Direct Materials Price Variance | | | Direct Materials Efficiency Variance | |
|---|---|---|---|---|---|---|---|
| (1) 55,000 | (2) 55,000 | | (1) 2,750 | | | (2) 5,000 | |

| Manufacturing Wages | | | Direct Labor Price Variance | | | Direct Labor Efficiency Variance | |
|---|---|---|---|---|---|---|---|
| (3) 117,600 | (4) 117,600 | | (3) 3,675 | | | | (4) 2,400 |

| Manufacturing Overhead | |
|---|---|
| (5) 91,600 | (6) 90,000 |

| Work in Process | | Finished Goods | | Cost of Goods Sold | |
|---|---|---|---|---|---|
| (2) 50,000 | (7) 260,000 | (7) 260,000 | (8) 260,000 | (8) 260,000 | |
| (4) 120,000 | | | | | |
| (6) 90,000 | | | | | |

## Requirement 3 (record overhead variances)

| Explanation | Debit | Credit |
|---|---|---|
| Production Volume Variance (1) | 3,000 | |
| Overhead Flexible Budget Variance (2) | | 1,400 |
| Manufacturing Overhead (3) | | 1,600 |

(1) the fixed portion of overhead costs ($3) times the difference between normal capacity and budgeted or, $3 \times 1,000$ hour = $3,000.

(2) the difference between actual overhead ($91,600) and the sum of the budgeted variable ($3 \times 15,000$) and normal fixed ($3 \times 16,000$) or, $45,000 + $48,000 = $93,000 - $91,600 = $1,400

(3) the balance in the manufacturing overhead account

## Requirement 4

Fun Fabrics
Standard Cost Income Statement

| | | |
|---|---:|---:|
| Sales revenue | | $400,000 |
| Cost of goods sold at standard cost | $260,000 | |
| Manufacturing cost variances: | | |
|    Direct materials price variance | (2,750) | |
|    Direct materials efficiency variance | 5,000 | |
|    Direct labor price variance | 3,675 | |
|    Direct labor efficiency variance | (2,400) | |
|    Overhead flexible budget variance | (1,400) | |
|    Production volume variance | 3,000 | |
| Cost of goods sold at actual cost | | 265,125 |
| Gross margin | | $134,875 |

**Study Tips:** The standard cost income statement reports cost of goods sold at standard cost, then modifies this amount by the variances for direct materials, direct labor and overhead. Debit variances reflect additions to cost of goods sold while credit variances are deductions. The standard cost income statement is for internal purposes only.

# Chapter 25 - Activity-based Costing and Other Tools for Cost Management

## CHAPTER OVERVIEW

As businesses attempt to remain competitive in an international environment they strive for competitive advantages. Some of these involve better management of costs, efforts to deliver higher quality products to the customer, and the introduction of systems which allow management to effectively plan for future operations. While we have been investigating a variety of topics concerning "costs" in recent chapters, we now turn our attention to some of the issues at the forefront of cost management. The learning objectives for this chapter are to

1. Describe activity-based costing (ABC) and develop ABC costs.
2. Use ABC costs to make business decisions.
3. Decide when ABC is most likely to pass the cost-benefit test.
4. Compare a traditional production system and a Just-in-Time (JIT) production system.
5. Record manufacturing costs for a JIT system.
6. Contrast the four types of quality costs and use these costs to make decisions.
7. Relate a life-cycle budget for a product to target costing and value engineering.

## CHAPTER REVIEW

### Objective 1 – Describe activity-based costing (ABC) and develop ABC costs.

**Activity-based costing** is a system that focuses on activities as cost objects and uses the costs of those activities as building blocks for compiling the costs of products and other cost objects. A **cost object** is anything (specific task, particular product, function) for which it is worthwhile to compile cost information. Activity-based costing can be implemented by any business—it is not associated only with manufacturing.

ABC is the result of the need by companies for more accurate information concerning product costs thereby allowing managers to make decisions based on accurate information. One way to express the relationship between various types of cost is

   Total cost = direct costs + indirect costs

Direct costs (materials and labor) are fairly easy to trace due to their cost drivers. The challenge addressed by ABC costing is the indirect costs, both manufacturing and non-manufacturing. ABC recognizes that frequently multiple cost drivers exist. When this occurs, applying costs on the basis of a single cost driver results in distorted product costs. Applying ABC to products requires these seven steps:

1. Identify the activities
2. Estimate the total indirect cost of each activity
3. Identify the primary cost driver as the application base for each activity's indirect costs
4. Estimate the total quantity of each application base

5. Compare the allocation rate for each activity:

   Allocation rate for activity = $\dfrac{\text{Estimated indirect costs of activity (Step 2 above)}}{\text{Estimated quantity of allocation base (Step 4 above)}}$

6. Obtain the actual quantity of each allocation base used by the cost object
7. Allocate the costs to the cost object:

   Allocated activity cost = Allocation rate for activity (step 5 above) × Quantity of allocation base used by the cost object (step 6 above)

> **Study Tip:** Note that steps 2 through 7 are identical to those used to allocate manufacturing overhead.

Organizing cost information by activity provides detailed information not available using a single application rate.

> **Study Tip:** Review carefully Exhibits 25-4, 25-5, and 25-6 in your text along with the narrative discussion regarding Chemtech.

### Objective 2 - Use ABC costs to make business decisions.

With ABC in place, managers are able to make more accurate decisions because they are based on more precise product cost information. Once the product pricing has been determined, other decisions based on product pricing can be made with accuracy. For instance, deciding whether to produce something or simply purchase it from a supplier can now be more accurately determined. In addition, ABC may highlight issues regarding production levels, product mix and selling price.

### Objective 3 – Decide when ABC costing is most likely to pass the cost-benefit test.

While ABC is a simple concept (products cause activities, and activities consume resources), ABC systems can be extremely complex and therefore costly. To implement ABC successfully, the benefits should exceed the costs. Generally, companies in competitive markets are more likely to benefit from ABC costing. In addition, companies with high indirect costs, multiple product lines using varying resources, and companies with varying production levels for those product lines are likely to benefit.

Existing cost systems may need revision when management cannot explain changes in profits, when bids are lost (or won!) unexpectedly, when competitors underprice the company but remain profitable, when employees "don't believe the numbers," where a single-allocation-based-system exists and when production has been re-engineered but the accounting system has not.

> **Study Tip:** Carefully review the ABC Decision Guidelines in your text so you become familiar with ABC costing.

### Objective 4 - Compare a traditional production system and a just-in-time (JIT) production system.

In a **traditional production system** large inventories are maintained. However, maintaining large inventories consumes cash that could be used for other purposes. In addition, problems caused by inferior quality, obsolescence, and production bottlenecks might be overlooked with large amounts of inventory.

The actual manufacturing processes in a traditional production system can also result in inefficiencies. The actual physical movement of goods in process can be quite long resulting in further inefficiencies. **Throughput time** is a term used to describe the time between the receipt of raw materials and the completion of a finished good. As an equation it is expressed as follows:

Throughput time = Processing time + waiting time + moving time + inspection time + reworking time

Whereas processing time adds value to a product, the other elements in the equation are **non-value-added** activities and considered waste.

**Just-in-time (JIT) production systems** (introduced in Chapter 19) are designed to eliminate the waste found in a traditional system. Underlying JIT systems are the following four concepts:

1. **arrangement of production activities** - processes are arranged so production is continuous without interruption.
2. **setup times** - the greater the amount of setup time the greater the amount of non-value-added activity. JIT minimizes the amount of time required for setup.
3. **production scheduling** - under JIT products are produced in smaller batches, frequently the amount needed to fill a specific order. In addition, production is not begun until an order is received. This is referred to as a "**demand-pull**" system because the customer's order (the demand) "pulls" the product through the manufacturing process. In turn, the product acts as a "demand" to "pull" raw materials into the manufacturing process. All of which results in less inventory and activities, and an early detection of production problems.
4. **employee roles** - in a traditional system employees are trained to complete a specific task. Under JIT employees are crossed-trained to perform multiple tasks. This means greater flexibility and lower costs.

Review Exhibit 25-9 in your text for a comparison of a traditional system with a JIT system.

## Objective 5 - Record manufacturing costs for a JIT costing system.

In Chapter 24 you learned about the traditional standard cost system where costs are tracked through the manufacturing process from raw materials to finished goods. Under JIT, a backflush costing system is used. Backflush costing is a standard costing system that starts with output completed and works backwards to apply manufacturing costs to units sold and to inventories. Backflush costing takes less time and is less expensive to use than the traditional standard costing.

In a JIT system, no distinction is made between raw materials inventory and work in process. Instead they are combined into one account, Raw and in Process (RIP).

When materials are acquired:

RIP Inventory                              XX
    Accounts Payable                        XX
Recorded at standard amounts

As conversion costs are incurred:

| | | |
|---|---|---|
| Conversion Costs | XX | |
|     Various Accounts | | XX |

Recorded at actual costs

When the number of units of finished product is known:

| | | |
|---|---|---|
| Finished Goods | XX | |
|     RIP Inventory | | XX |
|     Conversion Costs | | XX |

The amount for each account above is based on standard costs.

When goods are sold:

| | | |
|---|---|---|
| Cost of Goods Sold | XX | |
|     Finished Goods | | XX |

Recorded at standard amounts

Price variances are recorded at the time materials are acquired while efficiency variances are not recorded until goods have been completed. Over/underallocated conversion costs are transferred to Cost of Goods Sold.

## Objective 6 - Contrast the four types of quality costs and use these costs to make decisions.

**Quality** is the conformance of the attributes of a product or service to a specific set of standards.

Four types of **quality costs** are prevention costs, appraisal costs, internal failure costs, and external failure costs. **Prevention costs** are those a company incurred to avoid poor quality goods and services. **Appraisal costs** occur when a company wants to detect poor quality goods and services. **Internal failure costs** result when inferior goods or services are detected before delivery to the customer. **External failure costs** are those incurred after the customer has received the good or service. See Exhibit 25-11 in your text for examples of quality costs.

**Benchmarking**, the comparison of current performance with some standard, is used as a nonfinancial performance measure. Benchmarking recognizes that not all performance measures are financial but these nonfinancial measures do, nevertheless, affect profitability. See Exhibit 25-13 for some examples of benchmarking.

## Objective 7 - Relate a life-cycle budget for a product to target costing and value engineering.

To remain competitive, companies must continuously strive to improve their activities. The reduction of costs over a product's life cycle is one means of doing so. When a new product is planned, a life-cycle budget is prepared. A **life-cycle budget** lists projected revenues and costs before any reduction efforts are made. Based on this budget, managers decide whether or not the new product is worth pursuing. See Exhibit 25-14 in your text as an example of a life-cycle budget.

**Target costing** is a cost management technique that helps managers set goals for cost reductions through product design. First, cost reduction goals are set. **Value-engineering** (VE) is then used to meet these goals. Value-engineering refers to the process of designing products that achieve cost targets and meet specified standards of quality and performance. Careful analysis may highlight processes where costs can be saved while maintaining quality. Once identified, these amounts are used to reduce budgeted costs to target cost. Coordination between functional areas is necessary for target costing to work.

# TEST YOURSELF

All the self-testing materials in this chapter focus on information and procedures that your instructor is likely to test in quizzes and examinations.

**I. Matching**  *Match each numbered term with its lettered definition.*

_____ 1. product life cycle
_____ 2. throughput time
_____ 3. non-value added activities
_____ 4. appraisal costs
_____ 5. life-cycle budget
_____ 6. external failure costs
_____ 7. just-in-time costing
_____ 8. strategy
_____ 9. target costing
_____ 10. benchmarking
_____ 11. value-engineering
_____ 12. internal failure costs
_____ 13. activity-based costing
_____ 14. prevention costs
_____ 15. trigger points

A. the process of designing products that achieve cost targets and meet specified standards of quality and performance
B. points in operations that prompt entries in the accounting records
C. the time between receipt of purchased materials and completion of finished products
D. a cost management technique that helps managers set goals for cost reductions through product design
E. a set of business goals and the tactics to achieve them
F. the time from original research and development to the end of a product's sales and customer service
G. costs incurred to avoid poor quality goods or services
H. a budget that compiles predicted revenues and costs of a product over its entire life cycle
I. activities that do not increase customer value
J. costs incurred when poor quality goods or services are not detected until after delivery to customers
K. cost incurred when poor quality goods or services are detected before delivery to customers
L. comparison of current performance with some standard. The standard often is the performance level of a leading outside organization
M. a standard costing system that starts with output completed and works backward to apply manufacturing costs to units sold and to inventories
N. costs incurred in detecting poor quality goods or services
O. a system that focuses on activities as the fundamental cost objects and uses the costs of those activities as building blocks for compiling the costs of products and other cost objects

## II. Multiple Choice  *Circle the best answer.*

1. In manufacturing, all the following are non-value-added activities except:

   A. inspection time
   B. moving time
   C. processing time
   D. reworking time

2. Relative to actual production, all the following are downstream activities except:

   A. customer service
   B. distribution
   C. advertising
   D. product design

3. Raw Materials Inventory and Work in Process Inventory are combined in

   A. target costing
   B. value engineering
   C. activity based costing
   D. a JIT costing system

4. All of the following are characteristics of quality costs except:

   A. use of benchmarking for evaluation
   B. difficult to measure
   C. difficult to identify individual components
   D. types of financial performance measures

5. Which of the following are likely to use activity-based costing system?

   A. financial institutions
   B. retailer
   C. textile manufacturer
   D. all of the above

6. Which of the following is an example of an external failure cost?

   A. reworking time
   B. cost to honor warranties
   C. training program costs
   D. inspection costs

7. All of the following are nonfinancial measures of quality except:

   A. amount of machine "down" time
   B. return on sales
   C. unit failure
   D. training hours per employee per month

8. Value engineering is most closely associated with:

   A. just-in-time costing
   B. activity-based management
   C. target costing
   D. none of the above

9. Benchmarking is most closely associated with:

   A. target costing
   B. nonfinancial measures of quality
   C. value engineering
   D. activity-based costing

10. Cross-training employees is a feature of which of the following?

   A. target costing
   B. just-in-time costing
   C. activity based costing
   D. value engineering

## III. Completion   *Complete each of the following.*

1. The key to successful business management is _____.
2. The key distinction between the traditional product costing system and activity-based costing when applying overhead costs is _____.
3. Processing time, waiting time, moving time, inspection time and reworking time are all features of _____.
4. Four characteristics common to the just-in-time inventory are:
   1. _____
   2. _____
   3. _____
   4. _____
5. Combining raw materials and work in process inventories is a feature of a _____ system.
6. Identify the following acronyms:
   VE _____
   ABC _____
   RIP _____
   JIT _____
7. Quality costs are features of _____.
8. The four types of quality costs are: 1) _____,
   2) _____, 3) _____,
   and 4) _____.
9. Demand-pull refers to a production process where _____ triggers the manufacturing process.
10. Of the four types of quality costs, the one that is potentially the most devastating to a company is _____.

## IV. Daily Exercises

1. Classify each of the following quality costs as a prevention cost, an internal failure cost, an appraisal cost, or an external failure cost.

   a. direct materials and direct labor costs incurred to repair defective products returned by customers
   b. a training class for customer service representatives to teach them techniques for completing customer orders quickly, efficiently and correctly
   c. salary of a technician who randomly selects goods from the warehouse and tests them for conformance to company specifications
   d. time and materials costs incurred to rework those items determined by the testing technician as below standard
   e. $28,000 balance in Sales Returns for the return of defective products
   f. fee paid to pickup and dispose of rejected products

a. _____
b. _____
c. _____
d. _____
e. _____
f. _____

2. List the following ABC system steps in correct order (use 1 through 7):

    _____ A.  identify the primary cost driver as the allocation base
    _____ B.  identify the activities
    _____ C.  obtain the actual quantity of each allocation base used by the cost driver
    _____ D.  estimate the total quantity of each allocation base
    _____ E.  estimate total indirect costs of each activity
    _____ F.  allocate costs to the cost object
    _____ G.  compute the allocation rate for each activity

3. Zollner Tool and Die has collected the following information on overhead costs:

| ACTIVITY | AMOUNT | COST DRIVER |
| --- | --- | --- |
| Machine setups | $90,000 | Number of setups |
| Machining | 325,000 | Number of machine hours |
| Inspecting | 42,000 | Number of inspections |

During the period, Zollner estimates they will have 675 machine setups, 15,000 machine hours and a total of 1,350 inspections. Calculate the overhead rate for machine setups, machining and inspecting.

4. Trendy Tees manufactures specialty T-shirts sold at music festivals and uses a JIT costing system. The standard cost for their basic model is $4.50 for raw materials and $1.10 for conversion costs. For a recently completed order of 12,000 shirts, the following costs were incurred:

    Raw material purchases        $54,000
    Conversion costs               12,480

Prepare journal entries for this order using JIT costing.

## V. Exercises

1. Piggyback Container Manufacturing Co. uses activity-based costing to account for its manufacturing process. The direct materials in each container cost $3,700. Each container includes 60 parts, and finishing requires 15 hours of direct labor time. Each container requires 225 welds. The manufacture of 10 containers requires two machine setups.

| Manufacturing Activity | Cost Driver Chosen as Application Base | Conversion Cost per Unit of Application Base |
|---|---|---|
| Materials handling | Number of parts | $   5.00 |
| Machine setup | Number of setups | $800.00 |
| Welding of parts | Number of welds | $   3.00 |
| Finishing | Direct labor hours | $ 32.00 |

Compute the cost of each container.

2. Review the information in Daily Exercise #3, and assume the following additional information. Zollner manufactures one standard product (a drill bit used in furniture construction) and two specialty products, a gear and a corkscrew. Machine setups, machining hours, and inspections for the three products were:

| Activity | Drill Bits | Gears | Corkscrews |
|---|---|---|---|
| Machine setups | 520 | 90 | 65 |
| Machine hours | 8,900 | 3,200 | 2,900 |
| Inspections | 820 | 270 | 260 |

Calculate the total overhead costs for each of these three products.

3. Review the information in Daily Exercise #3, but assume Zollner uses a traditional cost allocation system for overhead. The allocation base is number of units produced, and during the current period Zollner's production was as follows:

| | |
|---|---|
| Drill bits | 520,000 |
| Gears | 90 |
| Corkscrews | 1,300 |
| Total units | 521,390 |

A. Calculate overhead costs based on production.

652  Chapter 25

B. Compare your results with these in Exercise #2. Which method is more realistic, and why?

4. Fab's Fashions Company uses a JIT costing system, with trigger points at the time of direct materials purchase and the transfer of completed goods to finished goods. The company has received an order for 20,000 sweaters at $15 each. The standard direct materials cost is $6.50 per sweater and a standard conversion cost of $5.50 per sweater. Direct materials were purchased for $129,000 and conversion costs totaling $110,400 were incurred. 20,000 sweaters were produced and shipped to the customer.

Prepare journal entries for the above transactions.

| Date | Accounts | Debit | Credit |
|------|----------|-------|--------|
|      |          |       |        |

Activity-based Costing and Other Tools for Cost Management

5. Port-o-Oven, Inc., is designing a new lightweight, portable microwave oven. The budgeted sales price is $550 with a desired manufacturing contribution of $120 per oven. Assuming cost reductions during the product's life cycle will be $25 per oven and the value-engineering cost reduction goal has been established at $40 per oven, determine the initial budgeted unit manufacturing cost in the life-cycle budget.

## VI. Beyond the Numbers

Clothing manufacturers typically produce 5% more units than called for in a contract. Called "overruns," these excess units are deemed necessary because of anticipated defects in some of the units produced. Usually, these defects are the result of faulty direct materials and/or workmanship. Part of the overrun cannot be reworked and is scraped. Other parts can be reworked but are not needed to fill the order. A third part is simply excess. Many times, the excess that is not scrapped is sold to a factor who then resells the merchandise to an outlet store where it is sold as "seconds."

Analyze a typical 5% overrun with respect to quality costs—prevention, appraisal, internal failure, and external failure.

## VII. Demonstration Problems

### Demonstration Problem #1

Lean and Mean hopes to manufacture a new multi-purpose piece of exercise equipment for in-home use. Demand over an estimated three-year life cycle totals 80,000 units, selling for $500 each. Research indicates the following per unit manufacturing costs:

| | |
|---|---|
| Direct materials | $123.00 |
| Purchased parts | 155.00 |
| Direct labor | 80.00 |
| Indirect materials | 4.50 |
| Indirect labor | 17.50 |
| Other variable conversion costs | 8.15 |

Fixed conversion costs for 80,000 units are:

| | |
|---|---|
| Indirect labor | $148,000 |
| Machinery depreciation | 720,000 |
| Other fixed conversion | 97,200 |

Upstream and downstream fixed costs are estimated as:

| | |
|---|---|
| Product development, design | $ 210,000 |
| Engineering, testing | 106,000 |
| Marketing | 1,750,000 |
| Other downstream fixed | 490,000 |

The exercise equipment will be sold through exclusive dealers who receive a 10% commission on each unit sold.

### Required:

Present an initial life-cycle budget based on sales of 80,000 units.

Lean and Mean Exerciser
Initial Life-Cycle Budget
80,000 units

## Demonstration Problem #2

Conor Cup Company manufactures environmentally friendly cups in two sizes for coffee bars offering carry-out service. The company uses a traditional system for allocating manufacturing overhead costs. Last year, the following results were reported:

|  | 8 oz. cups | 12 oz. cups | Total |
|---|---|---|---|
| Direct materials | $1,350,000 | $1,800,000 | $ 3,150,000 |
| Direct Labor | 400,000 | 600,000 | 1,000,000 |
| Overhead | 2,400,000 | 3,600,000 | 6,000,000 |
| Total | $4,150,000 | $6,000,000 | $10,150,000 |

Overhead costs were allocated on the basis of direct labor costs. Last year 510,000 cases of 8 oz. cups were manufactured (each case contains 500 cups) and 800,000 cases (each containing 300 cups) of 12 oz. cups were manufactured.

You have been asked by the company controller to analyze the allocation of overhead costs to the two products using an activity-based costing system. You begin by analyzing the specific components of the $6,000,000 in overhead costs assigned last year. Your investigation determines the following:

| Components | Cost |
|---|---|
| Indirect materials | $ 300,000 |
| Supervisor's salaries | 450,000 |
| Equipment depreciation | 3,150,000 |
| Equipment conversion costs | 1,500,000 |
| Miscellaneous overhead | 600,000 |
| Total | $6,000,000 |

In consultation with the controller, the following decisions are made regarding costs and cost drivers:

| Cost | Cost driver |
|---|---|
| Indirect materials | Direct materials |
| Supervisor's salaries | Direct labor cost |
| Equipment depreciation | Hours of equipment use |
| Equipment conversion costs | Number of conversions |
| Miscellaneous overhead | Cases of output |

Further investigation disclosed the following:

The equipment was used 70% for the 12 oz. cups and 30% for the 8 oz. cups. The equipment was converted a total of 120 times during the year, 90 times for the 12 oz. cups and 30 times for the 8 oz. cups.

**Requirements:**

1. Calculate the per cup cost for each size using the traditional system of overhead allocation.
2. Apply activity-based costing using the results of your investigation to allocate overhead.
3. Calculate the per cup cost given your results in requirement 2.

**Requirement 1**

**Requirement 2**

**Requirement 3**

# SOLUTIONS

## I. Matching

| | | | | |
|---|---|---|---|---|
| 1. F | 3. I | 5. H | 7. M | 9. D | 11. A | 13. O | 15. B |
| 2. C | 4. N | 6. J | 8. E | 10. L | 12. K | 14. G | |

## II. Multiple Choice

1. C  Non-value-added activities are those which do not add value to the product. Inspecting, moving, and reworking are examples of non-value added activities. Processing costs are value-added activities.

2. D  If production is the point of reference, downstream activities are those which occur after production is completed. Of the four choices listed, only product design would occur before production begins.

3. D  RIP (Raw and In Process) is a feature of just-in-time costing.

4. D  Because quality costs are difficult to identify and measure, benchmarking is one way to evaluate them. Quality costs are nonfinancial performance items.

5. D  Activity-based costing is a concept of accumulating costs using multiple cost drivers and is not specific to particular businesses or industries - it can be used by any organization.

6. B  External failures are those which occur after the product or service has been received by the customer. Of the four options, the only one which would involve a customer is the cost of warranties.

7. B  Return on sales is the only choice listed that can be expressed in financial terms.

8. C  Value engineering refers to techniques used to reduce the cost of a product while maintaining its satisfaction to the customer. Value engineering is one way to achieve target costing.

9. B  Target costing, value engineering and activity-based costing all relate to either cost measurement (ABC) or cost reduction (target costing and VE). Benchmarking is a way to evaluate nonfinancial measures of quality.

10. B  Cross-training is a prominent feature of just in time costing.

## III. Completion

1. intelligent decision making
2. the use of multiple cost drivers in the ABC system
3. throughput time
4. arrangement of production activities, setup times, production scheduling, employee roles (order not important)

5. JIT costing
6. VE = value engineering; ABC = activity-based costing; RIP = Raw and In Process; JIT = just-in-time
7. total quality management
8. prevention costs, appraisal costs, internal failure costs, external failure costs
9. the receipt of a customer order
10. external failure costs

## IV. Daily Exercises

1. a. external failure cost
   b. prevention cost
   c. appraisal cost
   d. internal failure cost
   e. external failure cost
   f. internal failure cost

2. 
   | | |
   |---|---|
   | 3 | A. |
   | 1 | B. |
   | 6 | C. |
   | 4 | D. |
   | 2 | E. |
   | 7 | F. |
   | 5 | G. |

3. Machine setups = $90,000/675 = $133.33/setup
   Machining = $325,000/15,000 hrs = $21.67/hour
   Inspecting = $42,000/1,350 = $31.11/inspection

4. 
   | | | |
   |---|---|---|
   | RIP Inventory | 53,400 | |
   |     Accounts Payable | | 53,400 |
   | | | |
   | Conversion Costs | 12,480 | |
   |     Accounts Payable | | 12,480 |
   | | | |
   | Finished Goods Inventory | 67,200 | |
   |     RIP Inventory | | 54,000 |
   |     Conversion Costs | | 13,200 |
   | | | |
   | Cost of Goods Sold | 67,200 | |
   |     Finished Goods Inventory | | 67,200 |
   | | | |
   | Conversion Costs | 720 | |
   |     Cost of Goods Sold | | 720 |

## V. Exercises

1.

| | | |
|---|---|---:|
| | Direct materials | $3,700 |
| | Materials handling (60 parts @ $5.00) | 300 |
| | Machine setup ($800 x 2 / 10) | 160 |
| | Welding (225 x $3.00) | 675 |
| | Finishing (15 x $32.00) | 480 |
| | Total cost | $3,315 |

2.

**Drill Bits**

| Activity | Number | Cost |
|---|---|---|
| Machine setups ($133.33) | 520 | $ 69,333 (rounded) |
| Machine hours ($21.67) | 8900 | 192,833 (rounded) |
| Inspections ($31.11) | 820 | 25,511 (rounded) |
| Total | | $287,677 |

**Gears**

| Activity | Number | Cost |
|---|---|---|
| Machine setups ($133.33) | 90 | $12,000 |
| Machine hours ($21.67) | 3200 | 69,333 |
| Inspections ($31.11) | 270 | 8,400 |
| Total | | $89,733 |

**Corkscrews**

| Activity | Number | Cost |
|---|---|---|
| Machine setups ($133.33) | 65 | $ 8,667 |
| Machine hours ($21.67) | 2900 | 62,833 |
| Inspections ($31.11) | 260 | 8,089 |
| Total | | $79,589 |

3.

A. Total overhead costs =   $ 90,000
                            325,000
                             42,000
                           $457,000

Drill bits = 520,000 / 521,390 × $457,000 = $455,782
Gears = 90 / 521,390 × $457,000 = $78.88
Corkscrews = 1,300 / 521,390 × $457,000 = $1,139

B. It is obvious a traditional costing system based on production drastically distorts the allocation of overhead. It would also be distorted if only one of the activities (setups, hours, or inspections) were the allocation base. Granted, this is an extreme example but it does serve to illustrate the point that activity-based costing can result in a more realistic application of overhead.

**Study Tip:** Remember, ABC relates only to overhead, not direct materials or direct labor.

4.

| | | |
|---|---|---|
| RIP Inventory | 130,000 | |
|    Direct materials price variance | | 1,000 |
|    Accounts Payable | | 129,000 |
| | | |
| Conversion costs | 110,400 | |
|    Various accounts | | 110,400 |
| | | |
| Finished goods | 240,000 | |
|    RIP Inventory | | 130,000 |
|    Conversion costs | | 110,000 |
| [($6.50 + $5.50) × 20,000)] | | |
| | | |
| Cost of goods sold | 240,000 | |
|    Finished goods | | 240,000 |
| | | |
| Accounts Receivable | 300,000 | |
|    Sales | | 300,000 |
| | | |
| Cost of goods sold | 400 | |
|    Conversion costs | | 400 |
| (to transfer underapplied overhead) | | |

5. The relevant formulas are:

Sales price - desired manufacturing contribution = life-cycle cost
Budgeted cost - value engineering reductions = target cost
Target cost - cost reductions = life-cycle cost

If life-cycle sales price is $550 and desired manufacturing contribution is $120, then the allowable life-cycle cost is $430 ($550-$120).

If life-cycle cost = $430, and cost reductions equal $25, the target cost = $430 + $25 = $455.

If target cost = $455 and value engineering reductions equal $40, then budgeted cost = $455 + $40 = $495.

The initial budgeted unit manufacturing cost in the life-cycle budget was $495.00.

## VI. Beyond the Numbers

Ideally, a manufacturer should strive for zero defects. However, this is not always possible. To obtain defect-free material, the manufacturer needs to work closely with the supplier(s). This is a prevention cost. During the manufacturing process, appraisal costs are involved as a result of inspection costs. In addition, internal failure costs are incurred to both rework (when possible) and to dispose of units that can neither be reworked nor sold as seconds. If you analyze the situation carefully you will see that there are no external failure costs. The clothing manufacturer ships only goods which conform to the order. Any excess goods that can be sold are factored to an outlet store. As long as the costs associated with the excess are considered when they are sold, no external failure costs are involved. As stated above, zero defects is the ideal and something companies should strive to achieve. However, given the 5% excess, clothing manufacturers seem to have adjusted well enough to cover the costs incurred with the excess (one of the fastest growing segments in retailing are the "outlets").

## VII. Demonstration Problems

**Demonstration Problem #1 Solved and Explained**

Lean and Mean Exerciser<br>
Initial Life-Cycle Budget<br>
80,000 units

| | | | |
|---|---|---:|---:|
| Sales @ $500 per unit | | | $40,000,000 |
| | | | |
| Direct materials @ $123 per unit | | 9,840,000 | |
| Purchased parts @ $155 per unit | | 12,400,000 | 22,240,000 |
| Materials contribution margin | | | 17,760,000 |
| | | | |
| Other costs direct to product: | | | |
| | | | |
| Variable conversion costs @ $110.15 per unit | | | |
|   Direct labor @ $80 per unit | | 6,400,000 | |
|   Indirect materials @ $4.50 per unit | | 360,000 | |
|   Indirect labor @ $17.50 per unit | | 1,400,000 | |
|   Other @ $8.15 per unit | | 652,000 | 8,812,000 |
| | | | |
| Product contribution margin | | | 8,948,000 |
| | | | |
| Fixed conversion costs: | | | |
| | | | |
|   Indirect labor | | 140,000 | |
|   Depreciation | | 720,000 | |
|   Other fixed | | 97,200 | 957,200 |
| | | | |
| Life-cycle manufacturing contribution | | | 7,990,800 |
| | | | |
| Other fixed costs: | | | |
| | | | |
|   Product development, design | | $210,000 | |
|   Engineering, testing | | 106,000 | |
|   Marketing | | 1,750,000 | |
|   Sales commission | | 4,000,000 | |
|   Other downstream fixed | | 490,000 | 6,556,000 |
| | | | |
| Life-cycle operating contribution | | | $ 1,434,800 |

---

**Study Tip:** The initial life-cycle budget is organized into four parts: the materials contribution margin, product contribution margin, life-cycle manufacturing contribution, and life-cycle operating contribution.

---

As the name implies, the initial life-cycle budget is the starting point. It shows all the costs (not just manufacturing) that can be traced to the product. After the budget is prepared, managers need to determine whether or not to proceed with the project. It is at this point where target costing techniques are applied to attempt further cost reductions, if needed.

**Demonstration Problem #2 Solved and Explained**

**Requirement 1**

8 oz. cups:
| | |
|---|---|
| Total cost | $4,150,000 |
| Total cups (510,000 cases × 500 ea) | 250,000,000 |
| Cost per cup ($4,150,000 / 250,000,000) | $0.017 |

12 oz. cups:
| | |
|---|---|
| Total cost | $6,000,000 |
| Total cups (800,000 cases × $500 ea) | 240,000,000 |
| Cost per cup ($6,000,000 / 240,000,000) | $0.025 |

**Requirement 2**

| Component | Cost | 8 oz. | Calculations | 12 oz. | Calculations |
|---|---|---|---|---|---|
| Indirect material | $300,000 | $128,571 | $1,350,000 × $300,000 / $3,150,000 | $171,429 | $1,800,000 × $300,000 / $3,150,000 |
| Supervisor's salary | 450,000 | 180,000 | $400,000 × $450,000 / $1,000,000 | 270,000 | $600,000 × $450,000 / $1,000,000 |
| Equipment depreciation | 3,150,000 | 945,000 | 30% × $3,150,000 | 2,205,000 | 70% × $3,150,000 |
| Conversion costs | 1,500,000 | 375,000 | 30/120 × $1,500,000 | 1,125,000 | 90/120 × $1,500,000 |
| Miscellaneous | 600,000 | 233,588 | $510,000 × $600,000 / $1,310,000 | 366,412 | $800,000 × $600,000 / $1,310,000 |
| Total | | $1,862,159 | | $4,137,841 | |

**Requirement 3**

8 oz. cups

| | | |
|---|---|---|
| | $1,350,000 | (Direct materials) |
| | 400,000 | (Direct labor) |
| | 1,862,159 | (Overhead - from Requirement 2) |
| Total cost | $3,612,159 | |

or $3,162,159 / 250,000,000 = $0.014 per cup

664 Chapter 25

<u>12 oz. cups</u>

|  |  |  |
|---|---:|---|
|  | $1,800,000 | (Direct materials) |
|  | 600,000 | (Direct labor) |
|  | 4,137,841 | (Overhead - from Requirement 2) |
| Total cost | $6,537,841 |  |

or $6,537,841 / 240,000,000   =   $0.027 per cup

# Chapter 26 - Special Business Decisions and Capital Budgeting

## CHAPTER OVERVIEW

In recent chapters you have learned about a variety of issues all related to the topic of "costs." Most of these issues looked at costs (and behavior) in the short run. When costs are correctly recorded and carefully analyzed, a business is in a better position to plan for future operations. We now turn our attention to some special decisions businesses frequently must make and to issues concerning the acquisition of long-term (capital) assets. The learning objectives for this chapter are to

1. Identify the relevant information for a special business decision.
2. Make six types of special business decisions.
3. Explain the difference between correct analysis and incorrect analysis of a particular business decision.
4. Use opportunity cost in decision making.
5. Use four capital budgeting models to make longer-term investment decisions.
6. Compare and contrast popular capital budgeting methods.

## CHAPTER REVIEW

### Objective 1 – Identify the relevant information for a special business decision.

To achieve business goals, managers must develop strategies by choosing among different courses of action. A **strategy** is a set of business goals and the tactics to achieve them. To do this, the manager must gather information and distinguish between the relevant information and that which is not relevant. This approach to decision making is called the **relevant information approach** (also called the incremental analysis approach).

**Relevant information** is expected future data or information that differs among the alternative courses of action. Information which does not differ is irrelevant and will not change a business decision. See Exhibit 26-1 in your text.

### Objective 2 – Make six types of special business decisions.

**Special sales orders** are evaluated by comparing the expected increase in revenues and the expected increase in expenses. If fixed expenses do not change, they are not relevant and should be ignored.

A quick summary analysis (Exhibit 26-3 in your text) subtracts the expected increase in expenses from the expected increase in revenues to arrive at the expected increase in operating income. An income statement analysis with and without the special order (Exhibit 26-4) compares total revenues, expenses, and operating income for both courses of action. (Both analyses should give the same result.)

## Objective 3 – Explain the difference between correct analysis and incorrect analysis of a particular business decision.

Correctly analyzing a business decision requires you to ignore **irrelevant costs**. A cost that is the same for all decision alternatives is NOT relevant and must be ignored. You should consider only those costs and revenues which change between alternatives.

The oil filter illustration is your text is an excellent example of this difference. Using the conventional income statement as the basis for the decision is not the correct analysis because of the nature of fixed costs. However, when the question is analyzed using the contribution margin format, the irrelevant costs (fixed expenses) are ignored and a better decision results.

When considering **dropping products, departments, or territories, with no change in fixed costs**, the only relevant information is the expected decreases in revenues and variable costs, which together show the contribution margin and change in operating income. Study Exhibit 26-5 in your text.

When considering the **dropping products, departments, or territories with a change in fixed costs**, the analysis must include the change in fixed costs as well as changes in variable costs and revenues. Refer to Exhibit 26-6 for an example.

When deciding **which product to emphasize**, it is necessary to determine whether a constraint or limiting factor exists. A **constraint** restricts production or sales. Constraints may be stated in terms of labor hours, machine hours, materials, or storage space.

The way to **maximize profits for a given capacity** is to maximize the contribution margin per unit of the constraint. Exhibit 26-7 in your text presents an example of how to maximize the contribution margin per labor hour.

The **make or buy decision** (often called **outsourcing**) determines how best to use available facilities. The relevant information for the make analysis includes: 1) direct materials, 2) direct labor, 3) variable overhead, and 4) fixed overhead. The relevant information for the buy analysis is: 1) the fixed overhead that will continue whether the part is made or bought and 2) the purchase price to buy the part. This analysis shows whether it is cheaper to make the part or to buy the part. Review Exhibit 26-8 in your text.

Sometimes facilities can be used to make other products if the product currently produced is purchased from an outside supplier. In the make or buy decision, the alternatives become: 1) make, 2) buy and leave the facilities idle, and 3) buy and use the facilities for other products. As indicated in Exhibit 26-9 the alternative with the lowest net cost is the **best use of the facilities**.

The **sell as-is or process further** decision compares the expected net revenue (revenue minus costs) of processing further with selling inventory as-is. Exhibits 26-10 and 26-11 illustrate the sell as-is or process further decision. Note that past historical costs of inventory are **sunk costs**—they cannot make a difference to the decision; the sunk costs are irrelevant because they are present under both alternatives.

## Objective 4 – Use opportunity cost in decision making.

An **opportunity cost** is the benefit that can be obtained from the next best course of action in a decision. An opportunity cost is not associated with a transaction and is therefore not recorded although it must be considered in decision making. Outlay costs are recorded. Suppose Alternative A will generate $5,000 income and Alternative B will generate $6,000 income. The opportunity cost of Alternative B is the $5,000 of income from Alternative A that you have given up.

## Objective 5 – Use four capital budgeting models to make longer-term investment decisions.

**Capital budgeting** is a formal means of analyzing long-range investment decisions for purchasing, using, and disposing of capital assets such as land, buildings, and machinery. Four **capital budgeting decision models** are presented in this chapter. They help managers evaluate and choose among alternatives. Capital budgeting focuses on cash and three of these models use net cash inflow from operations to analyze alternatives.

1) **Payback** is the length of time it takes to recover the dollars invested in a capital outlay. If annual cash inflows are identical each year, then:

$$\text{PAYBACK PERIOD} = \frac{\text{AMOUNT INVESTED}}{\text{EXPECTED ANNUAL NET CASH INFLOWS}}$$

If annual cash inflows are not equal, you might construct a table, as in Exhibit 26-13, to determine the payback period. Payback highlights cash inflows, but ignores profitability which is a major weakness of this model. However, it can be useful in eliminating some unwise alternatives.

2) The **accounting rate of return** measures the average rate of return from using an asset over its entire life:

$$\text{ACCOUNTING RATE OF RETURN} = \frac{\text{AVERAGE ANNUAL OPERATING INCOME}}{\text{AVERAGE AMOUNT INVESTED IN THE ASSET}}$$

$$\text{AVERAGE ANNUAL OPERATING INCOME FROM ASSET} = \text{AVERAGE ANNUAL NET CASH INFLOW FROM OPERATIONS} - \text{ANNUAL DEPRECIATION}$$

$$\text{AVERAGE AMOUNT INVESTED} = \frac{\text{AMOUNT INVESTED} + \text{RESIDUAL VALUE}}{2}$$

See Exhibit 26-14 for an example of this calculation.

Although the accounting rate of return measures profitability, it ignores the time value of money, a topic you were introduced to in Chapter 15.

The following two models consider the timing of the cash outlay for the investment and the timing of the net cash inflows which result. These models are the most commonly used in capital budgeting.

3) **Net present value** is a method used to compute expected net monetary gains or losses from a project by discounting expected future cash flows to their present values using a minimum desired rate of return. The **minimum desired rate of return** used to calculate present value is called the **discount rate** (also called the hurdle rate, required rate of return, cost of capital, and target rate.) Exhibit 26-16 in your text illustrates present value analysis in which 1) the annual cash inflows are equal (an annuity) and 2) the annual cash inflows are different. Note that when the annual cash inflows are equal, you use Exhibit 26-15, Present Value of an Annuity of $1, to find the present value factor. When the cash inflows are not equal, you use Exhibit 26-17, Present Value of $1, to find the present value factor for each year of the analysis. Exhibit 26-18 in your text includes in the analysis the residual value of an asset (an inflow of cash) that is expected to be recovered at the end of the asset's useful life.

The steps to determine the net present value of a project are:

1. Find the present value of annual cash inflows.
2. Find the present value of the residual, if any.
3. Add (1) and (2) to obtain the present value of the net cash inflows.
4. Subtract the investment (which is already in present value terms) from the present value of the net cash inflows (3) to obtain the net present value of the project.

The net present value method is based on cash flows and considers both profitability and the time value of money. A company should only consider those investments that produce at least zero net present value or a positive net present value in this calculation.

4) **Internal rate of return** is another discounted cash flow model. The internal rate of return (IRR) is the rate of return that makes the net present value of an investment project equal to zero. There are three steps in calculating the internal rate of return:

1. Identify the expected net cash inflows.
2. Find the interest rate that equates the present value of the net cash inflows to the present value of the cash outflows. For a single investment of cash followed by a series of equal cash inflows, use the following equation:

INVESTMENT = EXPECTED ANNUAL x ANNUITY PRESENT VALUE FACTOR
       NET CASH INFLOW

Solve this equation for the annuity present value factor. Scan the row in Exhibit 26-15 that represents the life of the project for the present value factor closest to your calculation. The percent for that column is the approximate IRR.

3. Compare the IRR with the minimum desired rate of return. Projects should be accepted if the IRR is greater that the minimum desired rate.

## Objective 6 - Compare and contrast popular capital budgeting methods.

Exhibit 26-20 summarizes some of the strengths and weaknesses of the four capital budgeting models described above. The two discounted cash flow models (net present value and internal rate of return) are favored because they consider both profitability and the time value of money whereas the payback model ignores both while the accounting rate of return considers only profitability.

**Study Tip**: Review the Capital Budgeting Decision Guidelines at the end of the chapter.

# TEST YOURSELF

All the self-testing materials in this chapter focus on information and procedures that your instructor is likely to test in quizzes and examinations.

## I. Matching    *Match each numbered term with its lettered definition.*

_____ 1. accounting rate of return
_____ 2. capital budgeting
_____ 3. decision model
_____ 4. time value of money
_____ 5. opportunity cost
_____ 6. relevant information
_____ 7. annuity
_____ 8. constraint
_____ 9. discount rate
_____ 10. net present value
_____ 11. payback
_____ 12. sunk cost
_____ 13. internal rate of return

A. a method or technique for evaluating and choosing among alternative courses of action
B. actual outlay incurred in the past and present under all alternative courses of action; irrelevant because it makes no difference to a current decision
C. expected future data that differs between alternative courses of action
D. formal means of making long-range decisions for investments such as plant locations, equipment purchases, additions of product lines, and territorial expansions
E. item that restricts production or sales
F. calculated as average annual net cash inflow from operations minus annual depreciation, divided by average amount invested
G. length of time it will take to recover, in net cash inflows from operations, the dollars of a capital outlay
H. management's minimum desired rate of return on an investment, used in a present value computation
I. the benefit that can be obtained from the next best course of action in a decision
J. method of computing the expected net monetary gain or loss from a project by discounting all expected cash flows to their present value, using a desired rate of return
K. stream of equal periodic amounts
L. the fact that one can earn income by investing money for a period of time
M. the rate of return on a project that makes the net present value equal to zero

## II. Multiple Choice    *Circle the best answer.*

1. Relevant information:

   A. is expected future data
   B. differs among alternative courses of action
   C. does not include sunk costs
   D. all of the above

2. The standard income statement categorizes expenses:

   A. into cost of goods sold and selling and administrative expenses
   B. into variable expenses and fixed expenses
   C. both A and B
   D. neither A nor B

3. The contribution margin income statement categorizes expenses:

   A. into cost of goods sold and selling and administrative expenses
   B. into variable expenses and fixed expenses
   C. both A and B
   D. neither A nor B

4. Select the correct statement concerning the payback period.

   A. The longer the payback period, the less attractive the asset.
   B. The shorter the payback period, the less attractive the asset.
   C. The longer the payback period, the more attractive the asset.
   D. Both B and C are correct.

5. The accounting rate of return considers:

   A. the timing of cash flows
   B. the time value of money
   C. profitability
   D. all of these

6. The net present value method of capital budgeting considers:

   A. only cash flows
   B. only the time value of money
   C. both cash flows and the time value of money
   D. the length of time to recoup the initial investment

7. If a potential investment has a negative net present value:

   A. it should be accepted in all situations
   B. it should be rejected in all situations
   C. it should be accepted if payback is less than five years
   D. it should be rejected if the accounting rate of return is less than 16%

8. The internal rate of return (IRR) method, while similar to the net present value (NPV) method, differs from it in the following respect(s):

   A. IRR identifies expected future cash flows.
   B. IRR identifies the excess of the project's present value over its investment cost.
   C. IRR identifies a specific rate of return for the investment.
   D. all of the above

9. Which of the following capital budgeting decision models is based on profitability?

   A. payback
   B. accounting rate of return
   C. net present value
   D. internal rate of return

10. In deciding whether to take a year off from college and work full-time or continue in school and work part-time, the opportunity cost is:

   A. the amount of money already invested in your education
   B. the amount saved from college expenses by working full-time
   C. the amount of earnings foregone by selecting one option over the other
   D. the difference between the projected total income of the two options

## III. Completion   *Complete each of the following.*

1. A(n) _____ income statement is more useful for special decision analysis than the standard income statement.
2. The item that restricts production or sales is called the _____ or _____.
3. Fixed costs are only relevant to a special decision if _____.
4. A(n) _____ is the cost of the forsaken next best alternative, or profit given up, by selecting one alternative over another one.
5. _____ costs are not formally recorded in the accounting records.
6. The major weakness of the payback is that it _____.
7. An investment should be rejected if its net present value is _____.
8. A project's internal rate of return (IRR) is that rate of interest that makes the present value of the project's cash inflows and cash outflows _____.
9. The _____ refers to earning income by investing money for a period of time.
10. GAAPs are based on accrual accounting whereas capital budgeting is based on _____.

## IV. Daily Exercises

1. Place the following in correct sequence (1 through 4):

   _____ a. gather information relevant for the decision
   _____ b. analyze the information to compare alternatives
   _____ c. identify the alternative courses of action
   _____ d. choose the best alternative to achieve the strategic goal

2. Compute the payback period given the following information:

   | | |
   |---|---|
   | Cost of new machinery | $450,000 |
   | Useful life | 9 years |
   | Annual depreciation | $50,000 |
   | Annual net income attributed to new machinery | $18,000 |

Special Business Decisions and Capital Budgeting   673

3. Continental Manufacturing produces a component which sells for $62. The manufacturing cost per component is $38. Variable manufacturing costs are $29 and fixed manufacturing costs are $9 per unit. Continental has received an offer for 8,000 components; however, the components will have to be slightly modified to conform to metric measurements. Modifying each component will cost 50¢. The buyer is willing to pay $33 for each component. Assuming Continental has excess capacity, identify the relevant and irrelevant factors in deciding to accept the offer.

4. Using the information in Daily Exercise #3 above, decide whether Continental should accept the offer.

5. Molinari, Inc., is planning to construct a new facility at a total cost of $25,000,000. The project will have a 20-year life at the end of which it will be abandoned. It is expected to generate net income of $3,750,000. Calculate the annual rate of return of the new facility.

6. Review the information in Daily Exercise #5 above and consider the following additional information. Net cash inflows from the new facility are expected to be $5,000,000. Calculate the cash payback period.

7. Review the information in Daily Exercises #5 and #6 above and consider the following additional information. Molinari has a 12% minimum rate of return on investment. Calculate the net present value, using the discounted cash flows. (Hint: you'll need the present value tables in your text.)

## V. Exercises

1. A clothing wholesaler has offered to pay $20 per unit for 2,500 hats. This offer would put idle manufacturing capacity in use and not affect regular sales. Total fixed costs will not change. There will be only half the normal variable selling and administrative costs on this special order.

   | | |
   |---|---|
   | Normal selling price per hat | $25.00 |
   | Variable costs per hat: | |
   |     Manufacturing | 14.00 |
   |     Selling and Administrative | 3.00 |
   | Fixed costs per hat: | |
   |     Manufacturing | 2.00 |
   |     Selling and Administrative | 2.50 |

   A. What is the relevant information associated with this special order?

   B. What difference would accepting this special order have on company profits?

2. Nicola, a bright young CPA, has provided you with the following information:

   | | |
   |---|---|
   | Salary at current position | $40,000 |
   | Revenues expected by opening his own office | 125,000 |
   | Expenses expected for the new office | 100,000 |

   A. What is the opportunity cost associated with working at her current position?

   B. What is the opportunity cost associated with starting her own business?

   C. From purely a quantitative standpoint, what should she do?

676  Chapter 26

3. Eric's Nursery is concerned that operating income is low, and is considering dropping its garden implements department. The following information is available:

|  | Total | Plants & Fertilizers | Garden Implements |
|---|---|---|---|
| Sales | $425,000 | $225,000 | $200,000 |
| Variable expenses | 239,500 | 91,500 | 148,000 |
| Contribution margin | 185,500 | 133,500 | 52,000 |
| Fixed expenses | 153,000 | 81,000 | 72,000 |
| Operating income (loss) | $ 32,500 | $ 52,500 | ($ 20,000) |

Eric can avoid $48,000 of his nursery's expenses by dropping the Garden Implements division.

Determine whether Eric should drop the Garden Implements department.

4. Cedar Industries is considering a long term capital project requiring an investment of $300,000. The project is estimated to have a useful life of five years with no residual value and produce net cash flows as follows:

| Year 1 | $85,000 |
|---|---|
| Year 2 | 88,000 |
| Year 3 | 82,000 |
| Year 4 | 79,000 |
| Year 5 | 76,000 |

Determine the cash payback period for the project.

5. Review the information in Exercise #4 above and calculate the net present value for the project, assuming Cedar's cost of capital is 10%. Refer to Exhibit 26-17 in your text.

## VI. Beyond the Numbers

Review the information in Exercise #2 and list additional considerations (both quantitative and qualitative) that might influence Nicola's decision.

_____
_____
_____
_____
_____

## VII. Demonstration Problems

### Demonstration Problem #1

A. S&L Inc., produces two products, S and L, with the following per unit data:

|  | Product S | Product L |
|---|---|---|
| Selling price | $50 | $24 |
| Variable expenses | 30 | 15 |
| Units that can be produced each hour | 4 | 8 |

The company has 8,000 hours of capacity available. Which product should the company emphasize?

B. Body Works, Inc., has the following manufacturing costs for 4,000 of its natural bath sponges:

| | |
|---|---|
| Direct materials | $ 6,000 |
| Direct labor | 3,000 |
| Variable overhead | 2,000 |
| Fixed overhead | 5,000 |
| Total | $16,000 |

Another manufacturer has offered to sell Body Works similar sponges for $3.25 each. By purchasing the sponges outside, Body Works can save $2,000 of fixed overhead cost. The released facilities can be devoted to the manufacture of other products that will contribute $2,000 to profits. What is Body Works' best decision?

|  | Alternatives | | |
|--|--|--|--|
|  | Make | Buy and leave facilities idle | Buy and use facilities for other products |
|  |  |  |  |
|  |  |  |  |
|  |  |  |  |
|  |  |  |  |
|  |  |  |  |
|  |  |  |  |
|  |  |  |  |
|  |  |  |  |

Decision:

## Demonstration Problem #2

The data for a piece of equipment follows:

| | |
|---|---|
| Cost | $40,000 |
| Estimated annual net cash flows: | |
| Year 1 | 12,000 |
| Year 2 | 12,000 |
| Year 3 | 12,000 |
| Year 4 | 12,000 |
| Residual value | 8,000 |
| Estimated useful life | 4 years |
| Annual rate of return required | 12% |

The present value of an amount of $1 at 12% is:

| Year | 1 | 2 | 3 | 4 |
|---|---|---|---|---|
| Interest factor | 0.893 | 0.797 | 0.712 | 0.636 |

The present value of an annuity of $1 at 12% is:

| Year | 1 | 2 | 3 | 4 |
|---|---|---|---|---|
| Interest factor | 0.893 | 1.690 | 2.402 | 3.037 |

**Required:**

1. What is the payback period for the equipment?
2. What is the accounting rate of return for the equipment?
3. What is the net present value of the equipment?
4. Indicate whether each decision model leads to purchase or rejection of this investment. Would you decide to buy the equipment? Give your reason.

**Requirement 1 (payback period)**

**Requirement 2 (accounting rate of return)**

**Requirement 3 (net present value analysis)**

**Requirement 4 (decision)**

# SOLUTIONS

## I. Matching

| | | | | | | |
|---|---|---|---|---|---|---|
| 1. F | 3. A | 5. I | 7. K | 9. H | 11. G | 13. M |
| 2. D | 4. L | 6. C | 8. E | 10. J | 12. B | |

## II. Multiple Choice

1. **D** Relevant information is the expected future data that differ between alternative courses of action. A sunk cost is an actual outlay that has been incurred in the past and is present under all alternatives. Sunk costs are irrelevant.

2. **A** Answer B describes the contribution margin format income statement.

3. **B** Answer A describes the "standard" income statement format.

4. **A** Payback is the length of time it will take to recover, in net cash flow from operations, the dollars of a capital outlay. The shorter the payback the better. The longer it is, the less attractive.

5. **C** The accounting rate of return is calculated by:
   Average Annual Operating Income ÷ Average amount invested.
   By looking at the numerator, answer C can be seen to be the best.

6. **C** The net present value method computes the present value of expected future net cash flows and compares that present value to the initial investment. Answer C covers this approach.

7. **B** The initial investment is subtracted from the present value of the investment's expected future cash flows. If negative, the investment does not recover its cost. If positive, the investment generates a return above the minimum required. Only projects with zero or positive net present value should be considered.

8. **C** Both the NPV and IRR methods make use of expected future cash flows (answer A). Answer B is not correct because it describes only NPV. Only the IRR method (and not NPV) generates a specific rate of return for the project.

9. **B** The accounting rate of return model is based on profitability; the other three models are based on net cash flows.

10. **C** The opportunity cost is the benefit obtained from the next best course of action, so if the decision is to remain in school the opportunity cost is the full-time wages not earned, whereas if the decision is to work full-time, the opportunity cost is the foregone part-time income.

## III. Completion

1. contribution margin (The contribution margin format highlights how costs and income are affected by decisions.)
2. limiting factor, constraint (Such things as the size of the factory labor force, available storage space, availability of raw materials, available machine time, or market share can act as constraints.)
3. fixed cost differs among alternatives (Recall: a cost is relevant only if it differs between alternatives. A cost can differ between alternatives and still be fixed for each alternative.)
4. opportunity cost (It is not the usual outlay (cash disbursement) cost. If you quit your job to start your own business, the salary from the job you gave up is the opportunity cost of starting your own business.)
5. Opportunity (Since these costs do not involve giving up an asset or incurring a liability, they are not recorded.)
6. ignores profitability and the time value of money (Because of these shortcomings, the payback period can lead to unwise decisions.)
7. negative (If negative, the investment does not recover its cost. If positive, the investment generates an acceptable rate of return. Only projects with zero or positive net present value should be considered.)
8. equal
9. time value of money
10. cash flows

## IV. Daily Exercises

1.
| | |
|---|---|
| 2 | A. |
| 3 | B. |
| 1 | C. |
| 4 | D. |

2. $450,000 / ($18,000 + $50,000) = 6.6 years (rounded)

3.
Relevant
Variable manufacturing costs ($29)
Additional 50¢ cost/component
Continental has excess capacity

Irrelevant
The $62 selling price
$9.00 fixed costs

4. If the offer is accepted

| | |
|---|---:|
| Sales (8000 x $33) | $264,000 |
| Less: Variable Costs (8000 x $29) | 232,000 |
| Additional Variable Costs (8000 x 50¢) | 4000 |
| Increase in Net Income | $28,000 |

Special Business Decisions and Capital Budgeting 683

5.
$$\text{Annual rate of return} = \frac{\text{Average annual operating income}}{\text{Average amount of investment in asset}}$$

$$= \frac{\$3,750,000}{(\$25,000,000/2)}$$

$$= 30\%$$

6.
$$\text{Cash payback period} = \frac{\text{Amount invested}}{\text{Net cash inflows}}$$

$$= \frac{\$25,000,000}{\$5,000,000}$$

$$= 5 \text{ years}$$

7.

|  | Present Value at 12% | Net Cash Inflow | Total Present Value |
|---|---|---|---|
| Present value of equal annual net cash inflows for 20 years | 7.469 | $5,000,000 | 37,345,000 |
| Investment |  |  | 25,000,000 |
| Net present value of new facility |  |  | $12, 345,000 |

## V. Exercises

1. A. The relevant information is the special order price of $20 per unit, the variable manufacturing cost of $14 per unit, and one-half the normal variable selling and administrative expenses which amount to $1.50 per unit ($3 x 1/2).

   B. Additional revenues from special order (2,500 x $20)        $50,000
      Less: Variable manufacturing cost (2,500 x $14)              (35,000)
      Less: Variable selling and admin. cost (2,500 x $1.50)       ( 3,750)
      Increase in profits                                          $11,250

2. A. The opportunity cost is the net revenue given up by keeping the existing position: $125,000 revenue - $100,000 expense = $25,000.

   B. The opportunity cost is the cost of giving up the existing position: $40,000.

   C. The current position pays $40,000. Going into business will net $25,000. Keeping the present position makes Nicola $15,000 better off.

3. The relevant information is the contribution margin that would be lost if the garden implements department is eliminated and the fixed costs that would be eliminated. The nursery would lose the

$52,000 contribution margin if the department is closed and would reduce fixed costs by $48,000. The lost contribution margin is $4,000 greater than the reduction in fixed costs ($52,000 contribution margin lost - $48,000 fixed costs eliminated), so the department should not be closed. The nursery is $4,000 better off by keeping it.

4.

| | |
|---|---|
| Year 1 | $ 85,000 |
| Year 2 | 173,000 |
| Year 3 | 255,000 |
| Year 4 | 334,000 |
| Year 5 | 400,000 |

Payback = 3 years + $45,000* / $79,000**
= 3 years + .5696 = 3.6 years (rounded)

* Amount needed to complete $300,000 recovery
** Amount of net cash inflow in Year 4

5.

| | PV Factor | Net Cash Inflow | PV of Net cash Inflow |
|---|---|---|---|
| Year 1 | 0.909 | $85,000 | $ 77,265 |
| Year 2 | 0.826 | 88,000 | 72,688 |
| Year 3 | 0.751 | 82,000 | 61,582 |
| Year 4 | 0.683 | 79,000 | 53,957 |
| Year 5 | 0.621 | 76,000 | 47,196 |
| | Total PV | | 312,688 |
| | Less Investment | | 300,000 |
| | Net PV of Project | | $ 12,688 |

## VI. Beyond the Numbers

Probably the most significant quantitative consideration is the potential increase in salary compared with the potential increase in income from the business. For instance, if salary increases are likely to average 10% over the foreseeable future while the business growth potential is 20% annually, in a few years the income from the business will surpass the salary. An important qualitative consideration is being an employee versus your own boss. Frequently, it is the intangible costs and benefits that cloud the issue and make decision making so complex.

## VII. Demonstration Problems

### Demonstration Problem #1 Solved and Explained

A. Product to Emphasize

|  | Product S | Product L |
|---|---|---|
| (1) Units that can be produced each hour | 4 | 8 |
| (2) Contribution margin per unit* | $20 | $9 |
| (3) Contribution margin per hour (1) X (2) | 80 | 72 |
| Capacity: Number of hours | X 8,000 | X 8,000 |
| Total contribution margin for capacity | $640,000 | $576,000 |

* Contribution margins: S: $50 - $30 = $20; L: $24 - $15 = $9

Decision: The company should emphasize Product S because its contribution margin at capacity is greater by $64,000.

Explanation:

When a constraint exists, such as the number of labor hours available, we must conduct our profit analysis in terms of the constraint. Since only 8,000 labor hours are available, our profit will be greatest if we produce those products which offer the highest contribution margin per labor hour. To compute the contribution margin per labor hour for each product, multiply the contribution margin per unit of each product times the number of units of each product that can be produced per hour.

**Study Tip:** The product with the highest contribution margin per hour will provide the highest profit.

B. Make or Buy

|  | Make | Alternatives Buy and leave facilities idle | Buy and use facilities for other products |
|---|---|---|---|
| Direct materials | $ 6,000 | - |  |
| Direct labor | 3,000 | - |  |
| Variable overhead | 2,000 | - |  |
| Fixed overhead | 5,000 | $ 3,000 | $ 3,000 |
| Purchase price from outsider | - | 13,000 | 13,000 |
| Total cost of obtaining sponges | 16,000 | 16,000 | 16,000 |
| Profit contribution from other products | - | - | (2,000) |
| Net cost of obtaining 4,000 sponges | $16,000 | $16,000 | $14,000 |

Decision: The company should buy the sponges and use the facilities for other products.

Explanation

Continuing to make the sponges will cost the same $16,000 that it currently costs. The current cost to produce is relevant because it will change if the sponges are purchased. If the sponges are purchased, the relevant information is the purchase price and the amount of fixed overhead that *will continue*. The problem tells us that $2,000 of fixed overhead will be saved. Since total fixed overhead is $5,000, $3,000 ($5,000 - $2,000) of fixed overhead will continue, and the sponges will cost $16,000. If the facilities are used to earned an additional $2,000 profit, the net cost of the sponges is $14,000 ($16,000 - $2,000). For this alternative, the additional relevant information is the profit from the other product that could be produced.

**Study Tip:** Relevant information differs among alternative courses of action.

**Demonstration Problem #2 Solved and Explained**

**Requirement 1 (payback period)**

When the annual net cash flows are constant, the payback period is equal to the amount of the investment divided by the annual net cash flows.

$$\$40,000 \div \$12,000 = 3.3 \text{ years}$$

**Requirement 2 (accounting rate of return)**

The accounting rate of return is average annual operating income from the investment divided by the average amount invested. Average annual operating income is equal to net cash inflows from operations (O) minus annual depreciation (D). Average amount invested is the sum of the investment (I) plus residual value (RV) divided by 2.

R = (O - D) ÷ [(I + RV) ÷ 2] = ($12,000 - $8,000*) ÷ [($40,000 + $8,000) ÷ 2] = 0.167 = 16.7%
* D = ($40,000 - $8,000) ÷ 4 years = $8,000

**Requirement 3 (net present value analysis)**

The steps to determine the net present value of a project are:

| | |
|---|---:|
| Present value of net equal annual cash inflows ($12,000 × 3.037) | $ 36,444 |
| Present value of residual value ($8,000 × 0.636) | 5,088 |
| Present value of the equipment | 41,532 |
| Investment | 40,000 |
| Net present value | $ 1,532 |

Explanations:

Since the annual cash flow is the same amount, $12,000, it is an annuity. Multiply the annual amount, $12,000, by the present value of an annuity for 4 years. The present value of the cash inflows is $12,000 × 3.037, or $36,444.

The residual value of $8,000 is discounted to its present value ($8,000 × 0.636 = $5,088).

The present value of the equipment is $41,532 ($36,444 + $5,088).

The investment is $40,000.

The net present value of the investment is the present value of the equipment minus the investment.

$$NPV \text{ of Equipment} = \$41,532 - \$40,000 = \$1,532$$

**Requirement 4 (decision)**

The payback period is less than the useful life of the equipment. The accounting rate of return is higher than the 12% required return. Both methods indicate favorable potential for the investment. The net present value is positive, which indicates that the rate of return exceeds the 12% required return. Since the net present value considers both profitability and the time value of money, and is positive in this instance, the equipment should be purchased.